T3-AKC-090

TAX HAVENS AND OFFSHORE FINANCE

Studies in International Political Economy will present new work, from a multinational stable of authors, on major issues, theoretical and practical, in the international political economy.

General Editor

Susan Strange, Professor of International Relations, London School of Economics and Political Science, England

Consulting Editors

Ladd Hollist, Visiting Associate Professor, Brigham Young University, USA

Karl Kaiser, Director, Research Institute of the German Society for Foreign Affairs, Bonn, and Professor of Political Science, University of Cologne, West Germany

William Leohr, Graduate School of International Studies, University of Denver, USA

Joseph Nye, Professor of Government, Harvard University, USA

Already Published

The Political Economy of New and Old Industrial Countries
The East European Economies in the 1970s
Defence, Technology and International Integration
Japan and Western Europe
France in the Troubled World Economy

Forthcoming Titles

International Political Economy — A Text
International Regimes for the Control of Nuclear Technology
The North-South Dialogue
Dependency Transformed
The International Gold Standard

TAX HAVENS AND OFFSHORE FINANCE
A Study of Transnational Economic Development

by
Richard Anthony Johns

St. Martin's Press, New York

St. Martin's Press, Inc., 175 Fifth Avenue, New York, NY 10010
Printed in Great Britain
First published in the United States of America in 1983

ISBN 0-312-35180-1

Library of Congress Cataloging in Publication Data

Johns, Richard Anthony.
The growth of offshore tax havens and finance centres.

Bibliography: p.
1. Banks and banking, International. 2. Banks and banking, Foreign. 3. Banks and banking--Great Britain. 4. Tax havens. I. Title. II. Title: Offshore tax havens and finance centres.
HG3881.J55 1983 332.1'5 82-10755
ISBN 0-312-35180-1

This book is dedicated
to my wife Brenda
and to my parents

Contents

Tables

Foreword

Every blind man who touches a part of the elephant learns some of the truth about it—but not the whole truth; and only the rare unfortunate is unlucky enough to be caught in generalizing about the elephant from an unrepresentative hand-hold on the tip of its tail. *

The subject of offshore finance centres is one that has not yet been approached within the context of the emerging global trends in international banking and international trade relations. This study attempts just such an analysis. In Part I a comprehensive conceptual approach is provided within which the emergence of and rationale for offshore centres is related. This approach is evolved in relation to the different types of pressure exerted on and the vacuums created for invisible production that is both domestic and external in origin by national economic friction structures and the derived but constrained competitive 'frictioneering' abilities of particular offshore economies. The business potential thereby created in terms of international invisible exchange located in offshore centres and made possible by developments in telecommunications and the growth of world-wide financial networks when actualized is revealed to constitute a new secondary trading system for transnational enterprise. Part II utilizes the above approach to demonstrate how a traditional 'guardian' onshore/offshore politico-economic friction matrix and 'currency bond' can, and has, interacted to transform tax haven centres into offshore finance centres that are globally orientated. This regional case-study of the transformation of the British Isle centres of Jersey, Guernsey and the Isle of Man outlines their differing development profiles prior to and subsequent to the rescheduling of the Sterling Area in June 1972 and the suspension of the 1947 UK Exchange Control Act in October 1979. Part III traces the global pattern of offshore haven centre development that emerged in the 1970s, and considers what changes might result from certain onshore deregulation and reregulation activities that have so far restructured the international friction matrix in the 1980s. As this topic is an area where information and statistics are often hard to come by, the author hopes that the results of his labours do not correspond with those of the rare unfortunate mentioned in the quote from Johnson above.

R.A. JOHNS

Department of Economics
The University of Keele
Staffordshire
April, 1982

*Johnson, H.G., 'Technological Change and Comparative Advantage: An Advanced Country's Viewpoint', *Journal of World Trade,* January/February 1975, p.13.

ACKNOWLEDGEMENTS

In the preparation of this book I have benefited from the insights, help and advice generously given by bankers and officials in the islands of Guernsey, Jersey and the Isle of Man, to whom I am most grateful. I should like to give particular thanks to Professor Susan Strange of the London School of Economics, who has been a source of great encouragement to me since my research on this project began in 1980; and to the University of Keele for granting me leave of absence in which to write the manuscript during the autumn term of 1981. This study would not have been possible but for finance obtained from a Bank of England Houblon/Norman Award and travel grants provided by the University of Keele. Further acknowledgement must be made to the staffs of the Reference Library of the Bank of England and the *Financial Times* for access given to their respective books, information files and press cuttings in December, 1981, which proved invaluable in the preparation of Chapter I of Part III. Finally, I wish to thank my wife, not only for tolerating me during the writing of this book, but also for typing most of the manuscript.

PART I
The General Economic Rationale for Offshore Finance Centre Development

Like water finding its own level, entrepreneurial business, when constrained in one place, will emerge in another. When restrictions in one place become too burdensome, too discouraging and perhaps too punitive, the businessman will look elswhere . . . As one door closes, another is opened. *

The emergence of, and rationale for, any offshore centre needs to be considered within the context of particular trends within the international trading system and its constituent onshore and offshore economic parts. Chapter I identifies the existence of onshore national friction structures and distortions therein as the prime factor motivating the international private sector demand for the financial development of tax havens. Chapter II seeks to explain the evolutionary mutation of these 'intermediate' economies in the light of transnational trends in the development of world capitalism in general and multi-national banking in particular. Chapter III surveys the countervailing power that may be exercised, particularly in the areas of fiscal protection and exchange control, to pre-empt or limit the erosion of onshore industrial infrastructures and tax bases. Chapter IV examines the competitive power of offshore states in terms of their ability to attract transnational business and to create such business.

*Hanson, D.G., *Service Banking,* Institute of Bankers, London, 1979, p. 272.

CHAPTER I
The Importance of National Friction Structures and Distortions Therein and the International Politico-economic Friction Matrix

Standard textbooks on international trade usually emphasize in their introductory chapters that, while the character of international exchange retains the specialization characteristics of internal national trade in respect of the territorial division of labour, the very process of internal integration of nation states creates the potential for government-induced frictions and factor immobilities. If activated by interventionist policies, such frictions will constrain and thereby provide discontinuities in the free inter-country flows of economic goods, services and resources, with consequences for the global location pattern of production. Ability to impose these frictions is derived primarily from the internal economic sovereignty accorded the government of a country as a decision-making unit in respect of its internal allocation of resources and its control over domestic external entry or internal exit of resources, goods and services. Naturally the number, bias, mix and importance of the frictions in force will change over time in relation to domestic needs, international obligations, and the general regime of international trade, as indeed do private sector market-induced frictions and imperfections, with changes *inter alia* in the concentration of business ownership, the spread of information, changes in technology, etc. The list below is indicative of the source and range of such economic frictions,[1] the first five of which are of particular relevance in this context:

1. The different systemic internal frictions resulting from the various types and mixes of economic control systems participating in the international economy and their underpinning taxation burdens, methods of monetary control and general economic policy objectives. *Inter alia* in respect of taxation, matters such as the relative burdens of direct and indirect taxation; the general provision, definition and treatment of tax deductibles; and rules for the transfer of losses and the allocation of reserves and profits will be important for business. In respect of monetary control, the existence or otherwise of a central bank, support provided by monetary authorities as lenders of last resort to banks experiencing liquidity difficulties, usury laws or interest rate controls, reserve requirements imposed on banks, and differential treatment accorded to domestic and foreign banks and other financial institutions of significance both for the internal allocation of credit and the external competitiveness of domestic financial institutions.
2. Banking laws and other financial laws with regard to entry (branching laws for domestic and/or foreign banks, attitudes to mergers and take-overs, etc.), licensing laws with respect to the type and functional diversification of

financial activities permitted and restrictions or the absence of restrictions governing linkage with other institutions; bank secrecy laws; authorization procedures; capital and capital adequacy requirements and provisions and the weights given to the categories of assets involved; deposit protection insurance schemes; systems of supervision and approaches to liquidity, prudential and solvency control; and the monitoring and regulation of institutions' foreign currency exposure. Such regulations can be constructive or abusive, pro-competitive or anti-competitive with regard to economic activities and financial flows. Some countries, Western Germany for example, may make the bank deposits of non-residents periodically subject to higher reserve ratios than residents, or impose special minimum reserve requirements for any increase in non-resident bank deposits. With respect to insurance and reinsurance, policies of nationalization, 'domestication' and prohibition of insurance business may obtain as well as repatriation requirements for profits earned abroad.

3. Selective foreign exchange regulations and capital controls with regard to 'inward' and 'outward' investment in debt instruments, equity and real estate: this includes interest equalization taxes, programmes of voluntary or compulsory restraint on foreign banking, etc.
4. Company laws relating to incorporation procedures, requirements as to filing accounts and disclosure, the setting of production standards, restrictive business practices, trade-mark and patent rules and consumer protection legislation.
5. Regulations concerning listing procedures and the fees charged on stock exchanges (minimum commission/negotiation/free price/fixed commissions); share ownership and control (in some cases banks are not allowed to own shares in the exchange itself); and whether the organization itself is a single capacity system or not (i.e., whether there is separation between broker and jobber functions).
6. The degree of interventionist control applied to the international value of each national currency.
7. The existence of different selective tariffs, quotas, bounties and domestic subsidies.
8. Anti-dumping regulations.
9. Immigration and emigration policies.
10. Restrictive customs procedures (rules and regulations for classifying and valuing commodities).
11. Restrictive state-trading policies and discriminatory government and private procurement policies that discriminate against the foreign sector and restrict foreign competition.
12. Restrictive administrative and technical regulations with regard to *inter alia* safety and health regulations.
13. Legislation affecting trade unions, wage costs and labour use: this includes factor expenditure levels such as social contributions made by producers, minimum age regulations for employment, equal pay, minimum wages, worker and factory protection, school leaving age and retirement age legislation.

TABLE I The growth of incomes compared with that of direct taxes on corporations and households in terms of per annum average percentages for the period 1970–78 in the main industrial countries

	Corporations Per annum av. increases in			*Households Per annum av. increases in*		
Countries	*Surpluses*	*Other* incomes*	*Direct tax*	*Wages & salaries*	*Indirect taxes*	*Direct taxes*
Japan	6.2	11.2	17.5	16.9	12.8	18.5
USA	13.0	11.8	9.2	10.0	8.8	10.2
Canada	17.3	12.7	14.8	13.6	13.4	14.2
UK	11.3	14.1	15.9	15.8	13.0	15.2
France	10.0	11.1	15.8	14.8	12.1	17.2
W. Germany	6.8	6.1	11.4	8.9	7.7	11.9
Netherlands	10.8	9.2	14.2	12.3	13.1	17.0

Source: derived from charts in Doggart, *Tax Havens,* p. 135.

*Entrepreneurial income, interest, rent and dividends paid to households.

National friction structures created by the above, whether overt or covert, will indicate the extent to which national intermediation is privileged over foreign intermediation, and the openness or otherwise of the economy to foreign companies and investors. Relative success in the achievement of policy objectives pursued will also have implications for national and international investors with regard to the currency and country risks involved in their activities. These policies may also pre-empt the development of any effective or pioneering role in the international money markets by indigenous banks or in domestic markets by foreign banks. In general within the international trading system, however, these frictions create localized production pressures and vacuums both for internal 'outward' business and external 'inward' business activities that encourage, whether desired or not, implicitly or even explicitly, industrial seepage and relocation of activity within the international trading system motivated by tax and regulation avoidance/evasion.

As regards systemic frictions, the period since the early 1960s has seen an extension of national tax bases to include within their nets capital gains taxation and a more comprehensive taxation of accumulated wealth and its transfer by gift or on death. Moreover, with the emergence in the late 1960s of inflation as a central macroeconomic problem, fiscal instability and pressures have been exerted on economic sectors through general and intermittent regulation of many types of earnings by means of incomes and/or prices policies. Doggart summarizes the impact of these trends thus in relation to the period up to the end of the 1970s:

> tax takes have increased a good deal faster than incomes in the last 20 years . . .
>
> 1. In six out of seven major industrial nations direct taxes on households grew at a consistently higher rate than incomes between 1970 and 1978 (the USA, Canada, Japan, France, West Germany and the Netherlands), the only exception was the UK . . .

TABLE II Changes in tax elasticities and total tax burdens of OECD countries in terms of a comparison of their average figures for the periods 1965–70 and 1970–78

	Tax elasticities		*Total tax burden %*	
Countries	*1965–'70 av.*	*1970–'78 av.*	*1965–'70 av.*	*1970–'78 av.*
Japan	1.08	1.23	19	24
USA	1.15	1.0	30	30
Canada	1.22	0.99	32	31
UK	1.22	0.90	38	34
Finland	1.08	1.13	32	37
Norway	1.18	1.19	39	47
Sweden	1.13	1.25	41	54
Denmark	1.34	1.06	40	43
W. Germany	1.04	1.76	33	38
Belgium	1.13	1.27	35	44
Netherlands	1.12	1.11	40	47
Luxembourg	1.06	1.55	32	50
France	1.02	1.11	36	40
Switzerland	1.13	1.32	24	32
Italy	1.02	1.16	28	33
Austria	1.03	1.17	35	42
Spain	1.17	1.32	17	23
Portugal	1.25	1.14	23	26
Greece	1.17	1.32	24	28
Ireland	1.20	1.03	31	33
Australia	1.08	1.14	26	29
New Zealand	1.15	1.10	28	30
+Countries		14		19
−Countries		8		3*

Source: derived from charts in Doggart, *Tax Havens*, p. 132.

*Includes the USA where there was no change.

2. Revenue raised by direct taxes on corporations outpaced the increase in corporate savings everywhere except in Canada and the USA . . .
3. All 23 (OECD) countries . . . had tax elasticities (the ratio of trend growth rate of total tax and social security receipts to trend growth rate of GDP) above 1.0 in 1965-70.[2]

The evidence for 1 and 2 is contained in Table I. In terms of 3 mentioned in the quotation above, changes in tax elasticity (the ratio of the growth of taxation to the growth of Gross Domestic Product: a figure greater than 1.0 means that a 1.0 per cent change in GDP is accompanied by a more than proportionate increase in taxation) are shown in Table II for OECD countries, together with changes in their national tax burdens as measured by tax revenue (including social security contributions) as a percentage of GDP at market prices. In respect of the twenty-two reported countries, there was an increase in tax elasticities in fourteen and an increase in tax burdens in nineteen cases. It is clear therefore that, as compared with the late 1960s, the 1970s was a period in which there was an overwhelmingly general increase in domestic taxation pressure in OECD countries, including even the traditional continental haven centres of Switzerland

and Luxembourg, although this pressure was not quite as strong in terms of national tax elasticities.

Given that some countries adopt a permissive regulatory environment and others a stringent one, disparities, gaps and differentials arise in national systems of regulation. These differences can lead to perverse competition in regulatory laxity and a gravitation by some institutions to the least regulated financial centres, although, as will be seen later, this does not always have long-term development benefits for such centres given the reputation they have with reputable international bankers and some national tax authorities. In so far as operational costs are lowered by for example, a lack of a deposit insurance scheme, banks located in such centres have a higher financial leverage potential which can enable them to operate on narrower spreads between payments to depositors and interest charges made to lenders. Dangers posed by such uneven regulatory practices led to the establishment of the Bank for International Settlements' Committee on Banking Regulations and Supervisory Practices (the 'Cooke Committee') in 1975, which established general guidelines in their Basle 'Concordat' of that year on 'The Supervison of Banks' Foreign Establishments', although these have as yet no mandatory force. Five general recommendations were made:

1. Surveillance and supervision of foreign banks should be the joint responsibility of parent and host authorities.
2. No foreign bank should be able to evade/avoid supervision.
3. Host authorities should have the prime responsibility of supervising the liquidity of such banks.
4. Solvency supervision should be a matter for the parent authority with respect to foreign branches and primarily the host authority's responsibility in the case of locally incorporated foreign subsidiaries.
5. Ideally, international co-operation should be promoted by information exchanges between host and parent authorities.

As regards control of parent banks, Western European governments are in the process of adopting a system of common procedures and directives that could in future be jointly activated in such a way as to render the offshore activities of their national banks subject to a common onshore control. This movement began with the Council Directive of 12 December 1977: Directive 77/780/EEC relating to the setting up and pursuit of the business of credit institutions advocated *inter alia* the elimination of the most obstructive differences between members states' laws governing such institutions. If activated, this directive would significantly lessen the degree of international financial regulatory differentials. Moreover, in June 1979 the Central Bank Governors of the Group of Ten (Belgium, Canada, France, W.Germany, Italy, Japan, the Netherlands, Sweden, the UK and the US) and Switzerland recommended that their supervisory authorities should adopt a system of supervision on the basis of consolidated accounts. This was taken up by the EEC Commission on 28 September 1981 and put to the Council as a proposal, which also provided for the removal of any legal impediments to the exchange of information without which consolidation cannot be implemented, and for the conclusion of bilateral agreements between member states and third countries in the interests of world-wide consolidation.

With respect to external economic frictions, some attempt has been made at collective action and policy harmonization in the advanced industrial countries. In 1951 a *Code of Liberalization of Current Invisible Transactions* was agreed by the seven countries of the then Organization for European Economic Co-operation, and subsequently the twelve members of the successor organization, the Organization for Economic Co-operation and Development, have agreed since 1961 to a *Code of Liberalization of Capital Movements*. However, implementation has only been partial and the liberalization commitment has only had the somewhat vague objective of being 'to the extent necessary for effective economic co-operation' (Article 1 of the 1961 Code). Derogation clauses have enabled the policies of what Bertrand has called 'Scandinavian syndrome' countries to persist.[3] Generally the expansion of mixed economy attempts at management of national economic activities have often resulted in controls on trade inflows and outflows as part of the system of resource allocation control. Moreover, even under the above Code, no obligations exist *inter alia* with regard to 'inward' short-term credit and loan transactions (with the exception of commercial credits) and direct investment; the issue of foreign securities (quoted securities are included) on domestic markets; foreign takeovers, mergers or acquisition of controlling interests in domestic companies or banks;[4] the sale of 'collective investment securities' such as mutual funds and investment trusts; 'outward' financial loans and credits of more than one year's maturity.

In the 'real' as opposed to the 'textbook' world of international exchange therefore, industrial specialization at the state level is both 'artificially' created and constrained by the existence of domestic and foreign national barriers to trade and other restrictive national and international government and business trade practices. Trade flows are determined by a whole host of complex factors that cannot be explained merely by relationships as simple as those posited in conventional general trade models and are the result of a whole series of multi-sectoral, inter-sectoral, and intra-sectoral decisions (with lags) taken and made, both domestically and in the rest of the world by consumers, producers (public, private, multinational), importers and exporters and departments of state and local government. Each sectoral group is, to a greater or lesser degree, inhibited or liberated in such decisions according to the existence of, and changes in, the nature of the particular regime and constellation of general world economic conditions, and the government-induced and sector-induced economic frictions obtaining. Such trade flows inevitably also reflect particular structural features and politico-economic ties historically determined by the past pattern of international economic development (colonial centre-periphery ties; trade bloc relations; the influence of post-colonial multinational firms etc.) and international politics.

The above-mentioned national friction structures may often have been imposed in an *ad hoc* manner and will probably have created in many instances a regime of control that has a life of its own which becomes progressively separated from any current policy logic. Such structures usually embody artificially created market distortions of three main types, applying Bhagwati's welfare terminology:[5]

a) *Endogenous distortions:* ones arising from private sector national, international or transnational market imperfections.

b) *Autonomous policy-imposed distortions:* ones that have prevailed unquestioned for many years (e.g. as a result of historical accident), and have no necessary direct relevance to current policy objectives or needs. These might relate to the political degrees of *de facto* freedom exercised by former colonial states and their preferential relationship with certain countries, etc. and also to national regulatory systems in the areas of credit control, for example, the British system prior to 1971 applied to the clearing banks but not to the burgeoning secondary banking system which was thereby given a *de facto* competitive bias; and the area of protection of investors in the non-banking sectors of the financial system: for example, the recent UK 'hotch-potch' criticisms of Professor Gower with respect to differential restrictions applied in the areas of securities and investment and the particularly rigid attitude taken with regard to unit trust issues. In the area of foreign entry regulation, domestic financial institutions are often overprotected for quasi mercantilist reasons.

c) *Instrumental policy-imposed distortions:* ones designed for particular short to medium term policy objectives often relating to balance of payments difficulties: for example, policy changes made within an existing regime of exchange control; attitudes towards the domestic flotation of foreign bonds, inward foreign money and capital flows etc.

It is important to realize that the existence of the above-mentioned frictions and the continued presence of their distorting effects have internal and external implications for resource allocation both nationally and internationally, such that the realization of potential comparative advantage, however defined, is restricted and replaced by quite other, often non-economic and/or 'artificial' motivations. In principle, however, these distortions could be removed by unilateral action at individual government level, or by multinational agreement at the regional and/or global level, thereby altering the operational context in which market forces interact.

In addition to state-induced economic frictions, the international location of potentially competitive production activities may also be constrained by private sector market imperfections resulting from the concentration of industrial ownership, the use of patents, and the presence of oligopolies and cartels. The existence of multinational firms will moreover tend to bring about a transnational allocation of processes and products according to global company advantage rather than country advantage.

When the general phenomenon of world exchange is viewed in the light of the above 'facts of economic life' perspective, it is evident that the combined national friction structures of the major industrial onshore trading nations, from which and to which the main global exchange flows emanate and gravitate, constitute an 'international friction matrix', the overt and covert characteristics of which divert, destroy, and create profitable trade activities. Within this matrix, international friction differentials and asymmetries, national friction loopholes, anomalies and discretionary procedures will cause some degree of industrial dislocation, relocation and *de novo* establishment. These tendencies will become marked when either the general matrix or a regional sub-matrix becomes more restrictive in complexion, whether this results from internal friction intensification or external trade friction intensification. Both of the latter frictions will create a need for an alternative secondary trading system to become established, motivated by regulation avoidance/evasion of the effects of the primary onshore trading system's friction structures and located in offshore lower cost zero/near zero friction states, especially in the case of invisible trade activities. Onshore intensification (relaxation) of these restrictions or distortions will stimulate (lessen) this need and will increase (circumscribe) their production possibility potential. In this regard, some national friction structures will be more important than others. In general, those of high GDP per-capita countries will be of greater significance than low per-capita countries, although the latter may not be as sophisticated in their ability to control trade flows, and may nevertheless possess extremely rich potential clientele for offshore services if incomes and wealth are very unevenly distributed.

The importance of the international friction matrix and the evolution of a secondary trading system is very well exemplified by the transformation of international monetary relations that resulted from the creation of the Eurocurrency Markets in the 1960s and their rapid growth and worldwide sourcing in the 1970s. This financial mutation will now be considered in some detail as it was a decisive initiating and sustaining factor in the rapid growth of international banking in this period: this development provided a significant externality for the process of onshore external centre evolution and the derived process of offshore tax haven transformation. The creation process arose from a particular sequence of US domestic regulations and deregulations that stimulated a series of US bank emigrations and invasions motivated by their avoidance or evasion.

During the years that followed the end of the Second World War, American banking reigned high in international finance. The US dollar acted as the world's unit of account for measuring prices and incomes internationally and became its standard for deferred payments. American banks led the world: in 1956 for instance, forty-four of the largest US banks were ranked in the world's top one hundred banking corporations. In the 1950s, a new financial market evolved as a vehicle for raising foreign loan finance on an international scale centred on New York—the international dollar bond market (the 'Yankee' Bond Market). However in the early 1960s, US domestic balance of payments and monetary policy imposed certain restrictions which encouraged borrowers to seek new funds in Europe and subsequently elsewhere within the world trading system, including American business corporations that operated overseas. This regional financial relocation was promoted both by the emergence of external US dollar currency deposits and the spread of international availability and use of Certificates of Deposit (CDs). An international (some would declare a supranational) private banking sector emerged which became increasingly transnational in its features as it became more extensively based on its lending and borrowing sourcing and diversified in its financial instrument offerings. Thus, the international dollar bond market of the 1950s re-emerged outside the US as the Eurodollar Bond Market to which new Eurocurrency markets were subsequently added.

The first such Eurobond was a $15m. fifteen-year bond issued on 1 July 1963 for Autostrade, the operator of toll motorways in Italy, guaranteed by IRI, the

Italian state industrial and financial holding corporation. These bonds, subsequently issued through international banks, were prohibited from being placed in the US or with US persons in contrast to Yankee bonds. Yankee bonds are issued on the domestic US capital market and are registered and subject to review by the US Securities and Exchange Commission and must first be publicly rated by one of the reputable independent bond agencies, such as Moody's Investors Service, Inc. and Standard and Poor's Corporation to meet legal investment standards for institutional investors and to broaden their appeal (the top four grades being AAA, AA, A and BBB). The Interest Equalization Tax imposed in the US for balance of payments reasons during the period 1963 to 1974 essentially closed the latter market to many non-US borrowers which encouraged them to seek Eurobond finance. Other non-dollar denominated Eurobonds evolved, although they were subject to varying degrees of government control, which included regulations with respect to issue size, and the calendaring of issues to maintain orderly market conditions. The first to develop was that for Deutschmarks following the imposition in March 1964 of a 25 per cent tax on domestic DM bonds held by non-residents and the exemption of this tax with respect to foreign issues launched by non-German institutions. Similar developments occurred in 1965 with respect to Euro-French franc and Euro-Dutch guilder bonds.

The other financial instrument promoting the beginnings and extension of global banking was the increasing availability of CDs: these are negotiable instruments mostly in bearer form evidencing a deposit with a commercial bank, which became an important financial asset used in the emerging inter-bank market. The first US domestic CD was issued in 1961 by First National City Bank and as from 1966 and 1968 Dollar CDs and Sterling CDs respectively were made available in London, not subject to any UK or US stamp and/or withholding taxes. These were followed in November 1968 by the launching of an Asian Dollar market in Singapore for offshore US dollar accounts and the development as from 1970 of a Far East CD market. Following a liberalization of the licensing system applied to issuing houses in respect of dollar CDs in September 1971, the London market became more globally based and participated in by the interntional banks (see *The Banker* Survey of the London dollar CDs in May 1976, pp. 607–20).

Unquestionably, the international privatization of international finance was furthered by a sequence of regulation changes in three main areas of US domestic policy between 1963 and 1974. These three areas were: (*a*) capital controls; (*b*) domestic regulation of external US branches and subsidiaries; and (*c*) interest rate and reserve controls.

(a) Capital Controls

There were three types of control which had the effect of encouraging US external business to seek funds from abroad rather than from the home market:

i) The Voluntary Foreign Credit Restraint Program (VFCRP) which operated between 1965 and 1974 to limit the size of foreign loans extended from US domestic banks but did not generally apply if extended from their foreign branches.

ii) The Foreign Direct Investment Program which arose from the control of the export of capital from American business corporations abroad. At first (in 1965) the demands were voluntary, but, after 1968 mandatory limits were imposed. This resulted in external financial pressure being exercised by such corporations in the Euromarkets and demands being increased on US foreign branches as intermediaries.

iii) The Interest Equalization Tax which was introduced in 1963 on the purchase of long-term foreign securities was extended to bank loans of more than one year's duration after 10 February 1965, whether from domestic or foreign branches. This measure was designed to eliminate the interest-rate differential between Europe and America and thus to discourage the outflow of American funds abroad. However, the lending activities of foreign branches were exempted from the tax as from February 1967 and the continued existence of these provisions until 1974 favoured such foreign branch activities.

(b) Domestic Regulation of External US Branches and Subsidiaries

Under S.25 of the Federal Reserve Act, all member banks of the Federal Reserve Board must apply for permission to establish foreign branches. In 1963, Regulation M was revised such that further branching in a country abroad where a branch was already located was not subject to permission, and branches could 'exercise powers that are usual abroad' and they could 'underwrite and deal in the obligations of the national government of the country'. Thus banks could now expand via their foreign branches in ways which were precluded at home by state laws and diversify into international business that would not become intermittently directly hampered by US balance of payments policy.

As regards subsidiaries, amendments were made to Regulation K to make it easier to set up Edge Act Companies (EACs) as holding companies purely for foreign banking within the areas laid down by Regulation Y.

(c) Interest Rate and Reserve Controls

Domestic US controls included the use of limits being set to the interest rates charged (Regulation Q) and reserve requirements being made in respect of deposits (Regulation D). Given the liberalization of controls on branching abroad mentioned in (*b*) above, both these regulations could be evaded or avoided in foreign branches. Thus, domestically Regulation Q limited the amount of interest payable by banks on savings deposits. From 1966 onwards it was deliberately kept within the 4-5¼ per cent range to freeze such rates below three-month money market rates as a means of deflating the economy when required (as in 1968-69, 1973-75, and from 1977 onwards). These interest rate ceilings imposed under Regulation Q could be avoided by the payment of rates above these limits at foreign branches. Initially this proved an especially attractive loophole, as it enabled a foreign branch to attract funds abroad with higher deposit rates and to relend them to its US domestic parent, especially during times of tight domestic monetary control: these 'captive' foreign branch funds accounted for 50 per cent of all funds from foreign branches in 1969, when a 3 per cent differential obtained between Regulation Q limits and London rates.[6] To counteract this, 30 to 90 day Certificates of Deposit (CDs) of over $100,000 were made exempt as from 24 June 1970, and larger CDs of longer maturities became exempt as from 16 May 1973, thereby ending the interest-rate benefits of foreign branches. However, additionally in 1969 a 10 per cent special reserve requirement was placed on increases in Eurodollar borrowings by US domestic banks above a base level, making borrowings from foreign branches subject to reserve ratios as if they were ordinary deposits. The use of this provision as a regulator continued to make the costs of dollar business lower abroad and effectively separated the US domestic money market from the huge pool of dollars held abroad.

Regulation D did not apply to deposits held in foreign branches. This meant that in countries where no reserve requirements were imposed on external currency deposits, as in the UK, it was possible to offer higher interest rates to depositors than in the US and to charge lower rates to borrowers, thereby contributing to the wholesale flow of Euromarket business, reinforcing its lower levels of operating costs. A similar logic lay behind the growth of other currency-denominated Eurocurrency deposits. Further internal friction structures existed with respect to the US banking system which made expansion abroad attractive. Being an economic system that envelops a series of federal states, certain endogenous distortions arise from the need for each state to protect its domestic decision-taking base, especially with respect to legislation against local concentrations of economic power. Such regulations have escalated and remained unchanged for many years without reference to the contemporary needs of business whether internally and/or externally oriented. The federal system of internal regulation is multi-tiered and complex and the plethora of autonomous policy-imposed distortions themselves give rise to inter-state frictioneering in relation to the location of economic activities. In addition to state bank regulatory authorities, there are three federal agencies, each independent and not subject to any co-ordinating mechanism: the Federal Reserve Board, which purports to act as a central bank for its (voluntary) bank members; the Comptroller of Currency, the primary controller of banks who have opted for federal rather than state supervision; and the Federal Deposit Insurance Corporation which administers the deposit insurance programme. Furthermore, the expansion or merger of banks is also subject to the general anti-trust laws exercised by the Department of Justice.

Nationally the most important of the arcane restrictions were, and remain, in addition to Regulation Q:

a) The McFadden Act 1927 and the Douglas Amendment which prevent branching from taking place outside a bank's home state and from acquiring banks in other states in most circumstances. As a result of this US nationwide banking development has been thwarted and thousands of small local banks have remained in business: in 1980, it was estimated that there were some 14,500 banks in existence. This geographical distortion was further intensified by legislation in many states that confine deposit-taking to one or a limited number of locations, and which, additionally, through 'usury' regulations limited the rates that lenders could charge borrowers. The above restrictions clearly ran counter to the existence of a modern financial services industry.

b) The Glass-Steagull Act 1933, which created and continues to create an artificial dividing line between commercial and investment banking, which thereby debars bank diversification into the Wall Street activities of corporate securities underwriting, stockbroking and mutual funds. Furthermore, this Act granted what are now some 4,400 savings and loan institutions the privilege of paying ¼ per cent more on savings deposits than that permitted to banks.

c) Banking laws further prevent banks from lending more than the equivalent of 10 per cent of their capital and reserves to a single borrower, whereas foreign banks from the US are free from this imposed limit. This regulation may deter domestic US banks from large participations in single Eurocredit loans.

The importance of state legislation is exemplified by the case of New York, which nevertheless has been at the forefront of commercial law reform to encourage freer competition in local and regional banking.[7] In 1934 the New York State Stephens Act partitioned the state into nine banking districts between which commercial banks could branch and merge, though the establishment of a *de novo* branch in a community other than New York City which is 'home office protected' (in which an independent commercial bank is headquartered) was prohibited except by the acquisition of an existing bank through merger. Some relaxations were made by the 1960 Omnibus Banking Act, but it was only when the 1971 Statewide Branching Law was passed that, after a 4½ year transition period, a single banking district was formed on 1 January 1976. Attempts to avoid state and federal regulation in these and other matters under the federal Bank Holding Company Act of 1956 by forming one-bank subsidiaries of a holding company parent were terminated by a 1970 Amendment to the Act, which withdrew this exemption although at the same time granting some opportunities for diversification to holding companies.[8]

As a result of these internal frictions, the US financial system became fragmented in an arbitrary way in terms of geographical dispersion, institution functions, and range of types of financial enterprise. Rationalization in terms of the needs of modern industry and banking practice has been thwarted. In common with the impact of controls on the financial system in the UK prior to 1971, these measures promoted a continually falling share of financial activities for the banking system, such that 'secondary' markets became more important as the core deposit base of the officially recognized system declined.[9] During the 1970s, this resulted in many innovatory developments being denied to domestic US banks: in particular, the commercial paper market, the financial futures market, and money market mutual funds drew away lending and deposit business from domestic US banks as the institutions involved were free of insurance fees, reserve requirements and ceilings.

Commercial paper is simply a corporate IOU sold to raise short-term money.

Buyers tend to be mostly institutional investors. This market is largely exempt from regulation: issuers do not have to register with the Securities and Exchange Commission, borrowings can be arranged at short notice, may have a maximum maturity of nine months, may not be sold directly to the public and must be used for current financings. Amounts and maturities can be tailored to the borrower's need and usually at a lower cost than bank lending and the Euromarkets. Whereas the amount outstanding in this market varied between $32bn. to $50bn. in the period 1970 to 1976, from 1977 onwards it rose steadily up to a total of $164bn. at the end of 1981.

The financial futures market was launched in 1972 in Chicago when the International Monetary Market (IMM), a division of the Chicago Merchantile Exchange, introduced foreign currency futures and subsequently 90-day treasury bills. The first traded interest rate futures were issued in 1975 by the Chicago Board of Trade in the form of Collateralized Depository Receipts called Government National Mortgage Certificates or 'Ginnie Maes' as they became known. These markets were developed to protect the value of money given fluctuating currency values and interest rates. Other markets followed. In 1978 Amex (the American Stock Exchange) opened a competitive futures market in New York to be followed in 1980 by the New York Futures Exchange, and in 1981 by a New Orleans exchange.

Money market mutual funds began in 1972 and became, within a few years, of nationwide significance, rising in value to around $190 billion by the end of 1981, when they were equal to about a tenth of all money held by individuals in US savings and current bank accounts. Being unregulated they were able to offer 17 to 20 per cent interest when banks were only permitted to offer 5¼ per cent, their growth becoming particularly marked after 1978 when interest rates soared. This new non-bank business was supported by specialist financial intermediaries, many of which were new conglomerates formed by merging different financial interests such as stockbroking, insurance and travel services expertise.

Some legitimate means were nevertheless available to banks to obviate the impact of some of the domestic restrictions, the most noticeable being the following:

1. Under the 1919 Edge Act, banks are permitted to open offices outside their home states ('out-of-state banking') to provide financial services exclusively linked to foreign trade purposes. Although most foreign trade business became externally located, nevertheless the setting up of Citizens and Southerns from the State of Georgia in Florida in 1969 began a trend in which a number of regional small external enclave businesses were set up onshore.
2. Building societies found ways to offer customers current account and cheque book facilities and banks found ways to move into mortgage business via holding companies.
3. The avoidance of Regulation Q was effected in some instances by unconventional means such as the offer of free china, radios and television sets.
4. Some banking disintermediation away from savings accounts to Certificates of Deposits that had market-related interest rates took place.

In addition to 'unfair' non-bank competition, domestic US banks increasingly felt competition at home from foreign banks who managed to penetrate and internationalize home banking. As Berger points out:

> Whereas at the end of 1972, there were 52 foreign banks in the United States, with about 100 installations, by the end of 1979, the number of installations had grown threefold, representing 151 foreign banks from 30 countries. By the end of 1979 foreign banks in the United States held assets of $80 billion, or 6.6 per cent of the total of American bank assets. Put another way, whereas from about the middle of the 1970s the assets of domestic US banks grew by around 10 per cent a year, the US assets of foreign banks grew at an annual rate of almost 30 per cent.[10]

Thus, US banks have been domestically hemmed in by archaic legal constraints and unfair competition which has constituted a state of 'financial repression'. However, while their domestic profitability and ability to compete have been seriously hampered, freedom to develop overseas has been a compensation. For example, Citicorp, the second largest bank in America, reported in 1980 that 60 per cent of its offices were outside the US and 64 per cent of its net income before securities losses came from non-US business, and that international consumer lending was almost half as large as domestic consumer lending, Eurocurrency business being specially important in this regard.

To return to our global discussion, from 1963 onwards, a series of onshore external markets were created where none had existed before, the distinctive feature of which were bank deposits denominated in currencies not native to the country of deposit location. Forms of paper debt evolved to cover short, medium and long term requirements denominated in single or even multiple currencies. The attractiveness of the markets resides in the fact that depositors are paid higher and borrowers lower interest rates than in domestic markets due to the lower costs of intermediation, absence of regulation and greater competition. Interest payments are made on a gross basis, free of withholding tax and other income taxes which is attractive to all participating economic sectors which invest or borrow therein. Discussion of the structural changes within the Euromarkets as they developed will be reserved for Chapter II that follows. It will suffice in the context of this chapter to indicate the aggregate growth in magnitude of these markets and their multi-currency diversification, and to list the centres that participated therein. Table III indicates how the Euromarkets have grown dramatically since 1964, and how the importance of the US dollar fell from 83 per cent in 1964 to 69 per cent relative to other currency-denominated activites.

It soon became clear that even lower cost differentials could be achieved in offshore tax haven centres despite the additional establishment costs. As a consequence, an intertwined network of onshore external centres and offshore tax haven centres developed, interlinked spacially by telex communication and air travel and commercially by institutional multi-centre industrial location. This enabled a functional pattern of business activity involving a separation between arranging and booking locations according to the particular circumstances of each transaction. Official statistics given by the Bank for International Settlements, Basle, indicate that for the period 1973–80, a select number of such off-

TABLE III: Growth of the Euromarkets by size and currency-denomination 1964–1980 as reported in the Bank for International Settlements, Basle, Annual Reports (US$m.)

		US $m.		*Other currencies*						
Year	*Gross assets*	*Total*	*% Tot.*	*Total*	*% Tot.*	*Deutschmark*	*Swiss frs.*	*UK £*	*Dutch guilder*	*French frs.*
1964	12	10	83.3	3	16.7	0.8	0.8	0.8	0.1	0.1
1965	14	11	78.8	3	21.2	0.9	0.9	0.7	0.2	0.1
1966	18	15	83.3	4	16.7	1	1	0.7	0.1	0.6
1967	22	18	81.8	4	18.2	2	1	0.8	0.1	0.2
1968	38	30	78.9	7	21.1	4	2	0.6	0.3	0.2
1969	58	48	82.8	11	17.2	6	3	0.6	0.4	0.2
1970	78	60	76.9	18	23.1	10	5	0.6	0.6	0.4
1971	100	72	72.0	29	28.0	16	8	2	0.7	0.7
1972	132	98	74.2	34	25.8	20	8	2	0.7	0.7
1973	188	132	70.2	56	29.8	31	15	3	1	2
1974	215	156	72.6	59	27.4	35	14	2	2	1
1975	258	190	73.6	68	26.4	42	15	2	2	3
1976	305	224	73.4	81	26.6	49	18	2	4	3
1977	385	268	69.6	116	30.1	70	24	5	4	3
1978	502	340	67.7	162	32.3	97	28	7	7	6
1979	640	428	66.7	212	33.3	124	39	11	8	8
1980	751	519	69.1	233	30.9	123	50	13	7	12

Source: BIS Annual Reports, December figures.

TABLE IV: Bank for International Settlements estimated total Eurocurrency funds and offshore banking centre percentage share 1973–80, (US$m.)

		Offshore centre share				*Net Lender +/ Borrower − Position*
Year	*Total Funds*	*Use*	*% Tot.*	*Source*	*% Tot.*	
1973	132.0	18.7	14.1	12.5	9.5	− 6.2
1974	177.0	26.7	15.1	17.8	10.1	− 8.9
1975	205.0	35.6	17.4	19.9	9.7	−15.7
1976	247.0	40.8	16.5	21.3	8.6	−19.5
1977	300.0	43.9	14.6	33.4	11.1	−10.5
1978	375.0	55.0	14.7	45.4	12.1	− 9.6
1979	475.0	67.5	14.2	52.8	11.1	−14.7
1980	575.0	73.0	12.7	68.0	11.8	− 5

Source: BIS Annual Reports, December figures.

shore centres (the ones starred on page 21) accounted for at least 14 per cent of the use of these funds and provided around 11 to 12 per cent of their supply, so that in each year they were net borrowers of the reported market flow as Table IV reveals. The figures in Table IV underestimate the global importance of offshore centres due to the narrow coverage of the reporting countries as will be seen in Part III Chapter I.

Although discussion of individual centre development profiles is reserved for Part III Chapter I, it should be stressed here that the transformation of some of these centres resulted from the tacit or complicit permissive attitudes of other, mainly onshore, countries and the production vacuums created by their explicit desire not, themselves, to directly participate in the business of attracting external trade activities—this was the case in respect of Luxembourg as a Euromarket centre for Deutschmark and Swiss francs; Singapore, as an Asian dollar market given the non-participation of the Japanese authorities; and Bahrain, as the Middle East's offshore centre, given the attitude of Saudi Arabia and other countries in the area. Once established, these centres created their own respective development logic and strategy for self-perpetuating survival, if not growth, when the process of US deregulation before 1974 and since became manifested.

CONCLUSIONS

1) The parametric context of the onshore international politico-economic friction matrix, with its national differentials, assymetries and accretions of endogenous, autonomous and instrumental policy-imposed distortions can, if intensified or relaxed, encourage or deter the possibilities of external international profit engineering by industrial dislocation, relocation, or *de novo* establishment.
2) The existence of regulations in any form encourages attempts at international avoiding or evasive action and stimulates the creation of an alter-

native global trading system, especially for invisible trade activities, in low or zero friction offshore state centres.

3) A prime real world example of the above has been the creation of the Eurocurrency onshore external and offshore haven centres, which have provided a transnational common property financial resource for companies, governments and persons.

Before the conflicting areas of onshore countervailing power and offshore competition are examined, an outline of the emergence of this new second generation secondary trading system must be given fully related to the increasing global trends in international trading relationships and international banking.

REFERENCES

1. Baldwin, R.E., *Non-tariff Trade Distortions of International Trade,* London, Allen and Unwin, 1971; 'Part D—The Official Regulation of Financial Institutions' in *The Development of Financial Institutions in Europe,* ed. by J.E. Wadsworth *et al.*, Leyden, Sijthoff, 1977; Krul, N., 'Financial Markets and Economic Nationalism', ch.6 of *The New Economic Nationalism,* ed. by O. Hieronymi, London, Macmillan, 1980; and Appendix No. 1, pp. 113-54 of Griffiths, B.N., *Invisible Barriers to Invisible Trade,* London, Macmillan, 1975; Inter-bank Research Organisation, *The Regulation of Banks in the Member States of the EEC,* Leyden, Sijthoff and Noordhoff, 1978; Department of the US Treasury, *Report to Congress on Foreign Government Treatment of U.S. Commercial Banking Organizations,* 1979; Fair, D, 'The Independence of Central Banks', *The Banker,* October 1979, pp. 31-41; and Thring, P. and Taylor-Jones, M., 'Harmonising Bank Annual Accounts in the European Community, *The Banker,* June 1981, pp. 51-4.

2. Doggart, C., *Tax Havens and Their Uses,* Economist Intelligence Unit Special Report No. 105, London, 1981, pp. 2-3.

3. Bertrand, R., 'The Liberalisation of Capital Movements—An Insight', *Three Banks Review,* No. 132, December 1981, pp. 3-22. See also 'Experience with Controls on International Operations in Shares and Bonds', OECD Secretriat, Paris, 1981; and 'Regulations Affecting International Banking Operations', Directorate for Financial and Fiscal Affairs, OECD Paris, 1981.

4. See as an example the UK Monopolies and Mergers Commission's 'Report on the Proposed Mergers—The Hongkong and Shanghai Banking Corporation, Standard Chartered Bank Ltd., and The Royal Bank of Scotland Group Ltd.', January 1982. The Hongkong and Shanghai Banking Corporation's bid was found unacceptable because difficulties over the Bank of England's supervison, if the new entity was allowed 'would in themselves engender unacceptable risks to depositors with Royal Bank Group banks if they were acquired by the Hongkong Bank. . . . The Bank (of England) questioned whether, given the key part played by the London and Scottish clearing banks in the UK economy, it could ever be right to allow control of any of them to pass into hands not fully committed to the UK public interest . . . possibilities of conflict of interest are inevitably opened up . . . [as] the parent company is bound to respond to the policy requirements of its own home government and, more generally, to give primacy to its responsibilities to the needs and interests of the people of its area . . . in some circumstances these requirements may well be inconsistent with enabling a subsidiary abroad to be fully responsive to the authorities in the country in which it operates.'

5. Bhagwati, J.N., 'The Generalised Theory of Distortions and Welfare', ch.4 of *Trade,*

Balance of Payments and Growth ed. J.N. Bhagwati *et al.*, Amsterdam, North Holland, 1971, pp. 73–4.

6. Kelly, J., *Bankers and Borders: The Case of American Banks in Britain,* Cambridge, Mass., Ballinger, 1977.

7. See Kidder, K., 'Bank Expansion in New York State: The 1971 Statewide Branching Law', *Federal Reserve Bank of New York Monthly Review,* November 1971, pp. 266–74; and Kunreuther, J.B., 'Banking Structure in New York State: Progress and Prospects', *Federal Reserve Bank of New York Monthly Review,* April 1976, pp. 107–15.

8. See Hayes, A., 'The 1970 Amendments to the Bank Holding Company Act: Opportunities to Diversify', *Federal Reserve Bank of New York Monthly Review,* February 1971, pp. 23–7.

9. Berger, F.E., 'The Emerging Transformation of the US Banking System', *The Banker,* September 1981, pp. 25–39.

10. Berger, op. cit., p. 35.

CHAPTER II
The Emergence of the International 'Intermediate' Economy and the Semiperipheral Global Secondary Trading System

The last decade and a half has witnessed radical changes in the need for, and organization of, international finance. One particular consequence of this has been the transformation of certain tax havens throughout the world into offshore finance centres. These centres can be formally identified as being located in

> economies which have made a deliberate attempt to attract thereto international trade-oriented activities by the minimization of taxes and the reduction or elimination of other restrictions on business operations, such that, within the jurisdiction of the centre, aggregate economic activity is substantially geared to the special global invisible trade needs of external enterprises and investors.[1]

These centres are to be distinguished from specific zones or areas within onshore economies that can be so described, such as the City of London and the offshore banking facilities available in New York since 3 December 1981, which may more properly be described as 'onshore external centres'. Furthermore they are also to be distinguished from free trade zones, free ports and transit zones which are established primarily for visible trade activities, although a number of financial centres also co-exist with these additional facilities: not all haven centres are suitable for this co-orientation either because of domestic labour shortages, space considerations or their remoteness from markets.

In practice, the offshore finance centre or offshore-aspiring tax haven tends to be a geographically small state and one of three kinds—inland enclave states, coastal enclaves and island states, each with their own immediate but different contiguous or otherwise possibility of onshore hinterland exploitation. Some thirty-five or more areas throughout the world have been reported as having made significant efforts in this direction, though not all have realized domestically the substantial take-off implied by the definition given above. These areas include the states listed in Table V. While a number of these have today become, and are becoming, important financial and business peripheries of the main onshore network of world trade flows, more often than not their growth momentum in the first instance derived, and derives still in many cases, from a particular historical tax-haven relationship with an onshore economy or continent in near proximity, such as the Channel Islands and the UK; the Bahamas and other Caribbean states such as the Cayman Islands and the Americas; Hong Kong and mainland China; Vanuatu (formerly the New Hebrides) and Australia; Luxembourg and Belgium, Holland and West Germany. As tax havens or low-tax areas, they had or have natural attractions both for rich *émigrés* and *rentiers* alike from these and other geographical areas, who desired or desire politically stable congenial areas of settlement in which to maximize the net value of their wealth.

TABLE V: A list of the various types of aspiring tax haven financial centres

Inland enclaves	*Coastal enclaves*	*Island states*	
Andorra	Costa Rica	Anguilla	Isle of Man
Campione	*Lebanon	*The Bahamas	Jersey
Liechtenstein	*Liberia	Bahrain	Malta
Luxembourg	Nicaragua	*Barbados	Nauru
Monaco	*Panama	*Bermuda	*Netherland Antilles
Switzerland	Singapore	British and US Virgin Islands	Philippines
	*United Arab Emirates	*Cayman Islands	Seychelles
		Cyprus	St. Vincent
		Guernsey	Turks and Caicos
		*Hong Kong	*Vanuatu (New Hebrides)

*Eurocurrency statistics included in Annual Reports of the Bank for International Settlements.

They also attract non-resident business and rich entrepreneurs who require a legal *situs* for their production activities and the derived receipt of incomes that is tax-efficient and may also permit wealth accumulation as a result of low taxed investment of these incomes. In the case of the former sector, the usual economic motive was and is the avoidance of wealth taxes, capital gains taxes and gift and inheritance taxes, for which *inter alia* family trusts and holding companies are often established. In the case of the latter entrepreneurial group, the setting-up of overseas trading and investment companies are the means by which a presence is registered.

During the last decade or so, some haven centres have evolved a further stage of development as a result of participation in the process of global internationalization of national money and credit markets subsequent to the creation of the Interbank Markets and the Eurocurrency and Eurobond Markets in the 1960s, and the general spread of transnational banking in the 1970s. These developments were promoted by an electronic revolution in fund transfer mechanisms which considerably lessened the costs and inconvenience of operation of banks in remote locations and made inter and intra time-zone business activity viable. This gave rise to the creation of international wholesale banking, where large denomination deposits held in a variety of currencies, obtained via extensive world-wide branch networks from non-resident corporate customers, banks, government agencies etc. are re-lent through such markets transnationally to similar sectors. These deposit-gathering, loan-distributing, network infrastructures also created the diversification possibilities of new transnational business superstructures, as well as the practice of international subcontracting via syndicated loan activities.

The above developments will now be considered in more depth in the following sequence of discussion:

The telecommunication revolution;
The evolution of the Interbank and Eurocurrency markets;
The growth of financial world-wide branching networks.

Subsequently consideration will be given to the emergence of 'intermediate' economies and a secondary global trading system that resulted therefrom.

THE TELECOMMUNICATION REVOLUTION

Over the last fifteen years or so, developments in telecommunications in respect of extensive and integrated transmission systems, switching equipment, and satellite communications have enabled a rapid spread of information in accessible form without regard for distance, permitting general commercial information to be widely and quickly diffused as well as on an intra-corporation basis. In respect of international banking[2] it gave rise to the spread and availability of information services in many vital areas: the foreign exchange market (e.g., Reuters' 'Monitor' service, the AP/Dow Jones 'Telerate' service); computer-assisted dealing services (e.g., Reuters' 'Money Dealing Service' and EUREX); computer-matched dealing services; fully automated dealing services; in-house 'back office' systems; automated settlement services such as the London Stock Exchange's Talisman service and the Eurobond Market's Euroclear and Cedel; automated funds transfer and message systems such as SWIFT (the Society for Worldwide Interbank Financial Telecommunication) which has 650 bank subscribers throughout the world,[3] and CHIPS (the Clearing House Inter-bank Payments System) in New York.

The above developments made it possible for international banking to become much more footloose in its location than heretofore. It was now possible to set up foreign branches as staging-posts within a worldwide development strategy with satellite peripheral bases which could be in direct communication with the pulse of daily activities on the money, capital and commodity markets of the world.

Kindleberger has pointed out that:

> difference in time is . . . (*a*) diseconomy of centralization that has supported the growth of North American markets as against European, the Eurocurrency market as against New York, and the West Coast of North America as against Toronto–Montreal and New York. Direct communication by telephone or telex must be simultaneous: when it spans many time zones, it involves a dislocation of the working day for at least one party.[4]

As regards the new potential offshore sites, business convenience tended to favour those areas within the same time zone as the main onshore financial centres and with convenient direct transport links with such centres because, in some circumstances, telecommunication is no substitute for face-to-face contact with bankers, lawyers, security-dealers, borrowers and lenders. The importance of location is illustrated in Table VI where a list of havens is given in terms of their places within the approximate diurnal time sequence standardized in relation to GMT. Thus in relation to a 24-hour clock based on Greenwich there is an overlapping sequence of business hours that ensures that banks and other institutions may do round-the-clock business in the money and stock markets of the world, with Japan and the Far East opening up in the early hours of the day followed by the Middle East, Europe, London, the eastern parts of the Carib-

TABLE VI: Offshore centres in relation to their GMT time zones and those of the main onshore centres

Main onshore centres	*Time zones*	*Associated offshore centres*
Los Angeles	− 8	
	− 7	Mexico
Miami	− 6	Costa Rica, Nicaragua
New York	− 5	Bahamas, Caymans, Panama
	− 4	Anguilla, N. Antilles, Bermuda, Turks and Caicos
London	GMT 0	Channel Isles, Isle of Man, Liberia
Paris Frankfurt	+ 1	Gibraltar, Lichtenstein, Luxembourg, Malta, Switzerland, Tunisia
	+ 2	Greece, Lebanon
	+ 3	Bahrain, Cyprus
	+ 4	United Arab Emirates, Seychelles
	+ 7½	Singapore
	+ 8	Hong Kong, Philippines
Tokyo	+ 9	
	+ 11	Vanuatu
	+ 11½	Norfolk Isles
	+ 12	Nauru

bean, New York and the West Coast of America. As regards the business activities of each offshore centre, it is unlikely that intra zone switching of business will occur at whim as secured clearing of balances imposes its own delay to deals, unless money has been deposited and reserved in advance of such contingencies.

THE EVOLUTION OF THE INTERBANK AND EUROCURRENCY MARKETS

(i) The Interbank Market

The interbank market emerged in the 1960s initially to re-lend money overnight to the UK local authority market at a ¼ percentage point or more above the discount market rate. More importantly, it soon developed to enable secondary investment bankers, domestic and foreign, to maximize their profits within prudential limits, by matching their liabilities and assets within the full range and currency spectrum of their short-to-medium-to-long-run maturities. Mismatching which would occur given that normal minimum deposit levels (in the early 1970s being £50,000 for the UK banks) tend to be much smaller than normal minimum lending levels (£500,000 in the early 1970s) and that the obtaining of business on either side of the balance sheet is unlikely to be synchronized, is thereby avoided. Thus, the interbank market enables daily dealings to occur to obtain or provide funds either side of these balance sheets to fill potential gaps in these maturity structures. This market supplemented the growth of the CD market (discussed in Chapter 1) and that of the Eurocurrency markets.

(ii) The Eurocurrency Markets

Chapter I has already accounted for the reasons underlying the creation of the Eurocurrency markets in the 1960s. It is necessary here to outline in more detail what they are and how they evolved, as once markets arise they develop their own logic and methods of self-perpetuation and these markets are a significant part of the story of offshore centre evolution.

Eurocurrency funds essentially consist of bond issues and Eurocurrency bank credits. Two technical innovations occurred during the 1970s that ensured the continuity of their development.

(a) Credit syndication. As debt grew, larger loans were made possible by being shared among several major banks and many smaller ones: perhaps over a hundred institutions might be involved in one large loan. Syndication thus made possible sovereign borrower financing and spread default risks more widely and internationally. Size was no longer a constraint on loan activities. The participation process usually involves a 'lead manager' institution being responsible for issues and working with a handful of co-manager institutions and perhaps another hundred major and minor under-writers and a similar number of other selling group banks. The banks that benefit most tend to be those with 'placing power' (ability to place at least £500,000 of a new issue) rather than mere connections with borrowers or marketing skills. This has given Swiss and Belgian banks advantages because of the 'in-house' discretionary funds that they have available to invest on behalf of their clients: Belgian banks are involved because the Belgian 20 per cent withholding tax is not levied on international bonds and domestic holders can cash their coupons in Luxembourg or Holland where there is a withholding tax.[5] By 1981, OECD estimated that the average size of individual Euro-credit syndicated loans were just over $110m. ushering in what has become known as the end of 'megadollar' deals.[6] By the middle of the 1970s the Association of International Bond Dealers listed 115 lead managers in the issue market and seventy-one market makers in the secondary market, although both are dominated by some twenty-five banks. Towards the end of the 1970s, the marketability of these loans was broadened through a system of sub-participation certificates which enabled the loan to be onsold at any time during its life.

(b) *The types of bonds available proliferated as the market developed.* Initially there was just the fixed rate 'straight' bonds issued for maturities varying between three and twenty-five years. Then came the variable floating-rate bond. In 1969 short-term rates rose above long-term ones, to protect the funding of medium-term assets through short-term liabilities, floating-rate loans were introduced in the 1970s shifting uncertainty over the directional change of interest rates to the borrower. Typically a new rate is fixed every six months on LIBOR, the lists prevailing in the London Interbank Market Offer Rate. The next mutation was the convertible issue, which could be converted if desired into the shares of the issuing company. To these were added at the end of the 1970s vehicles to further widen the choice of banks: (i) bonds guaranteed by an institution other than that of issue; and (ii) warranted Eurobonds which enable investors to buy further bonds of the same issue but at a fixed price. In early 1982 a further innovation occurred—zero coupon bonds: bonds priced at a very deep discount because they bear no interest but offer prospects of a substantial capital gain—especially attractive to investors located in centres such as offshore centres where such profits are exempt from taxation.[7] The burgeoning business that resulted from the Euromarkets directly encouraged participation by banks of all nations in the international financial intermediation process, the unregulated nature of the markets providing an ideal focus for international profit creation especially where onshore domestic market barriers were restricted and precluded business diversification. Financial packaging became increasingly sophisticated and complex. Witness for instance a report in the *Financial Times* of 3 February 1982 on p. 21 by Alan Friedman:

> *Denmark to Raise $800m. Eurocredit*
>
> The Kingdom of Denmark is raising $800m. through a floating rate note offer and two credits. Citicorp has received the mandate to arrange the financing.
>
> The first component of the package is a $100m. 10-year floating rate note issue with interest of 3/16 per cent above the London interbank offered rate (Libor). Investors will be able to redeem the paper at the end of the seventh year.
>
> The second component is a $200m. eight-year credit with a grace period of five years. Interest is to be paid at the rate of 3/8 per cent above Libor for the first five years and at ½ per cent thereafter.
>
> The largest portion of the package is a $500m. seven-year credit tied to the US prime rate. This is the first time the borrower has attempted a credit based on the prime rate and it signals a desire to tap the US market in future.
>
> There will be a four-year grace period and interest is to be 0.15 per cent over the Citibank prime rate or the adjusted CD rate for the first four years and 0.25 per cent thereafter. The idea is to syndicate this credit with regional US banks so as to introduce the Kingdom of Denmark to this market.

Estimates made by Hofmann in Table VII reveal the shifting pattern of Eurocurrency borrowing activity in the 1970s.[8] It is clear that the Eurobond market has increased in significance more than the Euro-syndicated loan market with the Foreign Bond Market growing even faster. The Eurobond market has

TABLE VII: Total Eurocurrency borrowing activity 1970–79

	1970–74		*1975–79*		
	$bn.	*% Tot.*	*$bn.*	*%Tot.*	*% 1970–74/1978–79*
(a) Eurobond Market	23.8	16.8	77.3	19.7	324.8
Euro-syndicated loans	94.4	66.7	226.5	57.8	239.9
Total (a)	118.2		303.8		
(b) Foreign bond market	23.3	16.5	87.9	22.4	377.3
Total (a)+(b)	141.5		391.7		

Source: Hofmann, 'Euromarkets in the Eighties'.

TABLE VIII: Eurobonds by category of borrower sector share 1970–80

Sectors	*1970–71*	*1972–74*	*1975–77*	*1978–80*
Companies	60.9	52.8	42.7	50.8
of which US	27.8	23.5	4.5	14.3
State enterprises	21.8	21.0	29.5	24.0
Governments	12.6	17.1	16.8	16.1
International Organisations	4.7	9.2	11.0	9.1
Value in $m. (average)	6,608	12,662	40,630	56,821

Source: Derived from *World Financial Markets,* Morgan Guaranty Trust.

TABLE IX: Nationality of the world's largest companies, 1962 and 1977

Company nationality	*1962*	*1977*
US	292 (60.5%)	240 (49.7%)
UK	51 (10.6%)	40 (8.3%)
Other European	91 (18.8%)	104 (21.2%)
Japanese	29 (6.0%)	64 (13.3%)
Developing countries	3 (0.6%)	18 (3.7%)

Source: Dunning, and Pearce, *The World's Largest Companies.*

been relatively freer than the Eurodollar market where there has been a periodic ban on Euro-Swiss franc and Euro-Belgian franc issues and limitations on the volume of new Euro-Deutchmarks, Euro-guilder and Euro-French franc issues by the German, Dutch and French authorities. It provides a supplementary channel beyond what is possible though foreign bond issues on some national markets where foreign bond issues are otherwise forbidden or are subject to rigid regulation (e.g., between 1971 and 29 July 1980 no foreign bonds were permitted in the UK: the so-called 'bull dog' bond market developed when the ban was lifted).

As regards the general pattern of borrowing, it is evident that while there were fluctuations, the borrower-mix changed considerably over the 1970s as Table VIII indicates. In the early years emphasis on multinational company borrowing was predominant with a 60 per cent share of which about half involved US companies. By the closing years of the decade about 50 per cent went to this sector, only 14.3 per cent of which was to US firms. The share of state enterprises, governments and international organizations had collectively increased somewhat. This is also a reflection of the world-wide relative decline in importance of the major US firms and banks. Dunning and Pearce have shown that top US industrial companies in 1962 accounted for 60.5 per cent of the largest world companies compared to 49.7 per cent in 1977 as is indicated in Table IX.[9] Moreover in respect of world banking, of the top one hundred banks in 1956, 44 per cent were American. By 1970 this had declined to 24 per cent although these banks accounted for 34.4 per cent of the total assets of the top one hundred banks.[10] Thereafter Japan had 21 per cent, Germany 12 per cent and Italy 10 per cent, with sixteen countries being represented in all. By 1981 the US share had fallen yet again to 14 per cent, with Japan becoming the top banker country—the

TABLE X: Distribution by nationality and position of Top 100 world banks and percentage share of resources of Top 100 banks in 1970 and 1981

(a) 1970 distribution of Top 100 Banks

Country	*No.*	*Positions in Top 100*	*% total deposits Top 100*
US	24	1,2,3,7,9,10,11,17,25,28,29,36,44,45,47,49,56, 62,63,66,70,84,89,92	34.9
Japan	21	5,18,20,21,22,32,37,40,41,48,53,57,59,64,65, 68,80,85,86,88,93	20.6
Germany	12	15,16,31,50,60,69,71,74,79,90,91	19.7
Italy	10	8,24,33,25,28,58,73,78,82,100	9.0
UK	7	4,6,23,34,51,75,97	4.9
Canada	5	12,14,26,46,55	5.5
France	5	13,19,27,72,94	4.1
Switzerland	3	39,42,43	3.1
Australia	2	52,76	1.4
Spain	2	81,98	1.0
Sweden	2	83,95	1.0
Holland	2	54,87	1.4
Belgium	2	67,99	1.1
Brazil	1	30	1.2
Hong Kong	1	86	0.5
Yugoslavia	1	96	0.5

Source: Derived from *The Banker,* June 1972.

(b) 1981 distribution of Top 100 Banks

Country	*No.*	*Positions in Top 100*	*% total deposits Top 100*
Japan	24	10,11,13,14,17,18,19,22,29,31,34,37,43,47,48, 54,62,66,70,74,76,79,83,86	25.1
US	14	1,2,12,21,26,44,46,58,59,65,69,80,94,97	15.5
W. Germany	12	7,15,20,24,32,41,50,57,60,75,78,87	12.4
Italy	10	45,49,61,63,67,68,73,83,90,92	6.6
France	7	3,4,5,6,23,64,93	11.8
UK	5	8,9,16,30,53	7.5
Canada	5	28,40,51,56,71	4.5
Belgium	4	52,72,77,84	2.6
Holland	4	25,36,38,81	3.9
Sweden	3	85,89,91	1.4
Switzerland	3	39,42,55	2.9
Australia	2	88,95	0.9
Abu Dhabi	1	33	1.1
Austria	1	96	0.4
Brazil	1	27	1.2
Hong Kong	1	35	1.1
India	1	100	0.4
Israel	1	99	0.4
Iran	1	98	0.4

Source: Derived from *Statist 71st Annual Review of World Banking.*

TABLE XI: Distribution of publicized Eurocurrency bank credits by type of country borrower 1970–80

Type of Borrower Country	*1970–71*	*1972–74*	*1975–77*	*1978–80*
Industrial countries	78.8	66.6	39.0	41.4
Developing countries	19.9	29.4	51.3	52.2
of which non-OPEC	14.2	21.2	35.7	37.5
OPEC	5.7	8.2	15.7	14.8
Communist countries	1.2	4.0	6.4	6.0
International institutions	0.1	0.04	0.4	0.4
Value in $m. (average)	8,693	57,910	91,478	230,373

Source: Derived from the Morgan Guaranty Trust Company's *World Financial Markets.*

larger number of representative countries[11] indicates a more even distribution of power in this area as Table X shows.

An examination of the publicized Euro Bank Credits reveals how the pattern of lending shifted more towards balance-of-payments and development finance and the financing of large industrial projects in Comecon countries (see Table XI). The industrial countries' market share almost halved from 78.8 per cent to 41.4 per cent in the 1970s, the main lending countries becoming the non-OPEC countries in need of finance for their escalating international debts. From 1973 onwards, world events put these markets to the fore following the quadrupling of oil prices as they became the ideal vehicle through which the OPEC 'petro-dollar' surpluses could be channelled, and from which the consuming nations—both the advanced and, increasingly, the non-oil less developed countries could shore up their balance of payments deficits, as the oil and Arab nations were unwilling and then unable to assume the credit risks implied by such recycling operations. Furthermore higher primary product prices generally increased the need for trade financing activities to take place. Henceforth the principal borrowers became sovereign ones rather than multi-national corporations and US and European Banks became the channels of such funds—a supra-national or transnational private sector emerged in banking where none had existed before, enhanced by the 'conditionality' provisions of the IMF.

THE GROWTH OF GLOBAL FINANCIAL BRANCHING NETWORKS

As regards world-wide branching Pringle[12] and Frankel[13] have charted the growth of American overseas branching before 1965 and in the period 1965–75. Already by the mid-1960s Bank of America, Chase Manhattan and First National City Bank had established a world-wide network. The first 'invasions' had followed the return to non-resident convertibility in Europe in 1958 and the rise in US trade and direct investment abroad. A crucial year seems to have been 1961, as excess liquidity manifested itself in the domestic banking system and links were made with Japanese bankers.

Thus the number of banks with overseas branches remained constant at seven throughout the 1950s although total branches grew from 105 to 124, 1954–60. By

TABLE XII: Overseas branches of US banks 1965–75[a] by country

Country of location	*1965*	*1966*	*1967*	*1968*	*1969*	*1970*	*1971*	*1972*	*1973*	*1974*	*1975*
Belgium-Luxembourg	2	4	6	8	9	11	11	8	8	15	15
France	4	4	4	6	7	11	12	15	17	15	17
Germany	3	6	8	9	14	17	21	22	27	30	30
Greece	1	1	1	2	5	8	9	13	14	16	18
Italy	1	1	1	2	2	3	4	6	7	8	10
Netherlands	3	3	3	3	5	7	7	7	6	6	6
Switzerland	1	1	2	3	3	6	7	8	8	9	9
United Kingdom	17	21	21	24	32	37	41	45	49	52	55
Total Europe[b]	32	43	48	59	80	103	116	128	142	157	167
Bahamas	2	3	3	3	8	32	60	73	94	91	80
Cayman Islands	—	—	—	—	—	—	—	—	2	32	44
Total Caribbean[c]	5	9	9	10	22	53	89	107	131	164	164
Argentina	16	17	17	25	33	38	38	38	38	38	37
Brazil	15	15	15	15	15	15	16	19	21	21	19
Colombia	5	6	6	8	17	23	26	28	28	32	36
Panama	10	12	15	19	21	26	29	29	32	33	33
Total Latin America[d]	72	79	93	123	155	182	191	195	190	195	198
Taiwan	—	2	2	2	2	2	2	2	3	5	7
Hong Kong	6	6	8	10	12	13	13	15	19	23	24
India	5	6	8	8	11	11	11	11	11	11	11
Indonesia	—	—	—	—	4	6	6	6	6	6	6
Japan	13	14	14	14	14	15	15	17	21	25	31
Lebanon	3	3	3	3	3	3	3	3	3	3	3
Persian Gulf[e]	2	2	3	3	3	3	8	11	10	10	11
Singapore	—	8	8	8	8	9	11	11	11	14	18
Total Asia[f]	45	55	63	69	78	83	91	98	112	126	143
Total Africa[g]	3	2	2	3	3	1	2	2	2	2	5
Overseas areas of the United States	23	23	29	31	35	38	43	47	50	55	55
Grand total	180	211	244	295	373	460	532	577	627	699	732
US member banks with overseas branches	11	13	13	15	26	53	79	91	107	125	125

Source: Frankel, 'International Banking', p. 5.

[a]As of January 1.
[b]Also includes Austria, Ireland, Monaco and Romania.
[c]Also includes Barbados, Haiti, Jamaica, Netherlands Antilles, Trinidad-Tobago, British Virgin Islands and other West Indian islands.
[d]Also includes Bolivia, Chile (no resident US branches as of 1 January 1975), Dominican Republic, Ecuador, El Salvador, Guatemala, Guyana, Honduras, Mexico, Nicaragua, Paraguay, Peru, Uruguay and Venezuela.
[e]Includes Bahrain, Qatar, Saudi Arabia and United Arab Emirates.
[f]Also includes Brunei, Fiji Islands, Israel, Jordan, Korea, Malaysia, Pakistan, the Philippines, Thailand and Vietnam.
[g]Includes Liberia, Kenya, Mauritius, and Nigeria (no resident US branches as of 1 January 1975).

1965 however total branches had grown to 180. Thenceforward as Frankel shows (see Table XII), the number of branches had risen to 732 by 1975 and the number of participating banks from 11 to 125. The earlier and much smaller banking 'invasion' of London had been made to acquire a sterling base, given at that time a quarter of world trade was financed in that currency. However the Eurodollar market soon became the main attraction—thus as of 31 December 1965 although the UK had only 21 (10 per cent) out of the 211 US overseas branches, it accounted for $4,257m. out of a total of $9,102m. (46.8 per cent) deposits of overseas US branches.[14] In the period 1965–75, it is evident that the largest relative regional growth took place in Europe (an increase of 521.9 per cent) where banks rose from 32 to 167, but the most spectacular growth took place in the Caribbean where branches rose from 5 in 1965 to 164 in 1975, an increase of 3,280 per cent! This was largely because the Bahamas, and to a large extent other countries, became a shelter for US Eurodollar deposits given the convenience of its location and similar business hours with New York with which it has a common time zone, thereby enabling many such branches—Baker[15] suggests eighty—to be merely 'shell' branches operated by parent institutions from the US mainland.

An example of such networking is given by Citicorp, the US bank which was the largest bank in *The Banker* top 100 banks of 1981: it had thirty-three domestic subsidiary companies; seventy-three international subsidiaries, eighteen of which were in twelve offshore haven centres; seventeen international affiliates, four of which were in two haven centres; branches in eighty countries, seventeen of which were haven centres and a further fourteen representative offices. A glance through the Bank Research Unit's *Who Owns What in World Banking* reveals that between a quarter and a third of the total number of the offices of many large British, American and Japanese Banks are located abroad. This tendency is not as significant for French and German banks, as Table XIII indicates with respect to these countries' representatives in the top 10 world banks in 1981.

As the size of individual packages increased, so joint-venture and consortium banks were set up as a mechanism for participation on a group national or group international basis.[16] This appealed particularly to Arab banks: *The Banker* survey of joint-venture and consortium banks in March 1981 identified 142 banks throughout the world, 65 of which were located in Europe, 34 of which were London based; 21 in the Middle East; 5 in Africa; 32 in the Far East, of which 9 were in Singapore and 7 in Hong Kong; 15 in Oceania and 4 in the Americas. Of these, between one-fifth and a quarter contained Arab interests.

A consequence of these different types of growth was that significant mutual penetration of banking systems took place, foreign banks with parent firms as their base engaging in 'coat-tail banking' following their traditional customers worldwide, participating in the new financial vehicles for the financing of trade and seeking entry to protected markets. In this way, intra-industry international trade has been extended by the cross-fertilization of financial activities—especially where banks have pursued product differentiation and specialization in particular market segments. Caves has called this activity 'cross-hauling' in the context of foreign direct investment.[17] Hence reciprocity of treatment has often been

TABLE XIII: Global networks of the Top 10 world banks in 1981

			International Subsid. Cos.			International Affiliates		Branches		Representative offices	
Top 10 banks 1981	*Nationality*	*Domestic subsid. (affil.) companies*	*Total*	*No. in havens*	*No. havens*	*No.*	*Havens*	*No. countries*	*No. havens*	*No.*	*Havens*
Citicorp.	US	33	73	18	12	17	42	80	17	14	–
Bank America Corp.	US	27	109	32	15			75	12	17	3
Caisse Nationale de Crédit Agricole*	French										
Banque Nationale de Paris	French	23	21	7	5	16	55	33	3	23	3
Crédit Lyonnais	French	38	9	4	4	29	44	22	6	20	2
Sociate General	French	19	7	2	2	28	66	10	2	19	1
Deutsche Bank	German	46	9	4	4	41	94	12	1	18	2
Barclays Bank Group	UK	40	53	20	10	29	75	34	17	9	0
National Westminster Bank Group	UK	26	5	2	2	4	11	16	6		
Fuji Bank	Japanese	18	6	4	3	12	2	2	6	11	2

Source: Information extracted from *Who Owns What in World Banking 1981–82,* Banker Research Unit.

*a semi-public institution with as yet few international links. *See* Lewis, V., 'Credit Agricole—French Bankers' "Bête Noir"', *The Banker,* May 1979, pp. 25–8.

required by national monetary authorities when granting entry to foreign banks.[18]

Davis[19] lists some thirteen specific objectives being pursued by Euro-banks that had set up external subsidiaries or branches to operate in the London onshore external market in 1975, these being to:

1. enable a commercial bank (particularly Japanese or American owned, in the context of Edge Act legislation) to diversify into investment banking activities such as underwriting, securities dealing and the taking of equity interests;
2. earn a higher return on capital than the parent can in its traditional activities;
3. place surplus funds generated by stockholder banks into the international interbank market and enable stockholders to participate in Eurocurrency syndicated loans;
4. enable banks with little international experience to become acquainted with the international deposit and lending market;
5. serve in effect as an international branch in a specific financial centre for stockholder banks which are unable to establish one due to local or home country regulations;
6. attract international funds to the country or region in which the stockholders are located or to the parent itself;
7. serve as a common vehicle for a formal or informal grouping of individual banks with similar interests or objectives;
8. represent the parent bank in a major international money market to expand its international network;
9. extend the range of international services provided for the parents' domestic customers, in particular if competitor banks already have a significant Euromarket base;
10. serve as a marketing vehicle for the syndicated loans generated by the network of a large parent bank;
11. serve as a focal point for a number of international banks interested in doing business in a particular country or region;
12. enable a non-banking institution to participate in the Eurocurrency market; and,
13. enable stockholders to participate in the medium-term Eurocurrency lending market in general or in a specific type of lending such as shipping or energy finance.

In general large branch banks, and initially American banks, had 'ownership specific advantages'[20] over other banks and *de novo* financial institutions in respect of their size, established position, access to multinational deposit networks of parent companies, greater awareness of project opportunities, management expertise and marketing systems, financial engineering skills and favoured access to US multinationals. Moreover Kelly[21] has shown tht US participation in London was dominated by the banks of New York City, Chicago and California, who, given domestic interstate restrictive laws and having access to the wealthier areas of their home country, were naturally larger and better able to bear the risks and costs of such activities. Internalization incentives were strong to become multi-purpose financial institutions abroad (given diversification was precluded at home) and to be at the forefront of 'department store' or 'one-stop' banking. 'Location specific advantages' were clearly available in London, Paris and other onshore financial centres for arranging financial packages which, depending on nearness to borrowers and lenders, and cheapness, could, if necessary, be booked at particular centres such as Hong Kong, the Bahamas etc. to benefit from their 'country specific' advantages for particular financial deals.

This internationalization process was extended to almost every sphere of trade activity and gave rise to the emergence of an increasingly 'global' as opposed to 'international' system of exchange.[22] The participating nations of the world trading system became both more vulnerable and more sensitive to economic conditions in other countries. Significantly for offshore centres, this world system exhibited tensions because of 'the continued existence of still mainly nationally based political systems' as Lindbeck has remarked.[23] Within nations, business and production factors became more aware of transnational business possibilities and decision-taking, and the associated need for international currency ease of movement, international 'tax planning', cash management and the need for trouble-free bases for the deposit of funds and the location of particular intra-firm activities. During the past decade or so high rates of inflation combined with a succession of governmental prices and incomes policies to create an environment that has intensified the reaction against high marginal rates of personal taxation. The concomitant existence of associated fiscal and monetary restriction throughout the world created a demand for low tax areas which could act as alternative financial centres wherein to evade or avoid such restrictions and regulations.

The above-mentioned trends and developments created circumstances whereby some tax havens have been transformed, within certain limits, into offshore currency area centres and/or eventually, truly international offshore centres with an extensive ubiquity of business operations within the inter-offshore economy network and flow pattern of the world invisible trading system. Not all such centres are of significance in terms of their share of world trade but even as staging posts the internal significance commands a high percentage—perhaps greater than 20 per cent—of their national products. Moreover participation in Eurocurrency business in many cases is not very important: this tends to be confined to a small number of such centres as Chapter I revealed.

Whatever the individual financial development mix of those tax havens that were transformed, all such centres have become production interfaces linked to, yet separate from, onshore world capital markets and invisible production centres. They have emerged as 'vehicle' centres, 'product enclaves', to effect international invisible exchange, nodal points within the network of inter-regional world trade—in essence they have emerged as what we shall call *intermediate economies,* i.e. economies concerned with an entrepôt trade comprising a centripetal inflow of non-resident funds deposits, incomes, earnings and intra-firm payments which, after financial intermediation result in a centrifugal outflow of worldwide investments and capital transfers. The establishment of a network of such centres, whether based on the Euromarkets or transnational banking, has constituted a new secondary trading system that is global in scope, unlike the preceding largely intra-continental one based in the traditional inland centres listed previously and including Panama, that were themselves reoriented in this direction. As economies of convenience, these so-called 'offshore' centres have provided, in varying degrees, an international common property resource for transnational private sector business in at least four basic respects:

a) As centres of domicile through which international companies whether financial or otherwise, can incorporate and operate commercial holding companies and overseas subsidiaries in the most advantageous fiscal and/or exchange control climate.
b) As locations from and through which to exploit international capital and money markets with a greater freedom of action than might be feasible from their countries of origin.
c) As secure havens for international earning, savings and pools of liquidity seeking investment in a tax-neutral environment.[24]
d) As assembly centres for components externally produced in onshore centres and re-exported thereto being linked to free trade zones.[25]

The demonstrated success of most of these centres and their liberalized financial regimes has to an extent rewritten the geography of world finance.[26] The development of specialized financial institutions has no longer been the preserve of onshore metropolitan centres, although many of them remain of apex and pivotal importance. This new tier of circuitry and conduitry, by fulfilling an international store of value function, has facilitated the global migration of funds which has provided a reversal of the previous pattern of agglomerative tendencies noted by past observers.[27]

This mutation within the world system—the intermediate economy—exemplifies internationally a phenomenon that has been observed with reference to both regional and national manufacturing activities—'situations whereby a large amount of ownership and control of enterprises in key sectors lies outside the region concerned'.[28] Regional economists and geographers have denoted the former manifestations 'branch plant economies' or 'externally-controlled economies'[29] where the production units, be they branches or subsidiaries, are *de facto* externally controlled from head offices located elsewhere. Whilst a number of issues arise from this of a legal tax and sovereignty nature, it is nevertheless likely that access to the financial resources of the parent and its bargaining market power and its world-wide supply of, and demand for, funds through its network system ensures greater stability than any possible via independent indigenous concerns.

In the context of offshore developments, a *sine qua non* for the growth of activities (*a*) to (*d*) specified above is the double coincidence of a liberal economic system that has macroeconomic and fiscal stability combined with an unchanging or harmonious political environment.[30]

In practice the above conditions tend to obtain in geographically fairly small islands or continental (often mountain) enclave states. Such areas offer little scope for (*d*) visible trade development in response to duty-free re-entry of product provisions offered by most onshore industrial countries, when offshore component assembly industries assemble onshore domestically produced components and re-export them to the country of component origin (with the exceptions of Hong Kong, Singapore, Panama and some Caribbean economies already listed). Our discussion is therefore primarily concerned with intermediate economies geared basically to activities (*a*), (*b*), and (*c*) above, i.e. concerned essentially with invisible trade activities. Of necessity the existence of these activities requires a 'tax-haven' economy or 'low-tax' external administration, the prior existence of which will bring about some geographical onshore relocation of economic resources and an offshore legal relocation of *situs* for business activity. However, unless and until the haven manages to diversify its financial structure, it will not become an 'offshore centre' capable of generating its own levels of business activity, thereby creating net additions to the effective aggregate supply and supply capacity of world invisible trade.

Globally there are two separate types of effects theoretically consequent on the establishment of intermediate economies orientated essentially to invisible trade that involve onshore industrial 'slippage' and an erosion of actual or potential tax bases:

*Invisible trade diversion:** where the overseas trade or investment activity merely uses the offshore centre as a routing or 'paper' centre, a location of record, where little or no actual banking or business is carried out other than the 'suitcase' variety; where institutions located elsewhere merely have a 'brass-plate' 'shell' presence or 'cubicle' existence. In this case the haven merely seeks to attract income leakages from the economies whence its clients originate and little 'real' financial centre development takes place with regard to international banking. Looked at autonomously from the centre's state point of view, access to the onshore centre is vital and an 'export platform' strategy needs to be pursued, to use Evans' phrase,[31] whereby invisible trade activity must be re-exported onshore for the expertise of financial intermediation to take place.

Invisible trade creation: where the trade or investment activity uses the offshore centre as a 'functional' centre where deposit-taking, final lending and financial intermediation is actually carried out. Such activity may be of a positive sum variety, whereby the supply of international financing facilities is actually added to, or of a zero-sum variety, whereby onshore activities are appropriated and replaced by offshore business. In the latter case this would amount to a 'subimperialist' strategy to borrow a word from Evans taxonomy of strategies for dependent development.[32] Here financial development becomes self-transforming and relatively self-directing. In theory the *raison d'être* of functional centres would be to recycle funds from the major international financial centres, such as London and New York, to final borrowers, whereas paper centres would be merely used by international business to minimize overall tax payments—functional activities therefore constitute 'pure' intermediate economy activities, whereas 'paper' intermediate economy activities are merely intra-

*In this case diversion is from a higher tax to a lower tax centre in contrast to customs union theory where Viner's 'trade diversion' is from a low cost to a high cost country.

corporate and intra-personal sector activities. However, in practice this distinction is a blurred one because telecommunication services permit a divergence between the legal and actual location of many of these financial activities such that centres will have a bias according to the commercial implications of their strategic locational position with regard to their onshore hinterlands and non-financial centre domestic activities. There will be a tendency for primarily deposit centres to exist in proximity to surplus unit locations (as in the case of Bahrain and the oil rich countries of the Gulf); primarily funding centres will tend to have a central location as regional entrepôt 'turntable' centres (as in the case of Singapore); primarily arranging centres,[33] where the financial packages are structured but not necessarily booked if fiscal or political practicalities favour an alternative location will tend to be in proximity to ultimate borrowers (as in the case in Hong Kong). Offshore subsidiary or branch business will tend to involve wholesale operations so that access to and standing in the local or nearest interbank market will be important for liquidity management and matching of the types and maturities of assets and liabilities. Moreover, retail banking—the direct taking of demand deposits may be limited *in situ* by:

a) the size and wealth distribution of the economy;
b) population constraints on the immigration of tax exiles seeking a place of domicile;
c) the banking licensing system that may preclude penetration of the domestic market for deposits by its system of licensing that may confine foreign bank activities to offshore banking only.

In practice there is a multi-locational roundabout chain of intermediation and interdependence along which the distinctly separate functions of deposit collection, interbank intermediation, transmission of information regarding actual and potential lenders and borrowers, and currency transformation for contractual and speculative purposes takes place. Stages within the chain involve comparatively large minimum deposit sums, which may subsequently be repackaged in ever larger amounts as the recycling process from the often geographically distant surplus unit lenders to the deficit unit borrowers is effected. The concomitant intermediation may involve maturity, currency and spatial switches of these monies. A good bank credit evaluation capability is essential if final lending risks are to be minimized.

Representation of individual institutions is essential in all types of centres both offshore and onshore—in precisely which centres will depend upon whether the institution has a clear vision of what is optimal for its particular global clients and objectives. On the non-banking side, additional use of the global network may be attempted in relation to company registration, company management and the routing of company profits given the availability of secrecy laws, no-tax guarantees and the reach exerted by onshore tax authorities.

Thus the 'facilitative' factors of extensive and integrated communication systems and international financial sub-contracting have led within international banking to its own internalization of the general industrial phenomenon noted by Caporaso[34] whereby:

different aspects of production, once integrated within the same work unit and work place, are now 'emancipated' to be carried out in different places . . . Firms are not so limited . . . by the necessity of carrying out the entire production of a product in one country; further, they are not constrained to carry out within one workplace different processing phases which might profit from work at several different locations.

In the sphere of international banking this has meant a significant degree of multinational multicentre financial sectoral integration. The emergence of the 'intermediate' economy as described above is thus an important mutation that has as yet been ignored and should be incorporated in the 'world system' analysis of Wallerstein[35] and others where:

all areas of the world . . . comprise . . . a single ongoing division of labour . . . where exchange . . . is based on differential appropriation of the surplus produced and positions are hierarchically ordered . . . [and where] the possibilities open to a given nation for capital accumulation or development are constrained by its structural position within this division of labour and shaped by the cyclical and secular evolution of the world system as a whole.[36]

Thus the existence of offshore financial haven centres interposed both horizontally and vertically between the onshore 'core' or 'polar' economies and their 'peripheries' constitutes a new type of 'semi-periphery' in the surplus extraction chain, whereby transnational capitalism, whether in the personal, business or institutional sectors, can extract the maximum profit possibilities even at the expense of the onshore core countries which are the loci of their parental lineage. In the words of Wallerstein:[37]

The core-periphery distinction . . . differentiates those zones in which are concentrated high-profit, high-technology, high-wage diversified production (the core countries) from those in which are concentrated low-profit, low-technology, low-wage, less diversified production (the peripheral countries) . . . the semi-peripheral countries . . . act as a peripheral zone for core countries and in part they act as a core country for some peripheral areas. Both their internal politics and their social structure are distinctive, and . . . their ability to take advantage of the . . . downturns of economic activity is in general greater than that of either the core or the peripheral countries.

Given the intermediate role outlined, peripheral financial capitalism can integrate both the intra-area multipolar capitalism of onshore centre countries and their vertical financial relations with periphery countries. An essential complementary element of semi-peripheral development has been the 'export-orientated industrialization' strategy of transnational transplanting of processing industries to 'Investment Promotion Zones', Export Processing Zones or 'Free Trade Zones'. Ping[38] estimates that these zones proliferated from zero in the early 1960s to more than eighty main areas in 1980 with another forty under construction or being planned, more than 50 per cent of which are in Asia, in the countries fringing the Pacific Basin. However Diamond estimates that in 1977 no fewer than 264 free trade zones, free ports and free transit zones existed in sixty-seven countries, two-thirds of which were in developing countries.[39] In return for local factory investment, multinational investors are generally offered fiscal freedom from corporate income tax, import duties and quotas, property taxes, and excise taxes; given fiscal incentives in terms of preferential low interest rates on loans, tax credits, subsidized rents and service charges etc; and offered socio-political incentives such as no minimum wages, no trade unionism, no strikes and exemptions from social security payments. The 'first wave' of industrial invasion enveloped countries such as Hong Kong, Singapore, South Korea and Taiwan. From the late 1970s a new phase of evolution was entered that had these main elements:

a) Relocation of industries from the above mentioned original cheap labour countries to the subcontinents of South Asia and China, the poorer ASEAN countries like Indonesia and Thailand, and to some small islands in the Pacific and Indian oceans.
b) The rise of indigenous Asian multinationals as a result of the 'first wave' activities and their participation in the industrialization invasion of the second wave.
c) New patterns of activity and refinements in the international division of labour resulting from the micro-electronic technological revolution, whereby the world-market factory of the multinational corporation emerged, wherein processing and assembling of components is undertaken for global rather than domestic or even regional distribution.

The financing of these activities and the investments generated from the profits that arose thus became an important potential market for the newly emergent offshore finance centres. In a number of cases these centres combined both financial and manufacturing semi-peripheral development as will be seen in Part III.

CONCLUSIONS

The following five points seem germane to offshore financial development:

(1) The growth of high taxation and restrictive policies and regulation procedure in mixed interventionist economies, combined with transnationalization of national money and capital markets, has given rise to an international or transnational private-sector need for tax havens, which has led to a transformation of some into offshore centres for external non-resident economic purposes.

(2) Offshore centres have consequently become international invisible production interfaces linked to, yet separate from, onshore world trade and capital markets, and have evolved as international intermediate economies, interposed between the main onshore centres of wealth and international exchange and of pivotal significance as shelters for incomes derived either from the horizontal

trade between such areas and their vertical trade relations with developing countries.

(3) This development has been made possible by a telecommunication revolution that has given immediate business access to financial information and the setting up of a global network of corporate activities. Such centres are necessarily dependent on world onshore markets for their business trading activities and as arranging centres wherefrom much of their wholesale banking derives. Although onshore disintermediation involves the use of many locations largely as booking centres, real activity and a diversification of their domestic financial systems may nevertheless take place in relation to other areas of external need.

(4) The creation of the Eurocurrency markets was crucial for the above sequence of events. The spread of external banking initially by the US and subsequently other national banks gave rise to a global network that arose out of regulation evasion or avoidance and began the development process. The banking 'invasions' that occurred were essential catalysts of change bringing with them the essential expertise and clientele linkage for transnational intermediation.

(5) The emergence of 'intermediate' economies as described can be seen as a form of semi-peripheral development supportive to the maintenance and furtherance of the world capitalist systems, integrating its inter-area multipolar onshore sources and their vertical financial relations with peripheral countries. Together with the extension of global free trade zone activity they constitute a global secondary trading system, the former for visible trade, the latter for invisible trade.

Despite these general outcomes, entry to the secondary trading system is not uncircumscribed and successful entry and survival does require a full understanding of the competitive abilities that can be exerted in such areas. Thus Chapter III will now consider the main ways in which onshore interventionist control can be exercised as a countervailing power to pre-empt and/or appropriate any onshore income leakages that might or do occur. The remaining chapter in this part will explore the nature of the offshore competitive process and how it can be exploited, onshore countervailing powers notwithstanding.

REFERENCES

1. This definition is a modification and fusion of two separate definitions given in Yassukovich, S.M., 'Multinational Companies and Offshore Centres', *The Banker,* May 1974, p.489; and McCarthy, I.M., 'Offshore Banking Centres: Benefits and Costs', *Finance and Development* December 1979, p.45.
2. See Clark, R. and Cherrington, M., 'Telecommunications and Financial Markets', *The Banker,* March 1980, p.97.
3. 'Survey: Technology in Banking', *The Banker,* March 1980, p.131.
4. Kindleberger, C.P. *The Formation of Financial Centers: A Study in Comparative Economic History,* Princeton Studies in International Finance No. 36., Princeton University, 1974, pp.10–11.
5. Mendelsohn, M.S., 'Eurobond Survey', *The Banker,* November 1976, pp.1235–54.

See also Goodman, L.S., 'The Pricing of Syndicated Eurocurrency Credits', *Federal Reserve Board of New York Quarterly Review,* Vol.5, No.2, Summer 1980, pp.39–49.

6. Montagnon, P. 'Syndicated Credits: Extending the Era of "Megadollar" Deals: Survey, Euromarkets', *Investors' Chronicle,* 18 September 1981, p.19 and 21.

7. Reported in the *Financial Times,* 18 January 1982, p.15.

8. Hofmann, H., 'Euromarkets in the Eighties: Survey, Euromarkets', *Investors Chronicle Survey,* 12 September 1980, p.5. There is a plethora of articles on these developments and their implications. Perhaps some of the best include: Paltzer, E.F., 'Internationalization of Banking by Foreign Bases and Addresses', ch.XI of *The Development of Financial Institutions in Europe, 1956–1976,* ed. by J.E. Wadsworth *et al.,* Leyden, Sijthoff, 1977; Ossola, R., 'The Vulnerability of the International Financial System: International Lending and Liquidity Risk', *Banca Nazionale del Lavoro Quarterly Review,* September 1980, pp.291–305; Lipson C., 'The International Organisation of Third World Debt', *International Organisation,* Vol.35, No.4, Autumn 1981, pp.604–31; Dematte, C., 'International Financial Intermediation: Implications for Bankers and Regulators', *Banca Nazionale del Lavoro Quarterly Review,* March 1981, pp.91–110.

9. Dunning, J.H. and Pearce, R.D., *The World's Largest Companies 1962–78,* London, Financial Times, 1980.

10. 'The Top 300 Banks', *The Banker,* June 1972, pp.813–21.

11. *Statist 71st Annual Review of World Banking,* Financial Times Business Publishing Ltd., 1981, pp.ix and xi.

12. Pringle, R., 'Why American Banks Go Overseas', *The Banker,* November 1966, pp.770–85.

13. Frankel, A.B., 'International Banking: Part I, Business Conditions', *Economic Review of Federal Reserve Bank of Chicago,* September 1975, p.5.

14. Pringle, op.cit, p.785.

15. Baker, J.C., *International Bank Regulation,* New York, Praeger, 1978.

16. Blander, M., 'Why Banks Choose to Work Together', *The Banker,* March 1981, pp.93–9.

17. Caves, R.E., 'International Corporations: the Industrial Economics of Foreign Investment', *Economica,* Vol.38, 1971, pp.1–27.

18. Dean, J.W. and Giddy, I.H., 'Strangers and Neighbors: Cross-Border Banking in North America', *Banca Nazionale del Lavoro Quarterly Review,* June 1981, pp.191–212.

19. Davis, S.I., *The Euro-Bank—Its Origins, Management and Outlook,* London, Macmillan, 1976, pp.31–2.

20. Dunning, J.H., 'Explaining Changing Patterns of International Production: In Defence of the Eclectic Theory', *Oxford Bulletin of Economics and Statistics,* Vol.41, 1979, p.277.

21. Kelly, J., *Bankers and Borders: The Case of American Banks in Britain,* Cambridge, Mass., Ballinger, 1977, p.91.

22. Madeuf, B. and Michalet, C., 'A New Approach to International Economics', *International Social Science Journal,* Vol.XXX, No.2, 1978.

23. Lindbeck, A., 'The Changing Role of the Nation State', *Kyklos,* Vol.28, 1975, Fasc.1, p.29.

24. Yassukovich, S.M., 'Multinational Companies and Offshore Centres', *The Banker,* May 1974, p.489.

25. See Finger, J.M., 'Tariff Provisions for Offshore Assembly and the Exports of Developing Countries', *Economic Journal,* Vol.85, 1975, pp.365–71; and 'Offshore Assembly Provisions in the West German and Netherlands Tariffs: Trade and Domestic Effects', *Weltwirtschaftliches Archive,* Band 113, 1977, Heft 2, p.237–49.

26. Kerr, C.F. and Donald, P., 'Some Aspects of the Geography of Finance in

Canada', in Irving, Robert M., ed., *Readings in Canadian Geography,* Toronto, Holt, Rinehart and Winston, 1965.

27. See Kindleberger, op.cit.

28. Firn, J., 'External Control and Regional Development', *Environment and Planning,* Vol.A, No.7, p. 394, 1975.

29. Watts, H., *The Branch Plant Economy: A Study of External Control,* London, Longmans, 1980.

30. Indeed it was once reported that an American syndicate, the Ocean Life Research Foundation, was contemplating the creation of a 400-acre island on a submerged coral reef called Minerva in the South Pacific between Tonga and Fiji as 'a combination of tax haven, retreat from bureaucratic government and headquarters for ecological and marine research.' see Doggart, T., 'Tax Havens—the Landscape Changes', *The Banker,* April 1972, p.539.

31. Evans, P., *Dependent Development: The Alliance of Multinational State, and Local Capital in Brazil,* Princeton, Princeton University Press, 1979, p.319.

32. Evans, op.cit., p.318.

33. Caouette, J.P., 'Hong Kong and Singapore—A Survey: Time Zones and the Arranging Centre', *Euromoney,* July 1978, pp.48–54.

34. Caporaso, J.A., 'Industrialization in the Periphery: The Evolving Global Division of Labor', *International Studies Quarterly,* Vol.25, No.3, September 1981, pp. 375-6.

35. Wallerstein, I., 'Dependence in an Interdependent World: The Limited Possibilities of Transformation Within the Capitalist World Economy', paper presented at Conference on Dependence and Development in Africa, Ottawa, Canada, 1973; 'Semi-peripheral Countries and the Contemporary World Crisis', *Theory and Society,* 3, 1976, pp.461-84; and 'A World-System Perspective on the Social Sciences', *British Journal of Sociology,* 27, 1976, pp.343-52.

36. Evans, P., 'Beyond Center and Periphery: A Comment on the Contribution of the World System Approach to the Study of Development', *Sociological Inquiry,* Vol.49, No.4, pp.15–16.

37. Wallerstein, I., 'Semi-Peripheral Countries and the Contemporary World Crisis', ch.5 of *The Capitalist World Economy,* Cambridge University Press, 1979.

38. Ping, H.R., 'Bargaining on the Free Trade Zones', *New Internationalist,* No.85, March 1980, pp.12–14.

39. Quoted by Doggart, C., in *Tax Havens and Their Uses,* Economist Intelligence Unit Special Report No.105, London, 1981, p.43.

CHAPTER III
The Onshore Exercise of 'Countervailing' Power to Pre-empt or Limit the Extent of Offshore Appropriation of Invisible Trade Activities

There are two principal areas of onshore policy that may pre-empt or limit the relocation and accumulation offshore of economic resources of onshore provenance, which independently or combined may constitute a powerful countervailing force against offshore appropriation of international invisible trade activities: fiscal protection policies against potentially transferable taxable business and financial activities to prevent onshore industrial seepage; and exchange control policies with respect to 'inward' and 'outward' financial flows that may also be designed to achieve the same objectives for balance of payments reasons as well as the development onshore of external trade activities. These policies will now be separately examined.

ONSHORE FISCAL PROTECTION AND THE PENETRATION OF OFFSHORE FISCAL TERRITORIAL JURISDICTIONS

In the absence of multilateral agreements (such as in territorial waters) concerning the geographical limits of national tax jurisdictions, it is a matter of national legal assertion as to the degree of extra-onshore domestic jurisdiction to be pursued, and the criteria to be adopted to determine the territorial *situs* of income. Thus the effectiveness of tax havens as refuges from onshore tax persecution may be to some extent thwarted by the fiscal protection policies and assertions of fiscal sovereignty adopted by onshore economies that seek nationally to internalize tax revenues their citizens may attempt to derive from their externally located activities. In practice here, as in the area of exchange control regulations, it is necessary to identify effective restrictive treatment from economically non-restrictive treatment: mere assertions of rights to tax to be effective require efficient information gathering and policing so that the actual impact of such regulations may in reality reach considerably under 100 per cent of the target activities.

Onshore fiscal attitudes to transfers of onshore income and business, whether specifically backed by legislation in the areas of Company Law, human migration or trade of particular industries, necessarily *per se* define and/or support by legislative force the areas of 'illegal' external trade as seen by onshore revenue authorities and as reinforced by the judgments of domestic Courts.[1] However, unilateral national assertion of rights to tax activities outside the geographical jurisdiction of the domestic country may not encounter universal reciprocity of need, treatment and cooperation. On the contrary, counter assertions may be made by other states with regard to the rights of their residents and/or external clients to fiduciary or numbered accounts, and the rights of their domestic monetary and fiscal authorities not to pursue identical approaches. The asymmetries of treatment thereby created will distort international invisible exchange flows accordingly.

In reality, there are many possible areas of 'fiscal leverage',[2] which administrations may seek to apply. It will suffice in this context merely to indicate four of the more important areas of general taxation and to indicate the variety of differences of approach that may be pursued. Differential provisioning in these areas and other such criteria governing the deductibility or otherwise of expenses will crucially determine the inter-country (and in federal economies intra-country) legal competitive framework to which particular nationals may have access including tax havens in general or in particular. Broadly these areas are:

i) general attitudes to tax avoidance/evasion;
ii) definitions of national fiscal boundaries;
iii) attitudes towards company management and place of domicile;
iv) treatment of branches and subsidiaries.

(i) General Attitudes to Tax Avoidance/Evasion

The apparent usurpation of the independence of offshore and other states may of course be legitimized in relation to the tax avoidance/tax evasion issue and the particular view of it taken by onshore economies legislation desirous of protecting the actual or potential erosion of their national tax base. Conventionally the ordinary citizen is regarded by some as having a right to so arrange his affairs within the law so as to minimize his tax obligations and payments. As Lord Clyde once remarked in relation to the UK:

> No man in this country is under the smallest obligation, moral or other, so to arrange his legal relations to his business or to his property as to enable the Revenue to put the largest possible shovel into his stores. The Revenue is not slow—and quite rightly—to take every advantage which is open to it under the taxing structure for the purpose of depleting the taxpayer's pocket. And, the taxpayer is, in like manner, entitled to be astute to prevent, so far as he honestly can, the depletion of his means by the Revenue.[3]

Thus, tax avoidance may be regarded as merely prudent financial management. However tax evasion implies that such activities are done fraudulently to escape legal obligations. In practice the complexities of the modern financial world do not easily comply with the niceties of this theoretical distinction such that the borderline between the two concepts may be a very fine one, especially in circumstances when a vigorous pursuit of tax avoidance constitutes an abuse of that right.

Within Europe some three differences of judicial attitude may be detected, although there is common ground in insisting that there must be a bona fide commercial purpose behind the territorial zoning of transactions in relation to issues such as the location of the effective management of the enterprise, the use of nominee directors and the place of registration of the firm. A group of European countries, including France and Holland, simply apply an 'abuse of rights' or 'abuse of forms' concept which calls for the existence of an offshore transaction to be ignored if the sole purpose is to avoid taxes which would be otherwise levied—as when a chain of offshore subsidiaries act as a conduit for profit accumulation with the *de facto* control of one person or company. Germany on the other hand has all-embracing anti-avoidance legislation which deems all tax haven unearned income to be the income of the German resident owner or beneficiary. Moreover, its Aussensteuergesetz legislation in 1972 seeks to ensure equality of tax treatment in international transactions when the effective level of foreign tax falls below 30 per cent. France introduced a system of substitute taxation in 1974.

The UK has traditionally taken a comparatively pragmatic view of tax avoidance internally and externally, although it has gradually moved away from the traditional view of Lord Clyde quoted above, perhaps following the thoughts of Lord Simon in 1943 that 'There is, of course, no doubt that they (tax avoiders) are within their legal rights, but there is no reason why their efforts . . . should be regarded as a commendable exercise of ingenuity or as a discharge of the duties of good citizenship' (*Latilla* v. *IRC*). This approach has hardened slightly in recent years as we shall see later in this book. As for the rest of the world, the US Internal Revenue Code contains extensive provisions to deal with tax avoidance, of which sub-part 'F' generally has the effect of nullifying any operations which can be shown to be designed to save tax rather than to have a commercial purpose.[4] Extensive anti-avoidance legislation has also been enacted in Australia, South Africa and New Zealand, the effect of which has been to give their revenue authorities power to attribute to a resident beneficiary any profits which might avoid tax through contracts or arrangements entered into for that specific purpose. Some attempts have been made to co-ordinate national policies in this area but have not as yet succeeded, e.g. the EEC Report on the Tax Arrangements applying to Holding Companies (COM (73) 1008 EEC) was followed on 10 February 1975 by an EEC Council resolution on measures against tax evasion and 'tax flight' which envisaged far-reaching and close co-operation between tax administrators. A Directive was issued on 19 December 1977 to abolish holding companies but was not approved by the Council although exchanges of information were approved.

(ii) Definitions of National Fiscal Boundaries

A basic decision to be made is that of which definition to use to circumscribe the onshore fiscal boundaries. Most nations apply one of a variety of at least three approaches to determine the scope of their activities:[5]

a) *the residence principle* that income should be taxed only in the country where the factor owner resides. Implication: taxes cannot be avoided by the mere export of factor services. Differential application of this principle may involve, as in the UK categorization on the basis of, for example, 'resident and ordinarily resident'; 'ordinarily resident but not resident'; 'resident but not ordinarily resident'; 'not resident and not ordinarily resident'.

b) *the source principle* that income is taxed only in the country where it is actually earned. Implication: taxes cannot be avoided by the emigration of factor owners.

c) *the world-wide principle* that income is taxed both in the country of residence of the factor owner and in the country where it is earned. Implication: no avoidance except by the simultaneous emigration of owners and services. This can be modified by double-taxation agreements limiting the scope of their jurisdiction and the share of tax revenue, as will be discussed in the next chapter.

A further principle (*d*) may be added, which has been adopted in the UK:

d) *the 'domicile' principle*—a concept quite separate from residence. In the UK it is regarded as the place to which an individual will ultimately return, which is normally regarded as the 'Domicile of Origin' of the individual's parents. To have acquired a 'Domicile of choice' all ties must have been severed with the 'Domicile of Origin'.

In addition to these principles attempts may also be made to assert the imposition of extended limited tax liabilities: for example, under the Capital Transfer Tax introduced in the 1975 UK Finance Act any person taking up residence in the Channel Islands or Isle of Man after December 1974 was nevertheless 'deemed' to be 'domiciled' in the UK for purposes of the provisions of the Act; also under the German International Transactions Tax Law of September 1972, paras. 2 and 3, any German nationals who emigrate subsequent to a five-year stay in W. Germany, are subject to full tax liability on all German assets and source income for a period of ten years. Taxes on capital may be levied without regard for any of the above particular principles but simply by an equalization tax to effectively eliminate differentials in rates of return on capital, as was the case in the US 1963–74.

(iii) Attitudes towards Company Management and Location of Registration

Countries which do not attempt an all-embracing anti-avoidance world-wide approach and seek to take a pragmatic point of view of commercial 'legitimacy' or otherwise of business purporting to be external and located in tax havens (particularly those in their immediate vicinity) have to make decisions which may be arbitrary or which, once laid down by statute or case law, may, in the words of the UK Board of Inland Revenue in their recent Consultative Document, be rendered 'artificial with the passage of time and technical innovation'.[6] Concepts of 'company residence' and 'company mangement' and 'control' are often resorted to. Clearly mere registration at a particular location may not be equated with actual residence, or, in the words of Article 4 of the OECD Model Double Taxation Convention 1977, 'the place of effective management', and the latter may not even correspond with 'where the directors' meetings are held', or 'the principal place of business', 'the place of practical day-to-day management' or 'the place where the principal administrative functions are performed'. Moreover, it is often the case that tax advantages for companies—whether they are truly onshore in origin and therefore 'illegitimate external companies' or 'controlled foreign companies', from the viewpoint of the onshore tax authority, or not—are more often derived from being registered as external companies in their 'haven of registration' and being separately controlled from a 'haven of management'.

The UK authorities have sought to introduce a tax on UK corporate shareholders with a direct or indirect interest of 10 per cent or more in an overseas company 'resident in a country with a privileged tax system' and which 'did not distribute by way of dividend to the shareholder a substantial proportion of its profits'. A 'privileged tax system' is defined as 'one in which a company was not subject to tax in its country of residence or was subject to taxes on profits and gains in that country which were significantly lower than those to which it would have been charged in the UK on the relevant profits or gains'.[7] However as the Institute of Directors pointed out, this is a very narrow view given that tax systems offer different tax allowances—'we do not consider a tax system with high rates of tax and generous reliefs, as in Britain, to be economically or morally superior to the typical haven structure with few reliefs but low rates of tax'.[8] Moreover the implicit assumption behind such measures that any reduction in tax avoidance though the use of havens would cause an equivalent or near equivalent increase in taxable UK commercial activity and therefore revenue seems optimistic. Nevertheless unhelpful selective value judgements—pursued by, on the one hand, some onshore authorities who are too ready to take the view that such haven centres are the *situs,* not of intermediate economies as we have described them, but the international equivalent of the domestic 'black', 'informal', 'underground', 'hidden' economy sectors,[9] the refuges of transnational moonlighters and tax evaders, which should be squeezed and, on the other hand, those extreme supporters of economic freedom at all costs, whose near anarchistic *incivisme* is unleashed against all bureaucracies and the impedimenta of government—may well cloud most discussions of this subject.

(iv) Treatment of Branches and Subsidiary Companies and their Earnings

An offshore branch of an onshore business is clearly a direct extension of the parent company and lacks a separate identity. However, in the case of a subsidiary, most onshore tax authorities would tax only the dividends remitted to the parent and not its total earnings: the US Revenue Act (1962) Subpart F, as amended in 1976, makes shareholders of certain controlled foreign corporations assessable for both undistributed and distributed earnings: this is also the case in the Netherlands. Moreover some exchange control systems require repatriation of both branch and subsidiary profits: in the UK full repatriation of branch profits was normally required and two-thirds of subsidiary profits. Such incoming profits to the parent's home country may be subject to different tax treatment dependent on the country involved, the existence of withholding taxes and double taxation agreements. Differential local taxes on branch and subsidiary profits, disclosure requirements and onshore account consolidation requirements make general statements in this area naïve.[10]

Japan applies a particular criteria rendering a foreign subsidiary not subject to its tax laws so subject when it is a 'specified foreign subsidiary', being defined as a foreign corporation with a head office or main place of business in a country where the tax burden is significantly lower than in Japan and more than 50 per cent of its stock is owned by Japanese residents. Income derived from genuine trading or business activities with unrelated persons is excluded from the scope of the charge. A foreign corporation is not a specified foreign subsidiary if it satisfies all of the following conditions:

a) its main business is not to hold securities, patents or copyrights or to lease ships or aircraft;
b) it has the necessary office, shop, factory or other fixed business premises to conduct its business in the country of incorporation;
c) it independently administers, controls and manages its business carried on in that country;
d) where its main business is wholesaling, banking, administration of trusts, dealing in securities, insurance, shipping or air transport, more than 50 per cent of its total gross receipts is derived from unrelated persons; and
e) dividends received from other specified foreign subsidiaries do not exceed 5 per cent of gross receipts.[11]

The UK Board of Inland Revenue proposed in their draft legislation document, *International Tax Avoidance,* to remove the tax advantage of accumulated income in low tax areas, unless a UK controlled foreign company satisfied either a 'genuine trading test' or an 'acceptable distribution test' or a 'motive test'. *Inter alia* genuine trading activities would not obtain where the main business of the companies is private investment business (which is intended to include the holding of securities, patents or copyrights; dealing in securities other than in the capacity of a broker; the leasing of any description of properties or rights; the investment in any manner of funds connected or associated with persons who, alone, or acting with others, have control of the company) or, in the case of a company principally engaged in financial business (which is to specifically include dealing in any description of goods wholesale rather than retail; banking or any similar business involving the receipt of deposits, loans and the making of loans or investments; the administration of trusts; dealing in securities in the capacity of a broker; insurance business of any description; the business of shipping or of air transport), where more than 50 per cent of its gross trading receipts are derived directly or indirectly from connected or associated persons, and in the case of banks where 15 per cent or more of the company's outstanding capital is so held, or where the proportion of the company's gross receipts that are attributed to distribution from other controlled foreign companies exceeded 5 per cent. 'Acceptable distributions' would arise in the case of trading companies where at least 50 per cent of profits are distributed in dividends to the UK and at least 90 per cent for all other companies. Bona fide commercial transactions will provide additional mitigating circumstances provided the 'motive test' demonstrates that avoidance of UK tax was not one of the main purposes of these transactions.

In addition to trying to attack international tax avoidance activities, onshore tax authorities may also seek to pre-empt offshore development by the conferring of particular tax advantages on external business. Thus the US Revenue Act 1971 established DISC—the Domestic International Sales Corporation under which US exporters are given a 'safe haven' relief from intercompany transfer pricing rules applied by the Internal Revenue Service (IRS) and a portion of total profits can be allocated thereto where it will be eligible for DISC tax-deferral privileges.[12] Moreover in federal onshore states there are possibilities of state laws which can be used as incentives for the location of patriate international business. For example, in the US the State of Delaware allows payment of foreign bondholders interest gross of withholding tax if 80 per cent of the gross income of the Delaware subsidiary for the prior three years is from foreign sources under the Investment Company Act of 1960, provided the US SEC (Securities and Exchange Commission) approves, and it is assumed that such securities will not be sold to residents.

Similar effects can be offered through tax-free zones for manufacturing for exports and external or offshore banking, as well as tax exemption being unilaterally offered for particular forms of investment, e.g. the UK tax-exempt gilts.

It should be borne in mind here that from the point of view of a globally footloose company, the overall tax climate of an economy is important, i.e. the combination of tax levels and tax allowances. Low taxes on income and profits when not combined with favourable depreciation allowances or an overall favourable economic climate may not provide as profitable location cost advantages as higher-tax, high-allowance economies.

THE EXERCISE OF EXCHANGE CONTROL POLICIES AND THE 'CURRENCY BOND'

There are many devices that may be used to reduce home demand for invisible imports from the rest of the world as well as the level of capital and other outflows to the rest of the world. Such devices include *inter alia:*[13]

1) restrictions on the free availability of foreign currency for foreign direct and portfolio investment purchases. This might involve the use of earmarked amounts of 'investment currency', the supply and price of which might be market-determined and so involve a 'premium' payment above official exchange rates,[14] and the designation of 'premium-worthy' investments securities;
2) restraints on foreign borrowing and lending;
3) control over individual and institutional ability to 'switch' security investment and to disinvest and reinvest with the proceeds;
4) requirements to lodge all certificates of title with 'authorized' depositories;
5) restrictions on the maximum interest payable by banks and non-banks on foreign-owned deposits;
6) constraints on insurance abroad of domestic property and the domestication of the supply of insurance at home;
7) localization or retention of part or all of the funds earned by foreign enterprises.

All these devices, the precise rationale for which may involve a mixture of politico-economic motives, balance of payments considerations etc. inevitably result in indigenous invisible industry protection and imposed control over the demand for foreign exchange for balance of payments purposes. Domestically, however, their effect will be to lessen the effective ability of onshore residents to exploit the production possibilities for invisible activities and intermediation offered by offshore centres. In such circumstances a company may seek the establishment of a foreign intermediate holding company abroad primarily not for tax reasons but to permit freedom of re-investment abroad if its corporate profits are externally earned.

Onshore fiscal protection and exchange control provide important constraints on offshore centre invisible production possibilities, yet the historical relationship of the offshore state with its onshore periphery can convey advantages of some substance that could constitute a crucial, though biased development 'externality'. Few prospective offshore centres have not had a past where a colonial relationship has not existed or where a 'guardian' relationship does not continue in the form of some economic dependency on an onshore centre, which does not still have some monetary and/or exchange control implications. In most cases, offshore local currency is pegged to the value of the onshore centre, and before 'going international', there is often a stage of development where the offshore centre acts essentially as an offshore centre for its particular currency zone only. Indeed the prospective offshore centre's development potential may be crucially affected by the international standing of the particular onshore currency. In Susan Strange's terminology[15] such currencies can be one of several types, although particular currencies may change their category status over time, and at any one period of time may be in a process of category transition:

> *Top currency status*—'the choice of the world market . . . the preferred medium of the international economy and financial system . . . most often and most widely used for a great variety of monetary purposes . . .'
>
> *Master currency status*—'where an imperial or hegemonial state imposes the use of its currency on other political entities, whether they are allied states, dependent protectorates, or colonies'. To which a further sub-category needs to be added, namely, 'or where, in a post colonial period monetary union continues, with the consent of both parties, such that the former dominant state in effect still retains considerable monetary sovereignty and control directly through its central bank or indirectly through 'authorized' banks'.
>
> *Negotiated currency states*—'where either the issuing state once had, but has subsequently lost, a position of political dominance; or, it once had and has subsequently lost a position of economic dominance'.
>
> *Neutral currency status*—'where the issuing state has no special political interests outside its own frontiers to seek or to protect and is politically indifferent towards the users' (e.g. Swiss francs; Deutschmark).

This taxonomy is naturally based on the country of issue. To this list should be added one further category—*non-national neutral currency status*—to cover the use of Eurocurrency money and bond markets which have evolved essentially since the mid-1960s because of excessive controls that resulted from demand management policies in particular mixed economies and constitute, as Mann[16] has remarked 'an international "grey market" or alternative system', and do not involve problems concerned with national withholding taxes when investments are made therein. In the absence of any exogenously exerted exchange control system and given the existence of neutral non-national currencies, international and indeed national users of money will be free to choose the currency which suits them best.[17]

In practice each actual or potential offshore centre is likely to be related to one of these onshore national currency groups. *Per se* this generates differential development potentials. There is likely to be a comparative advantage of financial expertise accessibility in cases where the natural onshore country's currency has 'top' currency status, or had such status and now has 'master' currency status, or where its own currency has a preferred 'neutral' currency status which it wishes to exploit. Naturally there may be elements of one or more types at play at any one time, for transitory reasons of particular short-term world currency market situations, or because of monetary adjustment lags in relation to a location-changed domestic international competitive situation. 'Master' currency status may not give a potential offshore centre much advantage where the master country has not had much significance in world trade. But when the currency has had a world trade significance it may continue to have a preferred currency status within the world hierarchy of traded master currencies. Thus the 'openness' for 'inward' investment of the 'guardian' currency country will make an important difference in certain cases to its 'offshore' states[18] some of which may reap considerable benefits from direct access to such onshore centres and/or where an autonomous policy-imposed distortion is created in their favour, as was the case in 1972 in the UK, when EC82 was issued rescheduling the Sterling Area to just the Channel Islands, Eire and the Isle of Man (to which list Gibraltar was subsequently added), so depriving Bermuda, the Bahamas and others of certain privileges they had when within the Scheduled Territories which were now concentrated on the countries on the narrower list. It was only natural that many of the Caribbean countries subsequently changed their currency bond to that of the US dollar which made them attractive to American Eurodollar activity managed from New York given the common time zone for business activity and the fact that New York was at that time the most open state for international banking activity location.

SUMMARY

1) Effective exploitation of the onshore friction matrix and non-resident international private sector access to these centres has been or is circumscribed by countervailing onshore economy attempts to impose exchange control systems and assert tax jurisdictions to pre-empt or control the type and amount of activities so diverted.
2) Differential onshore national attitudes to tax avoidance or evasion jurisdiction, differences in definitions of national fiscal boundaries and the problems of divergency between place of registration and place of effective management are not simply solved given the complexities of modern business methods and communication systems. Policies to protect the erosion of the national tax base may be seen as legitimate, but not if they are

mercantilist in intent or effect. Failure to evolve and apply a common policy within the global trading system does seem unfortunate in terms of equity of treatment of states and business activities both onshore and offshore.

3) Exchange control policies by adding to the international friction matrix provide negative incentives for regulation avoidance or evasion but within the context of the polar influence of the currency concerned may accord preferential treatment to some areas given their currency bond link. Equally in special circumstances it is possible for an embryonic offshore centre to change its currency bond as part of its development strategy.

Given the parametric context of the onshore international friction matrix as so far described, what does offshore centre development involve?

REFERENCES

1. See Bhagwati, N.J., 'Alternative Theories of Illegal Trade: Economic Consequences and Statistical Detection', *Weltwirtshafliches Archiv,* Band 117, Heft 3, 1981, pp.409–27.

2. See Saunders, R.M. *Principles of Tax Planning,* London, Finax Publications, 1978; and Sharp, P., *UK Fiscal Implications of International Trade,* London, Institute of Chartered Accountants, 1976.

3. Quoted by G.C. Powell on p.106 of *Tax Havens and Measures against Tax Evasion and Avoidance in the EEC,* ed. J.F. Avery Jones, London, Associated Business Programmes, 1974.

4. The Tax Reform Act of 1976 made several important changes: for the intricate complexities of this country's legislation see Syckoff, E.L., 'US Taxation of Foreign Trusts', *US Taxation of International Operations Service,* Englewood Cliffs, N.J., Prentice-Hall, 1979.

5. See Philip, K., 'On Location of Production, Factor Movements, etc., as Affected by the Social and Fiscal Policies of Individual Countries and Economic Communities' and 'Comment' thereon by Hufbauer, G.C. 'Taxation and Public Expenditures in an Open Economy', ch.8 of *The International Allocation of Economic Activity,* ed. by B. Ohlin *et al.*, London, Macmillan, 1977.

6. UK Board of Inland Revenue, *Company Residence, A Consultative Document,* January 1981, para. 2.

7. UK Board of Inland Revenue, *Tax Havens and the Corporate Sector, A Consultative Document,* January, 1981, para. 6.

8. UK Institute of Directors. *Submission on the Inland Revenue Consultative Document on Taxhavens of January 1981,* p.5, para.13, 26 June 1981. For a full discussion of the reliefs and investments available to both domestic and foreign companies see L. Blackstone and D. Franks, *The UK as a Tax Haven: A Guide to New Tax Planning Opportunities* Economist Intelligence Unit Special Report No.95, March 1981.

9. See Smith, A., 'The Informal Economy', *Lloyds Bank Review,* July 1981, pp.45–61.

10. See ch.7, 'International Taxation' in D. Wood and J.Byrne, *International Business Finance,* London, Macmillan, 1981.

11. Annex, p.4, of UK Board of Inland Revenue, *Tax Havens and the Corporate Sector.*

12. See Sethi, S. and Cuhney, A.F., 'The Domestic International Sales Corporation (DISC): Problems and Prospects' in *Management of the Multinationals,* ed. S.P. Sethi and R.H. Holton, New York, Free Press, 1974.

13. For a discussion of the arguments for such restrictions from the onshore country point of view see Cairncross, Sir A., *Control of Long-term International Capital Movements,*

Washington, D.C., The Brookings Institution, 1973, ch.1. For a general discussion of these matters see Griffiths, B., *Invisible Barriers to Invisible Trade,* London, Macmillan, 1975; and the IMF, *Annual Reports on Exchange Restrictions,* Washington for a continuous country by country review of such practices; and Parker, A., '*Exchange Control*', 3rd ed., London, Jordan and Sons, 1978.

14. See Woolley, P.K., 'Britain's Investment Currency Premium', *Lloyds Bank Review,* July 1974; also 'UK Exchange Control: A Short History, *Bank of England Quarterly Bulletin,* Vol. 7, No.3, September 1967, and, 'The Investment Currency Market', *Bank of England Central Bulletin,* Vol. 16, No.3, September 1976; and, 'Direct and Trade Investment in the Non-sterling Area', *Board of Trade Journal,* Vol.194, No.3710, 26 April 1968, pp.1263–7.

15. Strange, S., *Sterling and British Policy: A Political Study of an International Currency in Decline,* ch.1, *passim,* Oxford University Press, 1976.

16. Mann, D., 'The Role of British Banks After the End of Exchange Control', *The Banker,* January 1980, p.101.

17. See Vaubel, R., 'Free Currency Competition', *Weltwirtschafliches Archiv,* Band 113, 1977 Heft 3, pp.435–61 for a discussion of this controversial issue.

18. Thus the access Sterling Area offshore centres had to the London money and capital markets in the days of exchange control 1947–79 gave them the opportunity to benefit from the relative 'openness' of the UK monetary authorities compared say to those in the US. See Lees, F.A., *Foreign Banking and Investment in the US,* London, Macmillan, 1976, pp. 128–37.

CHAPTER IV
The Competitive Power of Offshore States and the Art of International Economic 'Frictioneering'

Previous chapters have established the production pressures and vacuums created for transnational and other business, both national and international, within the international trading system by onshore national, some would argue mercantilist, politico-economic friction structures. This chapter will attempt to analyse the preconditions necessary for offshore take-off, the production rationale for such centres, and the means by which their competitive powers may be exercised by their political administrations together with their personal, business and financial sectors, whether internally or externally located.

PRECONDITIONS FOR OFFSHORE TAKE-OFF AND THE DEVELOPMENT OF A GLOBAL NETWORK OF OFFSHORE CENTRES

As long as a 'tax haven' or 'low-tax' area has a nucleus of deposit and merchant banks and certain specific infrastructural facilities, a potential for financial sector transformation exists so long as any changes in the general industrial structure of their economies do not offend the indigenous population. While these economies may be countries of convenience for their non-resident and resident tax-avoiding patrons, it is essential that the 'enclave' foreign body institutions that constitute the offshore sector complement and harmonize with the other constituent parts of their indigenous industrial superstructures if incipient nationalist feelings are not to be awakened. Given the above, four basic infrastructural preconditions are necessary for initial and ongoing development and industrial diversification:

1. *Politico-economic and fiscal stability.* This is a *sine qua non,* without which there can be no long-term security for depositors, investors and institutions. International capital is very sensitive to serious doubts and uncertainties concerning the continuation of the status quo with regard to the exercise or non-exercise of non-interventionist domestic policies. From the viewpoint of the non-resident, states such as the Channel Islands and Hong Kong are ideal in this respect in that they have a non-party political administrative form of government. In certain parts of the world, such as the Caribbean, colonial marriages of convenience at independence have not proved particularly stable for some island states that were artificially brought together. Thus Anguilla managed to secede from its independence link with St. Kitts and Nevis and, as from 1 January 1981, regained its status as a Crown Colony, a step which several other islands in the area would like to emulate.
2. *A stable local currency and ease of use of international currencies.* As was previously

mentioned, in most cases, a particular historical onshore link continues to have monetary and exchange implications for the off-shore centre of a polar kind. On the monetary side this tends to manifest itself in the pegging of offshore currencies more often than not to particular 'guardian' onshore currency values. The resulting currency bond (albeit a 'top'/'master'/'negotiated' or 'neutral'/currency bond) will tend to have concomitant implications both for the current stability of particular offshore local currencies and the local ease of foreign currency use.

3. *Ready availability of expert professional services.* Growth of deposits and trading companies requires the presence of banks, solicitors, accountants, stockbrokers, trust companies and other management and financial services. Such specialist services become of crucial importance if an offshore centre is to develop and have access to transnational business networks. As such firms are rarely indigenously present, they have to be attracted which may create local resentment if there is already population pressure on local housing and office space, etc.
4. *Good communications.* The establishment of telex, telephone, mail and air services is essential. Given that many haven centres are also tourist centres, the travel communications infrastructure is usually already at hand and ready-made. For onshore clients these facilities will be important where face-to-face contact with offshore institutions is desired or warranted for confidential business discussions. At the institutional operational level, ease of contact with, and electronic access to, parent organizations and the major onshore financial markets is essential for the profitable timing of deals. The latter will be heightened if there is a time zone link with the operation of a major centre and the business hours of its money and capital markets are common.

The realized existence of potential island or continental sites for offshore activities and their geographical scatter will depend upon whether the infrastructural requirements mentioned above are:[1]

i) *'place-free'*, i.e. potentially available everywhere under the same conditions;
ii) *'conditionally place-bound'*, i.e. available at all or only some places under unequal conditions;
iii) *'unconditionally place-bound'*, i.e. present at a few mutually distant sites.

Given the real world differential growth of interventionist government activities of recent decades, only comparatively few areas can provide frictionless or low friction economic environments that are combined with a high degree of political and economic stability. Thus the initial global centre scatter is likely to be generally 'unconditionally place-bound', (despite regional clustering of small island centres, as in the Caribbean, that may constitute 'conditionally place-bound' exceptions), and the organic process of the development of a world network of offshore finance centres will tend to confirm this general location pattern, despite the continued existence of several small tax haven or low tax areas that remain untransformed. The following reasons account for this likely outcome:

1. Development takes place discontinuously. The externalities created by a new financial centre confers advantages of establishment that may preempt a subsequent extension to nearby potential bases, unless, in the case of small island communities, growth constraints are soon encountered.
2. Small island states often, for reasons of population pressure or industrial balance, tend sooner or later to adopt restricted entry procedures whereby expansion becomes based on growth by consolidation, new entry being confined to single representative institutions from countries not previously present within the domestic financial community.
3. Inevitably the world supply of mobile technical staff is limited and will tend to have its own locational preferences that may preclude any significant effective extensions of the world-wide chain of centres.
4. Political instability risks are attached to newly politically independent states which tend to favour consolidation activity even in the slightly higher 'low-tax' centres. This is especially so in cases where, after independence, development may take place in an unmonitored fashion resulting in a low international reputation being attached to the potential centre, which sterilises ongoing development. There were several cases of such false starts in the 1970s with belated attempts being made by administrations to 'clean up' local business activities.
5. It is often the case that particular onshore economies that were the original colonial masters of newly independent states continue to grant them by their autonomous or instrumental policy-imposed attitudes, covert, albeit limited, freedom, or, in some cases, positive preferences for these activities within scheduled currency areas, often on the basis of a continuing participation in monitoring these offshore activities.
6. The existence of time zones. In so far as there is a 24-hour business activity sequence permitting geographical switching of trading activity on a continuous basis, as each principal onshore world capital market proceeds through its working hours the termination of which overlaps that of others, locations within the same zone as the main onshore markets, or which overlap for much of their business hours, have distinct operational advantages over those not so located.
7. If the number of world centres were to proliferate on any basis other than an 'unconditionally place-bound' one, the disintermediation implied from onshore to offshore centres would, more than certainly, bring about a zealous onshore reorganization of friction structures such that onshore areas might themselves establish competitive banking free zones.

THE ART OF INTERNATIONAL ECONOMIC 'FRICTIONEERING'

So long as the above-mentioned pre-conditions are present, the superstructural development of offshore activities and their continuing evolution will depend on the potential of haven centres, actual and realized, to exploit, generate, identify and attract what I will call 'economic frictioneering activities', which I will define as *activities which promote personal, financial and business disintermediation and friction-busting from established onshore (and even other offshore) capital and financial markets and locations of business registration for sectoral profit and the net gain of the offshore state.* Such activities are of two kinds (i) offshore public sector frictioneering activities, and (ii) international private sector frictioneering activities.

(i) Offshore Public Sector Frictioneering Activities

This essentially consists in establishing an offshore low or zero friction non-interventionist structure to ensure a long-run stable environment to which business will be continuously attracted, consistent with an international reputation to inspire confidence and renown for respectable business standards. In the framing of the structure, regard will be had to the desirability or otherwise of having a two-tier system of minimum regulations which differentiates between internal domestic resident activities and external domestically-based activities, e.g. whether to have exemptions from income tax and withholding taxes on dividends, disclosure procedures for non-resident and resident trusts, etc. Essentially though, the offshore domestic friction structure should ideally be one where there is: *a well defined, yet flexible, background of law and procedures free from undue restrictions with regard to the establishment and operations of businesses, whether industrial, commercial or financial.* There are three central areas to be considered here:

a) *the relative ease of production entry,* licensing, local capital requirements, etc., regulations and monitoring of operations;

b) *company law and freedom from onerous local taxation* whether direct (profits tax, license fees etc.) or withholding taxes on dividends issued;

c) *the relative absence of local exchange control regulations,* if any, and freedom to use non-local currencies (ease of currency movement).

To the extent that local policy-induced restrictions obtain in these areas, there will be invisible trade-averting implications, if only to check total laissez-faire opportunism and financial expediency.

(a) Ease of production entry. Prudential questions of solvency and protection of depositors would seem to require some minimum regulations if any centre is to have a long-run reputation for business stability and security of investments. This is especially important with regard to banking regulations where under-regulation would tend to encourage unsound business and shady practices that would lower the reputation of the centre and particularly discourage transnational institutions whose prestige is essential for most of their clientele. As will be seen in Part III failure to understand the importance of this led to sterility of development in a number of potential centres in the Caribbean in the 1970s and in Panama. In extreme cases this led to onshore tax authorities taking the view that most activities in such were suspect and/or merely artificial 'shell' operations. To avoid this the local banking commissioner/commercial relations officer must pursue a course that is flexible enough to react to the requirements of genuine business, yet is able to lean hard on those who seek to abuse acceptable business

standards. Dependent on what is felt desirable in the individual circumstances of the offshore economy, bank licensing may involve the provision of general licences allowing both domestic and international banking to take place, or a series of different categories including separate licences for offshore banking, e.g. Bahrain and OBUs (Offshore Banking Units); Singapore and ACUs (Asian Currency Units), and representative offices. In an extreme case, as in Bermuda, all banking is confined to indigenous banks. Regulated entry may also be necessary for reasons of pressure on housing, office space, etc., and to minimize any local antagonism if growth threatens to be rapid in the short run. For this and other reasons a moratorium may be imposed, as was the case in Jersey in the early 1970s and in Hong Kong from 1965 to March 1978 and since August 1979. In the latter case offshore activity tended to be channelled primarily through investment companies owned by the international banking fraternity.

(b) Company law, commercial law and freedom from onerous local taxation. Here the art of public sector frictioneering lies in ensuring a minimum degree of requirements in respect of incorporation procedures, and yet to permit a range of company categories, such that revenues to the 'intermediate economy' are maximized. Requirements concerning subscribed and paid-up capital will set the tone to the reputation of the centre.

In the area of company law it is necessary to ensure that the scope of legal provisions is such as to permit the existence of forms of company incorporation that will appeal internationally (and yet not entirely fall foul of onshore tax authorities) and facilitate the existence of modern commercial practices. Essentially regulations concerning board and management structure may affect the scope of the activity permitted as well as minimum capital and debt/equity ratio requirements, disclosure of shareholders, and the filing of accounts. Consideration must be given to the question of local attitudes towards *inter alia* trusts, close companies and open-ended investment companies which may be restricted onshore.

In the area of trusts, it matters whether the domestic law has a common law tradition or a civil law tradition. Those with a common law tradition give rise to the foreign trust as the mechanism for much personal sector tax planning; the civil or continental law tradition lacks a trust law and so usually involves secret bank accounts or a private company. Under the former the title is usually owned absolutely by a trustee (often a bank) with absolute discretion in the management, investment and distribution of assets. Nothing is vested in the family.[2]

Close companies are ones that are director controlled, where one person, or a small group of people, are able to resort to measures such as the retention of profits beyond the needs of the business which would be impractical for a company the control of which is more diverse. Such companies are often made subject to special restrictions so that their close control does not place them in a privileged position with regards to tax. In the UK provisions were made in the Finance Acts of 1922, 1937, 1965, 1978 and 1980. To avoid such restrictions any artificial attempts to structure 'open' companies are subject to wide interpretations of words such as 'control', 'participator' and 'associate'.[3]

Open-end investment funds involve in principle a continuous issue and repurchase of shares/units on demand, with the price of the shares/units determined by the net asset value of the fund's portfolio divided by the number of shares/units issued. They are generally referred to as open-end investment funds, in the UK as unit trusts and in North America as mutual funds. Tight controls have been introduced in Western Germany, Switzerland and Luxembourg and a strong code of operation has been in force in most EEC countries[4] with guidelines being laid down by OECD and the Commission of the European Communities.[5] Restrictions in the form of invisible trade barriers may be erected onshore, e.g. under the UK Prevention of Fraud (Investments) Act 1958 Section 17, foreign open-end funds cannot be authorized for sub-section (*a*) stipulates 'The Managers and the trustee must be UK registered companies with registered offices in the UK for the despatch and receipt of all documents relating to the fund.' Offshore laws permit such unit funds, contrary to onshore provisions, to 'gear' and borrow money in addition to that subscribed in order to boost performance for unitholders. They may further promote funds investment in commodities and metals that are inherently risky ventures which may not be permitted onshore; and issue 'no par value' shares and bearer shares.

As regards commercial law, it is essential where there has been an indigenous system of laws, that they should be carefully revised to ensure that obstacles do not unwittingly preclude the pledging of 'moveables', that Usury Laws do not remain to keep interest rates artificially low, and that insurance/reinsurance business is permitted and catered for.

In the area of offshore taxation structures, regard must be had to onshore taxation structures and the mitigation of their effects in the international sphere. As long as competition for the location of footloose transnational activities can be influenced by structural differences in the various national tax systems, whether onshore or offshore, every transnational investment/business plan must take into account the relationship between onshore and offshore states with regard to their business objectives. Given that international economic interdependence has not as yet been accompanied by 'neutrality' of taxation in regard to international competition, problems of international double taxation exist where there is imposition of comparable taxes by two or more original sovereign tax jurisdictions on the same taxpayer in respect of the same tax object and for identical periods.

As was indicated in the previous chapter, modern inland revenue regimes do not regard themselves as being restricted in their national right to tax, or even in the imposition of extended limited tax liabilities, because there is as yet no system of public international law in this area other than general guidelines or models laid down by bodies such as OECD. Views concerning the appropriate national allocation of the tax base differ widely. Unilateral attribution rules of legal alignment are individually worked out in relation to the 'connecting factors' of particular activities as Knechtle has pointed out:[6]

> The tax subject is connected to the State by *domicile/residence* or *abode/sojourn* (as well as by nationality), while a tax object is subject to the territorial sovereignty of the State by virtue of the *place where it is located* (situs), and an act by reason of the *place where the act is carried on.* Accordingly the taxing power is sometimes held to belong to the State of domicile/residence or

> abode/sojourn ('fiscal domicile'), sometimes to the place where the object is situated (situs), and sometimes to the place of action. Hence . . . these have developed as primary connecting factors . . . and . . . *nationality* has lost its importance as a fiscal connecting factor.

Fiscal conflict and international double taxation is bound to occur as each state is a state of source in respect of incomes from its territory which flow abroad, and a state of residence as regards taxation of foreign incomes of persons resident within its territory. This conflict of overlapping tax claims exists independently of the international tax avoidance/evasion issue concerning 'artificiality' that may arise with regard to alleged residence of companies. National treatment given to income from moveable capital assets (dividends and interest) and royalties may well reflect the capital-exporting bias of creditor countries and the capital-importing bias of debtor countries (the former favouring the residence principle, the latter the source or origin principle) or for particular items, the inter-state balance of payments may suggest particular treatments. In so far as practical considerations may well place factual and legal obstacles on the operational enforcement of particular objectives, if these objectives are nevertheless legislated for, actual incidence of taxation may remain hypothetical for many potential taxpayers, or else onshore tax strategy will switch its emphasis towards onshore shareholding. Knechtle argues that the resulting international double taxation

> is a breach of the postulate of fiscal justice, since it is incompatible with equal taxation of all tax subjects in accordance with their economic capacity . . . and is . . . rightly considered to be discrimination against foreign investment activity and business activity . . . which should be avoided not only for economic reasons, but also for reasons of equity.[7]

In practice these difficulties may be mitigated by the use of unilateral or bilateral provision of tax credits or exemptions that may cause the overlapping systems to merely abut if they fully allow for withholding taxes paid elsewhere or may in the case of exemptions provide direct incentives for the relocation of international capital. Both treatments under bilateral provision can be made under formal double taxation agreements (DTAs),[8] tax treaties, etc., where waiving of taxing rights on the basis of reciprocity is negotiated, the scope of which may be very narrow or widely related to income taxes, property taxes and death duties in general.

In respect of local tax haven strategy, offshore centre decisions will have to be made concerning the right mix between unilateral exemption of income originating from abroad, and bilateral relief from foreign withholding taxes on dividends, interest and royalties connected with key onshore economies, particularly those with which there are close trading ties. On the positive side, DTAs can be attractive for rich *rentier* immigrants (where they are a relatively large section of the local population or important for reasons of general domestic revenue) and can facilitate offshore activity: this has particularly been the case with respect of the Caribbean havens and their DTAs with the UK and the US; and Switzerland. However, an absence of double taxation agreements does mean an absence of exchanges of information between offshore and onshore tax authorities, which may work in the potential friction-buster's favour. The tax legislation of many countries, including the US, the UK, Australia and Canada, generally recognizes the principle that the country of the income source (the host country) has priority in the taxation of income generated by the investment of non-residents, but their systems of foreign tax credits mean that when the sum of income tax liability the lending country would levy on this foreign-earned income is not extracted in the host country, it will be so extracted in the onshore lending centre. This will, in the case of zero tax havens, be the full amount and, in the case of low-tax areas, the residual amount. However, base-company income (accruing in the host country) is only usually so taxed when a distribution is made, thus giving the company deferral advantages and possibility of reinvestment in the low-tax countries[9] given the difficulties the offshore tax authority may have in trying to scrutinize the myriads of such global activities.

In general a common approach adopted in haven centres is to attract international trading companies, trusts etc., by having either provision for zero tax 'exempt' company status or a low-tax flat rate annual 'corporation tax company'. Given that each centre will have slightly different taxes, sets of company laws etc., inter-offshore centre substitution and disintermediation may well take place to maximize particular institutional benefits. Thus it may be easier to set up an externally-controlled (in the residence sense) company in one centre and to have its investment funds or management located in another offshore centre, where considerable tax exemptions are offered in the first centre. Here, the most crucial tax question is usually to ensure that the context and management of a company or partnership or the administration of the trust is in fact carried on in the chosen jurisdiction and is not deemed by other high tax mainland countries or higher tax offshore states to be located within their areas of influence. In certain circumstances the provision of unilateral relief against foreign withholding taxes may be an important way of broadening the investment inflow and investment base, as well as no-tax guarantees, bank secrecy laws and the provision of numbered bank accounts.

(c) Relative absence of local exchange control regulations. Despite political independence, it is not always true that monetary independence exists (e.g. the Channel Islands) which can mean that, if the monetary dominant mainland economy (usually with a 'master' or 'top' currency) cares to exercise a system of exchange control, the 'offshore' dependency, despite some areas of domestic sovereignty, in essence becomes a 'captive' offshore centre operating discretionally within an exogenous set of policy-imposed instruments and distortions. Its effective ability to frictioneer is circumscribed within a straightjacket of external control, which although not necessarily unduly repressive may so be modified in that direction by unilateral onshore decision.

(ii) International Private Sector 'Frictioneering' Activities

As offshore centres are the interposed financial and business peripheries of the general onshore network of world trade flows, as well as, in most areas, in effect adjuncts of particular onshore economies or continents, their evolution pattern will reflect the changing business needs of each. Of paramount significance is their ability to monitor the prospects for new forms of transnational business activity as the onshore national and international scene changes and, where possible, to take advantage of X-inefficiences in the offshore–onshore friction matrix created by legal anomalies, loopholes and discretionary procedures. Some changes may only be ephemeral and related to short-term balance of payments policy problems, others may be of more lasting significance for the 'sheltering' of business activities. Financial ingenuity and innovation are the essential means by which they seek to penetrate existing friction structures, in order to exploit, however transitory, new conditions brought about by relaxations in foreign frictions as a result of the abolition or modification of 'policy-imposed' distortions, such as *inter alia* the introduction of a wealth tax, the onshore creation of tax-exempt gilt funds or loopholes that are legitimately created by a new set of restrictive laws. It cannot be stressed too strongly that people with a wide experience of international finance must be present for effective frictioneering activities to take place. Chown[10] has identified three possibile main techniques for what others have called 'international profit engineering'[11] the potentials for which need to be considered by an incipient friction-buster:

i) *profit-creation:* 'actually setting up a commercial business within a low-tax territory' for domestic offshore activities;
ii) *profit-diversion:* an attempt to arrange that the profits that would otherwise accrue to a high-taxed country are diverted to a low-taxed one;
iii) *profit-extraction:* an attempt to mitigate the taxation of profits in a high-tax country by having a low-tax subsidiary charging management fees or royalties against these profits, especially where double taxation agreements exist between the low and high tax countries involved.

In terms of the offshore centre, external business can be created from the three main sub-sectors of the international private sector:

1. the international personal sector;
2. the international company sector;
3. the international finance sector;

1. The International Personal Sector

Essentially the supply of funds and offshore use from this sector includes

1) (*a*) Offshore resident, generally wealthy, *émigré rentiers* and businessmen; (*b*) Wealthy onshore individuals for whom onshore residence is not possible for a variety of reasons, who live in high-tax areas and/or who suffer actual or incipient political instability, or fears thereof, in their countries of residence.
   Both these groups seek to protect their fortunes during their life; and, at death to avoid or evade onshore estate duties.
2) Actual or incipient internationally mobile expatriates who require a secure

haven for their financial assets prior to, during, or subsequent to periods of work abroad.

3) Temporary service overseas by self-employed workers.

All these groups may well be at the mercy of onshore tax jurisdictions and exchange control systems. Even in the case of the resident *émigrés,* devices such as 'deemed domicile' for specific taxes may bring them within an onshore tax net. Category (1a) may well be severely restricted or not encouraged where offshore population pressures give rise to land and housing shortages. What is important for (1b) is the question of secrecy of bank accounts and a minimum of exposure if companies are formed. It is likely that within the 'intermediate' economy, international private sector inflow of funds will generally be transformed into international commercial sector activities as the funds so attracted are often used to establish private investment companies to continue the process of wealth accumulation for their owners. This is usually effected by means of an investment holding company which may be combined with a trust. Other opportunities for profit rest on the existence of the possibilities of family trust formation: in this case the residence of the trust for onshore exchange control purposes may be determined by the residence of the settler and the residence of the beneficiary. The existence offshore of professional trustees, legal services, etc., will be a *sine qua non* of frictioneering here. One further ploy may be an attempt to reduce tax by 'converting' income into capital thereby creating in general a lower taxed capital gain at the expense of higher taxed income, e.g. the right to income from a licence or royalties might be waived in return for a lump sum.

As regards (2), an increasingly transnational mobile work force (as distinct from once-and-for-all emigration) will often require financial facilities for salary dispersal schemes for employers, currency accounts, as well as trustee and other fiduciary services.

As regards (3), if, as is the case in the UK, self-employed workers are not eligible for tax exemption on their earnings on overseas assignments of over twelve months' duration, whereas contracted ones are, an offshore company may be set up to provide an employment contract, which, if recognized by onshore tax authorities, would enable tax exemption thereby to be obtained.

Possibilities for friction-busting in the international personal sector are very much institution-related and institution circumscribed.

2. The International Industrial and Commercial Sector

As indicated earlier, our discussion is essentially geared to basically very small economies and the evolution of trade activities consequent on a tax-haven orientation of the economic system. In general there will be little scope for profit-creation either from offshore domestic-economy oriented activities (which may not anyway be encouraged) or, with a few exceptions, from visible trade development of component assembly industries as previously mentioned. Whether domestic-oriented trade or intermediate visible or invisible trade is involved, however, the scope for an offshore-attracted presence and a resident foreign participation in frictioneering activities will be dependent upon offshore foreign company law regulations (if different from domestic ones) including exposure requirements laid down by registration procedures, the existence or otherwise of withholding tax requirements on dividends and other factors previously mentioned, and any special arrangements that might exist for particular industries (e.g. shipping). The objective will be to maximize company benefits from the asymmetries and constellations of cost differences created by different onshore international friction structures, relative individual offshore low-friction structures, and the possibilities of inter-offshore exchange and offshore/onshore exchange. In this regard onshore tax jurisdictions with an asserted and exerted worldwide net may severely restrict frictioneering potential, e.g. in 1962 the US brought in legislation concerning 'controlled foreign corporations'—companies registered abroad which receive foreign-based company income and in which a controlling interest is held by US residents—as have Australia, Canada, Germany and the Netherlands. Such legislation may *inter alia* make onshore resident shareholders, whether corporate or individuals, subject to anti-avoidance legislation (though in this area this may depend on a distribution actually being made, until which time benefits of deferral may be enjoyed) and/or require onshore repatriation of a certain percentage of non-resident overseas subsidiaries' profits. Within such limits, external trading companies and/or investment holding companies, can be set up to pursue profit-diversion and profit-extraction activities as described, especially when anonymity can be preserved legally by the use of nominees provided by local finance institutions. Establishment of such companies has appeal in cases where the promoter lives in a country subject to any one or combination of the following features: low political stability, high-level taxation, restrictive legislation. Trading profits may accumulate wealth in an unpublicized manner if there is no requirement to file annual accounts for public inspection or the disclosure of the identity of the beneficial shareholder or participants. Such holding or trading companies may be particularly appropriate for operations such as ship chartering, aircraft basing, film making, property development, and mining and oil production and development. What individual firms have to consider here is what is tax-effective from a net tax point of view. Low or zero tax areas with respect to particular forms of income may not have the range of tax deductibles with regard to depreciation and other allowances so that the net position may not be all that different from an onshore location. There may, however, be advantages of tax deferral as opposed to tax avoidance as well as political stability and/or greater security from the effects of the vicissitudes of policy following general elections. Knowledge of and monitoring of changes in laws, legal loopholes and discretionary procedures will be essential if the legitimate viability of activities is to remain intact. One token example of each is given below, taken from the UK experience.

Legal Loopholes. Under S.482 of the 1970 Taxes Act, while it is illegal for a UK resident company to transfer part or all of its trade to a non-resident company without Treasury consent, it is not illegal to sell an asset which is not part of a trade to a foreign company. Thus the intellectual property vested in the patent rights to a new invention patented overseas if so sold before trading commences does not infringe the law.

Similarly, in a much more roundabout way, it is possible to use a network of tax treaties and havens to obtain the best features of each as a means of avoiding onshore withholding taxes thus syphoning off particular forms of income. Doggart gives the following example[12] – a West German patentee seeks to license a US company without paying US or German tax by the following steps:

1) He (*a*) assigns patent to a Liechtenstein holding company (*b*).
2) (*a*) grants a licence to a Swiss letterbox company (*c*) which in turn licenses a US corporation (*d*).
3) (*d*) pays royalties to (*c*) which is free of US withholding tax (of 30 per cent) by virtue of the US/Switzerland tax treaty.
4) (*c*) pays royalty equivalent to (*b*) and suffers no withholding tax or profits tax.
5) (*b*) pays no profits tax (only net worth of 0.1 per cent per annum) and no tax distribution of profits. Royalties are accumulated until (*a*) requires them.
6) If (*a*) owns (*d*) and insures that the royalty rate is high he will absorb as much US profit as possible.

Thus multi-centre offshore disintermediation leads to a 'daisy-chain' of geographical exchange that successfully avoids onshore tax in more than one country.

Discretionary procedures. These are often embodied in exchange control policies and procedures associated with the clearance of, for example, the external status of companies, pension rights, etc. Discretionary powers may be exercised by *inter alia* the central bank, the revenue authorities, departments of ministries and the law courts. Thus in the UK whether a company is liable or not liable to profits and capital gains taxes rests with the decision of the Inland Revenue as to whether the alleged foreign non-resident company is trading 'with' or 'in' the UK. This decision turns on the answer given to the question – where do the operations take place from which the profits in substance arise? Again in the UK whilst tax avoidance schemes may be decided on the basis of form rather than substance, as in the case of *Wallesteiner* v. *Moir* 1974, Lord Denning was prepared to 'lift the veil of incorporation' to treat certain limited companies as the instruments of control not as separate legal entities.

The following frictioneering ploys are commonly resorted to by this sector:

a) The use of 'letterbox' companies to collect patent royalties, licensing fees, loan interest, etc. These companies can act, as Hermann has pointed out,[13] as 'turntables' for capital by reinvesting the funds received so that they again can earn tax exempt income. The funds can be placed at the disposal of the persons or companies controlling the holding company, providing them with the additional advantage of being able to deduct from the taxable income the loan interest paid to their own holding company which is not taxed at all or only at a very low rate.
Additional benefits can be obtained by combining letterbox companies with normally taxed companies as Hermann has shown. Withholding taxes in

one centre can be eliminated by the use of an intermediary company in a third country where there is no withholding tax, provided a double-taxation convention exists between that country and the country whence the royalties originate so that the income is routed through the third country to the offshore centre.

b) *'Invoicing'.* The technique of 'invoicing' or 'transfer pricing' involves the interposition of a subsidiary offshore trading company often external to the offshore place of residence between onshore exchange centres, through which invoices are routed and profits siphoned off by the simple device of re-invoicing, such that onshore tax payments on income are minimized (taking into account any exchange rate risks involved). Appropriate activities here might include property companies, equipment leasing, service companies, cash management, etc. Countries with a world-wide tax system that is closely monitored may seek to minimize such opportunities, e.g. Section 482 of the US Internal Revenue Code allows any transfer prices used to be challenged in those intrafirm transactions which diverge from any 'arm's length' standard they wish to apply based on real market costs. In the UK S.485 of the 1970 Taxes Act provides that where property is sold between associated persons, i.e. the seller controls the buyer or vice versa, or both are in common control, the Board of Inland Revenue may direct that the market price be substituted for the actual price. These provisions were tightened up by the 1975 Finance Act under which rights or powers of nominees and connected persons (spouse, relatives, partners) were specifically included in the definition of control and a situation where (*i*) one of the parties involved is a company resident outside the UK and a 51 per cent subsidiary of a company resident in the U.K. and (*ii*) the other party is the parent company or a 51 per cent subsidiary of the parent company.

c) *Share exchanges.* With large highly capitalized companies operating on an international basis, onshore overseas company investment can be effected, in cases where exchange control would not permit direct 'outward' investment, by means of an exchange of shares whereby the equity of an overseas company can be acquired against shares in an onshore company.

d) *The realization of capital gains in a tax haven from the disposal of overseas assets.* Where onshore tax jurisdictions have capital gains legislation, the possibility exists, depending on the specific provisions of the latter, that capital gains may be avoided if realized through a tax haven, though naturally such loopholes are liable to be closed from time to time. Thus the 1979 UK Capital Gains Tax Act S.15 sought to prevent non-resident companies being used in this way by holding companies acting as the receiver of such funds tax-free. This Act applies only to non-resident companies which would be close if resident in the UK but *not* if the subsidiary were controlled by a UK quoted company or if the subsidiary were open even if resident in the UK.[14] Similarly the use of holding companies by overseas residents who purchase property which they subsequently sell may avoid capital gains tax.

e) *'Upstream' loans.* Where profits earned overseas through a separate overseas company are only taxed onshore when they are remitted by way of dividends, it may be possible to repatriate them in a non-taxable form as an 'upstream' loan unless onshore legislation specifically regards such a loan as income if its international tax avoidance provisions classify it as such.

3. The International Institutional Financial and Investment Sector

(*i*) *International banking services.* The presence of international banks, especially merchant banks, is of pivotal significance for all offshore activities: they constitute a developmental externality without which intermediate economy transformation cannot take place. For frictioneering to flourish, the offshore banker must have the ability, given his protected offshore domicile, to:

a) By intermediation, create and tailor the denomination and type of securities issued so that he can legitimately attract mainland onshore funds. The underwriting of capital issues is important here.

b) Switch such funds into other currency areas where direct transfer would not be possible, or only possible by purchase of an earmarked investment currency at a premium rate, or where resale of securities is subject to a 'surrender rule' that operates as a tax.

c) In order to maximize the invisible production possibilities of (*a*) and (*b*), it may well be necessary for the international banker to ensure a concomitant presence directly or via joint ventures in the world-wide chain of offshore centres as each centre may be a vital link for the maximization of global frictioneering opportunities. Moreover a multi-intermediate economy presence may help to diversify his business-mix and exchange risks.[15] What is essential is flexibility with regard to investments.

Banks play the central role in the intermediate economy as providers of specialized technical knowledge which is essential for profit-creation financial activities and indeed, as has been seen, in the promotion of the accumulation process resulting from the profit-diversion and profit-extraction activities of other sectors. A diversified range of personal and corporate services offered may often include the following, often within a conglomeration of specialist associate subsidiary companies:

portfolio loans;
fund flotations;
deposit accounts in most of the world's major currencies;
management of salary dispersal schemes;
investment management;
cash management;
insurance brokerage;
emigrant financial services;
company management;
trustee and other fiduciary services;
merchant banking, including specialized corporate finance advice and the provision of individually tailored financial packages, and company registration services.

Their involvement with these services gives integrity to the activities involved. The very fact that a trust is administered, managed and controlled by a bank of international repute as trustee, provides incontrovertible evidence to onshore tax authorities of the legitimacy of the activity. Moreover, depending on any regime of exchange control obtaining in the case of a 'captive' single currency area offshore centre, its position as an 'authorized', or in some cases, 'concessionary' bank may be of crucial significance, without which no 'legitimate' activity may take place.

Some of the frictioneering techniques that are commonly resorted to include:

'Back-to-back' loans. In the case of loan portfolios the usual mechanism of transfer is the 'back-to-back' or 'counter' loan, whereby in essence a 'currency-exchange' is arranged by the intermediary institution which acts as a matchmaker, accepting one currency on deposit and making available the desired restricted onshore currency either locally or, given a world-wide representation chain, wherever the firm wishes to invest.

'Feeder funds'. A similar technique can be used in the flotation of foreign-currency-denominated funds, where so-called 'feeder funds' can be legitimately attracted offshore, which are then switched into funds regionally specialized or geographically diversified so as to penetrate currency areas with portfolio investments in ways that would not be permitted from their originating offshore centres because, for example, of particular exchange control restrictions.

'Parking' or 'garaging' funds. A typical procedure[16] might involve a bank branch trading a foreign currency position with a branch in another country, e.g. usually with an agreement to reverse the position later if it is used to avoid overnight exceeding of local bank regulations; or an attempt could be made to effect such trade at non-market rates for tax avoidance purposes.

'Gearing up' overall lending capacity. Where the parent country of a banking group does not have solvency requirements that are based on the consolidation of the group's worldwide accounts that include all assets and liabilities and in which intra-group items are offset (the general case until recent decisions to adopt this principle), subsidiary companies strategically located in no or low solvency requirement centres can be used as a conduit through which to extend the group's overall lending capacity beyond levels which are considered prudent by the parent country, the regulations of which can to some extent be thereby evaded or avoided.

(ii) Investment trusts. As Palamountain has shown,[17] an offshore base gives greater flexibility of investment by freeing managers from restrictions habitually imposed by the governments of their own countries. Thus, for example, an offshore fund might well be able to hold more than 5 per cent of its assets in one company, something prohibited both by the Securities and Exchange Commission in the US and the Department of Trade and Industry in the UK. It will probably be empowered to invest fairly widely in unquoted securities. It may be able to be established in such a way as to incorporate gearing ('leverage'), to deal in the

commodity futures markets or to indulge in 'hedging' operations. None of these would be open to an authorized unit trust in the UK and much of it would be precluded in the US. In addition there may be greater freedom with regard to the charging of management costs and expenses. Moreover, where the offshore centre has a particular relationship with the world capital market of a 'top' or 'master' currency onshore country where capital gains tax exists, it enables third country residents (whether of the personal or corporate sectors) who are not subject to such taxes domestically, to gain indirect portfolio investment access to the investments available therein. Naturally the absence of capital gains taxes offshore will mean that investment switches will not incur capital gains tax. Even if the investor is an onshore resident liable to such taxes, considerable sums of tax will be avoided in the process of rolling-up the value of his investments even where selling his investments results in a once-and-for-all capital tax payment. Investments in neutral currencies such as Eurodollars will avoid capital gains and interest income taxes being paid in onshore countries with world-wide tax jurisdictions. Potential ill-repute of such offshore funds can be avoided where its operation is placed in the hands of internationally known fund managers and is guaranteed by a custodian institution of repute.

(iii) Financial activities associated with transnational business.
(a) Cash management. Multinational companies possess cash assets and liabilities in several countries denominated in different currencies. Naturally, therefore, the management of cash flow and the 'netting' of balances in order to achieve maximum benefit from such liquid resources is a crucial activity. Account has to be taken of the offshore tax treatment of interest paid and received, their multinational onshore treatment, the choice between borrowing at onshore parent company level and seeking interest deductions against parent company profits: a company set up for the purpose in an offshore centre can build up net balances for investment purposes in a neutral tax environment. Fees, commissions, conversion and transmission costs of cash management can be avoided by leading and lagging techniques that have similar results. Thus speeding up the settlement of intra-company liabilities while permitting extended credit from a particular location may help fund operations in high risk locations, or help finance trade in a weak currency area if intracompany debts are denominated in stronger currencies. If the objective is to run down balances, early payment from the location and late debt payment can have the desired effect even though the results generate arbitrary transfers of profitability.[18]

(b) Pension funds. International executives and skilled workers who are highly mobile are faced with what Merriman[19] has called a 'Tower of Babel' effect with respect to the plethora of currencies, tax structures, exchange control regimes, social security systems, definitions as to right to benefit and specified year of state pensionable age, requirements to preserve accrued pension rights etc. Nevertheless retention of a pension scheme in the country of origin may subject the contributor to a tax penalty and/or no tax relief deductability. Naturally this subject is a very complex one and each combination of individuals and country(ries) of work and intended country of retirement has to be examined carefully before a

policy optimum for that individual can be determined. Merriman has categorized workers in the following manner with respect to their employment by multinational firms:

1) *home staff*—head office employees;
2) *local staff*—recruited for local service only by branches or subsidiary companies in particular locations;
3) *expatriates*—those recruited in one location, seconded to another location with the intention of return to the former location;
4) *transferees*—those recruited in one location and transferred permanently to another location;
5) *international staff*—specifically mobile international service staff.

Categories (3) and (5) are ones that legitimately require an international pension scheme, even if it is self-administered. Such schemes may include both insured pensions and life assurance arranged through participation in one of the international networks of insurance companies, wherein intra-firm transfers can be effected to suit the geographical changes of country of residence. Some onshore centres may actually encourage the location of such schemes onshore (as under S.218 of the 1970 UK Taxes Act) but discretionary clearance procedures may prove to be a deterrent.

(c) 'Captive' insurance. This can be an important industry for the diversification of the offshore industrial superstructure, as it brings with it the need for insurance brokerage and reinsurance expertise. It is an ideal transnational industrial mutation suitable for offshore development in cases where there is no law preventing insurance development and there is access to the reinsurance market, availability of insurance broking, and specialized risk management services.[20]

Essentially a 'captive' is a subsidiary insurance company created and owned by a non-insurance organization for the purpose of insuring the risks of its parent. If its underwriting is restricted solely to the business of its parent it is usually termed a 'pure' captive but if, in addition to that primary function, it underwrites risks for outsiders, it is described as a 'broad' captive. This concept is not a new one as captives were in existence a century ago as mutual operations involving more than one parent (especially in shipping), but in recent years the emergence of 'pure' captives as 'in-house' insurance companies has been noticeable due to the increased size of individual companies and the transnational nature of many of their activities. European (including UK) captives tend to be of two sorts (i) 'domestic' captives—old established companies based and operated from the parent's own country, participating in their parent's risks by way of co-insurance, and (ii) 'offshore' captives—which tend to accept the whole, or the greater part of a particular class of insurance and then reinsure on an excess of loss basis as part of a company's risk financing strategy. In the latter case onshore premiums will flow to the offshore centre under insurance contracts negotiated and signed offshore. 'Such income may take on the character of foreign source income and may be available to set against excess foreign tax credits available to the onshore parent. Essentially the captive performs an income-washing function'.[21]

In the offshore context, 'broad' captives may well be a useful way of pooling limited local insurance expertise. Premiums may be accumulated tax-free in what amounts to a tax shelter for unrepatriated and undistributed profits, thus extending the financial base of the parent company. Furthermore ease of foreign currency investment in the money markets of the world will enable profits to be created from the cash flow resulting from the intra-firm retention of a substantial proportion of the premiums previously paid to specialist insurance firms: the captive thus unlocks funds previously 'frozen in advanced premiums'.[22] Legitimate taxation benefits may be maximized as premiums paid to captives are tax deductible and not paid out of earnings on which tax has already been paid. Moreover the lower offshore tax payments on the insurance activity will enable investments to be made and interest to be earned that is either taxed at rates lower than in onshore centres, or, as in the Bahamas and Caymans, free of tax. Furthermore

> dividends from a captive may be paid to the multinational in the year or years when earnings are needed to enhance the parents' balance sheet. Equally, dividend payment to the parent may be postponed, or deferred, during 'good' years . . . The commercial necessity for the multinational to move money from one nation to another cannot be overemphasized. Major international companies cannot restrict the operations and activities of their foreign subsidiaries to a single country . . . Until recently, the major methods of transferring money have been by royalty payments and fees for technical assistance, know-how and management services. However, most countries now place limitations on such payments . . . In addition, the freedom to repatriate dividends has been steadily restricted . . . Flexibility is vital in maximizing the success of international operations and the captive insurance or reinsurance company is one of the few remaining major means of maintaining such flexibility.[23]

No firm estimates exist as the precise extent of this phenomenon. Some sources claim that in 1970 there were 163 captives throughout the world which had risen to about 1,350 by 1980, and that the number is likely to reach over 2,000 by the mid-1980s. Others have suggested that by the end of the 1980s something like 60 per cent of premiums formerly paid to commercial insurers will be going to captives. Clearly these trends indicate a considerable growth of potential business for offshore finance centres, other things being equal. What is important for such developments to occur within any one centre is that as reinsurance companies are necessary for and complementary to the existence of captive centres, it is essential that domestic offshore legislation must permit intra-centre business between captive and reinsurance companies, even if they are externally controlled.

(d) Leasing. The development of equipment leasing worldwide has created a need from the lessor's point of view to establish a base in a tax-efficient location to act as a recipient of payments when there is no withholding tax on payments of rent and dividends to the parent company's home country.

(e) Depository receipt companies. One method of firms acquiring funds to internationalize participation in a company where international equity issues are not possible is to make a Euro-equity issue under which an offshore depository cor-

poration issues receipts for shares owned which may then be traded. This financial mechanism also avoids formalities associated with obtaining listings on the New York and London Stock Exchanges. This device has been used by Japanese companies as such vehicles are permitted quotations on the Tokyo Stock Exchange.[24]

The above list is not exhaustive of all transnational activities suitable for haven location. Moreover further mutations and innovations cannot be ruled out. It is evident from the above discussion that the creation of externally controlled financial centres in intermediate economies has, in many ways, effectively integrated the capitalism of centre countries with that of the periphery ones as was indicated in Chapter I. While the indigenous centre and the user companies and individuals do mutually benefit, the former from job creation and the derived domestic income generation process, as well as the complementary support given to tourism in terms of the additional use made of travel facilities, hotels, restaurants etc. and the importation of ready-made marketing networks, nevertheless, these centres do tend to share the three basic limitations which Caporaso has noted with respect to general semi-peripheral industrialization:[25] 'limited room for new entrants, limited autonomy of industrialization and limited ability to change . . . position in the global division of labor.' In many cases however these constraints would tend to apply even in the absence of international financial transformation.

ENVOI

The production rationale for offshore finance haven centres is the creation, diversion and extraction of profit from the international frictioneering possibilities presented to them by the international friction matrix and changes therein. The following desiderata condition enterprise development:

1) The provision of a well defined, yet flexible, background of law and procedures free from undue restrictions with regard to the establishment and operations of business, whether it is industrial, commercial or financial.
2) In practice much of the above business will tend to be channelled into two basic forms of external non-resident company—trading companies and investment holding companies. Both types of company will seek to locate business and divert profits from areas that would in most cases have otherwise been subject to onshore higher tax jurisdictions. Their use of haven centres for 'legitimate' onshore tax-avoiding economic purposes will, even in the absence of double taxation agreements and the fear of information exchanges, be subject in some degree to onshore fiscal protection policies which may seek directly or indirectly to repossess monies so retained.
3) In reality much of the above company activity, as well as the transformation of the haven into a finance centre, requires the presence of international banks whose financial expertise and ability to penetrate the money and capital markets and deposit and lending centres of the world is unchallenged.

4) Once established, the externality of a pool of specialized financial and managerial knowledge tends to lead to a consolidation of business activity and a diversification of the centre's financial structure.
5) Despite the international tax avoidance/evasion issue there are nevertheless legitimate areas of transnational business suited to tax haven location which provide a respectable basis for the transformation of the latter into international intermediate economies.
6) The number of centres that can undergo this transformation process is limited as business convenience and the limited global supply of financial expertise tend to prescribe an 'unconditionally place-bound' location scatter of such production bases. Further additions to the global network may require new interregional shifts of international economic power.

Having established the above generalized view of offshore financial development, the points made will now be elaborated in Part II with respect to the British Isle development of Jersey, Guernsey and the Isle of Man during the period since 1960; and, in Part III, to the general development of the global network of tax haven financial centres that evolved in the 1970s.

REFERENCES

1. These concepts were first used by the author in 'The Locational Implications of Resource Scarcity for Fisheries Development', *Discussion Papers in Economics* No. 6, Department of Economics, University of Keele, March 1974.

2. Adams, C.W., 'Secret Account or Foreign Trust?' *The Banker,* April 1972, pp. 531 and 533.

3. See Gammie, M., *Tax Strategy for Companies,* 2nd edn., London, Oyez, 1981, p. 164.

4. Committee on Financial Markets, *Standard Rules for the Operation of Institutions for Collective Investment in Securities,* OECD, Paris, 1972.

5. EEC Draft Directive 1975.

6. Knechtle, A.A., *Basic Problems in International Fiscal Law,* translated from the German, edited and revised by W.E. Weisflog, London, HFL, 1979, p. 62.

7. Knechtle, op.cit. p. 46.

8. See Knechtle, op.cit., pp. 185–90 for history of double taxation agreements.

9. See Bergsten, C.F. *et al., American Multinationals and American Interests,* Brookings Institution, Washington, D.C., 1978, p. 462–3 and ch.6, pp. 165–212.

10. Chown, J., 'Who Uses Offshore Centres? 1. Multinational Companies', *The Banker,* April 1977, pp. 97–9.

11. Doggart, C., *Tax Havens and their Uses,* Economist Intelligence Unit Special Report No. 105, September 1981, p.9.

12. Doggart, op.cit., p.72.

13. Hermann, A.H., 'The EEC's Kidglove Approach to Tax Havens', *The Banker,* April 1972, pp.505 and 507.

14. Gammie, op.cit., p.252.

15. Brown, W.P., 'Who Uses Offshore Centres? International Banks', *The Banker,* April 1977, p.101.

16. As revealed in the Edwards allegations concerning the activities of Citibank in Paris, Frankfurt and Zurich. See *Financial Times,* 24 January 1979.

17. Palamountain, E., 'Thoughts on Offshore Funds', *The Banker,* August 1970, pp. 851–2.

18. Wood, D. and Byrne, J., *International Business Finance,* London, Macmillan, 1981, p.137.

19. Merriman, P., 'Pensions for International Executives', *Multinational Business,* Issue No.2, 1981.

20. Sennet, W.E., Ch.2 'What is a Captive?', and Ch.3 'Advantages and Disadvantages of Captives and Preconditions for Successful Operation', in *Papers in Risk Management, No.5: Captive Insurance Companies,* Keith Shipton Developments Ltd., 1976; and information supplied by Risk Management Ltd., Guernsey.

21. Doggart, T., 'Tax Havens—The Landscape Changes', *The Banker,* April 1972, p. 543.

22. Bank of America, *Captive Insurance Companies,* n.d., p.8.

23. Bank of America, op. cit., p.6.

24. Wood and Byrne, op. cit., p.211.

25. Caporaso, J.A., 'Industrialization in the Periphery: the Evolving Global Division of Labour', *International Studies Quarterly,* Vol.25, No.3, September 1981, p.380.

PART II
A Regional Case Study of the Development of British Isle Offshore Finance Centres

Tax havens have never boasted a gradual Darwinian process of evolution. Their origins and development owe most to a series of volcanic upheavals which, often overnight, throw up new islands, engulf existing havens, or remould established contours. *

The general survey given in Part I made the point that many tax havens or offshore centres have a special onshore dependency relationship, whether of colonial or post-colonial origin, and that there are monetary and exchange control implications of this relationship. One particular implication is that their development potential can be crucially affected by the particular international standing of the currency of the onshore 'guardian' economy, one possible type of which is the 'master' currency, to use Susan Strange's terminology. A further point was made that the precise onshore currency bond might confer special advantages or disadvantages in respect of the tranformation of havens as single currency area offshore centres prior to their achievement of a truly global international offshore status.

The evolutions of the Channel Isles and the Isle of Man centres are interesting examples of centres with an onshore 'master' currency bond that have not only manifested this pattern of development but, being separate administrative entities, have been regional competitors both within the Sterling Area as well as within the global secondary financial system. A case study of their separate and different development profiles and achievements is therefore instructive of the realities behind the transformation process.

Before an analysis is attempted of the evolution pattern of each centre, both prior to the abolition of exchange control (Chapters III, IV and V) and since (Chapter VI), it is necessary first to identify precisely the politico-economic context of their operations and the degree of local sovereignty obtaining in respect of insular decision-taking in the areas of money and finance. Chapter I will therefore be concerned with the constitutional parameters of island independence, and Chapter II will examine aspects of monetary union, including the sterling 'currency bond' and the UK exchange control regime in force from 1947 to 1979.

*Doggart, T., 'Tax Havens—The Landscape Changes', *The Banker,* April 1972, p.537.

CHAPTER I
The Effective Constitutional Parameters of Politico-fiscal Sovereignty of the British Isle Centres

In the concluding section of the *Royal Commission on the Constitution 1969–1973,*[1] the Committee remarked, in relation to the systems of government in the Channel Islands and the Isle of Man, that they were:

> unique and not capable of description by any of the usual categories of political science . . . [they are] full of anomalies, peculiarities and anachronisms, which even those who work the system find it hard to define precisely. We do not doubt that more logical and orderly races than the British would have swept all these away long ago and incorporated the Channel Islands and the Isle of Man into the United Kingdom as fully as the Orkney and Shetland Islands (whose position, if the accidents of history had fallen out differently, might so easily have been the same as the Isle of Man's) were incorporated first in the Kingdom of Scotland and then in the United Kingdom (para. 1459) . . . in some respects they are like miniature states with wide powers of self-government. (para. 1360)

What has evolved over the centuries and in recent years has been a spirit of what is asserted to be 'co-operative independence'. This spirit underlies most constitutional matters, as the *Special Committee (Jersey and the EEC)* reported in respect of Jersey,[2] though it applies to each isle:

> The history of the constitutional development of the Island in its relationship with the Crown during this century and the last clearly indicates that, without sacrifice of the basic rights of the Crown, the scope of insular legislative responsibility has continuously expanded and that, where overriding considerations have required that Acts of Parliament should be applied or extended to the island, its special constitutional position has invariably been recognized and the appropriate safeguards to preserve that position have been inserted after full consultation with the Insular Authorities. (para.102)
>
> Although the right of Parliament to legislate for [the islands] extends, as a matter of strict law, to every field of legislation, it is considered that that right is now limited, in two respects, 'by an unwritten rule which is founded upon custom and practices and tacit understanding', that is to say by constitutional usage.
>
> The two limitations are:
>
> (1) matters of purely domestic concern to the island; and
> (2) taxation. (para.103)

> In matters which are of purely domestic concern to the island, the decision whether or not to legislate invariably rests with . . . [the island government] . . . It cannot be conceived that the United Kingdom Government would be advised that it was proper to legislate for the island in such matters without . . . [its] . . . consent . . . This limitation on the constitutionality of such legislation, as opposed to its strict legality, is governed mainly by usage and it is difficult, therefore, to define with precision.
>
> There are certain domestic matters to which the limitation clearly applies, but it is possible to conceive of legislation relating to other matters of domestic application of which it might be difficult to say whether it did or did not infringe that constitutional usage. (para. 104)

Thus in terms of international law, these islands cannot be classed as states, much less as sovereign states. They are essentially dependencies of, and therefore owe allegiance to, the English Crown. They are neither part of the United Kingdom nor its colonies, and differ from other overseas dependencies in their proximity to the UK and in the antiquity of their connections with the Crown. On the one hand, they have their own legislative assemblies—in the case of Guernsey and Jersey their respective and separate 'States of Deliberation', and in the case of the Isle of Man, Tynwald and the House of Keys—each an individual system of local administration with its own fiscal and legal entities, yet, on the other hand, appointments to some of the chief posts in those local administrations rest with the Crown, and legislative measures passed by these insular assemblies depend for their validity on Orders in Council approved by the Crown.

The special position of the islands was recognized as early as 1801, when for matters of defence, foreign policy and allied government areas, their mainland supervision was exceptionally retained by the UK Secretary of State for the Home Office when a separate Secretary of State for the Colonies was set up for this purpose for the countries of the then British Empire. Since 1945, this special relationship has been confirmed *inter alia* by the 1948 British Nationality Act, whereby citizens of the islands, if they so wished, could be deemed citizens 'of the UK, Islands and Colonies'; the '1950 Declaration', whereby all foreign governments and international organizations were informed that, whereas in the past the islands had been regarded as part of the metropolitan territory of the UK, in future, any treaty or international agreement entered into by the UK government would not be considered as applying to the islands unless they were expressly included; and, in 1973, their independent status was significantly confirmed by Protocol 3 of the UK Treaty of Accession to the Common Market, which left the islands' fiscal independence intact and reaffirmed their freedom from imposition of duties and levies.

While the above circumstances generally hold for all three islands, very different historical backgrounds obtain to the Channel Islands as compared with the Isle of Man, which need to be established at this juncture. These backgrounds will now be provided in summary form: readers interested in a more detailed history of these constitutional matters are referred to the islands' submissions to the Royal Commission on the Constitution and to the references given.[3]

THE CHANNEL ISLANDS

In 933, the Channel Islands were annexed to Normandy and became part of the Duchy of Normandy. In 1066, William, Duke of Normandy, became King of England, so combining the titles of Duke of Normandy with that of the English Crown. After the collapse of the Norman empire, a break with 'continental' Normandy occurred in 1204, subsequent to which, official annexation of the Channel Islands to the English Crown was effected in 1254. Under the terms of annexation, a number of privileges and immunities were granted, which included entitlement to their own legislatures and the retention of their own judiciaries based on Norman Law. When the ducal title was surrendered, the English monarchs continued to rule as though they were Duke of Normandy, observing the laws, customs and liberties established by the Normans. At no time was there amalgamation with, or subjugation to the English governmental system. In 1341, Edward III granted a Charter to the People of Jersey, Guernsey, Sark and Alderney, whereby:

> We concede for ourselves and our heirs, to the said men of our aforesaid Islands, that they, their heirs and successors do hold and retain all the privileges, immunities, exemptions and customs, in their persons, properties, monies and all other things, in virtue of the concessions of our progenitors, Kings of England, or of other legitimate competancy, and that they fully enjoy and use them without imposition or molestation by ourselves, our heirs or our officers whosoever; even as they and their predecessors, inhabitants of the said Islands, have reasonably used and enjoyed them, which we now also confirm to them.[4]

In addition, immunity for Channel Islands' produce from English customs duties was confirmed by a Charter issued by Richard II in 1394, whereby it was declared that the Channel Islands would be 'ever free and exempt, in all towns, markets and parts of the realm of England of all tolls, exactions or dues, as fully and in the same manner as his faithful subjects in the Kingdom'.[5] These two rights were subsequently maintained and reaffirmed through the centuries to the present day. Rights were not autonomously controlled however. With respect to internal island financial affairs, all revenues could only be raised with the sanction of the Crown. Thus an Order in Council of 20th April 1771 declared that 'the States have no authority to pass any Act or law imposing [duties] without application having been made to Your Majesty for that purpose, and Your Majesty's consent and approbation to the Crown being first had and obtained.' In this and other areas, the Crown saw itself as *parens patriae* in the exercise of its prerogative powers. Gradually wide areas of autonomy were developed in the nineteenth century which considerably reduced any *ad hoc* resort to such discretionary exercise of power. In 1877, the 'Règlement sur la confection du Budget Annuel des États, et la regularisation des dépenses publiques' gave statutory force to the principles that annual States' expenditure should be balanced by annual revenue and an annual sum be retained to service any debt.

Internally, the Channel Islands are divided into two quite separate Bailiwicks – that of Jersey; and that of Guernsey, which also includes the islands of Herm, Jethou, Alderney and Sark. Each Bailiwick is separately administered and is a separate customs area, levying its own customs and excise duties. Within the Bailiwick of Guernsey, however, the island of Alderney had an independent existence with regard to finance until the Government of Alderney Law of 1948 placed it under Guernsey and subjected it to Guernsey taxes and duties in return for the latter's undertaking to settle the former's accumulated island debt. On the other hand, although Sark has its own legislature—the Chief Pleas—neither the Sark Reform Law of 1922 nor that of 1951 extended to the island the Guernsey income tax legislation which had been introduced in 1918.

THE ISLE OF MAN

This island has a legislative assembly—Tynwald—that dates back to the tenth century when the island was under the general control of the Kings of Norway. In 1266, the island was ceded to Alexander III of Scotland. After a period of dispute between Scotland and England, it was granted to Sir John Stanley in 1405 (who became the Earl of Derby) and, in perpetuity, to his heirs until 1736, when the 'Lordship of Man' passed by inheritance to the Murray family who were Dukes of Atholl. Problems arising from the use of the island for smuggling purposes ultimately led to the Crown repurchasing the Lordship for the sum of £70,000 on 10 May 1765. Formal transfer was effected through various acts of the UK parliament, beginning with the Isle of Man Purchase Act 1765 (5 Geo.III c.26) and ending with the Duke of Atholl's Rights, Isle of Man Act of 1825 (6 Geo.IV c.34). The 1765 Act, known as the 'Revestment Act' placed the island and its revenues under the direct control of the Crown, which immediately took action under an Act of 1767 to impose new and heavy customs duties to deter smuggling. Despite periodic increases in these duties, and petitions being made in 1837 and 1853,[6] the loss of insular control of finances continued until 1866. In that year the Isle of Man Customs, Harbours and Public Purposes Act was passed, which gave Tynwald a limited measure of control over insular expenditure, albeit subject to the approval of the UK Treasury and the local representative of the Crown, the Lieutenant Governor. This Act separated Manx revenues from those of the UK and required an annual payment of £10,000 to be made from local customs revenues into the UK Exchequer. Thenceforth, a gradual, at times uncertain and in several respects incomplete, devolution of powers took place, which now underlies the present constitutional relationship between the Isle of Man and the UK government. Despite such changes, sovereign self-determination has not been achieved, especially in the area of finance. Two aspects require consideration here, that of financial control and the related matter of the Common Purse Agreement.

While the Isle of Man (Customs) Act 1887 empowered Tynwald to levy or abolish customs and excise duties by resolution, such resolutions nevertheless required UK Treasury approval and confirmation by UK Act of Parliament within six months of their announcement.[7] This system continued until the 1955 (UK) Isle of Man (Customs) Act replaced Act of Parliament confirmation with that of Order in Council confirmation. The latter control was subsequently transferred to the office of the Lieutenant Governor by the Customs (Isle of Man) Act 1958, in whose hands financial powers were generally placed by the 1958 Finance Act. The formation of an insular Finance Board by Act of Tynwald as a result of the MacDermott Commission led to a sharing of these responsibilities until the 1976 Governor's Financial and Judicial Functions (Transfer) Act transferred many functions which had previously been the province of the local representative of the Crown, although formal overall responsibility for the financial affairs of the island was retained by that office. It still remains the case that all Manx legislation requires the approval of the British Sovereign, the Royal Assent being, in the view of the British Home Office 'not a mere formality'. In addition, the 1958 Loans Act permitted for the first time the raising of loans on the island without Treasury approval, and for the whole or part of the General Revenue, instead of only customs revenue as had been the case under the Isle of Man Loans Acts of 1880 and 1931.

Notwithstanding the above struggle for greater financial control, an increasing dependence on the UK Treasury took place with regard to indirect tax revenues. After the passage of the 1866 legislation referred to above, the Island Government did not always receive all duties payable on goods entering the island, as some arrived duty having been paid on the UK mainland. It was agreed that, in certain circumstances, some rates of duty could be kept lower on the island to encourage payment there. Finally, in compensation for this 'loss' a 'Common Purse Agreement'[8] was reached in 1894 in respect of tea and tobacco which was eventually extended to the sum total of all revenues (with the exception of beer) collected by HM Customs and Excise under the Agreement of 1957, and subsequently the collection and distribution between the UK and the Isle of Man of the EEC Agricultural Levy, Value Added Tax, Excise Taxes and the Pool Betting Duty. The arrangement is that revenue is shared on a per capita basis which includes a variable 'fiscal equivalent' in respect of island tourists. These funds accounted for approximately half of the Isle of Man Government income in the early 1970s. In addition a Continental Shelf Agreement was negotiated between the two governments in 1966 giving the Isle an entitlement to a share of the licence fees and royalties collected by the UK in respect of oil and gas exploitation of *all* UK waters. Whilst these agreements assured revenue incomes the 1957 Common Purse Agreement does very much control indirect taxes levied by the island government as articles 2-7 of the agreement make clear:

2. The Isle of Man Government agree to follow the United Kingdom in any tariff changes made by the United Kingdom (*a*) in their protective duties on imported goods, (*b*) in connection with Imperial Preference, and (*c*) in pursuance of commercial treaties or other international agreements. The Isle of Man Government also agree not to introduce any fresh difference in any of the duties involved in (*a*), (*b*) or (*c*) beyond that existing at present in respect of beer.
3. In the case of other duties, taxes or similar charges on goods, the Isle of Man Government will not introduce any fresh difference between their tariff and the United Kingdom tariff beyond that existing at present in respect of beer, whether by making insular charges or failing to follow

United Kingdom charges except after prior consultation with the United Kingdom Government.

4. The Isle of Man Government will keep their machinery law in regard to the duties, taxes and similar charges leviable on goods as far as possible in line with that operative in the United Kingdom.
5. The Commissioners of Customs and Excise will continue to collect the 'unequal' duties chargeable on goods brought into the Island and the unequal duty on Island beer, and will pay over to the Isle of Man Government periodically as may be arranged the proceeds of those duties, less expenses of collection and audit.
6. The Commissioners will also continue to collect the 'equal' duties on goods brought into the Island and the Purchase Tax chargeable in the Island and pay periodically to the Isle of Man Government their share of the total proceeds of such duties or taxes under Common Purse Agreements in operation at the time, less the expenses of collection and audit.
   In this and the preceding Article 'Unequal' duties means duties which are at different levels in the United Kingdom and the Isle of Man. 'Equal' duties means duties which are at the same level in both countries. No rebates will be given on any 'equal' duty goods consumed in the Island without prior consultation between the Two Governments.
7. In the event of the Isle of Man tariff of duties, taxes or similar charges leviable on goods getting unduly out of line with the United Kingdom tariff, or of any difference arising in machinery law which have not been discussed and agreed between the two Governments, the United Kingdom Government might find themselves unable to continue the arrangement at Articles 5 and 6 above and must accordingly reserve the right to discontinue them after giving due notice.

Up to March 1980 the customs and excise collection on the Isle of Man was directly administered by the UK Customs and Excise authorities.

The historical *de jure* creation of these politically hybrid systems of imperfect, compromised independence and their continued tacit or complicit acceptance by the UK constitutes an important politico-economic distortion of island sovereignty within which economic activities have had or have to be geared. Moreover, from time to time uncertainties have arisen with regard to *de facto* changes in this area. Internally, the islands have each benefited from an absence of frictions resulting from their respective non-party political environments, a low-level politicization of issues, and freedom from the vicissitudes of doctrinaire governments and changes thereof. These factors have minimized local interventionist policies and insular public sector expenditures—indeed, the Isle of Man's Financial Board is bound under Section 5(*c*) of the Finance Act 1958, as amended by the Governor's Financial and Judicial Functions (Transfer) Act of 1976, to budget each year for a surplus on its Revenue Account. As can be seen from Table XIV, each isle did indeed run a continuous surplus on revenue account during the 1970s.

TABLE XIV: Income and expenditure of the British Isle governments 1970–79

Year	*States of Guernsey*				*States of Jersey*				*Isle of Man Tynwald*			
	Income (1)	*Expenditure* (2)	*Surplus* (3)	% (3/1)	*Income* (4)	*Expenditure* (5)	*Surplus* (6)	% (6/4)	*Income* (7)	*Expenditure* (8)	*Surplus* (9)	% (9/7)
1970	7,627	5,433	2,194	28.8	11,643	11,639	4	0.0	9,654	11,083	1,429	14.8
1971	8,923	6,434	2,489	27.9	12,784	13,940	−1,156	—	10,160	9,314	846	8.3
1972	9,378	7,531	1,847	19.7	22,691	16,185	6,506	28.7	12,458	10,309	2,149	17.2
1973	11,954	8,751	3,203	26.8	27,434	19,508	7,926	28.9	15,601	11,857	3,744	24.0
1974	14,509	11,038	3,471	23.9	33,647	24,890	8,757	26.0	18,196	16,362	2,554	13.5
1975	18,950	15,562	3,388	17.9	46,984	33,780	13,204	28.1	23,353	24,777	1,424	6.0
1976	21,874	18,667	3,207	14.7	55,168	39,882	15,286	27.7	27,929	30,991	3,062	11.0
1977	27,849	21,518	6,331	22.7	63,981	48,860	15,121	23.6	33,928	39,450	5,522	16.3
1978	30,651	25,388	5,263	17.2	73,156	57,837	15,319	20.9	37,493	41,622	4,129	11.0
1979	36,435	30,203	6,232	17.1	84,699	67,920	16,779	19.8	43,723	44,605	882	2.0

Sources: Billets d'État, Guernsey; *Jersey Statistical Digests,* Economic Advisor's Office; *Isle of Man Digests of Economic and Social Statistics,* Treasurer's Office.

Notwithstanding the constitutional positions outlined, the effectiveness of the insular governments in terms of their fiscal sovereignties is circumscribed, as indeed is the power potential of any aspiring offshore centre for profit creation, diversion and extraction from the international trading system, by the desire and ability of onshore countries to exercise extra-territorial fiscal sovereignty over actual or potential frictioneering activities carried out by their non-resident or resident agents. Although global transformation has made the policies of all onshore countries important, naturally, the exercise of UK fiscal sovereignty has been of special significance, the main details of which are now considered.

Four general lines of approach have been adopted by the UK with respect to haven activities:

1) direct governmental approaches;
2) unilateral changes made in the UK annual Finance Acts;
3) general international tax evasion or avoidance legislation provisions;
4) Board of Inland Revenue action in the courts.

(1) DIRECT GOVERNMENTAL APPROACHES

Since 1918, there have been two main matters to which attention has from time to time been drawn by the UK government: (i) the so-called 'imperial contribution', an annual contribution towards the costs of defence and other services supplied by the UK to the islands not otherwise reciprocated, and (ii) the use and potential abuse of the islands as tax havens. The above matters were first raised in the 1920s. The following passage from Lord Coutanche's memoirs summarizes the events as seen from his viewpoint as Jersey's representative at the discussions held:

> In January 1923, the Channel Islands were invited by the British Government to make an annual contribution towards the expenses of Empire. In the case of Jersey, the amount suggested was £275,000 per annum. The States refused the invitation on constitutional and economic grounds. A Committee of the Privy Council, under the Duke of Atholl, was set up. It visited Jersey in October 1925, and conferred with Jersey's representatives. After this Conference, but before the Committee made its report to the Lord President of the Council, the States, in January 1926, decided to offer the British Government the sum of £300,000 as a one-time and final contribution towards the costs of the First World War.
>
> In due course the Duke of Atholl's Committee made its report. It considered the proposed gift of £300,000 inadequate, but suggested that any payment by Jersey should certainly be treated entirely as a war contribution and not regarded as payment for the benefits of Empire, which the Island had freely enjoyed for centuries. It recommended an annual payment of £120,000 for 100 years. The Committee did not omit to draw attention to certain individuals of considerable wealth who had migrated

from the United Kingdom to Jersey for tax avoidance purposes. The States refused these conditions, and asked for an opportunity to justify their views.

In April 1926 the British Government replied, asking for counter-proposals on the financial aspect. They said that a memorandum on the question of tax avoidance would probably follow, but asked that the two questions should be dealt with in separate communications.

When Lord Coutanche visited Sir John Anderson, the then Permanent Undersecretary of State at the Home Office, he firmly made the point that:

the question of how much we are able to pay will be conditioned to some extent by the way we run the Island. You are very anxious to put a stop to tax avoidance. We don't want tax avoidance either, but there must be a certain amount of liberty for new people to come to the Island, and we shouldn't be too critical of the fortunes which they bring with them, or of the houses which they buy, or of whatever else they do. These are two questions which I think must be dealt with at one and the same time and at the same conference. The amount which we can afford to pay depends on our economy.

On 22 February 1927, Sir John Anderson wrote to the island authorities regretting that Jersey was unwilling to undertake a proportionate share of the expenses of the war, but stated that:[10]

(HMG) do not propose . . . to take any steps to press the view which they entertain as to the obligation of the Island in this matter against the wishes of the Island community.

Without in any way pronouncing upon the constitutional issues involved or latent, they have approached the obligation not as a legal but as a moral obligation, and if the States decide to continue in their present attitude, HMG propose to leave the matter there . . . (the Isle of Man offered £760,000) . . . They still hope that the Island of Jersey, with resources exceeding those of the Isle of Man will feel that they should take at the very least an equal share of the costs of the war . . .

There is another matter of great importance for which HMG desire to ask the consideration of the States; that is the avoidance of UK taxation by British subjects who make use of the Channel Islands for this purpose. Very considerable losses have already been suffered by the Imperial Exchequer in this way, and the losses are likely to increase in the future as the means of avoiding taxation come to be better understood . . . HMG . . . hope to have the assistance of the States in dealing with the matter, which is regarded by HMG as one of urgency . . .

A committee was proposed with a view to the formulation of an agreed plan of action. The above letter was accompanied by what was later known as the 'Board of Inland Revenue Memorandum' which set out the main details of the problem as perceived by the UK authorities. However, despite a conference held at the UK Treasury on 15 and 16 July 1927, nothing very tangible resulted. Lord Coutanche summarized what transpired thus:[11]

The final agreement was that the legislation should not be directed against the Channel Islands in particular, but should be capable of application to any territory in which the problem arose *and which accepted the necessary arrangements for co-operation.*

The Island agreed to give such assistance as was possible so far as 'one man' companies were concerned, by effective enquiries into the objects and constitution of such companies prior to registration, and by requiring registers of shareholders, profit and loss accounts and balance sheets, and statutory declarations on the occasion of allotments and transfers.

There was no discussion on the question of a war contribution, because the British Government had by this time already decided to accept Jersey's offer of £300,000 . . . A Bill to implement the proposals for what, in general terms, may be called the reciprocal enforcement of Revenue judgments was introduced in to the British Parliament, but did not become law. It was understood that one, at least, of the self-governing Dominions saw major objections to the proposals.

And there the matter . . . still rests.

The detailed description given by the 'Inland Revenue Memorandum' does, however, provide a succinct statement of the dilemma created by the international transfer of incomes and places of company registration for the onshore UK authorities, and is reproduced below as quoted in the *Jersey Evening Post* of 1 March 1927.

Avoidance of British Direct Taxation by Removal of Residence, Domicile or Property of the UK
A note by the Board of Inland Revenue

1. There are two methods of avoidance of UK taxation through the use of countries outside the UK, each of which is illustrated by the case of the late Sir Robert Houston, which has recently attracted attention.
2. Under the first method, the taxpayer continues to reside in this country but transfers his property into such forms that the income therefrom is not subject to declaration of British Income Tax at the source. He then transfers the property to a 'one man' company established outside the UK, and in lieu of drawing dividends from that company, takes loans from it or allows the income to accumulate until the company is liquidated. Such a person may secure exemption from Income Tax and Super-tax without leaving the shores of this country, and the arrangements may also take such form as to prejudice the collection of Death Duties.
3. Under the second method, the erstwhile taxpayer removes his property to some place abroad or puts it into some form (e.g. registered War Loan) in which it cannot be taxed while owned by him as a foreign resident, and removes his place of residence abroad (to avoid Income Tax and Super-tax) and acquires a domicile abroad (to avoid Death Duties).
4. The place which at this present time is especially chosen for these purposes—both for registration of companies and for immigration—is the

Island of Jersey, but there are a good many avoiding companies and, so it is understood, a certain number of refugee taxpayers, also in Guernsey and its dependencies. If the abuse is terminated in these Islands, the Isle of Man may also come to be chosen, especially for the formation of companies.

5. If steps are taken to render it unprofitable to attempt avoidance in any of these islands, some at any rate of the candidates may resort to foreign countries. It must be recognised that as the present practices are driven further afield it will become more difficult to combat them, but it will certainly not be in any way impossible to do so. It seems reasonable to assume that from the point of view of residence the attraction of foreign countries will be less than those of the Islands, and the disadvantages will be greater. Probably a greater danger in the future would lie in the formation of private companies in foreign countries but on balance it may be anticipated that a large proportion of taxpayers who under present conditions have made use, or will make use, of the Islands for tax avoidance purposes would give up the game on the Islands ceasing to be available.

Registration of Companies in Jersey and Guernsey

6. There are considerable numbers of large private investment companies registered in Jersey and Guernsey. It would appear that the shareholders and directors are in the main nominees; it has so far been difficult to ascertain precisely what evasions they may conceal, but some such cases have been traced to definitely known British residents. The problem is already one of some magnitude. There seems little doubt that if nothing is done its importance will grow, and that Death Duties as well as Income tax and Super-tax will come to be affected.

7. The remedy which suggests itself is to reach an arrangement with the Governments of the Islands,* under which these Governments would dissolve such companies and prohibit the formation of any similar ones, in effect limiting the privilege of company registration in the Islands to
   (*a*) companies whose chief purpose is to carry on bona fide trading operations in the Islands, and
   (*b*) companies shown to the satisfaction of the Island authorities to be bona fide beneficially owned by native islanders.

Removal of place of residence and domicile to Jersey or Guernsey coupled with removal of property to places outside the UK

8. How many refugees from British taxation the Island of Jersey contains is not easy to ascertain. Reports from the Island suggest that numerous persons (perhaps some hundreds) who if they had remained here would have been large taxpayers have arrived since the end of the war, and the Islanders appear to believe that the numbers will swiftly increase. It seems clear that the total sum annually involved is a substantial one.

*'The Islands' is intended in the rest of this note to refer to Jersey, Guernsey and the Isle of Man.

9. In order to avoid the loss of British Income Tax and Super-tax, the following course is suggested—
   (1) To provide by law that any individual whose domicile of origin is in the UK and who was mainly resident in the UK during the ten years preceding the commencement of his period of residence (or first substantial period of residence) in one of the Islands shall, if resident in one of the Islands in any one Income Tax year, be charged to British Income Tax and Super-tax as if he remained ordinarily resident in the UK and were actually resident there for that year.
   (2) To arrange with the governments of the Islands to give the fullest assistance to the British Revenue authorities in ascertaining the names and addresses of persons likely to be liable to British taxation under this provision; to allow an office to be set up in each Island as may be required; and to permit the hearing of appeals by its Special Commissioners.
   (3) To take powers in regard to Income Tax in the Island territories, the service by the British authorities of notices, writs etc., and for obtaining judgment in the British Courts for taxes assessed and to arrange with the Government of each Island to execute in the Island any such judgment of a British Court in the absence of voluntary payment, and to pay the proceeds to the British Exchequer.
10. So far as concerns Death Duties, a somewhat similar procedure is suggested—
   (1) It would be necessary to provide by law that on the death of a British subject whose domicile of origin was in Great Britain† and who was mainly resident in Great Britain‡ in the ten years preceeding his period of residence (or first substantial period of residence) in one of the Islands, but who at the time of his death acquired a domicile of choice in one of the Islands, British death duties should be payable in respect of the property passing in some manner and to the extent as if he had died retaining his British domicile of origin. This may necessitate some slight amendment in the present law relating to duty on property abroad, and the opportunity should also be taken for effecting improvements which in any case are very desirable, in the existing machinery for recovery of duty especially in the case where the Executors in whom the administration of property situate abroad is vested are resident outside Great Britain.
   (2) It would be desirable to arrange that the Governments of the Islands should reveal and transmit to the British authorities, full particulars of the nature, value and destruction of the

†Death Duties in Northern Ireland are transferred taxes.

‡In this note the expression 'UK' is used to denote Great Britain and Northern Ireland.

estate of any such person passing under a will or intestacy dealt with in the Courts or by the authorities of the Island and that the Government of each Island would in the absence of voluntary payment, execute in the Island any judgement of a British Court against the executors or beneficiaries of such a person resident in the Island and transmit the proceeds to the British Exchequer. It would be desirable also, if it be practicable, to arrange (on the analogy of the procedure on grant of probate in this country) that the Island Governments should hold up probate pending the settlement of the British claim.

11. The Island authorities would no doubt be unwilling—indeed they should not be asked—to co-operate in the manner here suggested, if there were any danger of the proposals, through a miscarriage, hitting a native islander. For this reason it would be right to provide that any person aggrieved by a decision that he or the deceased whom he represents fell within the category of persons charged under this scheme should have the right of appeal to the Courts of the Island.
12. Two other points arise in a similar connection. Some of the Islands have an Income Tax and some may come to have Death Duties. The Island authorities would have a clear right to the first charge and this suggests that any duty paid to the Island authorities should be deducted from the amount of a British charge when levied under this scheme. Similarly any information acquired under this scheme by the British authorities as to the liability of particular tax payers should be made available to the Island authorities for purposes of their taxation and vice versa.
13. It may be said that these proposals to impose taxation on persons not domiciled or resident here in respect of income not arising here and property not situate here involves a great departure from tax practice. Precedent is not altogether lacking. The US impose this Income Tax on all their nationals wherever resident.
14. The formation of 'one-man' companies of the type in question in the islands by British residents appears to be purely a tax-dodging device, and it is difficult to see how any complaint of hardship could be legitimately raised by British tax payers against any proposals to dissolve such companies and to prohibit the formation of others.
15. As regards persons who have migrated to the Islands it will be observed that no attempt has been made in the proposals to analyse motives and to segregate those persons who have gone to reside in one of the Islands for the particular purpose of avoiding taxation; and this for the reason that such an analysis of motive is entirely impracticable. If it were felt necessary to make some attempt to separate those actuated from those not actuated by tax-dodging motives, it would be possible to devise expedients which would go some distance towards this end.

Leaving aside all constitutional proprieties, it is quite clear that activation of these proposals would have constituted a critical regressive step in the process of devolution of independence: a step taken by France with respect to French tax-payers in Monaco in an analogous situation some years later.

Despite the failure to arrive at a comprehensive intergovernmental offshore or onshore approach between the islands and mainland UK, some activities have been foreclosed or curtailed through three further lines of approach which will now be commented on.

(2) UNILATERAL CHANGES MADE IN THE UK ANNUAL FINANCE ACTS

Examples of these include:

(i) Tax-avoiding Monetary Arrangements

One such arrangement was rather novel in that it related to an ancient Norman anomaly—the 'rent hypothèque' whereby an investment made in this form counts as reality under Guernsey Law. Under the UK FA 1949 S.28 (2) with regard to UK estate duty

> property shall be deemed for the purposes of estate duty not to include any property passing on . . . death which is situate out of Great Britain if it is shown that the proper law regulating the devolution of the property so situate . . . is the law neither of England nor of Scotland and that . . . (*c*) . . . the property so situate is by the law of the country of which it is situate, immovable property . . .

Thus so long as it was possible for UK investments to be made in this form they classified as property held abroad and therefore not liable for estate duty. A considerable amount of such rents were created until 1962, when, under S.28 (1) of the Finance Act of that year it was removed.

Another such arrangement concerned the concessionary treatment of persons resident and ordinarily resident in the UK whereby under S.122 of the TA 1970, employment carried on outside the UK was exceptionally treated on a 'remittance' basis. This made the Islands attractive as centres for such funds during the periods in which this income was earned. However, the 1974 FA ended these concessions and thereby the business that they had generated.

(ii) Migration to Avoid New Taxes

The propensity to migrate for tax-haven purposes naturally intensified subsequent to the 1965 UK Capital Gains Tax, soon after which the first Housing Laws were introduced which stemmed this flow. Onshore emigration was, however, anticipated in the UK Capital Transfer Tax legislation contained in S.45 of the 1975 UK Finance Act (hereafter FA) as subsequently amended in S.29 of FA 1977. The latter legislation 'deems' a person for the specific purposes of capital transfer tax as domiciled in the UK who would not so otherwise be, for other tax purposes if that person was domiciled in the UK on or any time after 10

December 1974 and subsequently became domiciled on the island. Thus after this date 'deemed domicile' meant that it was not possible to avoid CTT by settling in the Channel Islands.[12]

(3) GENERAL INTERNATIONAL TAX EVASION/ AVOIDANCE LEGISLATION PROVISION

The main UK tax avoidance legislation of relevance to the Channel Islands is the 1970 UK Income and Corporation Taxes Act, Ss. 460 to 496—generally referred to in subsequent legislation as the 'Taxes Act' which is a general act covering the overseas aspects of the taxation of income and gains (hereafter TA).

Ss. 478–81 are concerned with provisions 'for the purpose of preventing the avoiding by individuals ordinarily resident in the UK of liability to income tax by means of transfers of assets . . . in consequence whereof . . . income becomes payable to persons resident or domiciled out of the UK' . . . such that they have the "power to enjoy" such income.' This section is directed at the avoidance of higher rate tax by UK resident individuals. It provides a defence against the individual who transfers assets into an overseas 'money box'—commonly a discretionary trust—so that the income arising escapes UK higher and additional rate tax (and may not suffer tax at all). The crux of this sort of avoidance is that, although the ownership of the transferred assets technically passes to a non-resident, the UK individual somehow retains the 'power to enjoy' the income, and the intention is that it can be repatriated or otherwise employed at some later stage in a non-taxable form for the benefit of the avoider or his family.

The House of Lords decision in the Vestey case in November 1979 held that the scope of S.478 was much narrower than had previously been thought, and there were proposals in the 1981 Finance Bill to amend the Section.

The Board of Inland Revenue is given very extensive powers in S.481 to obtain information not only from the taxpayer, but from his advisors. Any monies found to be transferred within the meaning of this provision will be deemed to have a fiscal domicile in the UK, except S.678 (3) where the transfer is a bona fide commercial transnational one not designed for the purpose of avoiding liability to taxation. One important implication of this as far as Guernsey and the Channel Islands are concerned is the question of offshore funds. Sumption[13] asserts 'there is nothing in the conception of an offshore fund which would avoid the effects of . . . [the] far-reaching provision [of S.478]. Obviously there must in all cases have been a transfer of assets within the meaning of the section.' However, whereas the above section makes an individual resident in the UK chargeable on the whole of the income

> The Revenue has informally indicated that provided that the fund is not brazenly operated for the purpose of tax avoidance, they will only assess an individual to the proportion of the fund's income attributed to his holding. An important reason for this attitude in the case of these funds managed directly or indirectly from the UK is that, being international in character, they represent a useful inflow of foreign currency.

As regards the formation of companies, the effect of S.482 is concerned with provisions in general to prevent the emigration or transfer abroad of trade or business by an established UK company and gives wide powers to the Treasury to grant or otherwise not grant general or specific permissions in certain sets of circumstances. Here the determination of the fiscal domicile is crucial and is not necessarily to be interpreted as being where its central management and control are situated. Under S.482 it is illegal, without prior Treasury consent, for a UK company to transfer shares in a non-resident subsidiary company it controls to any other person, e.g. an offshore holding company. In general, consent will only be given if the Treasury is convinced that the commercial advantages are substantial and 'even then, the Treasury will almost certainly require an undertaking that the offshore holding company will distribute the whole of its income to the UK parent in the form of dividends' (consent was also required under the Exchange Act of 1947 until October 1979—see Chapter II that follows). This section applies to UK resident companies which wish to migrate or to transfer their trade overseas, and provides that in such cases Treasury consent—which may or may not impose certain conditions—must be obtained. The Section was designed partly to prevent tax avoidance and partly to guard against losses of foreign exchange. In its present form, the Section (and the penalties it imposes on offenders) may no longer be appropriate and it was in the context of the possible repeal of S.482 that the consultative documents on *'Company Residence'* and *'Tax Havens and the Corporate Sector'* were issued. Furthermore, one result of the transfer of assets may be to put either a non-resident trust or a non-resident company into a position where it may realize an asset on which a gain is made, but, under S.42 FA 1965 this does not apply in the first case or S.41 in the second case, but under S.41, if a shareholder is both resident and domiciled in the UK, tax will be assessed as though a gain had been made in cases where ownership of more than 5 per cent of the total shares is concerned.[14]

S.485 of the 1970 TA is designed to counter artificial pricing arrangements between a UK company and an associated company in the same group, so as to prevent the former from, for example, selling goods at artificially low prices to the latter, which may then seek to sell to an ultimate purchaser at the full commercial rate and thereby divert the locus of profit to the haven centre. S.485 gives the Inland Revenue power to fix a more realistic price as if the two companies were trading at arm's length, and so to increase the UK company's tax liability accordingly.

(4) BOARD OF INLAND REVENUE ACTION IN THE COURTS

It is not intended to discuss the general matter of tax avoidance or evasion case precedents in the UK courts at this juncture, although some discussion is given in Chapter VI concerning some important judgments made therein in 1981. The point to be made here is that, very occasionally, the UK Inland Revenue authorities in their judicial pursuit of taxes bring cases before the Courts that involve one or other of the island centres, the solutions to which test, and conceivably might alter, the constitution status quo. These cases are very rare, but there have been two recent examples which are now outlined.

IRC v. Stype Investments (Jersey) Ltd

A substantive issue raised in this case by the Jersey investment company involved was that the immunities and privileges given to the Islanders by ancient Royal Charters prevented the UK Inland Revenue from serving any tax summons in Jersey in respect of capital transfer tax allegedly owed them in respect of the disposal of a large estate in England by Sir Charles Clore before his death in 1979 under the aegis of Stype Investments Ltd. The Inland Revenue claimed that the monies derived therefrom had been moved out of the jurisdiction of the English Courts to avoid the payment of tax, and that the investment company had 'intermeddled' with his estate, and were therefore liable to pay capital transfer tax. Mr Justice Goudling pronounced his decision in favour of the investment company on 12 March 1981, in respect of the 'intermeddling' charge: no judgment was made on the constitutional argument (reported in the *Jersey Evening Post,* 13 March 1981, p.1). Subsequently the Court of Appeal upheld the right of the IRC to serve proceedings under S.25(6) of the Finance Act for the payment of capital transfer tax (*Financial Times,* 30 April 1982, p.17). Leave to challenge this ruling in the House of Lords was refused on 17 June 1982 and the matter awaits resolution in the Jersey Courts.

The Savings and Investment Bank Case

In 1979, the UK Inland Revenue went to the Isle of Man and sought an order under the UK 1935 Bankers' Books Evidence Act requesting access to a bank account in respect of inquiries to assist court proceedings in Wales. Permission was refused by the island's First Deemster on constitutional grounds and an order was issued restraining Barclays Bank of Victoria Street, Douglas, Isle of Man from disclosing or permitting inspection of entries relating to account No. 50783064 of the Savings and Investment Bank Ltd. held by Barclays at that address. An attempt was made in the English Courts to demand access to the Barclays Bank master computer in Lombard Street, London. On appeal against an order made by Mr Justice Skinner on 12 February Lord Justice Denning found in favour of the Savings and Investment Bank. In his findings, His Lordship declared that he did not think that Barclays branch in Douglas should be considered any differently from an Irish or American branch bank there which was not subject to UK jurisdiction: as Barclays had to get a licence to operate there, the branch should be considered as a separate entity (reported in the *Isle of Man Courier,* 13 March 1981, p.7).

CONCLUSIONS

1. The exercise of individual insular sovereignty is hedged about with a somewhat unusual anachronistic exogenous political link with the UK mainland that gives each island constrained political independence and a conditioned statehood. Certain areas of decision taking are subject to *de facto* mainland contro, and others are given limited independent *de jure*

autonomy. It may be that ultimately in the long run all freedoms are at the discretion of the UK government, as the islands are dependencies of, and therefore owe allegiance to, the English Crown. In terms of the above freedoms, the Channel Islands of Jersey and Guernsey have had a wider measure of historical independence than the Isle of Man, and this latter island has had to fight for its financial independence since 1961, which has placed it in an inferior position with respect to financial development in the early 1970s.

2. Despite the above formal constitutional positions with regard to politico-fiscal sovereignty, and the failure in the 1920s to incorporate through Act of Parliament limitations on tax avoidance abuse by changed domicile or changed place of registration, the UK has, nevertheless, created an exogenous constraint on insular fiscal sovereignty through unilateral changes in its annual Finance Acts, general provisions against international tax avoidance and attempts at appropriating constitutional powers through the Courts, each of which have had implications for particular types of fric-tioneering activities and the inhibitions that may surround them in the precise locations of the British Isles.
3. Internally the islands have benefited from an absence of party-political government and the policy vicissitudes occasioned by changes of government, which has made for a greater degree of potential political stability than might otherwise be the case, as well as fiscal stability.

Additional to the frictions arising from (1) and (2) above are those arising from the monetary union between the islands and the UK and, in the period 1947 to 1979, from UK exchange control regulations. These matters are now discussed in Chapter II.

REFERENCES

1. 'Relationships between the UK and the Channel Islands and the Isle of Man', (Part XI of Volume 1 of the *Report of the Royal Commission on the Constitution, 1969—1973,* together with the relevant extract from Volume 2). London, Home Office, HMSO, 1973.

2. *Report and Recommendations of the Special Committee of the States of Jersey Appointed to Consult with Her Majesty's Government in the UK on All Matters Relating to the Government's Application to Join the European Economic Community,* States of Jersey, 1967.

3. In terms of constitutional relationships the following references are recommended: For the Channel Islands: Le Hérissier, R.G., *The Development of the Government of Jersey 1771-1972,* States of Jersey, 1972; Heyting, W.J., *The Constitutional Relationship between Jersey and the UK,* the Jersey Constitutional Association, 1977; Loveridge, Sir J., *The Constitution and Law of Guernsey,* La Société Guernesiaise, 1975. For the Isle of Man: Kermode, D.G., *Devolution at Work: A Case Study of the Isle of Man,* London, Saxon House, 1979; Kinvig, R.H., *The Isle of Man. A Social, Cultural and Political History,* Liverpool, Liverpool University Press, 1975.

4. Quoted in Heyting, op.cit., p.98.

5. Report . . . of the Special Committee of the States of Jersey, para.80, p.37.

6. Kermode, op. cit., p.30.

7. See Sargeaunt, B.E., *An Outline of the Financial System of the Isle of Man Government,* Douglas, Isle of Man, 1925.

8. See *Review of the Isle of Man/UK Common Purse Agreement,* London, August 1976.

9. Pocock, H.R.S. (ed.), *The Memoirs of Lord Coutanche,* Sussex, Phillimore Press, 1975, pp.62–3.

10. *Jersey Evening Post,* 1 March 1927, p.2.

11. Pocock, *The Memoirs,* pp.66–7.

12. There is one possible exception, namely, if a very determined UK domiciled taxpayer first acquires the domicile of a third country and then acquires 'island' domicile, so that he would not have been domiciled in the UK immediately before emigrating there. See Coombes, J., *Capital Transfer Tax,* London, Professional Books, 1977, pp.168–9.

13. Sumption, A., *Taxation of Overseas Income and Gains* 3rd edn., London, Butterworths, 1979, p.180.

14. Sharp, P., *UK Fiscal Implications of International Trade,* London, Institute of Chartered Accountants, 1976, pp.76–7.

CHAPTER II
UK Monetary Union and the Sterling 'Currency Bond'

Despite general domestic internal fiscal sovereignty, the islands remain, their constitutional rights notwithstanding, economies *manqués* as they have, in practice, very limited monetary independence being in monetary union with the UK. *Per se* any insular pursuit of an independent monetary policy is thereby precluded. Moreover, the associated currency bond effectively renders these islands especially vulnerable to any exchange control policies adopted on the UK mainland. These currency bond and monetary links have not always existed and have only been forged in comparatively recent times. This chapter seeks (*a*) to outline how the individual island currency bonds emerged; and, (*b*) to outline the exchange control system in force in the islands and applied by the Bank of England in the period 1947 to 1979.

THE FORMATION OF THE ISLAND-UK CURRENCY BONDS

Guernsey

During the period prior to 1873, many different currencies and monies were treated in effect as semi-legal tender on the island. Despite an early reference to a Guernsey coinage in an *Ordinance* dated 6 October 1623 (a 'furluque': one twenty-eighth part of a French penny), which subsequently disappeared, domestic currency chaos existed[1] and the island remained an emporium of several national currencies until issues of local States notes were made and currency order established in the early decades of the nineteenth century. The first States note issue was made in 1816, and the first modern regulated coin issue made in 1830 (the Guernsey penny was an eight double piece: a term used until decimalization). During the nineteenth century there was no one-to-one link with English money and a rate of exchange of 250 equivalent Guernsey pence to the 240 pence sterling pound obtained. Between 1848 and 1870, both English and French currencies were recognized as legal tender,[2] though English currency was ultimately given supremacy in 1873, since when, States notes have had a joint legal tender status with Bank of England notes. Despite this condominium of note issues, local clearing banks are nevertheless required to issue States notes to customers unless otherwise requested: the 'seigniorage' value of the difference between the costs of local note issue and its monetary face value thus gives the Island administration what amounts to an interest-free loan and a partial local exercise of a central banking function. Complete monetary union was not confirmed until April 1921, when a one-to-one link was finally established between the Guernsey pound and the pound sterling, so permitting greater ease of exchange between the local and the mainland currencies. This has remained the case to the present time. Joint decimalization of the two currencies was effected in the late 1960s, and with the option of identically divided coinages the currency bond was made complete.

Jersey

In comparison with Guernsey, Jersey achieved monetary union with the United Kingdom about fifty years earlier, but developed its own paper currency some 145 years later. Prior to 1834, the legal currency of Jersey was the French livre.[3] As the main medium of exchange on the island had been the six livre piece, which the French Government withdrew in that year, the States of Jersey were forced to consider what should henceforth be the island's legal tender. Eventually an act was passed on 18 September which made British sterling legal tender and regulated the value of the sovereign as equivalent to twenty-six livre. Despite the demotion of the livre tournois currency, all transactions, with the exception of banking, continued to be carried on in that currency. Shop-keepers tended to render their accounts in Jersey currency and at the bottom of their statements to declare the equivalence in British currency. On 13 July 1840, the States were granted the privilege of issuing copper currency that was denominated in both French and English amounts—the two sou, one sou, six deniers (half-sou) pieces were also stamped 1/13th, 1/26th and 1/52nd of an English shilling respectively. The higher denomination equivalents were 24 livres = one Jersey pound = 18s. 5¼d. English money; 20s. British = £1-1s-8d. Jersey currency (1s. British = 13d. Jersey). The resulting confusion and annoyance gave rise to many local businessmen demanding that the local currency be assimilated to that of England. After much debate, an act of assimilation was finally passed in February 1876 which made twelve local pence equal twelve British pence, and all subsequent issues of local copper coinage were stamped 1/12th, 1/24th and 1/48th of a shilling. The printing of local States paper currency did not take place until 1961.

The Isle of Man

During the seventeenth century, the Isle of Man suffered a glut of forged coins in circulation—'Duketoons'[4]—such that in 1646 it was made a capital offence 'to falsify, forge and counterfeit chip and diminish any kind of current coin'. Thereafter English coins circulated with Irish tokens that included St. Patrick halfpences and farthings (c.1660–67), Mic Wilson's tokens (1672) and Limerick tokens (1679). After a ban placed by Tynwald on the Irish pieces, indigenous coinage was encouraged such as 'Murrey's pence' produced by a local merchant as early as 1668. However, a Tynwald Act of 1710 authorized that the Earl of Derby's coinage first issued in 1708 would henceforth be the legal tender and all other issues were declared illegal. Thereafter an Atholl coinage followed in 1758. After the revestment of the island in 1765 George III copper coins were introduced in 1786, some eleven years before copper pence circulated on the mainland. Shortages of coin and a proliferation of the use of token money resulted in an Order in Council of 10 April 1839 which required the Royal Mint to strike pence, halfpence and farthings for the Isle of Man. An Act of Tynwald of 4 May 1840 – An Act for the Assimilation of the Currency of the Isle of Man to that of Great Britain – gave notice that the local coinage would henceforth be demonetized with effect from 21 September 1840, so that the Manx coinage would be of an equivalent value to that of the mainland: previously there had been fourteen Manx pence to the English shilling. This 20 per cent devaluation led to local unrest in 1840 known as the 'Copper Riots'. Thereafter only mainland coinage was used with the addition of Irish coins in the twentieth century. The issue of notes[5] did not become a matter of insular government control until 1961. Local banks were empowered to issue their own notes under licence granted under the 1817 Bankers' Notes Act passed by Tynwald. This Act also abolished all cards and notes under a value of 20 shillings. Local private sector note issue continued until the 1961 Isle of Man Government Notes Act, which revoked all such licences as from 31 July of that year, since when, the island Treasurer, with the sanction of the Governor and the approval of Tynwald, is empowered 'to issue notes to such an amount and of such denominations and in such series as he shall be so authorized'. For this purpose the Isle of Man Bank Ltd. (founded in 1865 and owned since 1969 by the National Westminster Bank, UK) acts as the agent of issue.

In addition to the 'currency bond', the above direct monetary link means that each island is faced with a domestic inability to conduct any domestic monetary policy with respect to, for example, the local money supply or interest rates. This makes the islands very much captives of, and subject to, exogenously instrumental policy-imposed distortions resulting from the vicissitudes of UK domestic monetary policy credit control, and regulations concerning capital movements, and exchange control policies.

Thus credit ceilings imposed by the UK have a direct effect on the availability of overdraft facilities in the islands. This point was raised in the early 1970s by G.C. Powell in his *Economic Survey of Jersey,* p.157, paras. 483–4.

> It may be asked why the need for restraint in the UK should automatically place pressure on business in Jersey. The customary response is that the exclusion of Jersey from the UK restraint could enable UK individuals to circumvent the restrictions, given the existence of the monetary union between the two areas. However, a much bigger potential loophole in the restraint policy exists in Northern Ireland, where several banks have a Dublin head office while others are fully owned by the London clearing banks, there is a free flow of funds between the two parts of Ireland, and the Bank of England is usually far less severe in its exhortations of restraint. In general, the loophole is not exploited because of banking co-operation: that is the Irish banks will not lend money to UK businesses. It would appear that a similar practice could operate in Jersey if the banks were so minded.

> There is no fundamental reason why, if the banks act responsibly, Jersey should be affected by UK ceiling restraints, particularly so since the advances ratio in the Island is currently below 25% and the existence of separate statistics allows the authorities to keep an eye on the situation . . . the position of Jersey borrowers at times of UK credit restraint should be raised with the UK authorities with a view to increasing the degree of local independence in this area.

In terms of extra island trade, the islands are structurally dependent on the UK as the focal point to which, and through which, exports and imports are necessarily oriented, either for final consumption or re-export, and for which, there is a heavy reliance on mainland UK transport services. In effect, therefore, the various island administrations act with powers that are rather greater than any UK local authority, but rather less than a fully autonomous government of a sovereign state. Thus trade policy as such is not an area of government discussion, and comprehensive balance of payments statistics are not published as, anyway, the usual use of policy instruments such as exchange rate policy, tariffs etc. is not appropriate. Yet, these administrations are free to run island lotteries, and to raise their own taxes in ways which are not subject to central UK government direct control, and they can also seek to wrest new freedoms that may give them further tax or revenue advantages, as when, under the 1969 UK Post Office Act each island was able to set up its own Postal Authority, which was then able to reduce intra and extra island charges for post and telecommunication services (which *inter alia* have kept such costs lower for business activity and *per se* have provided philatelic revenue as an important new source of administrative revenue from global sales to stamp collectors).*

THE 'STRAIGHT JACKET' OF EXCHANGE CONTROL 1947–1979

Given that *de jure* political sovereignty of the islands is constrained by their Crown colony status, and that monetary union has arisen *de facto* over the last century, the existence of mainland (onshore) exchange control policies has been an important exogenous autonomous policy-imposed distortion on the frictioneering ability, though, it should be emphasized here, the primary objective was the balance of payments objective of safeguarding the UK foreign exchange reserves. No concerted activities and approaches were organized between the Bank of England, the executive custodians of these policies, and the UK Inland Revenue, whose needs for financial intelligence information often coincided and whose activities could have been made more effective as a result of such information pooling. Though not constitutionally part of the United Kingdom, the islands were nevertheless subjected to the UK Exchange Control Act of 1947 by means of a Statutory Instrument issued under this Act and so were rendered subject to its general regulations as supplemented by the Notices and Memoranda, issued by

*Guernsey and Jersey from 1 October 1969 and the Isle of Man from 5 July 1973.

the UK Treasury, and administered by the Bank of England directly or indirectly through 'authorized' banks and depositories (ECI). Whereas from 1947 until June 1972 the islands were just three of an extensive number of Scheduled Territories (ST) that comprised the British Commonwealth (except Canada; and Rhodesia after 1965), the Irish Republic, British Trust Territories, British Protectorates and Protected Areas, Iceland, Jordan, Kuwait, Libya, S.Africa and S.W. Africa, and W. Samoa, from 23 June 1972, under EC83, they were three of only, eventually, a select five Rescheduled Territories, outside the UK, that included the Republic of Ireland and subsequently Gibraltar. In both time periods, the general exogenous autonomous policy-induced UK friction structure was periodically intensified and relaxed according to the instrumental policy-induced frictions required by the current needs and state of the UK economy. However, as will be shown later, this latter period conferred definite development advantages on them resulting from such an almost exclusively privileged position. Both periods, however, had in common a set of monitoring and institutional procedures policed by the Bank of England that ranged over the formation of companies, trusts, partnerships and securities transactions. These regulations created a kind of straight-jacket within which, while areas of freedom were nevertheless allowed to exist, pinching constraints in certain places effectively regulated developments of any significance.

The precise details of each area of regulation are intricate and contained in unpublished Notices and Memoranda issued under the 1947 Act, a simplified survey of which is now given:

(a) Company Formation

Companies were regarded as resident for exchange control purposes unless they were specifically designated non-resident by the Bank of England. The advantage of external company status was that, once incorporated, capital would be free to move between non-residents, although 'internal' sterling area business was precluded (a few exceptions existed). In order to obtain such status, permission had to be sought from the Bank of England (*EC Notice 18*) by application giving the name, address and object(s) of the company, the name and address of the promoter or the beneficial shareholder, and information as to the proposed share structure and any additional finance required. Permission, if given, would be subject to the following restrictions (*EC Memorandum 2794*):

i) The share capital had to be designated in foreign currency other than Swiss francs and held beneficially by non-residents.[6]
ii) Any transaction in securities in or with S.T. residents had to be conducted through an Authorized Depository (which might be a bank, an advocate, or an accountant) authorized under permission of the Bank of England.
iii) Consent had to be obtained from the Bank of England before any issue or transfer of shares.
iv) The company and Authorized Depository had to give an undertaking accepting compliance with the Bank of England's conditions.

v) Share capital and finance required by the company had to be acquired from non-resident sources.
vi) Annual submissions to the Bank of England by the Authorized Depository and confirmation of ownership and compliance with conditions, together with a statement of the companies' activities were required.[7]

Dividend, interest and capital payments were also subject to Bank of England control, and, in the case of an investment company, no borrowings were permitted in the UK. Due to this mantle of control, several external residents found it easier to form a company elsewhere, e.g. Panama, and nevertheless to have their company's financial and banking administration located in Guernsey. As regards company formation, the following types of structure were possible:

1) The establishment of an overseas branch of a UK resident company. No consents were required under S.482 of 1970 TA but exchange control permission was necessary as discussed above.
2) The establishment of an overseas resident subsidiary. This required consent both under S.482 of the 1970 TA and exchange control consent if its operations were outside the sterling area.
3) Partnerships: Bank of England permission was required to form a mixed-residence partnership, in which any one or more of the proposed partners is resident for exchange control purposes outside the Scheduled Territories with persons resident within the islands, or, for such a partnership, once formed, to undertake trading activities outside the ST. This foreclosed the use of any non-resident nominee devices to enable residents to obtain a non-resident 'leak' for their assets.

(b) Trusts

The residence of a trust for exchange control purposes was determined by the residence of the settler at the date of the creation of the trust (Exchange Control Act 1947, S.29(1)). A trustee which was accorded non-resident status could operate without restriction outside the ST. On the other hand, Bank of England permission was required to create a trust in which a resident settler sought to benefit a person resident outside the ST. The Bank treated each case on its merits. The attraction of this was that an individual could divorce himself from the ownership of assets, whilst entrusting professional trustees to apply those assets in a manner of which he approves. In addition to private discretionary or family trusts, 'open-ended' unit or investment trusts[8] offer an attractive vehicle for portfolio investment wherein, being offshore, the incidence of capital gains tax of the unitholder may be postponed and managers have greater flexibility of investment not being subject to restrictive laws impinging on their distribution of investments, etc.

(c) Pension Funds

The islands provided a tax neutral location for the domicile of employee benefit plans and pension funds for overseas employees. Such funds could be invested or maintained in any appropriate currency with a local Bank or Trust Company as Trustee.

(d) Emigrant Expatriate Funds

The use of low-tax areas by emigrating UK residents as bases for investment holding companies in which to retain their sterling assets, which would become decontrolled after emigration, was similarly regulated by the Bank of England through the 'Authorized Banks' mechanism of control.

(e) Portfolio Investment in Foreign Currency Securities

The Bank of England exercised very rigid rules in relation to financial transactions between the ST and the rest of the world. These controls intensified in some respects during the 1960s, but became gradually liberalized in the 1970s, until complete abolition was effected on 23 October 1979. Essentially these controls related to making foreign exchange and regulating foreign currency borrowing. It would be impossible to summarize in a simple way the plethora of such regulations, their intricacies, and the niceties of changes therein over the twenty-two years of operation of exchange control although other writers have attempted this.[9] It will suffice here to concentrate on a few central ones from the *EC7* (*second issue*) *Document* of 17 July 1978 dealing with portfolio investment and certain of its forty or more issued Supplements, and the *EC18 Document* dealing with direct investment.

The main methods of extra ST investment permitted included the following:

(i) The use of 'investment currency'. Outside the ST, no official exchange was allowed for portfolio investment unless it was purchased by permission through the *'investment currency'* market, the 'pool' or size of which was largely dependent on foreign exchange made available by sales abroad by UK residents of direct and portfolio investments in non-ST areas, the demand for which usually exceeded supply giving rise to a 'dollar premium' which could buy anything between 10 per cent and 50 per cent depending on market conditions.[10] Moreover, from April 1965 onwards, any sale of UK held foreign securities were subject to a 25 per cent 'surrender rule' whereby 25 per cent of the proceeds had to be exchanged for sterling at the official rate (abolished with effect from 1 January 1978 by *EC7 Supplement 34,* 22 December 1977) without reinvestment rights through an Authorized Dealer (30-35). After June 1972, the securities of the now designated Overseas Sterling Area became similarly treated.

(ii) The use of borrowed foreign currency. At the end of 1970, professional managers were generally permitted by *EC7 Supplement 4* (23 December) to acquire securities other than by the use of investment currency by direct borrowing of foreign currency, or to arrange such borrowing on behalf of resident clients from UK banks, or through 'back-to-back' loans, from persons outside the ST for the purpose of

investment in foreign currency securities. Under S.1 of the above, 'Portfolios of foreign currency securities acquired with the money borrowed will be exempt from the 25% requirement on "switching" . . . foreign currency securities'. S.3 stipulated that 'During the lifetime of the loan, borrowers will be expected to maintain excess cover of at least 15% (over the amount outstanding) in the form of foreign currency securities transferred . . . (over) a 3 month period . . . ' (S.6) (abolished by *Supplement No. 41* 13 June 1979 S.2(*a*)). In the area of loan portfolios the most common finance mechanism was that of the 'back-to-back' or 'counter loans', whereby either a foreign-based multi-national might be willing to lend foreign currency against a UK borrower making equivalent sterling loan facilities available to the former's subsidiary or associated company in the UK, or as a 'currency exchange' a UK bank (usually foreign owned) acted as a 'match-maker' and put together the entire package.

(iii) The use of sterling feeder funds. A large proportion of small-scale resident portfolio investment was made by means of investment in Unit Trusts and Mutual Funds, which, to obtain foreign currency, issued units expressed in sterling (so that no investment currency is involved), that is collateralized and foreign currency obtained from a bank acting as trustee to a foreign currency loan portfolio. The purchases by institutional portfolio investors of such units was limited to a maximum of 20 per cent of the overall value of the purchaser's portfolio of foreign currency securities and investment currency.

(iv) Foreign currency capital issues. Permission could be given to issue foreign currency bonds under the rules applying to foreign currency borrowing for portfolio investment purposes. In this case, it was customary for public advertising not to be allowed in the UK. Bonds might also be permitted in the UK, to finance outward direct investment.

The rigid existence of the onshore 'master-currency' bond meant that, although locally there was in fact a flexible background of law and procedures in theory free from undue restrictions with regard to the establishment and operation of business, in practice the exchange control system, which acted to support the master currency in its decline, gave considerable power to the Bank of England through the vetting and monitoring procedures that this involved: as did the extension of onshore fiscal jurisdiction in certain areas. Necessarily, the fric-tioneering freedoms that might otherwise have been possible were curtailed. However, without the economic link, the islands would not have benefited from the positive side of the relationship.

Exchange control did allow for the initial development of the islands as offshore sterling centres during the period 1960–72 and, as a result of the new sterling area created in 1972, gave a further consolidating impetus that enabled the subsequent establishment of a more truly internationally based offshore centre. These developments were positively related to the direct access available to the London markets and the large City reservoir of technical expertise, and the positive attempts being made by the British authorities in furthering the development of

London as a relatively open international financial entrepôt and onshore external financial centre, in an attempt to maintain its earnings given the weak and declining world position of sterling. These policies included:[11]

a) The adoption of a liberal 'open-door' policy towards foreign banks wishing to establish London offices, as part of their emphasis on competition in banking after 1971.
b) Attempts to stimulate London as the Eurodollar centre. Following the first issues of Dollar Certificates of Deposit in 1966 and Sterling Certificates of Deposit in 1968, London soon became the important wholesale centre for Eurodollar transactions and the flotation of Eurobonds. British authority flexibility over these activities, even though these markets became a way of by-passing periodic national needs to attempt domestic credit control, were in distinct contrast to the bureaucratic approaches being taken on the continent and in the US. This inspired the formation of specialized London-based consortia banks (such as the Orion Group which came to Guernsey in 1973), which specialized in medium-term multinational Eurocurrency financing.
c) The 'other business' brought in as a result of the above expansion. The new foreign industrial infrastructure brought with it direct access to the London market for its clientele, and provided at the same time information concerning business investment opportunities elsewhere for domestic economic sectors.
d) UK authority attitudes towards tax exemption of external gilt funds, which directly and indirectly encouraged particular forms of individual investment and offshore fund activity in the islands. These resulted from the following UK provision:
   1) Under S.7 paragraph 5 of the FA 1975, the following were specifically exempted from UK Capital Transfer Tax (which otherwise applied to all former UK domiciled citizens emigrating to the three isles after 10 December 1974): 'Savings by persons domiciled in the Channel Islands or the Isle of Man (War Savings Certificates, British National Savings Certificates, Premium Bonds, National Savings Bank and trustee bank deposits and tax-exempt contractual savings schemes.'
   2) Government securities free of tax while in foreign ownership. This relates to securities issued by the Treasury subject to a condition authorized by F(No.2)A 1931 S.22, or F(No.2)A 1914 S.4 as exempt from taxation as long as they are and remain in the beneficial ownership of persons neither domiciled nor ordinarily resident in the UK. A list of these stocks is given in the Appendix at the end of this chapter. These stocks could not be exploited under UK tax laws through a unit trust, but this did not apply in the islands and they were an attractive investment for non-resident UK expatriates.
   3) Under S.2 paragraph 1 of the 1979 Capital Gains Tax Act, all British Government issues in the gilt-edged market are exempt from capital gains if held for more than twelve months.

Thus in many ways *de facto* the City of London and the attitude of the UK monetary authorities provided an important externality for offshore development of the islands.

CONCLUSIONS

1) As Crown dependencies the islands of Guernsey, Jersey and the Isle of Man possessed/possess a number of distinctive features, which although constituting exogenous and endogenous distortions in respect of their full politico-economic independence with respect to insular resource allocation, have somewhat paradoxically enabled them to develop indigenous offshore international banking centres with world-wide coverage because of this special relationship.
2) The sequence of circumstances and events that gave rise to this development could not have been anticipated in the early 1960s, given the external aegis of the UK 'guardian' currency control over inward and outward Sterling Area capital flows, its superior governmental position within the monetary union, all of which was incompatible with full insular independence, and the spirit of constitutional freedoms granted by historical Acts of Parliament and Charters. However, on balance, the tax–exchange control friction matrix, while providing constraints on insular frictioneering activities, brought with it quite considerable benefits to the islands as a result of certain positive exogenous autonomous policy-imposed distortions. These included: (i) A continuous benefit from the 'expertise externality' provided by the Bank of England's monitoring procedures exerted under the 1947 Exchange Control Act. This ensured, as far as possible, a high degree of propriety in and viability of those businesses permitted residential establishment. (ii) The rescheduling of the Sterling Area under EC83 in 1972 enabled the final process of transformation from a sterling offshore centre to an international offshore centre to take place.
3) As a result, the arrangements and circumstances of 'co-operative independence' have helped to promote and never to threaten the sustained political and economic stability within the islands that has been an essential element in the establishment, continued existence and pursuit of offshore invisible trade activities.

REFERENCES

1. See Jacob, J. Esq., *Annals of the Bailiwick of Guernsey,* Vol. 1, London, Marshall and Simpkins, 1830, pp.409–11.
2. See Anstead, D.T. and Latham, R.G., *The Channel Islands,* revised E.T. Nicolle, 3rd edn., W.H. Allen, 1893, Appendix A.; Marshall-Fraser, W., 'The Coinages of the Channel Islands', *La Société Guernesiaise Report and Transactions,* 1948; and 'A History of Banking

in the Channel Islands and a Record of Bank Note Issues', *La Société Guernesiaise Report and Transactions,* 1949.

3. Falle, R., *Some Notes on the Jersey Currency,* undated, Local History Collection File, Jersey Public Library, pp. 1-2.

4. Mackay, J.A., *The Pobjoy Encyclopoedia of Isle of Man Coins and Tokens,* 2nd edn., Pobjoy Press, 1978, p.12.

5. Quarmby, E., *Banknotes and Banking in the Isle of Man 1788-1970,* London, Spink and Son Ltd., 1971.

6. The stipulation of Swiss francs as an exception was voluntarily acceded to by the Bank of England in response to a Swiss government request.

7. No statistics are available from the Bank of England of the number of permissions given as records were not kept.

8. See Corner, D.C. and Stafford, D.C., *Open-end Investment Funds in the EEC and Switzerland,* London, Macmillan, 1977.

9. See Parker, A., *Exchange Control,* 3rd edn., London, Jordan and Sons, 1978.

10. See Woolley, P.K., 'Britain's Investment Currency Premium', *Lloyds Bank Review,* July 1974; and 'The Investment Currency Market', *Bank of England Quarterly Bulletin,* Vol. 16, No. 3, September 1976.

11. Lees, F.A., *Foreign Banking and Investment in the US,* London, Macmillan, 1976, pp.128-37.

APPENDIX

List of British government tax-exempt securities for non-residents of the United Kingdom

*5¼% Funding Loan 1978/80	*6% Funding Stock 1993
13% Exchequer Stock 1980	*13¾% Treasury Stock 1993
11½% Treasury Stock 1981	*14½% Treasury Stock 1994
9¾% Treasury Stock 1981	*9% Treasury Stock 1994
12¾% Exchequer Stock 1981	*12¾% Treasury Stock 1995
*8½% Treasury Stock 1980/82	*9% Treasury Stock 1992/96
3% Treasury Stock 1982	*15¼% Treasury Stock 1996
14% Treasury Stock 1982	*13¼% Exchequer Stock 1996
*12% Treasury Stock 1983	*13¼% Treasury Stock 1997
*5½% Funding Stock 1982/84	*8¾% Treasury Stock 1997
*8½% Treasury Stock 1984/86	*6¾% Treasury Stock 1995/98
*6½% Funding Stock 1985/87	*15½% Treasury Stock 1998
*7¾% Treasury Stock 1985/88	*9½% Treasury Stock 1999
13% Treasury Stock 1990	*8% Treasury Stock 2002/06
*8¼% Treasury Stock 1987/90	*5½% Treasury Stock 2008/12
*5¾% Funding Loan 1987/91	*7¾% Treasury Stock 2012/15
*12¾% Treasury Stock 1992	*3½% War Loan
*12½% Treasury Stock 1993	

9% Treasury Convertible Stock 2000 (not readily available)

* May be purchased in Bearer Form.

Interest payments on the above are made gross, on application, to established non-residents of the United Kingdom, with the exception of 3½% War Loan, the interest on which is paid gross automatically.

The United Kingdom Government does not, at present, intend to issue any further tax exempt securities.

CHAPTER III
The Development of Jersey as the British Isle Offshore Banking Centre 1955–78

Jersey was the last of the three islands to adopt an income tax and the first island to establish a low tax rate of 40 per cent in the post-1945 period and so was the first potential centre ready for offshore development in the 1960s. Jersey's income-tax legislation was enacted as late as 1928, as compared with that of the Isle of Man in 1918 and Guernsey in 1919. Prior to 1928, Jersey had relied on indirect taxation as its main source of revenue for insular government expenditure, the only direct taxes being the equivalent of parish and States rates, which were not based on income. As can be seen from Table XV, Jersey's rates as a consequence of the above were set at higher levels than Guernsey. This Table, based on estimates made by E.P. Hellyer, the Jersey States Accountant-Auditor,[1] indicates how both Channel Islands were low indirect tax areas as compared with the Isle of Man and Great Britain, there being little difference between the latter two areas with the exceptions of spirits and beer. The late 1920s however, were years in which increased expenditure was being foreshadowed with respect to debt servicing, harbours and drains, and poor relief in Jersey. Estimates made for the period 1928–34 indicate that revenues would have had to increase by some 67 per cent if these objectives were to have been achieved without deficits being incurred. In these circumstances, resort to a local income tax was seen to be expedient, especially as it was shown[2] that the spending capacity of Jersey had increased by some £99,166 by the financial year of 1926–27, as compared with that of 1919–20, of which 40 per cent was attributed to visitors but 60 per cent to residents who had settled on the island since 1918; and that Jersey had a direct taxable capacity of £888,942 (on a UK basis of assessment) on a population base of 49,494 (as compared with the Isle of Man's £884,919 with a population base of 49,270 and that of Guernsey with £687,414 with a population base of 38,285) that could be exploited.[3] A single rate structure of 6d. or 2½ per cent was adopted in 1928, compared with that of 10d. or 4.1 per cent in Guernsey in that year and 1/6d. or 7.4 per cent in the Isle of Man. This rate was largely maintained until 1939 (with the exception of a 4d. rate in the period 1933–35). The general restructuring of rates at the beginning of the Second World War resulted in Jersey adopting a relatively high income tax rate of 4/- or 20 per cent, compared with the 10½d. rate in Guernsey and the 2/7d. top rate in the Isle of Man. Unlike the other islands, Jersey did not adopt a surtax in that year and, whereas after 1945 Guernsey's rate rose to 25 per cent, Jersey maintained its 20 per cent rate thereafter. Surtax was not abolished in Guernsey until 1955 and in the Isle of Man until 1961, and the 20 per cent income tax level was not achieved in Guernsey until 1960, and in the Isle of Man until 1980.

As regards company formation, no distinction of treatment was made in Jersey as between resident and external company status until 1940, unlike Guernsey,

TABLE XV: Statement of the tax revenue of the States of Jersey for the year 1926–27, together with the rates of taxation then in force. Added for comparison are the rates of similar taxation (where known) in force in Guernsey, the Isle of Man, and Great Britain

Source of revenue	*Yield, 1926–27*		*Rates charged*			
			Jersey	*Guernsey*	*Isle of Man*	*Great Britain*
			Per gallon	*Per gallon*	*Per gallon*	*Per gallon*
Spirits.	61,891		20/–	11/–	67/6	72/6
Spirits Perfumed.				(at 90°)	115/–	120/–
Cordials—						
50° and over.	1,300		7/7½	5/6	—	—
Under 50°	222		3/9½	(at 45°)	—	—
Wines						
Under 30°				*Claret*		
Cask.	1,363		1/2	3/– 1/6	2/6	2/6
Bottle.	2,131		2/3	4/– 2/6	4/6	4/6
30° and over						
Cask.	782		1/7½	3/–	6/–	6/–
Bottle.	413		2/8½	4/–	8/–	8/–
Sparkling			—	5/6	15/–	15/–
Subtotal		68,102				
Tobacco			*per lb.*	*per lb.*	*per lb.*	*per lb.*
Manufactured	3,446		2/8	2/2	10/4½	10/4½
Cigarettes	13,394		3/9	2/4	12/7	12/7
Cigars	2,345		3/9	2/4	15/7	15/7
Leaf	17,001		1/7	1/6	8/2½	8/2½
Subtotal		36,186				

Beer			*Per barrel*	*Per barrel*	*Per barrel*	*Per barrel*
Imported	3,370		18/6	15/–	74/–	100/6d.
Local	10,797		18/–	9/–	69/–	100/6d.
Subtotal		14,167				
			per lb.	*per lb.*	*per lb.*	*per lb.*
Tea		6,116	3d.	4d.	4d. & 3⅓d.	4d. & 3⅓d.
			See Act 27			
Inport Dues		22,008	June, 1924	—	—	—
Stamp Duties		2,323	—	—	—	—
			See Act 27	½d. on		
Amusement Tax		8,628	Aug. 1921	every 5d.	—	—
Company registration		433	1/6 per £100 Nom. Capital	1/– per £100 Nom. Capital	—	£ per £100 Nom. Capital
Motor Cars						
Cycles	624		£1	£1 5 0		
Cycles and Sidecars	354		£1 10 0	£1 10 0	—	—
Cycle Cars	82		£2			
Motor Cars	6,225		£3	6/– & 7/6d		
Exceeding 20 H.P.	489		5/– per H.P.	per cwt.		
Exceeding 2 tons	445		£1 per ½ ton			
International passes	125		£1 1 0			
Subtotal		8,344				
Immigration		1,064				
Licences and Dog Tax		3,747				
Total tax revenue		£171,118				
Occupiers' Rate		23,326				
Grand total		£194,444				

Source: Hellyer, *Rapport au comité hommé le 19 août 1927*, Exhibit IV.

which had introduced a separate Corporation Tax for external companies in 1936. In 1940, Jersey imposed a flat rate of tax on companies registered in the island albeit on a discriminatory basis—an annual rate of £50 if the company was controlled within the British Empire, and a tax equivalent to local income tax if controlled from outside the British Empire. This tax was repealed in 1956 and replaced with a £100 tax on companies controlled within the British Commonwealth and a tax of £150 if controlled outside the Commonwealth. In 1970 discrimination was removed and a flat rate of £200 levied annually on all external companies that was raised to £300 in 1974.

In respect of double taxation, an agreement between Jersey and the UK was made in 1951, which was in some respects less advantageous to island residents compared with residents of colonial and former colonial territories: in relation to dividends and debenture interest payable to UK companies, Jersey residents had no exemption and had to pay 41¼ per cent up to April 1971, and Jersey residents were liable to UK surtax if income liable to UK tax exceeded surtax limits. Jersey residents are also exceptionally liable to UK standard rate tax on royalties, annuities and commercial pensions relating to the UK. However, capital gains legislation does not apply on estate duties, although in respect of the latter Jersey does not permit the official transference of UK assets to a Jersey private investment company until a three year residence requirement has been satisfied—a restriction not applied in Guernsey where automatic transfer is permitted when residence is taken up.

There have apparently been three phases of development: (1) the period prior to 1971; (2) the period 1972–75; (3) the period 1976–78.

(1) THE PERIOD PRIOR TO 1971

After 1945, the Channel Islands experienced a considerable boom in tourism which, unlike the Isle of Man, was not just an immediate post-war phenomenon but lasted throughout the 1950s. The sunshine records of the islands, their proximity, lack of currency complications and cheap drink and tobacco, made them obvious holiday centres for UK residents. Thus in Jersey the number of passenger arrivals increased from 243,000 in 1950 (93,000 by air) to some 546,000 (390,000 by air) by 1961. The concomitant development of communication links and facilities on the island also commended it to two groups of migrants: UK expatriates returning, or expecting to return given the political instabilities actual or incipient, from the shrinking British Empire and new Commonwealth, who required a place of retirement which would maximize the real value of their pensions; and the *nouveaux riches* of the UK post-war boom, who desired the further protection of their newly acquired wealth from the tax consequences of UK estate duty liabilities. In consequence, there was quite a significant demand both actual and latent for trust companies and the associated professional services of lawyers, bankers and accountants. In the period 1961–71 the island resident population grew from around 62,500 to 72,300. Of this increase 3,400 is accounted for by births exceeding deaths, and 6,400 arose from net immigration.[4] The 1971 census revealed that there were 19,000 people who had taken up residence since 1960.

TABLE XVI: Jersey bank arrivals and deregistrations 1955–71

Year	*New bank arrivals*	*Year deregistered*	*Net total*
1955	Acme Investments Ltd.		6
1957	Guarantee Trust of Jersey Ltd.	1970	7
1961	Hill Samuel and Co. (Jersey) Ltd.		8
1962	Jersey Savings and Loan Corporation Ltd.	1970	
	Kleinwort Benson (C.I.) Ltd.		
	Royal Trust Company of Canada (C.I.) Ltd.		
	Walford Merchant Banking Corporation Ltd.		12
1963	Williams and Glyn's		13
1964	Jersey International Bank of Commerce Ltd.		
	United Dominions Corporation (C.I.) Ltd.		15
1965	Channel International Bank Ltd.		16
1966	Central Finance (C.I.) Ltd.	1971	
	Julian S. Hodge Bank (Jersey) Ltd.		
	Standard Bank (C.I.) Ltd.		
	Whyte, Gasc and Company (C.I.) Ltd.		
	Williams & Glyn's Investment & Finance Ltd.		21
1967	Hambros (Jersey) Ltd.		
	Midland Bank Finance Corp. (Jersey) Ltd.		
	National Westminster Bank Finance (C.I.) Ltd.		24
1968	First National City Bank (C.I.) Ltd.		
	Lombard Banking (Jersey) Ltd.		
	National and Grinlays Bank (Jersey) Ltd.		27
1969	Barclays Bank Finance Company (Jersey) Ltd.		28
1970	Bristol Street Group (C.I.) Ltd.		
	Lloyds Bank Finance (Jersey) Ltd.		
	New Guarantee Trust of Jersey		
	Slater Walker (Jersey) Ltd.		30
1971	Lloyds and Scottish Finance (C.I.) Ltd.		30

Source: Commercial Relations Office, Jersey.

Prior to the 1950s, banking on the island was essentially in the hands of branches of the main so-called 'big' UK clearers that had established themselves over the years—Lloyds Bank in 1919, Barclays in 1921, National Provincial in 1926 and Martins in 1951. The Jersey Savings Bank had existed since 1835 and several insular banks had been formed in the ninteenth century which had had a chequered existence, culminating in a banking crisis of 1873.[5] At the beginning of the 1950s there were some five banks. From the mid-1950s onwards the numbers grew until by the end of 1971 some thirty banks were present on the island, as Table XVI indicates.

As early as 1947, the States of Jersey had asserted their right to provide for the regulation of the borrowing and raising of money, the issue of securities, and the circulation of offers of securities for subscription etc. under the Borrowing(Control)(Jersey) Law 1947 Article 2. The Finance Committee activated these powers in the Control of Borrowing (Jersey) Order 1958 which gave them considerable control over the issue of shares, unit trust schemes, non-UK government securities, and to the activities of would-be rather than established financial institutions or finance companies. A general curb was firmly placed on financial ar-

TABLE XVII: New Jersey company incorporations 1955–70 (a) and number of corporation tax companies 1961–70 (b)

Year	*(a)*	*(b)*	*Year*	*(a)*	*(b)*
1955	46		1963	222	25
1956	35		1964	269	66
1957	57		1965	345	110
1958	43		1966	388	172
1959	70		1967	437	210
1960	90		1968	628	282
1961	134	12	1969	607	400
1962	153	17	1970	392	474

Source: Commercial Relations Dept., Jersey.

rangements that might have given rise to possible overt tax-evasive developments. Henceforth both bodies corporate incorporated under the law of the Island (S.4 (2)-(3)) and those not so incorporated (S.4(4)) could not, without the consent of the Finance Committee, issue any shares or securities (S.4(7)) where the whole or any part of the consideration for the issue is the transfer of any property or, if the purposes or effects of the transaction consist of or include: (*a*) the raising or borrowing of money outside the island, *unless* the borrowing is in the ordinary course of its business and is from a person carrying on a banking undertaking, and the money is made available in the scheduled territories; and (*b*) the exchanging or substituting of new securities for redeemable securities already issued by the body corporate, unless such new securities are not redeemable or are redeemable not earlier than the earliest date on which the securities already issued are redeemable.

These measures combined with the 'authorized depository' status conferred by the Bank of England under the UK Exchange Control regulations clearly ensured that a high degree of legitimacy was attached to all financial activities. A first wave of banking arrivals occurred in the period 1961–62 when the number of such institutions rose from seven to twelve. Included in this wave were important English merchant banks and the first non-UK institutions—the Royal Trust Co. of Canada. It was perhaps no accident that 1962 was also the year in which the old vestiges of usury control embodied in Jersey's Code of 1771 were abolished by the Code of 1771 (Amendment) (Jersey) Law of 2 October 1962, under which interest rates had been officially constrained to a maximum of 5 per cent. Given this expansion, closely followed by a second invasion wave in 1966 and the population increase by immigration already referred to, new company incorporations grew apace in the 1960s as Table XVII reveals. By 1968, this distribution of all companies by type was as follows:

Local Trading Companies	289	46%
Private Investment Companies	267	42.5%
Overseas Trading Companies	53	8.4%
Public Investment Trusts Merchant Banks and Financial Concerns	19	3.0%

TABLE XVIII: Publicized offshore funds launched in Jersey 1931–71 by type of issue

(a) General Statistics

Year	*UK equities*	*Investment trusts*	*US funds*	*Far East funds*	*International funds*	*No. new funds*	*Total no. funds*
1931		1				1	1
1960		1				1	2
1962		1				1	3
1965	2					2	5
1967	1					1	6
1968	1					1	7
1969			1	1	2	4	11
1970	2			1		3	14
1971	1					1	15

(b) Funds by type, name and value

Type of Fund	*Year*	*Name of fund*	*Value as at 1 October 1980*
Investment	1931	Jersey General Investment Trust Ltd.	
	1960	Channel Islands & International Investment Trust Ltd.	
	1962	International Trust Company of Jersey Ltd.	
UK Equities	1965	Save and Prosper Trust Channel Islands Ltd.	£2.5m
		The M and G Jersey Island Fund	£7.0m
	1967	Hambros Channel Islands Fund	£2.2m
	1968	Save & Prosper Channel Capital Trust Ltd.	£2.7m
	1970	Bandts Jersey Fund*	£1.3m
		Duncan Lawrie Sterling Fund	£0.3m
	1971	Britannia Growth Investors Trust	£5.6m
US	1969	Save & Prosper North American Fund Ltd.	$13.2m
Far East	1969	Britannia Far East & International Fund	£2.9m
	1970	Save & Prosper Jardine Far Eastern Fund	$12.1m
International	1969	Save & Prosper International Growth Fund Ltd.	$10.3m
		Tyndall Overseas Fund	$ 9.9m

Source: Trevor, Matthews and Carey, Ltd., *Channel Island Investment and Unit Trust Review*, October 1980.

*Became Tyndall Jersey Fund in 1976.

Private Investment Companies were of the following four types:

Principals resident in Jersey less than 3 years	59	22.1%
Principals resident in Jersey more than 3 years	104	39%
Principals non-resident	89	33%
Other	15	5.6%

By 1970 the division between local companies and those whose principals were non-resident was roughly 50:50 according to G.C. Powell, the Economic Adviser to the States of Jersey.[6] In order to supervise these developments in a more co-ordinated way a Commercial Relations Department was established at the end of 1971.

A modest beginning was made in terms of indigenous launching of funds in this period, as Table XVIII shows. Whereas before 1960 only one indigenous fund

TABLE XIX: Bank deposits made in Jersey 1960–70 (in £ms.)

Year	*UK clearing banks*	*Jersey Savings Bank*	*Other banks*	*% Total*	*Total deposits*
1960	27.2	12.11			39.31
1961	29.50	14.75			44.25
1962	32.09	18.10			50.15
1963	33.01	21.87			54.88
1964	35.76	25.74			61.50
1965	42.05	26.54			68.59
1966	48.15	28.79	36.5	32.2	113.44
1967	54.68	33.30	71.3	44.8	159.28
1968	55.15	34.78	118.0	56.7	207.93
1969	66.40	35.82	194.1	65.5	296.32
1970	70.15	40.88	325.0	74.5	436.03
% growth 1966–70	45.7%	42%	790.4%		284.4%

Source: derived from Table 5.11, p. 177, of Powell, *Economic Survey of Jersey.*

had existed, by the end of 1971 the total had risen to fifteen. Initial development was in unit trusts and no doubt as a result of the UK wealthy immigrants who wished to continue to invest in the UK, there was a concentration on UK equities, in particular growth equities. Jersey's venture into global offshore funds began in 1969 with the first dollar denominated funds. It is clear that Save and Prosper Management (Jersey) Ltd. was an important instigator of many of these funds. The M. and G. Jersey Island Fund is a feeder fund for Jersey investors only for the Guernsey based M. and G. Island Fund launched in 1965.

As a result of the growth of banking from six institutions in 1955 to twenty-one in 1966, the States of Jersey enacted as from 28 July 1967, the Depositors and Investors (Prevention of Fraud) (Jersey) Law 1967 to 'provide for the registration of persons carrying on the business of accepting money for investment on deposit, to penalise fraudulent inducements to invest money, and generally to provide for purposes connected with the matters aforesaid'. The provisions of the Act require annual registration of institutions and permit the Finance Committee to 'attach such conditions as it thinks fit to the registration of any person and . . . at any time vary such conditions' (Article 5 (2)). Local reporting requirements of annual returns date from 1966.

The latter part of the 1960s from 1967 to 1971 saw a further twelve new institutions incorporated, almost half of which were subsidiary companies of the main UK clearing banks set up to give an independent legal identity for their trust businesses. The others include some notable British merchant banks and also, in 1968, the first American arrival—the First National City Bank (CI) Ltd.. Insular bank deposits now began to increase very significantly as can be seen from Table XIX. The importance of 'Other' banks is reflected in the figures from 1966 onwards: their market share of Jersey deposits rising from 32.2 per cent in 1966 to about three-quarters of total deposits in 1970. Powell in his *Economic Survey of Jersey* indicates that 'it is likely that, in relation to the resident population, bank deposits in Jersey are significantly higher than in any other similar area in the world':[6] in late 1969, total deposits per head were £4,100 in Jersey compared with £740 in Malta, £250 in Hong Kong and £200 in Singapore; and compared to £1,558 in Guernsey and £564 in the Isle of Man.

The above expansion of deposits in Jersey was not an insular reflection of deposit growth on the UK mainland, where 'growth was related to the build up of the Eurodollar market, a significant proportion of deposits being held by American banks seeking to obtain funds which had been denied to them in the USA because of the ceiling on interest rates'.[7] Apart from deposits placed by 'wealthy' immigrants seeking the tax advantages of Jersey residence and deposits placed by overseas residents in territories where the political situation had led to, or was likely to lead to, controls on the mobility of funds, it was nevertheless true that some 28 per cent of deposits of non-clearer institutions were from UK 'residents'. Powell ascribes these sources as being fivefold:[8]

1. Those contemplating residence in the Channel Islands or abroad who find it convenient to build up deposits in anticipation of that move.
2. UK residents who have participated in the growth of international business who have sought tax advantages by having a company account in Jersey in which profits earned abroad are deposited and from which international business can be financed.
3. Employees of UK firms working abroad who legally repatriate earnings to Jersey, or have earnings surplus to their requirements paid direct to Jersey, provided they are not repatriated to the UK on return to employment there until a new tax year has begun.
4. UK residents domiciled abroad whose investment income can be usefully accumulated in a Jersey bank.
5. Certain local banks had lower reserve requirements and limits on balances than their London parents, and so could attract UK money which could not otherwise be accommodated.

However by the end of this period, general local economic circumstances were forcing on the authorities an evaluation of the evolution of the finance sector in the light of its concomitant contribution to the island's population pressure. Whereas in the period 1951 to 1961, net immigration was maintained at a rate of 300 per annum, between 1961 and 1967 this more than doubled to a rate of 700 per annum and to over 2,000 per annum in the years 1968 and 1969. As a result, an immigration policy was exercised through housing controls applied under the Housing Law of 1949. Henceforth any future growth involving the import of the banking expertise of senior staff and concomitant property acquisition would be carefully viewed and controlled within a long-term macro-economic context, of which housing policy would be an integral part. As Powell remarks in his *Survey:*

> The continued expansion of banking, light industry and the number of wealthy residents should be facilitated to extend the degree of diversification, but the effect of unlimited expansion of these sectors on tourism and agriculture, allied to their vulnerability to the effects of action taken by other countries, suggests that some restraints may be required in the in-

> terests of future economic stability. The greatest contribution to continued prosperity must continue to come from the tourist industry . . . [which] is dependent on the preservation of the Island's amenity resources, and an important part of this preservation will be played by the continued existence of a prosperous agricultural sector.[9]

By 1971, banks and finance business were contributing 15 per cent of Gross Domestic Product, compared with 11 per cent in 1968: tourism accounted for 45 per cent, agriculture 8 per cent and light industry 7 per cent respectively.

(2) THE PERIOD 1972–75

As Jersey was already in the process of re-evaluating the growth of the finance sector as a result of the banking invasion of the 1960s when the rescheduling of the Sterling Area took place in June 1972, it did not seek to yield to the renewed pressure from external banks for entry to that sector. During this period as a whole, only eight new banks were allowed to register, and as three deregistered (Acme Investments and Whyte Gasc and Co. (CI) Ltd. in 1974; and the Bristol Street Group (CI) Ltd in 1975), there was a net increase of only five.* In the same period there was a net increase of twenty-five in Guernsey and seven in the Isle of Man. The reason for this comparatively small increase was essentially the decision taken by the States of Jersey in October 1972 to freeze all new bank registrations pending an appraisal being made of the state of the economy. As a first step, a special committee of the States—the Immigration Committee—had been set up in September 1972. This committee reported to the States in March 1973 and concluded that the recent rate of immigration had indeed been excessive, and recommended that the annual average net rate of immigration should henceforth be controlled such that by 1995, the island's population would be contained below the figure of 80,000; that a 25-year development plan should be established, and that *inter alia* an island census should be held every five years commencing in 1976. A Policy Advisory Committee was set up in March 1973 to advise on the scale and pattern of development in Jersey for the next five years, to which some twenty-nine financial institutions submitted a report on 29 October 1973 on their contribution to the finances of the island.[10] The Policy Advisory Committee made its report in early 1974, and emphasized that 'the Island's low tax status is . . . fundamental to [its] continued existence as a prosperous, independent economy,[11] but stressed that two overriding factors should shape future industrial strategy: 'the desire to obtain that necessary additional income growth without population growth and without excessive demands on space, and . . . the need to obtain that income through a balanced expansion of a number of activities'.[12] In this context, a maximum number of fifteen net additional immigrants was recommended conditional on a general income tax contribution requirement in real

*There were three changes of name in 1974: Hedge Finance (J.) Ltd. became Julian S. Hodge Bank (J.) Ltd., Lloyds & Bolsa Finance (J.) Ltd. became LBI Finance (J.) Ltd., and National & Grindlays Bank (J.) Ltd. became Grinlays Bank (J.) Ltd.

TABLE XX: Bank arrivals in Jersey 1972–75

Year	*Name of bank*
1972	Bank of America (Jersey) Ltd.
	Bank of Nova Scotia (CI) Ltd.
	Morgan Grenfell (Jersey) Ltd.
	Wallace Bros. Sassoon Bank (Jersey) Ltd.
1973	None
1974	Algemene Bank Nederland (Jersey) Ltd.
	Commercial Bank of Wales (Jersey) Ltd.
	Hongkong & Shanghai Banking Corporation (CI) Ltd.
1975	Charterhouse Japhet (Jersey) Ltd.

Source: Commercial Relations Office, Jersey.

terms of a minimum sum of £150,000 per annum. As regards finance centre activities, the Committee concluded that:

> Future emphasis must be on the development of activities which generate the greatest stream of income with the least demand on resources, either directly through the requirements of office space or indirectly through the demands on housing. At this point in time banking generally appears to be the most rewarding in this respect[13] . . . with particular reference to corporate business and the handling of assets on behalf of very wealthy non-resident clients[14] . . . [thus] high labour/income ratio activities such as the handling of small trust and small customer current account facilities should be discouraged, as also should be the cutting of cake into smaller pieces through the multiplicity of money-broking, stockbroking and other financial service activities[15] . . . It is the view of the Committee that if a number of Continental banks, or those who can show a relationship with an area of business not already well represented in the Island present themselves to the Island they should not be turned away. It should prove possible in the first year of the five year period to introduce three or four new banks of stature drawn predominantly from the Continent.[16]

The banks that were allowed registration are given in Table XX. Jersey's 'dithering'[17] caused some twenty-five or so banks reported to be awaiting entry to go elsewhere, essentially to the neighbouring island of Guernsey.[18] The arrival of three new UK accepting houses was as a result of their acquisition of existing banking institutions, the parents of two of which had been subject to Bank of England 'lifeboat' support following the UK secondary banking crisis at the end of 1973. Charterhouse Japhet acquired Bristol Street Group Finance (Jersey) Ltd. and became registered under its own name in 1975; the other two were not actually registered until 1976—they were S.G. Warburg who acquired UDT (CI) Ltd. and Lazard Brothers who acquired Slater Walker (Jersey) Ltd. Thus during this period, there was a net increase in the number of financial institutions from thirty at the end of 1971 to thirty-five by the end of 1975. Bank deposits rose by 231.9 per cent over the 1971 total of £470m. as Table XXI reveals, and stood at £1,090m. at the end of 1975.

New company registrations continued to rise as is evidenced in Table XXII.

TABLE XXI: Jersey bank deposits 1971–75 (£m.)

End year	*Bank deposits*
1971	470
1972	590
1973	950
1974	1060
1975	1090

Source: Economic Advisor's Office, Jersey.

TABLE XXII: New company registrations and total number of companies registered 1971–75

Type of company registered	*1971*	*1972*	*1973*	*1974*	*1975*
Trustee and finance companies	8	47	62	49	24
Private investment companies					
Jersey residents		255	314	224	169
Other Sterling Area residents	259	315	369	375	225
Non-Sterling Area residents			245	255	173
Overseas trading companies	77	97	227	322	404
Local trading companies	217	461	548	232	261
Total new registrations	561	1175	1765	1457	1256
No. companies at year's end	4746	5769	7354	8445	9121
No. corporation tax companies	571	796	1300	1779	2015

Source: Commercial Relations Office, Jersey.

During this period, the total number of registered companies rose to 9,121 from a base of 4,746, i.e., by 92.2 per cent. A significant trend therein was the rise in importance of Overseas Trading Companies, which at seventy-seven had only accounted for 13.7 per cent of new registrations in 1971, but in 1975, despite downturns in other entries, had risen to 404, an increase of 424.7 per cent, and now accounted for 32.2 per cent of new registrations – a clear indication of a shift in the direction of extra-UK global financial business development. Meanwhile the GDP share of Banks and Finance rose from 15 per cent in 1971 to 20 percent in 1975, the share of tourism having declined from 45 per cent to 40 per cent in the same period. These changes reflect not only the Sterling Area rescheduling, but also the fact that the Island's future relationship with the EEC had been secured at the end of 1971. Perhaps mindful of the need to encourage 'reputable' growth, the States Economic Advisor emphasized in his Report on the Budget for 1973 that:

> In seeking to foster a continuing development of finance centre activities it is important that Jersey maintains an image of respectability. Not only is there no need for the Island to encourage those activities which are at the edge or outside the pale of legitimate tax avoidance but there are obvious dangers in pursuing such a policy. The proper sale of the services which Jersey as an international finance centre wishes to offer to the outside world

TABLE XXIII: Number of offshore funds by type launched in Jersey 1972–75

Type of funds	*Previous total*	*No. New Fund Launchings* 1972	1973	1974	1975	*Total at end 1975*
UK gilts	0		2	1		3
Money market	0				1	1
Bonds	0			1	1	2
Commodity	0				2	2
US	1			2		3
European	0	1				1
UK equities	7	1		1	2	11
International	2	3	1	2	4	12
Other	5					5
Totals	15	5	3	7	10	40

Source: derived from Trevor, Matthews and Carey Ltd., *Channel Islands Investment and Unit Trust Review*, October 1980.

TABLE XXIV: Jersey offshore fund issues by type and name 1972–75

Type of fund	*Year*	*Name of fund*	*Reported value 1 October 1980*
Gilts	1973	King & Shaxson Gilt Fund (Jersey) Ltd.	£25.6m
		Save & Prosper Sterling Fixed-interest Fund Ltd.	£18.4m
	1974	Unicorn Overseas Income Fund	£11.3m
Money market	1975	Central Assets Ltd.	£22.9m
Bonds	1974	First International Reserve Securities Trust Ltd.	$ 8.7m
	1975	King & Shaxson International Government Securities Trust First Sterling Ltd.	£ 0.7m
Commodity	1975	Save & Prosper (Jersey) Commodity Fund Ltd.	£ 4.4m
		Surinvest Copper Trust Ltd.	£ 0.9m
US	1974	Britannia Jersey Energy Trust	£ 3.5m
		Transatlantic Market Trust Ltd.	£14.3m
European	1972	Common Market Trust Ltd.	£25.6m
UK equities	1972	Trustee Savings Bank Unit Trust	£ 4.4m
	1974	Kemp-Gee Capital Fund	£ 1.2m
	1975	Kemp-Gee Income Fund	£ 1.2m
		Hill Samuel Channel Islands Fund	£ 1.1m
International	1972	Anchor International (Jersey) Trust	£ 0.5m
		Barbican International Fund	£ 1.3m
		Neptune International/Jersey Fund	£ 0.2m
	1973	Tyndall Overseas Fund (Sterling) Ltd.	£ 7.4m
	1974	Britannia Worldwide Fund	n.a.
		Lloydtrust Overseas Fund	£ 3.9m
	1975	Arbuthnot Eastern & International Trust (CI) Ltd.	£ 0.5m
		Britannia/Schlesinger International Fund (Jersey) Ltd.	£ 0.9m
		117 Jersey Fund Ltd.	£ 2.1m
		Unicorn Unidollar Trust	$13.8m

Source: derived from Trevor, Matthews and Carey Ltd., *Channel Islands Investment and Unit Trust Review*, October 1980.

> should also be through the medium of professional contacts not by emulating the selling techniques of those other areas which more appropriately merit the simple description 'tax havens'.[19]

This posture was in line with the Brussels Commission which 'implicitly accepted the argument that if refuges for funds are to be created and used it is better that they are within the spheres of influence of the high tax areas than completely outside'.[20]

The above trends came at an opportune time, for under the 1974 UK Finance Act, the 'remittance' basis for repatriated funds was withdrawn, under which Jersey had been used as a staging-post of deposit for funds prior to expatriate redomicile in the UK.

Substantial growth had also occurred in the launching of new offshore funds during this period as Table XXIII indicates, the total number rising from 15 in 1971 to 40 by the end of 1975. What is particularly striking here is the growth of the international funds, which increased dramatically from two to twelve and comprised approximately one-third of the total and were responsible for 40 per cent of the growth in this period. In addition a diversification took place in the types of issue, such that, for the first time, gilt funds, money market funds, bonds, commodity funds, and a European fund were created where none had existed before. The names of these funds and their reported values are given in Table XXIV.

(3) THE PERIOD 1976–78

During this period the net number of financial institutions rose from thirty-five at the end of 1975 to forty-two by the end of 1978, the details of which are given in

TABLE XXV: Bank arrivals and deregistrations in Jersey 1976–78

Year	*Arrivals*	*Deregistrations*
1976	Algemene Bank Nederland NV	First Nat. City Bank (CI) Ltd.
	Bank of America National Trust and Savings Association	Slater, Walker (J.) Ltd.
	Chase Bank (CI) Ltd.	Standard & Chase Bk. (CI) Ltd.
	Citibank (CI) Ltd.	United Dom. Trust (CI) Ltd.
	Citibank NA	
	Hongkong & Shanghai Banking Corporation	
	Minden Securities (Jersey) Ltd.	
	S.G. Warburg and Co. (Jersey) Ltd.	
1977	Bank of India	Channel International Bank Ltd.
	Brown Shipley (Jersey) Ltd.	Julian S. Hodge Bank (J.) Ltd.
	Standard Chartered Bank (CI) Ltd.	
1978	Banque Nationale de Paris S.A.	Minden Securities (J.) Ltd.
	Bilbao International Bank (Jersey) Ltd.	Wallace Bros. Bank (J.) Ltd.
	Lazard Brothers and Co. (Jersey) Ltd.	
	Morgan Guaranty Trust Co. of New York	

Source: Commercial Relations Office, Jersey.

Table XXV. An important feature of the new expansion was the putting into effect of the development policy outlined in the previous section which is manifested in Table XXV in two respects:

i) The further promotion of Jersey as a loan centre by the 1976 amendment to the 1967 Depositors and Investors (Prevention of Fraud) (Jersey) Law to permit institutions to be registered as branches rather than as local bodies corporate: a change that was immediately taken advantage of by four banks—Citibank, the Bank of America, Algemene Bank, and the Hongkong and Shanghai Banking corporation—which now established branches alongside their existing subsidiaries without putting much more pressure on island resources.
ii) The other new arrivals indicate a further develoment of extra-UK global offshore activity, given the presence of banks from France, Spain, India and the Far East.

Total bank deposit figures rose more modestly during this period—an increase of 137.6 per cent over the three year period on the previous base, as compared with 184.7 per cent for the period 1973–75: the yearly figures were £1,090m., £1,950m., £2,250m. and £3,500m. for the years 1975, 1976, 1977 and 1978 respectively. The significant development was the growth of the international loan business created by the non-UK institutions. D.K. Bonnar summed up the potential thus:

> To put the finance centre activities in a worldwide perspective, there is a presence in the Island of the first, second, and sixth largest banks in the world (all American), the largest bank in Holland, the fourth largest bank together with the largest trust corporation from Canada, the largest bank in the Far East (excluding Japan) and from the UK the five major clearing banks, nine of the seventeen international merchant banks, and two of the largest Commonwealth banks.
>
> In addition, permission has been given for the second largest Indian and the fifth largest Spanish bank to open here.
>
> With eleven out of the hundred biggest banking institutions in the world it is indeed an exclusive 'club' of quality, rather than the quantity of other offshore banking centres.[21]

The international loan business grew from a negligible amount in 1975 to £500m. in value by the end of 1976, and to something in excess of £2 billion by 1978.

The global direction of offshore development is further confirmed by the statistics of new company registrations as demonstrated in Table XXVI. Overall, the number of new companies increased by 37.2 per cent in these three years on the previous base. What is significant is the growth of overseas trading companies of 87.9 per cent and of non-sterling area residents of 98.8 per cent: by 1978, the former accounted for 43 per cent of the new entry (compared with 32.2 per cent in 1975) and the latter 19.5 per cent of the new entry (compared with 13.8 per cent in 1975). In terms of the Jersey economy as a whole, the estimated contribution made by banking and finance rose from 20 per cent in 1975 to 25 per cent in

TABLE XXVI: New company registrations in Jersey 1975–78

Type of company registered	*1975*	*1976*	*1977*	*1978*
Trustee and finance companies	24	48	74	51
Private investment companies				
Jersey residents	169	143	114	102
Other Sterling Area residents	225	192	256	208
Non-Sterling Area residents	173	295	337	344
Overseas trading companies	404	484	630	759
Local trading companies	261	375	358	301
Total new registrations	1,256	1,537	1,769	1,765
Total No. companies at year end	9,121	10,134	11,387	12,513
No. Corporation Tax Companies	2,015	2,350	2,920	3,600

Source: Commercial Relations Office, Jersey.

1978. The States Economic Advisor was able to conclude his review of 1977 with the statement that:

> The Island(s) . . . position as an offshore finance centre . . . is not simply a product of a special relationship with the UK to be weakened by changes in the fiscal legislation of the latter, but a centre of standing and integrity capable of attracting business from all parts of the world.[22]

Given the nature of this transformation, it was necessary to see that the reputation of the island was enhanced as much as possible. In 1978, two labour MP representatives from the National Executive of the UK Labour Party visited the Channel Islands, their visit being prefaced by the official statement that 'HMG has no plans to alter the constitutional status of these Islands. If they were ever to seek to do so they would certainly not proceed without the consent of their peoples.' Despite the publicity attached to such an unaccustomed visit, no new proposals were made which might have threatened the future viability of offshore activities. Internally, however, there was a need to consider reform, particularly in relation to company law, insurance, insolvency and mortgaging of moveable property, given that Jersey laws in these areas had not been substantially altered since 1861.

Since his appointment as the first Commercial Relations Officer in the early 1970s, David Morgan had been undertaking just such a review in a series of four reports issued from August 1973 to October 1975, which had been motivated as a result of certain commercial difficulties experienced in 1969 and 1970. Apart from questions of insolvency, the central concerns as far as offshore business was concerned were three in number which are now briefly outlined.

(1) Deficiencies of the Loi (1861) Sur Les Societées à Responsabilité Limitée as modified up to 1968

As an indication of the failure of Jersey company law to provide for modern business practices, it will be sufficient in this context to outline the twelve main matters that Morgan lists in his *Commercial Law Reform Report* No.2 October 1975(para. 15, pp.4–5) as requring alteration or addition to the above body of law:

a) Inability to alter the objects of a company without recourse to winding up the company and incorporating a new company.
b) Inability to incorporate any type of company other than a company limited by shares.
c) No specific provision in the law relative to directors or auditors or secretary and their duties and publication of such officers.
d No provisions as to public issues or take-over bid procedures or procedures to facilitate company reconstructions.
e) Insufficiency of data required to be available for public inspection by prospective creditors of a company.
f) Statutory requirements as to meetings, particularly the necessity to hold two meetings in certain circumstances, an impediment to the easy administration of companies having a small number of members.
g) Inadequate provision for voluntary liquidation of a company.
h) No provision for registration of external companies who establish a place of business in the Island.
i) No provision for the protection of minority interests.
j) No provision for the creation of debentures and in particular the creation of floating charges, which have become widely recognised as an accepted method of financing a company's operations.
k) Inadequate, or complete lack of, provisions for enforcement of statutory requirements.
l) Prohibition on establishment of incorporation of insurance companies, and thus preventing the Island offering the fullest extent of fiscal services provided in other similar financial centres.

Item (1) clearly deprived Jersey of the development of captive insurance, which Guernsey, as will be seen in the next chapter, was able to capitalize on after 1972.

(2) The Lack of a Trust Law

As Morgan makes clear in his *Commercial Law Reform Report* No.3 of 24 October 1975 (p.1):

> despite decisions of the English Courts which supported the proposition that the Jersey courts recognized the existence of trusts, and the fact that it has been commonplace for trusts to be created in the Island or transferred to the Island there [is no] specific law relating to the creation of trusts and the obligations of trustees, and both the customary and case law of Jersey upon the subject are very sparse . . . and . . . the full development of trust business is impeded by the failure to have such definite laws and . . . business has been lost, and will continue to be lost . . . until a Trust Law is introduced.

TABLE XXVII: Offshore funds launched in Jersey by type 1976–78

Type of fund	*Previous totals*	*No. new launchings* 1976	1977	1978	*Cumulated total*
Gilts	3	1	2	10	16
Money market	1	1		3	5
Bonds	2	1		3	6
Commodity	2	2			4
American	3	5	1	2	11
Far East	2	1	2	2	7
European	1			1	2
UK equities	11	1			12
International	12		3	1	16
Investment trusts	3				3
Totals	40	12	8	22	82

Source: derived from Trevor Matthews and Carey, Ltd. *Channel Islands Investment and Unit Trust Review,* October 1980.

(3) The Problem of Pledge

Jersey law with respect to moveable property requires that such property be pledged with the lender who must retain it and return it to the borrower on proper redemption of the loan if a valid security is to be obtained. This requirement makes the provision of credit and finance difficult in law on the island, and so a Chattel Bond was proposed to obviate this problem.

Local response to some of the above proposals, especially with regard to the disclosure of beneficial ownership under (1) and to issue (3), was hostile and resulted in all issues being shelved for second thoughts. Moreover no special urgency was seen in the resolution of these problems, given the considerable high income developments that were taking place, already noted, in offshore banking.

In the area of offshore funds, a dramatic increase took place as is shown in Table XXVII. The number of such funds increased from forty at the end of 1975 to eighty-two by the end of 1978. While new issues were made of all types of fund, with the exception of investment trusts, significant growth took place in gilt issues (total issues increasing from three to sixteen) and American funds (total issues increasing from three to eleven). The names and reported values of these funds are given in Table XXVIII.

In terms of island development, it was evident that the immigration policy adopted in the early 1970s was beginning to have an effect: the 1976 Island Census revealed that the rate of growth of the population had actually fallen, and that per annum net immigration had dropped from 640 in the period 1961 to 1971 to 450 in the period 1971 to 1976; the resident population rose from 72,303 in 1971 to 74,470 in 1976.[23]

TABLE XXVIII: Jersey offshore fund launchings by type, name and reported value 1976–78

Type of fund	*Year of issue*	*Name of new fund*	*Reported value 1 October 1980*
Gilt	1976	Tyndall Gilt Fund Ltd.	£14.3m
	1977	Britannia/Schlesinger Gilt Fund Ltd.	£12.7m
	1978	Allen Harvey & Ross Gilt Edged Fund Ltd.	£15.6m
		Arbuthnot Government Securities Trust Ltd.	£15.3m
		Britannia High Interest Sterling Trust Ltd.	£ 9.8m
		Brown Shipley Sterling Bond Fund Ltd.	£ 2.3m
		Clive Gilt Fund (CI) Ltd.	£ 3.7m
		Gartmore Gilt Fund (Jersey) Ltd.	£15.3m
		Lloydtrust Gilt Fund Ltd.	£ 6.9m
		Quest Sterling Fixed Interest Fund Ltd.	£ 2.0m
		TSB Gilt Fund Ltd.	£15.0m
		TSB Gilt Fund (Jersey) Ltd.	£ 2.1m
Money Market	1976	Lazard Brothers Sterling Reserve Fund Ltd.	£42.3m
	1978	Mercury Money Market Trust Ltd.	£ 8.2m
		Save & Prosper Sterling Deposit Fund Ltd.	£12.7m
		The English Association Sterling Fund Ltd.	£ 6.2m
Bonds	1976	Save & Prosper Dollar Fixed Interest Fund Ltd.	$ 3.7m
	1978	Britannia World Bond Fund Ltd.	$ 1.4m
		Quest International Bond Fund	$ 1.6m
		Unicorn Unibond Trust	$ 3.6m
Commodity	1976	Stronghold Managed Commodity Trust	£ 0.3m
		Wardgate Commodity Fund Ltd.	£ 5.0m
American	1976	Britannia/Schlesinger American Investments Ltd.	£ 4.3m
		Britannia/Schlesinger American Options Ltd.	$ 2.6m
		Duncan Lawrie International Fund	$ 0.6m
		Surinvest American Index Trust	£ 0.1m
		Tyndall American Fund Ltd.	£ 4.9m
	1977	Britannia American Smaller Companies Fund Ltd.	£ 1.1m
	1978	G.T. Dollar (Sterling) Fund Ltd.	£ 2.0m
		Albany Dollar Fund CI Ltd.	$ 4.2m
Far East	1976	G.T. Asia (Sterling) Fund Ltd.	£11.4m
	1977	Berry Pacific (Sterling) Fund Ltd.	£ 9.5m
		Surinvest Japanese Index Trust Ltd.	H.K.$41.2m
	1978	Britannia/Schlesinger Far East Fund Ltd.	£ 0.9m
		Tyndall Far Eastern Fund Ltd.	£ 3.8m
European	1978	Tyndall European Fund Ltd.	£ 0.6m
UK equities	1976	Emson & Dudley Investors Capital Trust Ltd.	£ 0.3m
International	1977	Britannia Universal Dollar Trust Ltd.	$ 7.1m
		Lazard Brothers International Capital Fund Ltd.	$14.0m
		117 Jersey Overseas Trust	£ 7.6m
	1978	Quest International Securities Fund	$ 7.2m

Source: derived from Trevor, Matthews and Carey Ltd., *Channel Islands Investment and Unit Trust Review,* October 1980.

CONCLUSION

Jersey was ideally suited for transformation from tax haven to offshore finance centre. Undoubtedly it was the most prosperous of the three British Isle havens, and had a good amenity and communications infrastructure which had largely been created by a booming tourist industry after 1945 and a wealthy immigrant community. Considerable financial development had taken place well before the 1972 watershed for development brought about by the Sterling Area rescheduling. However, internal pressure on housing and other island space resources necessitated a particular choice being made with regard to the expansion of the banking and finance sector which emphasized a degree of concentration being placed on the international loan business. This was in accord with the general development remit laid down by the Policy Advisory Committee's preference for specialization on activities which would generate the greatest stream of island income with the least demand on local resources. This specialization decision and the delay involved prior to the making of the assessment of the island's future needs, together with a failure to update local commercial laws, played a critical role in the instigation of offshore take-off in Guernsey, the other Channel Island centre, as will now be outlined.

REFERENCES

1. Hellyer, E.P., *Rapport au comité nommé 19 Août 1927 pour faire l'étude de la révision de la législation financière de l'isle,* 4 November 1927.
2. Hellyer, op. cit., p.8.
3. Policy Advisory Committee, *Report and Proposition Regarding the Scale and Pattern of Development in the Island over the Next Five Years,* 8 January 1974, States of Jersey, p.5 para. 8.
4. Ibid.
5. See Le Rossignol, S.J., *Notes on Banking and Political Events in Jersey,* Jersey, 1915, pp.8–23.
6. See Powell, G.C., *Economic Survey of Jersey,* States of Jersey, 1971, p.180. This survey is an invaluable source of information for the period up to 1970.
7. Powell, op. cit., p.149, para. 450.
8. Powell, op. cit., p.159, para. 486.
9. Powell, op. cit., p.160, para. 490.
10. Powell, op. cit., p.261, para. 850.
11. Coopers and Lybrand, *Report on Financial Institutions registered under the Depositors and Investors (Prevention of Fraud) (Jersey) Law 1967,* Jersey, 29 October 1973.
12. Policy Advisory Committee, op. cit., p.44, para. 13.
13. Policy Advisory Committee, op. cit., p.45, para. 17.
14. Policy Advisory Committee, op. cit., p.46, paras. 24–5.
15. Policy Advisory Committee, op. cit., p.33, para. 63.
16. Policy Advisory Committee, op. cit., p.33, para. 63.
17. Policy Advisory Committee, op. cit., p.46, para. 25.
18. See 'Jersey in Two Minds', *The Banker,* July 1973, p.747–8; and 'Jersey Still Dithering', *The Banker,* February 1974, p.90.
19. Powell, C.G., 'Does Jersey Have a Future as an Offshore Financial Centre?' *The Banker,* May 1974, p.501.

20. Jersey States Economic Advisor, *Report on the Budget 1973,* p.76.

21. Bonnar, D.K., 'Fitting into the Banking Jigsaw', *Jersey Evening Post Finance Supplement,* July 1978. See also 'Finance in Jersey Survey', *Jersey Evening Post Supplement,* August 1980.

22. States Economic Advisor, *Report on the Budget 1978,* p.80.

23. Policy Advisory Committee, *Report and Proposition Regarding Economic Strategies and Immigration Control Policies,* States of Jersey, 9 May 1978, p.5.

CHAPTER IV
The Diversified Development of Guernsey 1960–78

The importance of Guernsey as a low-tax area and its attractiveness as an international location of personal and company activities on any scale is substantially a post-1960 phenomenon. Before discussing its development as an offshore finance centre, however, it is necessary to outline briefly how its low-tax status came about.

THE DEVELOPMENT OF LOCAL TAXATION 1918–60

The principle of an income tax was first accepted in Guernsey in February 1918 and first applied in the year 1919. It was introduced as an expedient (*a*) with a view to meeting the then existing States deficit and its future general expenses, and (*b*) to cover half of the £100,000 contribution made by the States, the island government, to the Imperial War Expenses.[1] The first rate set was 7d. in the £ which by the 1930s stabilized in the range 10–11d.

Company formation was naturally fairly modest during the depression years of the interwar period but, nevertheless, considerable increase did occur as Table XXIX reveals; the number of registered companies almost doubling during this period from 409 to 797 in 1939.

As was reported in Chapter I of this part, since 1927 an informal agreement to limit the formation of companies aimed at avoidance of UK taxation had been made. Nevertheless some growth occurred, although it was not statistically verifiable. Such an increase naturally attracted possibilities of an extension of the domestic tax base such that on 24 April 1935 a Corporation Tax of £50 per annum was thence levied 'on all Companies which are registered in Guernsey but which, by reason of their being controlled from a place outside Guernsey, do not and are not liable to pay local Income Tax'.[2] The gross revenues reported in the States' *Billet d'État* reveal that in 1936 some £2,275 was raised by this tax (indicating the existence of about forty-five external companies) which had risen to £3,070-16s.-8d. in 1938 (indicating a company statistic of sixty-one). The supervision of the tax was at first in the hands of the States Supervisor and was not transferred to the Tax Administrator until 1949, at which time the gross revenue was £3,533-6-8d. (sixty-six companies).[3]

The island's post-1945 low tax structure came about, ironically, as a result of a 'trial and error' experiment with higher taxes at the end of the 1940s. In 1945 the standard rate of tax stood at 25 per cent, with a surtax of 25 per cent on income over £10,000. Following a decline in the predominant horticulture industry immediately after a post-war boom, the standard rate of income tax was increased to 26.5 per cent and surtax to 37½ per cent on income over £10,000 in an at-

TABLE XXIX: Number of companies registered in Guernsey 1918–39

Year	*Total*	*Net Change*
1918	409	
1919	421	12
1920	446	25
1921	467	21
1922	497	30
1923	524	27
1924	549	35
1925	564	15
1926	580	16
1927	589	9
1928	600	11
1929	614	14
1930	626	12
1931	635	9
1932	663	28
1933	686	23
1934	701	15
1935	719	18
1936	741	22
1937	759	18
1938	774	15
1939	797	23

Source: Guernsey Greffe.

tempt to recoup lost revenue: the immediate result was a stagnant economy. As F.W. Veale, former Commercial Relations Officer, reflected some years later:

> It was borne in upon us that there were lessons to be learnt. It seemed to us that there was sufficient evidence to show that high taxation was a disincentive and that there was little substance to the argument that high taxation was deflationary. It might have been if the product was used to repay existing debt, but not if the effect was merely to move spending from the private to the public sector. Neither could we see any virtue, at least in the circumstances in which we were placed, in promoting a system of high taxation which would become increasingly expensive to collect, and at the same time, forcing ourselves into a position in which we might have to establish an equally expensive system in order to pay money back to those industries which it was thought to be necessary or desirable to promote. Step by step we began to take a new course . . . [4]

This new course had three main elements:

1. Double taxation agreements were made with the UK (1952)[5] and Jersey (1955) to enable residents to claim relief from local tax on income arising from real estate and earned income in the UK.
2. In the absence of other bilateral double taxation agreements, unilateral relief (up to half the Guernsey rate or half the foreign tax suffered, whichever is the lower) was allowed with respect to income arising in Com-

monwealth Countries in 1953: and, in 1962, was extended to other parts of the world: the latter relief not being available in Jersey, to Guernsey's advantage. Moreover, the absence of double taxation agreements meant no mutual exchange of information with tax authorities of other countries, thus preserving the privacy of island transactions.

3. In 1955 surtax was abolished and the standard rate reduced to 26 per cent and, finally, to 20 per cent in 1960.

By 1960, then, the essential low friction tax structure had been formed. Since 1960 income tax had continued to be levied at a rate of 20 per cent per annum: contemporary Guernsey taxation provisions are contained in the consolidating Income Tax (Guernsey) Law 1975. There are no island surtaxes, value added taxes, capital gains taxes (with the exception, since October 1973, of a Dwellings Profits Tax), mandatory withholding taxes on interest and dividends, and above all estate duties.

Since 1960, therefore, the incipient friction-busting UK resident has been faced with the alternatives of tax-avoidance schemes located in the Channel Islands or elsewhere; or, the ultimate, expatriation and a change of residence and domicile: the latter course not always being possible, in so far as personal and business ties may make such a move potentially unattractive, although less so than more far distant locations. Moreover in the latter regard, increasingly island restrictions have been imposed on new resident immigrant rentiers through Housing Control Laws (e.g. 1969 and 1975) in the wake of immigration pressure following the 1965 UK Capital Gains Tax. As regards company registration, provided assurances are given that avoidance of UK taxation is not the motive for island registration, and provided that exchange control requirements were met, companies could seek either Corporation Tax status or ordinary status. In the latter case the company would be subject to the 20 per cent Guernsey income tax. In the former case, under the Corporation Tax (Guernsey) Law 1950, S.4, any company which is either controlled in Guernsey or, if not so controlled, maintains an established place of business and conducts a substantial part of its activities there, is not subject to the annual tax, but is instead chargeable in accordance with Guernsey income tax legislation; any company which does not fall within either of these classes will be subject to the flat rate tax (S.3)—certain conditions must, however, be observed:

i) The beneficial owners should be resident abroad.
ii) No business should be carried on in Guernsey, other than company administration.
iii) It should be impossible for a governor of the board to consist of directors resident in Guernsey.
iv) All directors' meetings should be held outside Guernsey.

This tax was reaffirmed at £50 in 1950 and increased to £200 by the Companies (Stamp Duty and Corporation Tax) (Amendment) Law, (XXIII) 1969, and to £300 under The Corporation Tax (Guernsey) Ordinance (XLVIII) 1973. As regards (iii) and (iv), as Sark is not part of the jurisdiction of the Guernsey Tax Authorities, board meetings held there qualify within the law as 'outside' Guernsey. Certain information must be provided on incorporation and in an Annual Return to the Greffier (the registrar of companies): *inter alia* this includes a Share Members' register.

THE GROWTH OF OFFSHORE ACTIVITIES 1960–78

In the absence of any published island national income statistics, the published 'Analysis of Business Profits' gives the only reasonable indication of the changing industrial structure of the island. It is evident from Table XXX that, whereas in 1960 horticulture was the predominant industry, by the end of the 1970s, a considerable diversification had taken place, such that Conseiller Grut, President of the Advisory and Finance Committee, in a speech to the States in March 1980, characterised the progression as a change from the two 'legs' of horticulture and tourism to the four, largely equal, legs of horticulture, tourism, light industry and finance, the latter being by far the most important.[6] The growth of the Financial Sector (Group 21 in Table XXX) has been dramatic as is evident from the statistics: over the period 1960–78 profits from finance grew from £340,000 to £17,900,000. This overall growth can be divided into three separate distinct periods, the end of each period corresponding with a particular growth watershed, the general statistics of which are given below, prior to an evaluation of each period.

The three periods were as follows:

Period 1960–66: the relative importance of 'finance' remained fairly constant at 7.5–8 per cent, with an overall per annum growth of 111.5 per cent or 18.6 per cent over the six year period, slightly below the normal rate of growth of business profits as a whole. The number of banks increased from six clearing banks to a total of eleven. The number of registered companies grew from 445 to 899: revenue from Corporation Tax companies rose from seven to fourteen; and external income grew from £1,499,000 to £2,845,000; the first issues of offshore funds, some six in number, were made.

Period 1967–71: the relative importance of 'finance' increased enormously to nearly one-fifth of business profits, an overall per annum increase of 227.2 per cent or 56.8 per cent for the four year period, while business profits as a whole only increased by 63.6 per cent or 12.7 per cent per annum. The number of banks rose from eleven to twenty-one; the number of registered companies increased from 1,020 to 2,004; Corporation Tax revenue rising from £15 to £65; and external income rose from £3,875,000 to £6,274,000 or 161.9 per cent, the greater proportion of which was now interest and income rather than dividends. The number of new funds launched was four.

Period 1972–78: the relative importance of 'finance' substantially grew from about one-fifth of total business profits to over one-third for the island as a whole, an overall increase of 354.1 per cent or 59 per cent per annum; external income rose from £7,197,000 to £22,639,000 or 314.4 per cent; the number of banks rose from twenty-one to forty-three; the number of

TABLE XXX: Analysis of business profits in Guernsey 1960, 1966, 1967, 1971, 1972 and 1978* (£'000s)

Group no.	Industrial sectors	*1960–66*		*1967–71*		*1972–78*	
		1960	*1966*	*1967*	*1971*	*1972*	*1978**
1	Horticulture	1,235	3,200	2,296	2,811	2,847	4,634
2	Mixed horticulture and agriculture	89	132	130	94	120	176
3	Agriculture and fishing	84	139	148	171	233	764
4	Trades directly related to groups 1–3	197	284	361	368	335	868
5	Hotels and catering	256	596	718	836	907	2,549
6	Wines, spirits, brewing, public houses and tobacco	160	352	364	855	340	730
7	Luxury trades	73	133	163	242	329	845
8	Entertainment	13	49	53	68	59	179
9	Foodstuffs	343	452	478	650	660	1,528
10	Clothing and footwear	87	185	211	294	323	851
11	Consumer durables	160	316	315	440	497	1,061
12	Miscell. domestic and personal supplies	50	92	133	153	186	605
13	Miscell. domestic and personal services	67	123	148	238	263	888
14	Fuel	143	217	217	222	255	293
15	Building and allied trades	289	567	713	1,250	1,467	3,538
16	Builders merchants and allied trades	66	96	136	260	220	394
17	Engineering and allied trades	70	169	135	283	320	1,949
18	Shipping and transport	60	286	259	443	543	1,315
19	Extractive industries	15	15	2	—	—	—
20	Professions and vocations	284	493	568	897	1,232	4,190
21	Banking, finance, insurance, investment management	340	719	952	3,115	3,942	17,900
22	Miscell. manufacturing	132	554	660	1,118	867	4,446
23	Other miscellaneous	138	438	431	884	745	3,824
	Total	4,351	9,607	9,591	15,692	16,650	53,527
	(a) Group 21 as % of total	7.8%	7.5%	9.9%	19.9%	23.7%	33.4%
	(b) % growth of Group 21 over period		111.5%		227.2%		354.1%
	Annual % growth over period		18.6%		56.8%		59.0%
	(c) % growth of all other Groups over period (Total −21)		121.6%		45.6%		180.4%
	Annual % growth over period		20.3%		11.4%		30.1%

Source: Figures for 1960, 1966, 1967, 1968 and 1972 taken from *Survey on Commerce and Light Industry* States Advisory and Finance Committee *Billet d'État,* XI, 1974. Figure for 1978 taken from Appendix V, *Billet d'État,* VI, 1981.

*Provisional figures.

registered companies from 2,421 to 6,162 and Corporation Tax Revenue from £80 to £578. The number of new funds was seventeen.

Each of these periods will now be fully discussed.

Stage 1: 1960–66, the Tax Haven Stage

Until the early 1960s, island banking was purely locally oriented, its primary purpose being to serve the needs of domestic commerce and industry. Guernsey's offshore significance was largely confined to that of being a 'tax-haven', where residents and non-residents could seek to receive income and/or own assets without paying high rates of tax thereon. Moreover, such tax advantages were coupled with certain limited extra UK freedoms, albeit of a discretionary nature, with respect to international capital movements under the 1947 Exchange Control Act, as has been indicated in Chapter II. In essence the UK was the main source of its clientele, Guernsey providing a haven for UK *émigrés,* whether locally resident or expatriate working abroad, and/or anticipating onshore repatriation following the wind-up of parts of the former British Empire, or temporarily working abroad as UK residents whose earnings were taxed in the UK on a remittance basis; or UK residents contemplating work abroad, but looking for a convenient location to place their sterling assets. These activities led to a building-up in this and subsequent periods of money placed on deposit, the different categories of depositors outlined above often tending to consolidate their assets and deposit them in fairly liquid form. Moreover, 'many of the local banks (had) lower limits on balances than their London parent and this (tended to) attract UK money which could otherwise not be accommodated'.[7]

During this period, the first five merchant banks arrived which complemented the six clearing banks already present, the contemporary names of which are Barclay's Bank Ltd., Midland Bank Ltd., Lloyds Bank Ltd., National Westminster Bank Ltd., Lombard North Central Ltd., and Williams and Glyn's Bank Ltd. The first merchant bank arrival was Kleinwort Benson Ltd. in 1963 inspired mainly by a desire to provide a service for its East African clients who at that time were experiencing certain very serious difficulties. This arrival was closely followed by Hill Samuel and Co. in 1964 and Southern Investment Corporation Ltd. and Rea Brothers Ltd. in 1965. These institutions were able immediately to attract local *rentier* and business clientele, as well as to pioneer the UK resident and external resident use of the islands, once they had gained 'authorized' status as a bank or depository from the Banks of England under the 1947 Exchange Control Act, by channelling their UK and overseas clients thereto in appropriate circumstances. General indicators of change are given in Table XXXI.

Trust and personal investment company formation now began to flourish, especially after 1965 capital gains legislation in the UK. The number of registered companies doubled from 445 to 889, as did revenue from Corporation Tax companies during the seven year period.

The beginning of offshore fund flotation occurred with six issues, the first five of which were open-ended investment trusts, the last a UK Equity Fund, as shown in Table XXXII. Towards the latter part of the period, further increases in

TABLE XXXI: General indicators of finance centre activity in Guernsey 1960–66

	Finance		*Companies*		*Estimated external income arising to persons (inc. companies) resident and non-resident in Guernsey from outside sources*		
Year	*Annual profits from banking, finance, insurance and investment management (£'000s)*	*Money on deposit (clearing banks only) (£m.)*	*Registered at year end (No.)*	*Revenue from Corp. Tax Cos. (£'000s)*	*Total (£'000s)*	*Dividends (£'000s)*	*Interest + other income (£'000s)*
1960	340		445		1,499	1,122	377
1961	384		486		1,731	1,268	463
1962	389		503		1,862	1,318	544
1963	458		603	7	2,150	1,545	605
1964	593	14	695	9	2,360	1,744	616
1965	677	14	794	12	2,619	1,923	696
1966	719	16	899	14	2,845	2,088	757

Source: Billets d'État and Commercial Relations Office, Guernsey.

TABLE XXXII: Guernsey offshore fund flotations 1959–66

Type	*Year*	*Name of fund*
	1959	The Investment Trust of Guernsey Ltd.
Investment trusts	1960	The Channel Islands & International Investment Trust Ltd.
	1962	The International Investment Trust Co. of Jersey Ltd.
	1963	First Guernsey Securities Trust Ltd.
		Kleinwort Benson Guernsey Fund
UK equity	1965	The M and G Islands Fund

taxes on the mainland and especially the 1965 UK Capital Gains Tax, encouraged a further inflow of rich émigrés to the island. The chargeable investment island income derived from sources outside Guernsey rose from £1.5m. in 1960 to £2.8m. and reflects this expansion.

Stage 2: 1967–71, the Sterling Finance Haven Centre

This period witnessed a more comprehensive development of merchant banking such that, by 1971, Guernsey had been transformed into a sterling financial offshore centre served by twenty-one banking institutions. The significant arrival of two important merchant banks—N.M. Rothschild and Sons Ltd., and Hambros Bank Ltd.—was followed by a succession of another five: the subsidiaries of the clearing banks—National Westminster Bank Finance (CI) Ltd., in 1967, the Midland Bank Trust Corporation (Guernsey) Ltd. in 1968, Williams and Glyn's

TABLE XXXIII: Guernsey offshore fund flotations 1967–71

Year	*Name of Fund*	*Value as at 1 October 1980*[*]
1967	Hill Samuel Guernsey Trust	1.5
	Hambros Channel Islands Fund	2.2
1967	Kleinwort Benson (Guernsey) Fund	5.4
	Kleinwort Benson (Guernsey) 2nd. Fund	3.6

[*]As quoted in Trevor, Matthews and Carey Ltd., *Channel Islands Investment and Unit Trust Review.*

Bank Investments (Guernsey) Ltd. in 1969, Barclays Finance Co. (Guernsey) Ltd. in 1970, and Lloyds Bank International Trust Corporation in 1971. This diversification was a natural extension of the traditional personal trust and investment company business essentially derived from the UK mainland and represents the island's first banking 'invasion' which put Guernsey on the map of emergent finance havens. The requisite institutional means and expertise in international merchant banking was therefore provided and a capacity for frictioneering activities, on which and with which a considerable superstructure of trust, personal investment and trading companies, portfolio investment activity and offshore fund flotation was to be built in the 1970s. As a result of this considerable expansion, a fuller range of services was now offered in the areas of company management, expatriate investment, investment management and, above all, offshore fund management. In the latter case, whereas prior to 1967 some seven funds had been floated in Guernsey, six of which had been investment trusts, some four new funds were launched in the period 1967–71, of which two were international funds, two were in UK equities, as is shown in Table XXXIII, all of which were the result of imported expertise.

While the number of deposit institutions increased from eleven to twenty-one the growth of profits was quite phenomenal—45 per cent per annum over the period as a whole—almost three times that of the per annum growth in the preceding period 1960–66, as Table XXXIV shows.

External income rose from £2,845,000 at the end of 1966 to £6,274,000 at the end of 1971, the proportion of interest and other income becoming of greater significance than dividends, indicative of the greater importance of trading companies as compared to resident rentier dividend income: one result of the introduction of the first Housing Laws in 1969 which put a break on new *émigré* entrants to Guernsey.

At this time the island authorities had seen a need to introduce some degree of local regulation, partly in response to the UK Protection of Depositors Act 1963. As a result of a Resolution of the States of 26 June 1968, wide discretionary enabling powers were conferred on the States Advisory and Finance Committee by the Protection of Depositors, Companies and Prevention of Fraud (Bailiwick of Guernsey) Law, 1969 in respect of the regulation of deposit-takers for the Protection of Depositors (Part I), the control of such businesses (Part II) and the use of words in the title of businesses (Part III). Powers were assumed under this law in the Protection of Depositors (Bailiwick of Guensey) Ordinance 1971 which was

TABLE XXXIV: General indicators of finance centre activity in Guernsey 1967–71

	Finance		*Companies*		*Estimated external income arising to persons (inc. companies) resident and non-resident in Guernsey from outside sources*		
Year	*Annual profits from banking, finance, insurance and investment management (£'000s)*	*Money on deposit (clearing banks only) (£m.)*	*Registered at year end (No.)*	*Revenue from Corp. Tax Cos. (£'000s)*	*Total (£'000s)*	*Dividends (£'000s)*	*Interest + other income (£'000s)*
1967	952	17	1,020	15	3,875	2,287	1,588
1968	1,550	20	1,297	20	4,307	2,447	1,860
1969	1,643	20	1,728	32	4,724	2,449	2,275
1970	2,312	22	1,952	88	5,398	2,672	2,726
1971	3,115	25	2,004	65	6,274	2,251	4,033

Source: Billets d'État and Commercial Relations Office, Guernsey.

enacted as from 1 January 1972. Under this Ordinance, Banks must seek annual registration and, if accepted, are grouped into one of three categories:

i) Branches of institutions recognized as banking or discount companies under the 1967 UK Protection of Depositors Act (S.19 of Ordinance).
ii) Subsidiaries of companies who are recognized as banking or discount companies under the UK Act (Sub-section 2, Section 6 of Ordinance). These are required to present detailed accounts to the Committee at least twice a year.
iii) All other financial institutions who have the same obligation as (ii) but in addition must send detached accounts to their shareholders and depositors.

These minimum regulations were fortuitously to prove an important framework for the significant 'take-off' which was about to occur and could not have been anticipated.

Stage 3: 1972–78, the 'Captive' International Offshore Centre

As a result of a sequence of events and a conjuncture of circumstances, Guernsey became an international offshore centre, albeit under the aegis of UK Exchange Control, in the period down to 23 October 1979, when that method of onshore UK control was terminated. The number of financial institutions, which was twenty-one at the end of 1971 doubled by the end of 1978 as Table XXXV indicates.

The general indicators of change in this period are given in Table XXXVI. During the period as a whole, Guernsey became considerably diversified and internationalized as a financial centre. The period naturally divides into two

TABLE XXXV: Banking arrivals and deregistrations in Guernsey 1972–78

Year	*Arrival*	*Deregistration*	*Net change*
1972	Morgan Grenfell (Guernsey) Ltd.	Barnett, Christie (A.) Ltd.	
	Barfield Trust Co. Ltd.		
	Leopold Joseph & Sons (G.) Ltd.		
	Citibank (CI) Ltd.		
	Channel International Finance (G.) Ltd.		
	Ocean Savings Corporation Ltd.		
	Henry Ansbacher & Co. (CI) Ltd.		
	Whyte Gasc & Co. (CI) Ltd.		
	Goulston Finance Corporation (G.) Ltd.		
	Barnett, Christie (Alderney) Ltd.		
	Barnett, Christie (Finance) Ltd.		
	Commercial Finance Corporation Ltd.		
	Dunbar & Company (G.) Ltd.		
	Sterling Industrial Securities (G.) Ltd.		+13
1973	Manufacturers Hanover Bank (G.) Ltd.	Ocean Savings Corp. Ltd.	
	Bank of Bermuda (G.) Ltd.	Commercial Finance Corp. Ltd.	
	Australian & New Zealand Banking Group (CI) Ltd.		
	The Royal Bank of Canada (CI) Ltd.		
	The Italian International Bank (CI) Ltd.		
	Orion Bank (G.) Ltd.		
	The Royal Trust Company (G.) Ltd.		
	First National Finance Corp. (G.) Ltd.		
	Cripps Newell (CI) Ltd.		
	Guinness Mahon (CI) Ltd.		+ 8
1974	First National Bank of Chicago (CI) Ltd.	Whyte Gasc & Co. (CI) Ltd.	
	Chemical Bank & Howard de Walden Ltd.	First National Finance Corp. (G.) Ltd.	
	First National Bank of Boston (G.) Ltd.	Guinness Mahon CI Ltd.	
	Union Discount Co. of London Ltd.	Cripps Newell (CI) Ltd.	
	Co-operative Bank Ltd.		
	Bank of America (G.) Ltd.		+ 2
	Chase Manhattan Bank (G.) Ltd.	Sterling Industrial Securities (G.) Ltd.	
	Hansen (G.) Ltd.		
	Barclaytrust International Ltd.	Bank of America (G.) Ltd.	
	Allied Bank International (G.) Ltd.		+ 2
1976		Goulston Finance Corp. (G.) Ltd.	
		Citibank (CI) Ltd.	
		Barnett, Christie Finance (G.) Ltd.	− 3
1977	Guinness Mahon (G.) Ltd.	Channel International Finance (G.) Ltd.	
	Brown Shipley (G.) Ltd.		0
		Henry Ansbacher & Co. (CI) Ltd.	
1978		Dunbar & Co. (G.) Ltd.	− 1
		Net Increase 1972–78	21
		Previous total 1971	21
		1978 total	42

Source: information supplied by Commercial Relations Office, Guernsey.

TABLE XXXVI: General indicators of finance centre activity in Guernsey 1972–78

	Finance				*Companies*			*Estimated external income arising to persons (inc. companies) resident and non-resident in Guernsey from outside sources*		
		Money on deposit (£m.)								
Year	*Annual profits from banking, finance, insurance and investment management (£'000s)*	*Total*	*Clearing banks*	*Other banks*	*Registered at year end (No.)*	*Corp. Tax Cos. (No.)*	*Revenue from Corp. Tax (£'000s)*	*Total (£'000s)*	*Dividends (£'000s)*	*Interest + other income (£'000s)*
1972	3,942	162	29	133	2,421		80	7,197	1,934	5,263
1973	5,669	279	34	245	3,260		117	8,534	2,504	6,030
1974	7,184	410	52	358	3,611		237	10,573	2,944	7,629
1975	9,602	552	55	497	3,955	1,165	236	12,105	3,244	8,861
1976	11,746	631	57	574	4,347	1,308	291	14,437	8,830	10,607
1977	17,109	728	65	651	4,924	1,606	364	18,305	4,704	13,601
1978	17,900	842	74	760	5,526	1,903	447	22,639*	5,262*	17,377*

Source: Billets d'État and Commercial Relations Office, Guernsey.

*Provisional figures.

phases, that of 1972–75, a period of take-off; and that of 1976–78, a period of controlled consolidation. Each phase will be separately discussed.

(i) The international offshore centre take-off, 1972–75. A particular sequence of concomitant events brought about a development mutation such that a take-off to international status was suddenly achieved:

1) In 1971 an agreement was made with the EEC whereby the island's historic autonomy on fiscal matters was preserved and could not be eroded by any UK accession to the Treaty of Rome.
2) The rescheduling of the Sterling Area in 1972 which led to a desire by London merchant banks and others to relocate their activities when previous Scheduled Territories havens such as Bermuda and the Bahamas became descheduled. This relocation brought with it non-resident business and a greater world-wide expertise and potential to seek additional business abroad. This represented a second 'banking invasion' much of which came from the new Overseas Sterling Area.
3) The decision of the States of Jersey in October 1972 to temporarily halt the entry of any new deposit institution, pending a report of its Policy Advisory Committee and its subsequent discussion by the States of Jersey which did not take place until 19 February 1976. In contrast to the cautious attitude of Jersey, Guernsey adopted a welcoming attitude as was made evident in its 1972 Economic Development Plan (*Billet d'État,* XI, 1972), in which the States Advisory and Finance Committee declared:

   > The Committee regards the further development of the Island as a finance centre as highly desirable. It believes that given the political will and given the minimum of restrictions consistent with the protection of depositors there is scope for considerable further development.

   During the period October 1972–February 1974, some eleven new banks were registered, several of which had actually been on the Jersey waiting list: this included the First National Bank of Chicago, the Australian and New Zealand Banking Group, the Italian International Bank, and Manufacturers Hanover.

Within this short period a truly worldwide business coverage was achieved. As the Economic Policy Document of 1974 (*Billet d'État,* XIV) states (S.456):

> In Guernsey there are now financial operations which draw major proportions of their business from South America, Australia and New Zealand, the United States, Canada, the Middle East and Africa. Although there are banks with connections in Italy and Germany, the growth of direct continental interests is negligible.

However, this expansion had been rapid and had created some problems for the island, as the above report went on to describe:

> *S.460* Considerable strain has been put on the Island's supply of clerical and professional staff . . . certain training and experience can only

be obtained outside the Island. There are many young Guernseymen being trained but at present such training is not rapid enough to keep pace with expansion.

S.461 Clearing banks are having the greatest problems with staff shortage. They have lost many employees to incoming merchant banks who can offer rates of pay well above the UK scales of the clearers.

S.462 Some banks are forced to buy open market housing for their employees. There is thus a reduction of income to the Island from the loss of rentiers, in addition to the loss of revenue from banking profits reduced by the use of working capital for housing.

S.463 The Committee believes that recruitment of new banks should now be severely restricted, and such banks should generally be associated with areas from which there is no existing business. Unless such restrictions are imposed to limit additional demands for white collar workers, it may not be possible for the existing finance sector (or other commercial activities) to build up the stabilities of staff which are essential to efficient operations.

The aim was now 'to widen the Island's role as an international and not as a Sterling Area Centre'.[8] A direct spur in this direction was soon given by the events of the succeeding years which significantly diversified the financial structure:

a) The 1974 FA ended the 'remittance' basis of income assessment available to persons resident and ordinarily resident in the UK from employment carried on outside the UK,[9] which had been available under S.122 of the TA 1970. This made the Channel Islands less attractive as a centre for such funds.

b) The 1975 UK Finance Act and its 'domicile' provisions in relation to the Capital Transfer Tax (already discussed) attacked some of the UK private sector motivations behind Guersney 'frictioneering' activities.

c) The fundamental attractiveness of fiscal and political stability compared with areas such as Bermuda and the Bahamas where some uncertainty about stability existed.

During this period, profits increased from £3,942,000 to £9,602,000 or 143.6 per cent or at a rate of 35.9 per cent per annum, money on deposits grew from £162m. to £552m. or 240.1 per cent, of which the relative importance of non-clearing banks rose from 82.1 per cent to 90.0 per cent; the number of registered companies rose from 2,421 to 3,955 (of which 1,165 were Corporation Tax Companies); and external income rose from £7,197,000 to £14,084,000, of which interest and other income rose from £6,030,000 to £10,409,000. Naturally, as a result of the wider business-mix of clientele, a greater range of money and capital market issues of offshore Finance Funds now became viable with a greater global orientation as Table XXXVII shows. Some six funds were created during this four-year period (compared with only eleven created over the previous decade or so) which included the first gilt funds, American funds and insurance-linked funds. One main incentive behind this was the increasing attractiveness of the US market. 'The dollar devaluations of 1971 and 1973 coupled with the downward

TABLE XXXVII: Guernsey offshore fund flotations 1972–75

Type of fund	*Year of issue*	*Name of fund*	*Value as at 1 October 1980*
Gilt funds	1972	Anchor Gilt Edged Fund Ltd.	£25.8m.
		Unicorn Guernsey Income Fund	£11.2m.
American fund	1973	Old Court American Fund	$ 6.5m.
UK	1972	TSB Guernsey Unit Trust	£ 4.3m.
equities	1973	Old Court Smaller Companies Fund	£20.9m.
Insurance-linked funds	1974	Cornhill International Managed Fund	n.a.

Source: derived from Trevor, Matthews and Carey, *Channel Island Fund Review,* October 1980.

stock market trend in the period 1972–74 have made US investments more attractive to foreign business firms.'[10] This trend was intensified by the removal of the American Interest Equalization Tax and the exemption to the 30 per cent US withholding tax for any new borrowings on the Eurodollar market by US multinational subsidies. The 1974 UK Finance Act imposed limitations on the outflow of capital to encourage investors abroad to use local or currency markets and required direct investment in the EEC and OSA to be financed mainly by such currency borrowing.

(ii) Controlled consolidation 1976–78. Although some twelve bank deregistrations took place in the period 1972–76, they were offset by new entrants for the most part. Although some of these deregistrations occurred as a result of bank mergers off the island, one or two did take place in relation to the fringe banking crisis of 1973–74 and one bank, Barnet Christie (Finance) Ltd., was an actual local failure, for which no local 'life-boat' operation was mounted. The attitude of the Authorities, therefore, was to restrict entry not only in line with the 1974 Report discussed above, but also from the prudential point of view. No new banks were actually admitted in 1976 or 1978. With a view to the consolidation of Guernsey as a sound and efficient international finance centre, the Advisory and Finance Committee's attitude was to encourage international banks of standing, but only where it could be clearly demonstrated that their proposed activities would be of significant benefit to the island. One reason for this, as was made explicit, was an increasing awareness of the island's physical growth limits and density of population, and a need to contain the expansion of the financial sector within these limits. The 1976 Report of the States of Guernsey Advisory and Finance Committee envisaged the following development profile: 'it is anticipated that within the foreseeable future the major growth in the banking sector will come from those companies already established here'. The objectives were strength based on financial diversity by the attraction of business from as many different sources and geographic areas as was prudent, and to maintain the highest standards of expertise and service at a competitive price combined with the capability to respond quickly and effectively to changing conditions. Although such a policy

TABLE XXXVIII: Guernsey offshore fund flotations 1976–78

Type of fund	*Year of issue*	*Name of fund*	*Value as at 1 October 1980*
Gilts	1978	King and Shaxson on Guernsey Gilt Fund Ltd.	£1.1m.
Bonds	1976	Hambro International Bond Fund	$5.3m.
	1978	Kleinwort Benson International Bond Fund Ltd.	$5.8m.
Commodity	1976	Old Court Commodity Trust	£27.7m.
	1977	Old Court Dollar Commodity Trust	$24.4m.
American	1977	Kleinwort Benson US Growth Fund Ltd.	$20.7m.
	1978	GT Dollar (Sterling) Fund	£2.8m.
Far East	1976	Kleinwort Benson Far East Fund Ltd.	$13.8m.
	1977	Berry Pacific (Sterling) Fund	£14.9m.
International	1977	Hambro International Equities Fund	$1.6m.
	1977	Hambro International Savings Fund	$1.7m.

Source: derived from Trevor, Matthews and Carey, *Channel Islands Financial Review*, October 1980.

would superficially appear restrictive in intent, it was nevertheless the case that the Commercial Relations Office tried to play a very positive role by an informal process whereby they sought in a participative way to assist the establishment of new applicants that satisfied the above ideal objectives.

During the period 1976 to 1978 there were eleven new offshore issues made in Guernsey as Table XXXVIII shows, increasing the total of Guernsey offshore funds to twenty-eight.

In general there were five main features of Guernsey's development over the period 1972–78:

1. As a direct result of EC.18, an important structural change took place in the range of financial services, namely, the growth of an insurance industry based on 'captive' insurance companies. Briefly, a 'captive' is a subsidiary insurance company created and owned by a non-insurance organization for the purpose of insuring the risks of its parent. Where its underwriting is restricted solely to the business of its parent it is usually termed a 'pure' captive, but when in addition to that primary function it underwrites risks for outsiders, it is described as a 'broad' captive. The rescheduled Sterling Area of 1972 precluded UK companies from establishing captives in Bermuda, the world centre for such companies, and other distant offshore centres. As it was and is not possible to incorporate an insurance company in Jersey under Jersey law, Guernsey became the offshore Scheduled Territory centre for this activity. Tax exemption was offered to such companies on the insurance underwriting side of their operations if they did not seek corporation tax status, so that income tax was only payable on their funds. Precise offshore requirements of such companies additional to the general ones already discussed included:[11] (i) The avoidance of administratively onerous protection laws. In the case of Guernsey, the only present regulation is in respect of the aforementioned Protection of Depositors, Companies and

Prevention of Fraud (Bailiwick of Guernsey Law, 1969, Part III, where the use of the word 'insurance' requires permission if it occurs in the business name, in which case capitalization of £100,000 is required. Under Protocol No. 3 of the United Kingdom Treaty of Accession to the EEC, it is anticipated that Guernsey-based companies should accept the full burden of any effects of insurance law harmonization at some future date. The States took enabling powers to control the insurance industry under the Protection of Depositors, Companies and Prevention of Fraud (Amendment) (Bailiwick of Guernsey) Law III 1977, and will no longer permit any insurance company to be incorporated with corporative tax status, i.e. where management and control would be situated outside the jurisdiction of the Island Authorities. Supervision of insurance companies will be formulated under the provisions of a new Ordinance which was envisaged in 1979 to come into force in 1980, but had not yet materialized. Despite its exchange control powers, the Bank of England recognized the balance of payments value of this activity and, although insisting that foreign-owned captives had to have their capital in sterling, did permit them to lend back monies to their parent organizations, and to retain premiums in the currencies in which claims would be paid so guarding against currency risks that might otherwise have been incurred. (ii) The availability of expertise. A full range of services in terms of insurance broking, underwriting, risk management institutions and Chartered and Certified Accountants was available in Guernsey especially from 1977. (iii) Access to reinsurance. The proximity to the major reinsurance market of London and its technical consultants was important. The number of these companies grew from about fifty in 1976 to over a hundred in 1979. Of this total, some 50 per cent were UK quoted companies. In addition several overseas groups from Canada, the US and Europe were represented as well as companies engaged in the provision of assurance and employee benefits for overseas residents. There was a tendency to develop 'broad' captives,[12] the acceptance of third-party business being a useful way of pooling limited local insurance expertise as well as of extending the financial bases of parent companies.

2. A continuous increase in new companies of international parenthood. The 1978 States Advisory Report, S.38, mentions that one-third of new companies formed were by non-residents of the Scheduled Territories.
3. Consolidation of existing institutions and a commitment to Guernsey offshore finance by investment in purpose-built new premises and larger office accommodation. Many institutions began to diversify into local mortgage business for which there was a demand, given that the 1962 UK Building Societies Act did not apply to the islands under S.133(5) and there was no institutional building society base.[13]
4. The development of Guernsey as an international funds management centre.
5. Financial diversification into the general business areas of overseas pensions funds, cash management and currency dispersal salary schemes for expatriates.

CONCLUSIONS

1. Guernsey's pattern of economic evolution as an offshore centre exhibits a three-stage process: (*a*) a tax haven stage 1960–66; (*b*) a sterling finance haven stage 1967–71; (*c*) an international offshore stage, sub-divided into: (i) a period of take-off, 1972–75, and (ii) a period of controlled consolidation, 1976–78.
2. A crucial factor bringing about the transformation from stage (*a*) to stage (*b*) was the presence of merchant banks with their world-wide contacts and 'authorized' status under the Exchange Control Act of 1947. The subsequent transformation from stage (*b*) to stage (*c*) required the presence of non-UK international banks, many of which came during the period of the Jersey moratorium on new entry following the rescheduling of the Sterling Area. Both the above transformations could not have been accomplished without a banking 'invasion' of external technical expertise.
3. Given the presence of these external institutions, a more diversified financial base was created by the growth of (i) 'captive' insurance, the growth of which in Guernsey was aided by restrictive Jersey insurance laws that had not been modernized; and (ii) international fund management with a global investment coverage.
4. The above structural changes took place under the aegis of mainland UK onshore control and with regard for the standards of financial respectability applied by the City of London.

REFERENCES

1. *Ordre en Conseil,* No.1, 1920: Ratifiant un Projet de Loi Intitulé Loi Ayant Rapport à La Taxe sur Le Revenue, 10 January 1920.
2. *Ordre en Conseil,* No.1 1936: Ratifiant un Projet de Loi Intitulé Loi Instituant une Taxe dite 'Corporation Tax', 3 January 1936.
3. *Billet d'État,* 6 May 1949, pp. 431–2.
4. Veale, F.W., 'Open Door to Expansion of Finance Industry', *Guernsey Evening Press and Star,* 14 October 1975.
5. For full text see Division F4.S Guernsey: 24th June 1952: S.I.1952/1215, *Simon's Taxes,* Vol.F.—Double Taxation Relief and Agreements, 3rd edn., 1976, pp.1387–91.
6. Reported in the *Guernsey Evening Press and Star,* 27 March 1980, p.1.
7. '1972 Economic Development Plan', *Billet d'État,* XI, 1972, S.75.
8. States of Guernsey Advisory and Finance Committee, *Economic Report for 1976, Billet d'État,* VII, 1977, S.31.
9. Sumption, A., *Taxation of Overseas Income and Gains,* 3rd edn., London, Butterworths, 1979, p.80.
10. Lees, F.A., *Foreign Banking and Investment in the US,* London, Macmillan, 1976, p.77.
11. See Sennet, W.E., *Papers in Risk Management No.5—Captive Insurance Companies,* Keith Shipton Developments Ltd., 1976, *passim.*
12. States of Guernsey Advisory and Finance Committee, *Economic Report for 1979,* S.39, *Billet d'État,* V, 1980, p.216.
13. See Mills, J., *Building Society Law,* London, Steven and Son, 1976, p.10.

CHAPTER V
The Isle of Man and the Problem of Offshore Take-off 1961–78

The Isle of Man has been officially described as 'a small independent land at the centre of the British Isles . . . [it] lies in the middle of the Irish Sea with England to its east, Ireland to its west, Scotland to the north and Wales to the south-east. It is shaped a little like a fish with its open mouth at the northern end and its tail tapering gradually to the south'.[1] However, as a 'fish with its mouth open' it has not always been free to so position itself to benefit from any scraps of financial business that may escape from the UK or any other onshore mainland. These and subsequent developments had to be striven for actively by Tynwald whose general objective, as stated in the Evidence Submitted by Tynwald to the Royal Commission on the Constitution was:

> to promote and continue the evolution of the constitutional relationship between the Isle of Man and the United Kingdom towards 'more complete self-government', in accordance with the declared and accepted policy of the United Kingdom for the self-determination of the peoples of dependent territories. This objective thus includes not only the right and the principle of self-determination, but also, in application of them, assured autonomy in respect of the Island's internal affairs.[2]

The Stonham Report while asserting that:

> The government and legislature of the Isle of Man are autonomous in respect of matters which do not transcend the frontiers of the Isle of Man (which includes the land mass, territorial waters, ground beneath territorial waters and airspace above the land mass and territorial waters,[3]

did not properly resolve what constituted 'domestic affairs' and which matters 'transcend the frontiers of the Island': clearly some aspects of tax haven operation could be asserted as belonging to the latter category.

Earlier chapters have already established how the Isle of Man's insular autonomy has been subject to a greater degree of supervision with regard to financial control and matters of taxation as compared with the Channel Islands and that its relative independence in these areas is of very recent origin. Prior to 1961, it was essentially the case that the Lieutenant-Governor appointed by the Crown acted as Chancellor of the Exchequer. Members of the island legislature could not bring forward money resolutions without his consent. Acts of 1866 and 1880 earmarked the use of domestic revenues and controlled the borrowing powers of Tynwald. The island legislature was not in a position to exert and develop a coherent industrial/financial policy in relation to autonomously set domestic objectives. The possibilities of indigenous direction of financial affairs begin essentially with the passing of two Acts in the early 1960s, as a result of which (*a*) in 1961 the Finance Board was formed to which executive power over financial matters was gradually transferred, a process largely completed in 1976, and (*b*) since the 1962 Income Tax Act, as confirmed by the 1970 consolidation Act S.104 'income tax . . . shall form part of the general revenue of the Isle of Man'.

Despite the above with respect to the exercise and gaining of effective administrative control of the instrumental means necessary for the insular conduct of independent economic policy, the traditions of low taxation had been established, as with the Channel Islands in the early part of this century.

Prior to 1918, there had been a flour subsidy to keep the price of bread low. This had been financed by the Isle of Man Accumulated Fund in accordance with the provisions of the 1866 Act. However, the Governor of the day and the UK government in 1918 insisted that henceforth the £25,000 required for the continuance of this arrangement must come from direct taxation. The House of Keys accordingly agreed to pass an Income Tax Bill for this purpose but insisted that any surplus while the subsidy was payable, and the whole of the tax proceeds when the subsidy ceased, should be under the sole control of Tynwald. HMG found this proposed action unacceptable and intimated:

> While His Majesty's Government are not able to accede to the demand of the Keys that expenditure from monies raised by direct expenditure from monies raised by direct taxation in the Island shall not be subject to the final approval of His Majesty's Government, they are willing in order to avoid raising the constitutional point in the present instance, that a provision should be inserted in the Income Tax Bill to the effect that the proceeds of the Tax shall be applied exclusively for the purpose of the Flour Subsidy, so long as the subsidy continues, and thereafter to such purposes as may be determined by legislation.[4]

The Bill was therefore amended and received the Royal Assent on 13 August 1918. Two new obligations were placed on the island's administration. Firstly, although the Flour Subsidy was terminated as from 31 March 1921, a provision contained in Section 5 of the Old Age Pensions and National Health Insurance Act, 1920 required that, after the Flour Subsidy had been provided for, the cost of the defrayment of the new provisions should be borne as to two-thirds by the Income Tax Fund and as to one-third by the Customs Revenue. Secondly, the 1922 War Contribution and Income Tax Appropriation Act empowered Tynwald to apply any surplus funds towards payment of an annual sum of £250,000 as a contribution from the Island to the Imperial Government towards the War Debt. Furthermore, not only were taxes higher than those applied in the Channel Islands but, unlike the Channel Islands, a graduated four grade income tax was imposed, with income tax commencing at 1s. 6d. on incomes not exceeding £500, rising to 2s. 7½d. on all incomes exceeding £1,500. By 1939 some eleven rates had also been introduced, with 9d. in the £ for incomes under £500 and a top rates of 2s. 1d. for incomes over £5,000. In 1939 a surtax was introduced on all incomes over £2,000 to provide the means for increasing the Island's contribution to the national defence of the UK. Amending Acts over the years led to consolidations in 1946 and in 1970, but the establishment of a low tax structure, competitive with that of the Channel Islands, took place only slowly over the period

1961–80. With effect from 6 April 1961 personal surtax was abolished, and the standard rate of income tax reduced from 22.50 per cent (4s. 6d. in the £) to 21.25 per cent (4s. 3d. in the £) as the top rate of tax, at which it remained surprisingly unchanged until 1978/79 when it was further reduced to 21 per cent and then 20.5 per cent in the financial year 1979/80.

The isle has only one double taxation treaty, namely with the UK, made on 29 July 1955. Under this treaty, certain types of income are exempt from tax in the other country: shipping and air transport profits, certain trading profits and remuneration of temporary visitors for personal and professional services. Dividends and debenture interest payable by companies are not covered and credit for double taxation must be claimed under unilateral relief provided by both countries.

In terms of direct taxation other than value added tax, a zero tax structure nevertheless obtained in relation to surtax, death or estate duties, gift or capital transfer taxes, wealth or capital levies, and capital gain tax (with the exception of the Land Speculation Tax of 20.5 per cent introduced in May 1975 on short-term capital profits arising from certain land transactions on the island).

The move towards low taxation had been pursued in order to revive the dwindling fortunes of the island's economy that had become apparent in the 1950s. Initially tourism was the first activity to suffer a decline. Following a post-1945 boom of more than 600,000 visitors per year in 1947–9, the numbers fell and stabilized at around 475,000. Rising living standards in Britain, improvements in transport abroad, and the high cost of transport to the island relative to mainland home holidays and holidays abroad, placed the island in a disadvantageous position, its attractiveness not being furthered by indirect taxes uniform with the mainland under the Common Purse Agreement. Moreover, while the island is larger than any of the Channel Islands, its climate tends to be not as moderate and sea mists or low cloud on its hills are far from unusual and winds can be severe.

During the 1950s there was an actual decline in the population, from 55,253 in 1951 to 48,133 in 1961. The government were in considerable difficulties as the *Second Bi-Annual Report from the Industrial Advisory Council to Tynwald* (1963) makes clear. The main sources of these difficulties were:

1. Scarcity of skilled labour combined with housing shortages.

> There is no surplus of skilled male workers and most new industries will require to bring with them a high proportion of key personnel. It is unlikely that such men will be persuaded to assume residence on the Island unless sufficient housing of a suitable standard is available for rental and unfortunately there is an acute shortage of such housing on the Island at the present time.

These conditions were continously referred to in subsequent Industrial Advisory Council Reports, e.g. the Nineteenth Report for 1970 announced that:

> Expansion of manufacturing industry in general is still severely restricted by the scarcity of labour and of housing in which imported labour could be accommodated.

> It is believed that a number of firms that are already established here have abandoned or at least modified their plans for expansion and have decided to sub-contract certain processes to United Kingdom firms. It is a fact that certain Island firms are operating at or below break-even level because they cannot get sufficient labour, and it is also a fact that one firm has recently decided to close down, giving labour scarcity as one of its reasons for so doing.

2. High cost disadvantages of the Isle of Man; as the Second Report of 1963 commented:

> From the outset it was appreciated that the Isle of Man could not equal the generous financial incentives offered elsewhere but this disadvantage was, to some extent, offset by the more attractive Manx tax structure. However, as an increasing number of development areas compete for his attention, an industrialist considering moving or expanding is now inclined to be more selective and to pay less regard to the tax advantages and more attention to apparent disadvantages. In the Isle of Man he is, to a certain extent, isolated from his market, while freight charges on raw materials and on the finished products increase his costs. These are increased, also, by the generally higher charges for services, particularly light and power. Therefore, it is not surprising that many industrialists decide that they can afford to ignore any Manx tax advantages in favour of remaining in close contact with existing markets and having a supply of skilled labour, cheaper services and operating costs and generous financial assistance.

There was, therefore, an urgent need to stem the outward drift of population, to maintain a viable tourist industry, and to broaden the base of the Island's economy by industrial diversification. This has had to take place within the context of the process of wresting of constitutional economic powers from the Governor and the mainland (already outlined in Chapter II) and the obligations that existed under the Common Purse arrangement. One further anachronism remained that became increasingly evident and surprisingly was not abolished until 1978: the Usury Act. Since 1648 the rates of interest permitted to be paid had been controlled by its *Usury Act* that had been inflexible both in boom and depression. Despite its abolition in England in 1854, this Act was not repealed on the Island until 1978, despite attempts to do so. As long ago as 10 February 1877 the leader columns of the *Isle of Man Times* declared that: 'I wonder that the Isle of Man is not made the laughing stock of the commercial and industrial world of Great Britain for retaining upon its statute book a law which defies and ignores the very elementary principles of political economy.' The problem resulting from this arrangement were well set out in a memorandum issued by W. Dawson, the Isle of Man Treasurer on 29 December 1976:

> If it is the wish of the majority of people in the Island to maintain a standard of living at least equal to that in the United Kingdom, then the Island's economy must expand in line with that of the United Kingdom . . .
>
> Within the Island, Government encourages investment, with the object

TABLE XXXIX: Comparison of interest rates: UK and the Isle of Man under the Usury Act

	London clearing banks base rate %	*UK 3 months deposits with Local Authorities* %	*Isle of Man Usury Act rate* %
1968	7	7¾	6
1969	8	9	8
1970	7	7¼	8
1971	4½	5	8
1972	7½	8¾	9
1973	13	17	10
1974	12	13¼	12½
1975	10½	11	12½

Source: 1975 *Economic Survey,* Table 26, p. 89.

of expanding and diversifying the economy. Yet, in times of high interest rates the Usury Act reduces the availability of finance for investment, because financial institutions in other parts of the sterling area can offer more attractive terms to lenders than can be obtained in the Island, and so funds flow away from the Island.

The financial institutions in the private sector are placed in an invidious position through the Usury Act. They are responsible for assisting in financing much of the investment in the Island, but when interest rates are high they are unable to charge the market rate on the advances they make. In fact, in terms of earnings on their funds, it would pay them to invest entirely on the London money market. Fortunately for the Island's economy the financial institutions have adopted a very responsible attitude in the present circumstances, and continue to provide finance for investment projects despite being unable to obtain a market return on advances. But loans for more risky projects, where a higher rate of interest would normally be charged to compensate for the higher risk, are unlikely to be made available. Yet the riskier projects are potentially those of greater benefit to the economy. The fact that the Usury Act fixes the lawful rate of interest for an advance on the most risky project at a level below that charged on 'blue chip' advances in the United Kingdom surely points to the absurdity of our present system.

The Usury Act is a blunt instrument of monetary policy. In so far as it succeeds in holding down interest rates in the Island it benefits the rich more than the poor; indeed, it is possible to borrow in the Island at rates depressed artificially by the Usury Act, and then re-lend the money in the United Kingdom at a considerable profit.

In practice the damaging side effects of employing the Usury Act to hold down interest rates in the Island have threatened to be so great that in recent years the maximum legal rate has been increased by Tynwald in line with market rates. The Act has also been sidestepped by financial institutions who have lent and borrowed at higher rates than the Usury Act maximum. Although these rates are not legally enforceable they have been accepted in good faith, and the wheels of commerce have continued to turn.[5]

Table XXXIX taken from the 1975 *Economic Survey*[6] suggests that this was an intermittent problem and one that could prove awkard in particular years, as was the case in 1968–69 and 1973–74. Given these circumstances, how did the financial sector develop and rise in terms of its insular importance? While a statistical record of the development of finance is not possible because computation of Manx accounts for industrial sectors only began with respect to the financial year 1969 and regular reporting of bank deposits only dates from 1973, it is possible to discern from the statistics available, shown in Table XL, that three phases of development manifested themselves in the period prior to 1978.

TABLE XL: Estimated Manx National Income for the years 1969, 1971, 1972, 1974, 1975, and 1978 and the relative importance of banking

Industrial sectors	*1969*	*1971*	*1972*	*1974*	*1975*	*1978*
1. Agriculture, forestry, fishing	1,219	1,697	3,119	1,483	1,231	4,855
2. Manufacturing, food, drink	765	1,025	1,106	1,670	2,051	3,171
Engineering etc.	6,195	5,631	5,844	9,707	9,359	16,009
3. Construction	2,522	3,892	6,107	6,383	7,989	11,932
4. Gas, electricity, water	1,022	1,433	1,898	1,885	2,153	3,552
5. Transport & communications	3,071	3,664	3,965	6,232	8,802	11,505
6. Wholesale distribution	1,505	1,616	2,440	2,771	5,008	5,472
7. Retail distribution	2,896	3,493	4,883	6,866	8,278	12,046
8. Insurance, banking, finance & business services	3,770	6,280	8,306	18,246	22,997	37,138
9. Professional & scientific services	2,463	3,208	3,904	6,595	8,223	15,251
10. Tourist accommodation	1,792	1,268	1,844	2,468	3,124	3,355
11. Other catering & entertainment	913	935	1,443	2,296	3,151	3,285
12. Miscellaneous services	1,315	1,643	1,965	2,867	3,356	6,256
13. Public administration	1,003	1,352	1,376	2,242	4,187	6,418
Total earned from Manx sources	30,451	37,137	48,200	71,711	89,909	140,245
Ownership of dwellings	2,720	3,293	3,839	4,756	5,232	6,963
(less adjustments)	(1,170)	(1,976)	(2,538)	(7,425)	(7,445)	(12,100)
Income from Manx sources	32,001	38,454	49,501	69,042	87,696	135,108
Net income from abroad	2,574	3,237	3,651	4,790	7,315	9,321
14. Gross National Income	34,575	41,691	53,152	73,832	95,011	144,429
% share of (8) in MNI	10.9%	15.9%	15.6%	24.7%	24.2%	25.7%
% growth of (8) in period	66.6%		119.7%		61.5%	
Av. per annum		33.3%		59.9%		20.5%
% growth of (14–8) in period	15.0%		23.9%		49.0%	
Av. per annum		7.5%		12.0%		16.3%

Source: Isle of Man Digest of Economic and Social Statistics, 1980, pp. 15–16.

1) *The Period Prior to 1972.* A period of expansion of domestic banking. In the years 1969–71 the percentage share of this sector of Manx national income (MNI) rose from 10.0 per cent to 15.9 per cent, there being a 66.6 per cent growth overall or 33.3 per cent per annum. This compares with only a 15 per cent overall growth in MNI (excluding finance) and a per annum growth of 7.5 per cent. The number of financial institutions rose to ten from six at the beginning of the 1960s.
2) *The Period 1972–74.* A period of rapid expansion and offshore growth. In these years, the percentage share of the finance sector rose from 15.6 per cent to 24.7 per cent: in absolute figures there was an increase of 119.7 per cent over the period as a whole, or 59.9 per cent per annum. MNI (excluding finance) rose at a faster rate than previously—23 per cent overall or 11.5 per cent per annum. The number of financial institutions increased from ten to nineteen.
3) *The Period 1975–78.* A period of stable growth but without much diversification of financial activity. In this period, the sectoral share only increased slightly from 24.2 per cent to 25.7 per cent of MNI: its overall period growth was 61.5 per cent or 20.5 per cent per annum. MNI however grew by 49 per cent or 16.3 per cent per annum. The relative growth momentum had severely slowed down, despite the growth of financial institutions from nineteen to thirty.

Each of the abovementioned development phases will now be individually discussed.

(1) THE PERIOD PRIOR TO 1972

Given the imprecisions in the constitutional relationship between the Isle and the UK mainland, its slightly higher tax structure, the Usury Act, industrial decline, and its slightly further location from the City of London not compensated for by its Irish onshore hinterland, the Isle of Man did not prove attractive to those British merchant banks which started to move offshore in the 1960s and to establish their bases in Jersey and Guernsey. Its limited local investment opportunities and general air of de-industrialization, gaps in the provision of air services for the business traveller, slow development of telephone facilities for links with international exchanges, and lack of first class hotel facilities also weighed against its suitability as a centre for prime offshore activities. In the judgment of the P.A. 1975 *Economic Survey,* in 1969 the entire activities of the domestic finance sector serviced Manx needs only.[7] Nevertheless it was a more buoyant Manx economy that was emerging at the end of the 1960s compared with the situation at the end of the previous decade. For one thing the population fall of the 1950s had been dramatically turned around. Whereas the population fell from 55,000 to 48,000 in the period 1951 to 1961, a slight increase to 49,300 in 1966 was followed by a rapid increase to 53,200 by 1971. This brought in its wake a demand for banking and financial activities which were naturally increasing anyway with the general spread of the banking habit and higher standards of living. Thus there was a need for the provision of extra banking capacity for an expanding resident population and a greater range of banking services. In the period 1958 to 1971 nearly 14,000 immigrants came to the island, most of whom came in the latter part of the period. Interestingly, the proportion of immigrants over the age of 60 fell slightly and those under 45 rose. The number of financial institutions rose from six to ten by the end of 1971, but in general there was nothing to amount to a merchant bank invasion of a scale comparable to that of the two Channel Islands already discussed. The vast majority of the banks were clearing banks and there was only a small merchant bank presence. The preconditions for international take-off did not occur as in the Channel Islands, where Hambros, Rothschilds and Kleinwort Benson had been established since the mid-1960s. The main clearing banks had previously been established in the island in addition to the Isle of Man Bank (founded in 1865 and taken over by the National Westminster Bank in 1969), Barclays Bank Ltd., and what is now the National Westminster Bank in 1890; the Midland Bank in 1900; the Trustee Savings Bank North West in 1920; Lloyds Bank Ltd. in 1932. To these six institutions were added the following four prior to 1972 making the total representation ten: 1969—the International Finance and Trust Corporation Ltd., The Savings and Investment Bank Ltd., and Singer and Friedlander (Isle of Man) Ltd.; 1970—Williams and Glyn's Bank (IOM) Ltd. As has already been stated, regular reporting of bank deposits did not occur until 1973, but IOM Treasury estimates them to have been at about £20m. in 1965[8] and to have risen to £39m. by mid-1973.

In the area of new company formation, considerable increases occurred as shown in Table XLI. Thus, from 1961 to 1971 the number of new companies on the register rose from 43 to 636, an increase of nearly fifteen-fold: no disaggregated statistics are available of such companies, but prior to 1974 when the UK repealed its Estate Duty, private investment companies were often resorted to by people domiciled on the Isle or elsewhere outside the UK to avoid liability to UK Estate Duty in respect of property situated within the UK by investing ownership therein and converting such possessions into Manx estate. This and

TABLE XLI: Number of new companies registered in the Isle of Man 1960–71

Year	*Number of companies*
1960	40
1961	43
1962	76
1963	102
1964	138
1965	106
1966	199
1967	186
1968	288
1969	401
1970	343
1971	636

Source: IOM Digest of Economic and Social Statistics, 1980, p. 29.

other motives for company formation were encouraged by the fact that prior to 1974 companies incorporated on the Isle, but residing elsewhere and deriving their income from sources outside, were untaxed. Some beginnings of insular trust activity was evident but only on a modest scale. Private trust formation is regulated in accordance with the Isle of Man Trustee Act, 1961, which is closely modelled on English law, the principal exception being that a Manx Trust is free to accumulate income. Trust deeds do not require to be publicly filed, except when the trust purchases land. There are no Manx duties or taxes upon their formation. Manx companies are also used for the provision of consultancy services externally from an individual's country of residence. During the period up to 1971 the first unit/investment trusts were formed, these being as follows:

July 1965, Barclay's Unicorn Australian External Trust;
March 1966, Barclay's Unicorn Manx Mutual Fund;
November 1977, Barclay's Unicorn Australian Minerals Trust;
April 1969, Stellar Growth Unit Trust (became Gartmore International Growth Trust in 1977);
November 1971, First Viking Commodity Trust.

The initial spate of activity brought in its wake the Prevention of Fraud (Investments) Act 1968 based on the UK Prevention of Fraud (Investments) Act 1958, vesting powers of authorization, investigation and rights to information in the Governor. Under this legislation the Trustee must have an issued capital of not less than £500,000, of which at least half must be paid up at all times; or it can be the subsidiary of a larger company, provided that the parent owns at least 80 per cent of the share capital in the subsidiary. The relative freedom of Manx unit trusts to invest in assets other than quoted securities encouraged the formation of commodity funds.

(2) THE PERIOD 1972–74

As the statistics given in Table XL have already indicated, this was a period of very rapid growth. Throughout these years there was a large inflow of immigrant population: in the census period 1971 to 1976, a further 10,563 immigrants came to the island, so that by the mid 1970s less than half the then resident population had been born locally. In 1972, a Select Committee of Tynwald was established to investigate the effects of this influx. Despite the fact that on 16 May 1973 Tynwald resolved to create a register of new residents and proposed that a licence system be introduced for the purchase or leasing of property, the resultant Registration of Residents Bill 1975 failed to be approved. Nevertheless the increased population and the rescheduling of the Sterling Area in June 1972 did encourage a significant expansion in the number of registered financial institutions in island terms, which was not as large as might have been expected given the freezing of new registrations in Jersey already referred to. The annual pattern of new arrivals is given in Table XLII, the total of new institutions rising by nine to an aggregate of nineteen. A close look at these institutions reveals that the 1972 intake was of UK origin only, the majority of which consisted of subsidiary com-

TABLE XLII: New bank registrations in the Isle of Man 1972–74

Year	*Name of institution*
1972	Barclays Finance Company (IOM) Ltd.
	Barclaytrust Isle of Man Ltd.
	Midland Bank Trust Corporation (IOM) Ltd.
	Rea Brothers (IOM) Ltd.
	Standard Chartered Bank (IOM) Ltd.
1973	Anglo Manx Bank Ltd.
	Commercial Bank of Wales (IOM) Ltd.
	Peel City Bank Ltd.
1974	Mannin Trust Bank Ltd.

Source: Commercial Relations Office, Isle of Man.

TABLE XLIII: Isle of Man offshore fund launchings 1972–74

Centric table	*Year*	*Fund*
1.	1972	Barclays Unicorn Greater Pacific
2.		Vanin International Securities
3.	1973	Tyndall Equity Fund International
4.		Tyndall Fixed Interest Fund International
5.		Tyndall Managed Fund International
6.		Barclays Unicorn Isle of Man Trust
7.	1974	Lamont International Income Trust*
8.		British Convertible Trust
9.		Capital Convertible Warrant Trust
10.		Manx Exempt Trust

*Became Gartmore International Income Trust in 1977.

panies of the UK clearing banks: there were no American ones. In the other two years several were new local banks not having worldwide deposit branches. Clearly the adverse natural factors had diluted the offshore image of the island. Moreover, the new economic administration of the island had not yet concerned itself, as the Channel Islands had, with producing up-to-date banking and insurance legislation which banks of international reputation tend to feel is necessary in order that their offshore activities may seem legitimate and subject to responsible controls. Thus, despite the rapid growth outlined above, the Isle of Man had been outmanoeuvred by the Channel Islands and thereby deprived of an international banking presence that would have subsequently been instrumental in diversifying the local financial sector base. Reported bank deposits rose from £39m. in mid-1973 to £50m. in mid-1974. During this period ten new Isle of Man offshore funds were launched as shown in Table XLIII. With the exception of 3, 4 and 5, which were US dollar denominated, all funds were sterling denominated. Some, such as 6 and 7, were very specifically not available to UK residents, purchasers being required to declare that they were 'not resident or ordinarily resident in the UK for tax purposes and . . . not acquiring the units as the nominee(s) of any person(s) so resident', as each trust invests in UK securities and is intended to provide a channel for indirect foreign investment in the UK.

During this period the number of newly registered companies rose from 785 in 1972 to 1,607 and 677 in the years 1973 and 1974 respectively.

(3) THE PERIOD 1975–78

As previously stated, this was a period of stable growth, there being no significant change in the financial sector's share of Manx national income. This period begins with a series of Acts of Tynwald that seek to provide a legislative framework within which Island supervision, control and rights to information are set to give the finance sector legitimacy and certainty to surround its operation and activities. This framework is contained in three main areas of legislation.

(i) The Banking Act 1975 (Government Circular No. 86/75) and Associated Regulations (G.C. No. 87/90)

This provided for the annual licensing of banks at a fee of £500 (No. 87), inspection of their records and control of their activities (No. 86, 88), and financial advertising regulations requiring any firm offering financial and investment advice to be licensed annually at £250, excepting stockbrokers, authorized unit trusts, the Bank of England and provident societies (S.7 No. 86). These regulations give the Treasurer complete discretion with regard to the issue and revocation of licences and the imposition of any conditions attaching to a licence. There are two important modifications, however:

1. Under S.1 certain categories of bank are specifically exempted from inspection and investigation, these being:

   'a clearing bank, being a bank entitled to the privileges of the London Clearing House, and any branch or subsidiary thereof; members of the London Accepting Houses Committee and any branch or subsidiary of such member'.

2. S.5 of No. 86 provides essentially for confidentiality of the affairs of bank customers:

   '(8) Nothing . . . shall apply in respect of the affairs of any particular customer of a bank except and in so far as it may be necessary for the purpose of an inspection and investigation (by the Treasurer] . . .
   (9) Any person who communicates, or attempts to communicate, any information relating to the affairs of a particular customer of a bank obtained by him by virtue of an inspection and investigation made [by the Treasurer] except
   (*a*) in so far as it may be necessary for the discharge of his functions under this Act; or
   (*b*) with the consent of the said customer, shall be guilty of an offence.'

The Banking Act 1977 imposed restrictions on the use of the word 'bank'.

(ii) The Company Registration Tax Act 1974

As a result of the above Act and the Company Registration Tax Regulations made and put into operation as from 11 December 1974, henceforth all external Isle of Man companies that do not trade and are not controlled in the island but registered there, were made subject to a tax of £200 per annum and required to submit returns in a form approved by the Income Tax Assessor and any other company information the Assessor may require. The Finance Board is empowered by S.1(2) to prescribe any special arrangements they see as necessary. The number of new company registrations increased perceptively from 714 in 1975 to 1,024, 1,490 and 1,890 in 1976, 1977 and 1978: the latter figure was an almost threefold increase on the annual averages of the early 1970s. Clearly, the expertise and clientele brought in by the new institutional arrivals had furthered this development.

(iii) The Companies Act 1974 and Captive Insurance/Insurance Regulation 1976/1978

Clearly, the advances made by Guernsey in this field, capitalizing from the post-1972 Rescheduled Sterling Area situation was seen as a development option for the Isle of Man, and one from which the island Treasury would benefit. However, the initial framework laid down was rather muddled and ineffectual in that no such company had been set up by the end of 1978. The Companies Act 1974, was described as

> An act to amend the Companies Acts 1931–1968; to provide that a subsidiary company shall not own shares in its holding company; for the conduct of business by insurance companies; for the registration by a company of substantial interests in its own shares; for the investigation of a company's affairs; prohibiting a company acting as a director; and for various matters relating to the administration of companies.

This provided an up-to-date definitional and supervisory context within which company formation and operation was henceforth to be subject. As far as insurance is concerned, S.3 and S.22 introduced for the first time a measure of official control via the Finance Board. Under these powers the Board issued the Companies (Insurance Business) Regulations in 1977 (G.C. No. 148/77). Insurance companies are allowed if already authorized in the UK by the Department of Trade or would be lawful in the UK, or are so authorized by the Finance Board. An annual licence fee of £500 was introduced in 1977 to be paid by those companies indigenous to the Isle of Man. In exercise of the powers conferred on the Finance Board by S.3 and S.22 of the 1974 Companies Act, the Board also sought to license and control the hoped for expansion of captive insurance companies, unfortunately in a rather muddled way.

The first scheme of regulation was the Companies (Captive Insurance Business) Regulations of 1976 (G.C. No. 84/76). Under these regulations, S.3 required that application be made to the Treasurer 'who, on behalf of the Finance Board, will issue or refuse a licence, or impose conditions'. A fee of £5,000 was payable under S.4 upon the issue of any such licence and payable thereafter annually if the licence was renewed. These regulations were clearly not likely to be financially attractive and indeed proved so, such that the above regulations were revoked and replaced by the 1973 Companies (Captive Insurance Business) Regulations (G.C. 84/78). These specified an initial registration fee of £250, a once only charge with no annual renewal fee. Moreover, to attract captive in-

TABLE XLIV: Isle of Man bank arrivals and the value of total bank deposits 1975–78

Year	*Name of bank*	*Total IOM bank deposits (£m.)*
1975	Kleinwort Benson (IOM) Ltd.	
	Lombard Bank (IOM) Ltd.	
	Rossminster Acceptances (IOM) Ltd.	119
1976	Allied Irish Banks (IOM) Ltd.	
	Royal Trust Bank (IOM) Ltd.	230
1977	Bank of Credit and Commerce International SA	
	Celtic Bank Ltd.	
	Northern Ireland Industrial Bank (IOM) Ltd.	280
1978	Bank of Scotland Trust Co. (IOM) Ltd.	
	The English Association in the IOM	
	Kingsnorth Bank Ltd.	315

Source: Commercial Relations Office, Isle of Man.

surance business to the island, S.1 and 2 of the 1978 Income Tax Act excluded the underwriting profits or losses arising in respect of captive insurance from the computation of the company's total income for Manx income tax purposes. Profits arising from re-insurance contracts are not, however, so eligible for exemption. This considerable rethink on licences seems to indicate that the 1976 regulations were rather premature and unfortunate.

In the general areas of banking and offshore funds modest consolidation took place during this period. Eleven new banks were registered such that the total number of institutions rose from nineteen to thirty: the new arrivals being the ones shown in Table XLIV. It is noticeable that the new arrivals were mostly British or Irish, a few were purely local, but, with the exception of the Bank of Credit and Commerce International S.A., none were of extra-UK parentage: more particularly, it is noticeable that no international US bank had been attracted to the island. Bank deposits nevertheless rose dramatically from £50m. in 1974 to £315m. in 1978, a more than fivefold increase, despite the fact that the Usury Acts Repeal Act was not passed until 1978.

In the area of offshore funds, a further eleven were added to the previous total of fifteen, as indicated in Table XLV. Most of the above were intended exclusively for non-UK residents and documents concerning these funds are subject to the restriction that they 'must not be distributed in the UK, the Isle of Man or the Channel Islands otherwise than to persons whose business involves the acquisition and disposal, or the holding, of securities (whether as a principal or as an agent)'. The commodity trusts are designed as investment media for those who seek above average returns for part of their investment portfolio and are prepared to accept the risks normally associated with potentially high rewards. Usually one or more special limited dealing companies are set up, wholly owned by the trust to which monies are lent and invested but which provide a limit to any loss incurred. It would appear that no foreign-currency denominated issues were made.

TABLE XLV: Isle of Man offshore funds launched 1975–78

Year of Issue	*Fund*
1976	The Silver Trust
	Tyndall (IOM) Equity Fund
	Tyndall (IOM) Fixed Interest Fund
	Tyndall (IOM) Managed Fund
	Tyndall (IOM) Property Fund
	Tyndall Commodity Fund International
	King & Shaxson Isle of Man Gilt Trust
	Barclays Unicorn International Income
1977	Commodity and Natural Resource Holdings (Canrho)
	Bishopsgate Commodity Services Ltd.
1978	Wren Commodity Trust

CONCLUSIONS

1. Among the three British Isle centres for external financial activities, the Isle of Man was unique in that, at the beginning of the 1960s, important vestiges of imperial control remained which circumscribed or inhibited autonomous insular control of economic affairs.
2. Establishment of insular autonomy was a slow and drawn-out process, and, in terms of creating a friction structure conducive to offshore development, the Isle of Man lagged behind its other two Channel Island rivals. Moreover, its geographical situation, climatological regime and recent industrial past, were not ones that provided a good image for a systemic transformation from tax haven to offshore financial centre.
3. It seems clear that the more regimented guardian relationship exercised by the UK thwarted any early attempt at positive public sector frictioneering. As a result of the failure to establish freedom of control of economic affairs, the constraint provided by the Common Purse Agreement caused a delay that was crucial for the subsequent development of a global industrial infrastructure. UK merchant banks were not established in the island prior to 1972 as they were in the Channel Islands and this was crucial when the rescheduling of the Sterling Area occurred in 1972, for there was no nucleus to which international, and more particularly US, banks could be attracted.
4. Despite the above difficulties, an effective transfer of economic powers did take place, and a substantial presence of extra insular economic/financial activity was achieved by 1978, such that the financial sector represented some 25% of Manx National Income by the end of the period.
5. There appear to have been three main phases of development:
   (*a*) the pre-1972 period: a period of internal financial development;
   (*b*) the period 1972–74: a period of rapid institutional growth largely as a result of a UK banking invasion;
   (*c*) the period 1975–78: a period of stable growth with consolidation of financial activities but an absence of diversification of the sector's base.

6. The lack of structural change in period (*c*) is evident in the following:
   (*a*) the resident financial institutions were very largely of UK parentage or of indigenous origin, lacking the authority of extra-UK institutions of a world-wide reputation;
   (*b*) the small number of indigenous unit trusts characterized by a lack of significant foreign currency-denominated funds and high proportion of commodity (high risk) funds;
   (*c*) the banking institutions themselves had a much lower level of deposit support from all sources.
7. The failure to maintain an increasing growth trend resulted from:
   (*a*) the relative dynamism in the Channel Islands promoted by their second extra-UK financial invasion in the years after 1972;
   (*b*) failure of the Isle of Man authorities to react fast enough, and in the right manner, in terms of establishing friction structures conducive to financial development. This includes in particular the comparatively late institution of banking laws and regulations: the failure to abolish the Usury Laws until 1978; and, the slowness and muddled attitude adopted towards captive insurance in the period 1976 to 1978.
8. Consequently, despite the unrivalled availability of space for development within the island, actual development appears to have fallen a little short of a fully-fledged offshore centre status. Consolidated growth seems to have occurred more in the area of company formation.

REFERENCES

1. *The Isle of Man: A Small Independent Land at the Centre of the British Isles,* Isle of Man Bank Ltd., Douglas, Isle of Man, 1980 Edn., p.7.
2. Royal Commission on the Constitition 1969–1973, *Isle of Man—Joint evidence of the Home Office and Tynwald,* HMSO, p.22.
3. *Report of the Joint Working Party on the Constitutional Relationship between the Isle of Man and the United Kingdom* ('The Stonham Report'), 1969, p.3, para.4.
4. Sargeaunt, B.E., *An Outline of the Financial System of the Isle of Man,* Douglas, Isle of Man, 1925, p.8.
5. Dawson, W., *Usury,* memorandum from W. Dawson, Government Treasurer Isle of Man, dated 29 December 1976.
6. *Economic Survey of the Isle of Man,* P.A. International Management Consultants, London, 1975.
7. *Economic Survey,* op.cit., p.82.
8. Information supplied to the author by Mr P. Duncan, Commercial Relations Officer, Isle of Man.

The reader is also referred to the following two sources which provide useful compendia of legislative details and technical discussion:

Solly, H.W., *Anatomy of a Tax Haven Vol.1 The Isle of Man,* 2nd edn., 1980, *Vol.2 Manx Income Tax,* 1979, Douglas, IOM, Shearwater Press.

Kermode, D.G., *Devolution at Work: A Case Study of the Isle of Man,* Farnborough, Hants., Saxon House, 1979.

CHAPTER VI
The Drive to 'Independent' Industrial Maturity Since 1979

At one stroke on 23 October 1979, the myriad of orders and onshore UK instrumentally imposed distortions were swept away and the British Isle/UK mainland friction matrix radically altered and liberalized. This implied that *de facto* a much greater freedom of administrative action would henceforth be possible in respect of each of the insular authorities. This unilateral measure of financial decontrol thus created an entirely new set of circumstances in which:

i) Official Bank of England direct control and monitoring of financial activity under the 1947 Exchange Control Act was at an end;
ii) UK sterling funds were no longer restricted largely to the Sterling Area, such that UK and island residents had greater freedom to invest overseas.

The implication of (i) was that thereafter, unless the island authorities decided otherwise, there would be no external company status other than corporation tax status. Moreover, disclosure of information to the Bank of England, albeit formerly confidentially given, would no longer be a factor possibly inhibiting some potential overseas clients from seeking company registration in the islands. In respect of banking, some degree of UK influence nevertheless remained, for although the 1979 UK Banking Act did not extend to the islands, it had implications for many locally incorporated subsidiaries, given that the 'listing' procedures thereunder would govern their access to the London money markets via their UK-based parent organization or branch in accordance with the status given to that institution by the Bank of England under the Act.

There was an initial fear that the London money dealers would regard the isle banks as being outside the UK's monetary system and charge 'commercial' as opposed to the more favourable interbank rates of interest on any borrowings, thereby raising the cost of access to the London money market. However, an informal agreement was soon reached in relation to 'listed' banks as the *Guernsey Evening Press and Star* reported on 24 March 1980 in relation to the following statement made by Mr Bruce Riley, the Guernsey Commercial Relations Advisor:

> No local banks will be penalised by the introduction of the UK's Banking Act. The status quo will continue as far as monetary control purposes are concerned. This means that banks here will accept the same monetary controls . . . as in the UK and will be required to report as before to the Bank of England.

This was apparently a choice voluntarily made, for the Guernsey paper observed that:

> It is understood that without such a voluntary agreement the Channel Islands might have to face the possibility of establishing themselves as com-

> pletely independent territories financially with their own currency, backed by a central bank, and with local exchange controls, a situation which seems both unacceptable and impracticable.

Thus the banks on the islands continued to act within structures imposed by the necessities of UK monetary policy and its adopted system of financial control. However, currency switching and freedom to choose the composition of currency-denominated investments had now been established, as well as the right and freedom to hold foreign currency accounts.

Exchange decontrol could not have come at a more fortuitous time for, as has been revealed in former chapters, certainly both Channel Islands had already achieved international offshore status, and each isle, having been nurtured in infancy and adolescence under the aegis of Bank of England control, had obtained thereby an integrity resulting from a demonstrated record of achievement of a decade or more. The central question now was whether offshore financial disintermediation (credit flows by-passing the domestic UK banking system) via the Eurosterling market would pose a threat to and lead to a disintermediation of flows from the island financial centres. Would the islands, given the end to their privileged status within the rescheduled Sterling Area, actually be in a position to compete to retain their holding of sterling funds and to continue to obtain other overseas business? The period of 'guardianship' was now over. In the new circumstances the islands would henceforth be more exposed to global foreign competition from the other offshore centres. They would have to be able to maintain their world market shares in the event of out-frictioneering attempts being made by the latter as well as selective defensive defrictioning of international financial activities in onshore economies to extend thereby or create *de novo* their own onshore external centres.

Certainly in the cases of Jersey and Guernsey, a global industrial infrastructure had been established that was sufficiently diversified as between representation from and participation by the UK clearing banks, British merchant banks, non-UK international banks and international fund management. Would these infrastructures now be undermined?

Despite the greater freedoms implied by UK exchange decontrol and the possibilities of profit resulting therefrom, the new era was greeted with anxiety. The *Guernsey Evening Press and Star* of 5th July 1980 reported the following series of statements by Mr Riley:

> Banks could foresee the loss of much lucrative 'back-to-back' business . . . whereby (formerly) customers borrowed foreign currency against the security of sterling deposits to avoid paying the investment currency premium.
>
> Fund managers saw their sterling feeder funds, which provided a vehicle for residents of the sterling area to invest overseas, becoming obsolete.
>
> At least some of those involved in the management of captive insurance companies feared that many new UK owned captives would be set up in Bermuda and other no tax areas.

What path would the drive to industrial maturity now take in island centres? Indeed might industrial maturity be pre-empted? In the case of the Isle of Man, a

TABLE XLVI: New company registrations in Jersey 1978–81

Type of company registered	1978			1979			1980			1981		
	No. of companies		%	*No. of companies*		%	*No. of companies*		%	*No. of companies*		%
Trustee, finance & mutual fund companies		51	2.9		46	2.3		35	1.5		38	1.5
Private investment companies		654	37.1		656	32.5		801	35.0		734	29.7
Jersey residents	102		5.8	88		4.4	71		3.1	58		2.3
British Isle residents	168		9.5	202		10.0	209		9.3	149		6.0
Others	384		21.8	366		18.1	521		22.8	527		21.3
Trading companies		1,060	60.1		1,318	65.2		1,452	63.5		1,702	68.9
Jersey residents	301		17.1	310		15.3	283		12.4	302		12.2
British Isle residents	256		14.5	310		15.3	300		13.1	322		13.0
Others	503		28.5	698		34.6	869		38.0	1,078		43.6
Total new registrations		1,765			2,020			2,288			2,474	
Total no. companies at end year			12,513			13,813			15,210			16,643
No. corporation tax companies			3,600			4,215			4,760			5,670

Source: Commercial Relations Office, Jersey.

TABLE XLVII: Origin of owners of new companies registered in Jersey 1978–81

	1978		*1979*		*1980*		*1981*	
Ownership origin	*No. Cos.*	*% Tot.*	*No. Cos.*	*% Tot.*	*No. Cos.*	*% Tot.*	*No. Cos.*	*% Tot.*
Jersey residents	403	22.9	398	19.7	354	15.4	360	14.6
British Isle residents	424	24.0	512	25.3	509	22.2	531	21.5
Residents outside British Isles	887	50.3	1,064	52.7	1,390	60.8	1,605	64.9

much narrower base had been established. Would its failure to attract non-UK international banking participants in these new circumstances be a real barrier to further development? Tentative answers to these questions will now be indicated in respect of each British Isle centre based on the experience of the period 1979 to 1981 and the availability of statistics. These individual records will be followed by comparative summaries of the development achievements of the three centres and an outline of recent UK attitudes with respect to haven activities.

Thus total new registrations increased by 40.2 per cent to 2,474 in 1981 compared with 1978, and net total end year registrations increased by 33 per cent from 12,513 to 16,643 in the same period. What has been notable has been the rapid increase in overseas trading companies and to a lesser extent private investment companies external to the UK, the former increasing by 114.3 per cent from 503 to 1078, the latter by 37.2 per cent from 384 to 527. It has been estimated that about half of the companies incorporated for non-residents were for beneficial owners in European countries, and one-third for Africa and the Middle East. If the private investment and trading companies statistics are added together as in Table XLVII, it is evident that extra-UK company incorporations grew from 50.3 per cent of the total to 64.9 per cent, while those for Jersey residents fell both absolutely and relatively, and those for UK residents increased slightly absolutely but decreased relatively. In terms of international banking, the following new registrations were allowed:

1979 Bank Cantrade Switzerland CI Ltd.
Chase Manhattan Bank NA
Royal Trust Bank (Jersey) Ltd.
1980 Bankers Trust Company
Standard Chartered Bank Ltd.
1981 Barclays Bank Finance Company Jersey Ltd.
Allied Irish Bank
Berliner Handels und Frankfurter Bank

One deregistration occurred in 1980, so that the net total of registered banking institutions rose from forty-two in 1978 to forty-nine in 1981. During the period 1978–81 bank deposits rose from £3,500m. in 1978 to £5,500m., £7,700m., and £10,000m. in 1979, 1980 and 1981 respectively, a rise of 286 per cent. The extension of trust business and international loan business were crucial factors here, the main medium for the latter being the international loan syndication market and Euro-currency lending. Whereas in 1970, deposits had been £400m. of which 80 per cent was in sterling, by June 1980, the deposit figure of £7.7 billion

TABLE XLVIII: Money on deposit in Jersey as disclosed in annual published accounts for 1980 by locally incorporated banking institutions

Name of banking institution	*Reporting date in 1980*	*Money on deposit (£m.)*	*Reported deposits from ass. cos. (£m.)*
Midland Bank Trust Corp. (J.) Ltd.	31 Oct.	339.1	
Nat. West. Bank Finance (CI) Ltd.	30 Sept.	316.0	
Citibank (CI) Ltd.	29 Feb.	260.7	209.6
Bank of Nova Scotia (CI) Ltd.	31 Oct.	223.3	207.1
Barclays Bank Finance Co. (J.) Ltd.	31 Dec.	218.6	
LBI Finance (J.) Ltd.	31 Mar.	165.8	0.2
Williams & Glyn's Bank (J.) Ltd.	31 Mar.	147.5	4.4
Grinlays Bank (J.) Ltd.	31 Dec.	144.0	26.0
Trustee Savings Bank C.I.	20 Nov.	121.3	
Bank Cantrade A.G. Zurich	31 Dec.	120.7	110.0
Morgan Grenfell (J.) Ltd.	31 Dec.	119.7	3.1
Kleinwort Benson (CI) Ltd.	31 Dec.	112.0	1.8
Standard Chartered Bank (CI) Ltd.	31 Dec.	108.2	0.8
Royal Trust Bank (J.) Ltd. & The Royal Trust Company of Canada (CI) Ltd.	30 Nov.	87.1	17.1
Chase Bank (CI) Ltd.	30 Sept.	86.9	8.9
Hill Samuel and Company (J.) Ltd.	31 Mar.	73.2	0.7
Lazard Brothers & Company (J.) Ltd.	31 Dec.	65.2	2.2
Lombard Banking (J.) Ltd.	31 Mar.	56.2	
Hongkong & Shanghai Banking Corp. (CI) Ltd.	31 Dec.	53.7	4.4
Hambros Bank (J.) Ltd.	31 Mar.	50.7	0.1
S.G. Warburg & Company (J.) Ltd.	31 Mar.	46.8	1.6
Jersey International Bank of Commerce Ltd.	31 Dec.	39.0	0.5
Bilbao International Bank (J.) Ltd.	31 Dec.	38.1	
Brown Shipley (J.) Ltd.	30 Sept.	14.2	13.0
Bank of America (J.) Ltd.	31 Dec.	12.5	12.4
Commercial Bank of Wales (J.) Ltd.	31 Dec.	11.9	0.1
Charterhouse Japhet (J.) Ltd.	31 Dec.	11.4	0.1
New Guarantee Trust of Jersey Ltd.	31 Dec.	10.8	0.01
Lloyds & Scottish Finance (CI) Ltd.	31 Mar.	4.0	0.01
Jersey Savings & Loan Corporation Ltd.	31 Dec.	2.0	
Totals		3,060.6	624.12

included 70 per cent in foreign currencies. In respect of the local importance of individual banks, Table XLVIII has been constructed on the basis of the available published accounts, although it excludes the clearing banks and local branches of international banks whose accounts are not published.

Given that the official figure for Jersey deposits in 1980 was £7,700m., it is evident that locally incorporated institutions accounted for very approximately 39.7 per cent of total deposits, the remainder being accounted for by the branches of the UK clearing banks and the international banks. Even given the partial coverage of these institutions and the different reporting dates it does appear that about 20 per cent of deposits have emanated from parental institutions in general

TABLE XLIX: New offshore funds launched in Jersey by type 1979–81

Type of fund	*Previous totals*	*1979*	*1980*	*1981*	*Cumulated total*
Gilts	16	5	1		22
Money market	5	3	1		9
Bonds	6	2	1	1	10
Commodity	4		1		5
American	11		2	1	14
Far East	7			2	9
European	2				2
UK equities	12	3			15
International	16	1	2	1	20
Investment trusts	3				3
Totals	82	14	8	4	109

Source: derived from Trevor, Matthews and Carey Ltd., *Channel Islands Fund and Unit Trust Review,* and *The Expatriate's Guide to Savings & Investment 1981–1982,* Financial Times Business Publishing Ltd.

with very high percentages in the case of some of the international affiliates such as the Bank of Nova Scotia (CI) Ltd.

New offshore fund launchings were initially high in 1979, but then tailed off in the succeeding two years as Table XLIX demonstrates. In 1979, the estimated total value of offshore funds was in excess of £600m., 60 per cent of which involved investment policies directed away from UK gilts or equities. The names of the publicized new offshore funds launched in the period 1979 to 1981 are given in Table L.

In the new circumstances, the Jersey authorities were determined to maintain their past business standards. The Economic Advisor in his *Budget Report* in October 1980, p.8, warned of:

> The need to continue to focus attention on preserving the image of respectability that the island has succeeded in building up over the years. On occasions the steps to sustain this image may not have obvious appeal for those who may see the prospect of short term profit opportunities thereby being frustrated . . . the institutional and legal framework must both be appropriate to the needs of the commercial business being undertaken and provide for a realistic basis of control of business standards.

In his previous *Report* (p.8) he had indicated what he had meant by this:

> The close vetting of company registration, with a restriction of new unit trusts and banking activity to those institutions of stature, and the pursuit of a 'low profile' policy in advertising the attractions of the Island low tax status.

As to the legislative framework referred to above, 'reform of local Commercial Law, with priority being placed on the drafting of a Trust Law' was required.

Preliminary results of the 1981 Census reveal that the island's population grew

TABLE L: Jersey offshore fund launchings by type, name and reported value 1979–81

Type of fund	*Year of issue*	*Name of fund*	*Reported value 1 December 1981*
Gilts	1979	Clive Hambro Gilt Growth Fund Ltd.	£1.7m
		Fidelity Sterling Fixed Interest Trust Ltd.	£0.6m
		Hill Samuel (Jersey) Fixed Interest Fund Ltd.	£2.0m
		Midland Drayton Gilt Fund Ltd.	£2.4m
		National Westminster (CI) High Income Fd. Ltd.	£4.7m
	1980	Craigmont Gilt Fund (Jersey)	£1.1m
Money market	1979	Arbuthnot Sterling Fund Ltd.	£1.8m
		Britannia Capital Deposit Trust Ltd.	£5.3m
		Brown Shipley Capital Fund Ltd.	£3.3m
	1980	Britannia Managed Currency Fund Ltd.	£0.2m
Bonds	1979	Save & Prosper Deutschmark Bond Fund Ltd.	DM 3m
		Save & Prosper Yen Bond Fund Ltd.	Y 162m
	1980	National West. (CI) International Bond Fd. Ltd.	£1.3m
	1981	Midland Drayton International Bond Fund	$1.0m
Commodity	1980	Britannia Gold Fund Ltd.	$1.8m
American	1980	Allen Harvey & Ross US Dollar Income Fund	$5.6m
		Britannia American Smaller Companies Dollar Trust	$1.8m
	1981	Arbuthnot Dollar Income Trust	$5.1m
Far East	1981	Britannia Australian Performance Fund	£2.5m
		Mercury Far East Trust Ltd.	£9.7m
UK equities	1979	The English Association Income Fund	£0.2m
		The English Association Equity Fund Ltd.	£0.6m
		National Westminster (CI) Equity Fund Ltd.	£1.8m
International	1979	Selected Market Trust Ltd.	£8.7m
	1980	Britannia Managed Currency Fund	£4.2m
		Hill Samuel International Growth Fund	£0.4m
	1981	Vanbrugh Currency Fund	£4.2m

Source: derived from Trevor, Matthews and Carey Ltd., *Channel Islands Fund and Unit Trust Review,* and *The Expatriate's Guide to Savings & Investment 1981–1982,* Financial Times Business Publishing Ltd.

from 74,470 in 1976 to 76,050 in 1981 and that, at the latter date, 8,226 or 10.8 per cent had taken up residence in Jersey since 1976.

GUERNSEY

As in Jersey, developments since 1978 have continued to be encouraging despite the world depression. As can be seen from Table LI, new company registrations were up 14.2 per cent by 1980, the net number of companies on the register then reaching 6,690. Whereas in 1978 one-third of the new companies formed were for non-residents of the Scheduled Territories, by 1980, with the removal of exchange controls, this proportion had risen to over three-quarters.

The 1979 *States Advisory and Finance Committee Report* makes clear that Guernsey had adopted a similar constrained expansion policy to that of Jersey:

TABLE LI: Guernsey company registrations, money on deposit and financial institution profits 1978–81

Year	*Company registrations*		*Money on deposit (£m.)*	*Finance sector profits (£m.)*
	New	*End year totals*		
1978	878	5,526	842	10.5
1979	898	6,162	1,070	14.4
1980	1,003	6,690	1,800	18.5
1981	1,072	7,295	2,691	n.a.

Source: Commercial Relations Office Guernsey.

TABLE LII: Money on deposit in Guernsey as disclosed in annual published accounts for 1980 by locally incorporated banking institutions

Name of banking institution	*Reporting date in 1980*	*Money on deposit (£m.)*	*Reported deposits from ass. cos. (£m.)*
Manufacturers Hanover Bank (G.) Ltd.	31 Dec.	307.8	245.0
N.M. Rothschild & Sons (CI) Ltd.	30 Sept.	137.6	
Barclays Finance Company (G.) Ltd.	31 Dec.	102.8	0.002
Royal Bank of Canada (CI) Ltd.	30 Sept.	97.5	27.7
Kleinwort, Benson (G.) Ltd.	30 June	59.4	
Orion Bank (G.) Ltd.	31 Dec.	57.2	
Midland Bank Trust Company (G.) Ltd.	31 Oct.	50.0	
First National Bank of Chicago (CI) Ltd.	31 Dec.	45.7	29.3
Australia & N. Zealand Banking Group (CI) Ltd.	30 Sept.	44.0	7.1
Bank of Bermuda (G.) Ltd.	31 Dec.	34.7	
Williams & Glyn's Bank Investments (G.) Ltd.	30 Sept.	32.6	1.8
Lloyds Bank International Trust Corp. (G.) Ltd.	30 Sept.	32.5	
Hambros Bank (G.) Ltd.	30 Sept.	30.1	
Rea Brothers (G.) Ltd.	31 Dec.	27.9	
Guinness Mahon Guernsey Ltd.	31 Oct.	24.0	
Italian International Bank (CI) Ltd.	31 Dec.	23.5	
Julian S. Hodge (G.) Ltd.	31 Dec. 79	19.0	
First National Bank of Boston (G.) Ltd.	20 Dec.	17.7	10.9
Morgan Grenfell (G.) Ltd.	31 Dec.	17.6	3.8
Leopold Joseph & Sons (G.) Ltd.	31 Dec.	14.6	0.6
Hill Samuel & Company (G.) Ltd.	31 Mar.	13.4	
Barfield Trust Company Ltd.	31 Dec.	12.7	
Ansbacher (CI) Ltd.	31 Mar.	7.1	
Hansen Guernsey Ltd.	30 Sept.	4.3	
Guernsey Savings & Loan Corporation Ltd.	31 Dec.	4.3	
Brown Shipley (Guernsey) Ltd.	31 Mar.	3.2	
Hume Corporation (G.) Ltd.	31 Dec.	2.7	
Chemical Bank & H. de Walden Ltd.	31 Dec.	2.6	0.3
Allied Bank International (G.) Ltd.	30 June	1.6	
Totals		1,228.1	326.502

> expansion of the finance sector (must be contained) within limits consistent with the overall policy on population growth . . . for the time being those institutions which are already established in the Island and have a record of substantial growth and profitability must have first claim on available resources.

During this period, two banks deregistered—Julian S. Hodge (Guernsey) Ltd., and Chase Manhattan Bank (Guernsey) Ltd.— and were replaced by three new banks—The Standard Chartered Bank, which in effect took over Julian S. Hodge (G.) Ltd., Lazard Brothers and Company (Jersey) Ltd., and, significantly, the Manufacturers Hanover Trust Company—in 1979. As can be seen from Table LI money on deposit more than doubled in this period and Finance Sector profits rose from £10.5m. to £18.5m.

As regards the local importance of banks, some idea of the relative significance of each may be gained from the published deposit figures of some twenty-nine out of the thirty-seven banks operating in 1980: this excludes the UK clearers and branch banks who do not publish separate Guernsey accounts in their annual figures. As Table LII reveals, the locally incorporated banks accounted for approximately £1,228.1m. deposits or 68.2 per cent of the annual total of £1,800m.: of their total £326.5m., or 26.6 per cent, was accounted for by deposits placed by associated company affiliates. Manufacturers Hanover Bank (Guernsey) Ltd. has clearly established itself as the largest locally incorporated bank and contributed 17.1 per cent of the total island deposits. This bank, an affiliate of Manufacturers Hanover, the fourth largest bank in the United States, subsequently launched yet another new venture in November 1981—Manufacturers Hanover Asset Management Ltd.—through which two new Guernsey-based unit trusts were instantly created: Geofund Liquid Assets, and Geofund Multi-Currency Income Trust.

The Advisory and Finance Committee had made clear in its 1978 *Report* 'the strength of the financial community rests . . . on the diversity of the activities in which it is engaged and in the fact that it now draws its business from many different sources and geographic areas.'[1] This diversity was confirmed in the three main areas of captive insurance, offshore fund flotations and offshore pension funds.

(a) Captive Insurance

A record number of new captives were registered in the six months up to the end of March 1980, even though captive insurance companies were no longer permitted to be corporation tax companies and had to pay income tax on their funds, although an exemption is still given to the underwriting side of their operations. This development occurred despite the fact that, with the removal of exchange control, UK companies could more easily go overseas to lower tax or no tax areas. Recent captive arrivals include Marks and Spencer Insurance Ltd. (linked to the Prudential subsidiary Merchantile and General for reinsurance), Woolworths, the Roman Catholic Church and other well-known international business concerns! Thus the emphasis on quality and sound insurance management seems to have paid off. Moreover, the island's capacity to attract and service captive and reinsurance business was enhanced by the formation of two management companies by two major insurance groups.

(b) Offshore Fund Flotations

Such was the volume and success of investment activities that by October 1981, a fourth stockbroking firm had opened on the Island. During a period when, in the eighteen months following October 1979 some £3.05 billion was invested in overseas companies by UK institutions, new offshore flotations kept up very well, Guernsey perhaps benefiting a little from Jersey's slightly more restrictive attitude reported above. During the period 1979 to 1981, the number of island offshore funds more than doubled, increasing from twenty-eight to sixty-three and giving the finance sector a good spread in the type of funds offered as is indicated in Table LIII.

The names of these publicized new offshore funds are given in Table LIV. Five new points of interest surround some of these flotations:

(i) The Royal Bank of Canada (CI) Ltd. set up RBC Investment Managers Ltd., a wholly owned subsidiary, which will offer management services in respect of individual investment portfolios with assets in excess of $250,000 US. This development is to be linked to the first of a series of Guernsey-based mutual funds designed to attract overseas investors largely through that bank's branches and subsidiaries in forty countries. The first fund, the RBC International Income Fund, was the first of its kind locally to offer bearer deposit receipts: this will allow shareowners to retain anonymity. Previously exchange control had limited the availability of such shares to UK investors and the Guernsey authorities had not been disposed to generally permit such issues. Moreover the fund is geared to investments 'without restriction on an international basis' to exploit the new cir-

TABLE LIII: New offshore funds launched in Guernsey by type 1979–81

Type of fund	*Previous totals*	*1979*	*1980*	*1981*	*Cumulated total*
Gilts	4	1		1	6
Money market	—	3	3		6
Bonds	2	1	5		8
Commodity	2				2
American	3		2	2	7
Far East	2		1		3
European	—	1			1
UK equities	5	1	2	1	9
International	4			3	7
Insurance-linked	1	4	4		9
Investment trusts	5				5
Totals	28	11	17	7	63

Source: derived from Trevor, Matthews and Carey Ltd., *Channel Islands Fund and Unit Trust Review*, and *The Expatriate's Guide to Savings & Investment 1981–1982*, Financial Times Business Pub. Ltd.

TABLE LIV: Guernsey offshore fund launchings by type, name and reported value 1979–81

Type of fund	*Year of issue*	*Name of fund*	*Reported value*
Gilts	1979	Baring Henderson Gilt Fund Ltd.	£3.6m
	1981	Schroder Sterling Fixed Interest Fund	n.a.
Money market	1979	Capital Reserve Fund Ltd.	£14.0m
		Old Court Sterling Fund Ltd.	£46.2m
		Kleinwort, Benson Sterling Asset Fd. Ltd.	£3.6m
	1980	Guinness Mahon International Fund Ltd.	n.a.
		Leopold Joseph Sterling Fund Ltd.	£5.5m
		Old Court International Reserves Ltd.	$20.7m
Bonds	1979	Kleinwort, Benson Eurobond Fund Ltd.	£2.9m
	1980	RBC International Income Fund Ltd.	$10.6m
		NEL International Fixed Interest Fund	£0.1m
		NEL Sterling Deposit Fund	£0.2m
		NEL Sterling Fixed Interest Fund	£0.1m
		NEL Sterling Managed Fund	£0.3m
American	1980	Henderson American Offshore Fund	$1.1m
		RBC North American Fund Ltd.	$11.4m
	1981	Schroder Dollar Equity Fund	n.a.
		Schroder Dollar Fixed Interest Fund	n.a.
Far East	1980	Old Court Hong Kong Fund	HK $11.3m
European	1979	Marianne (Sterling) Fund Ltd.	£0.7m
UK equities	1979	Hambro Special Situation Fund Ltd.	£0.2m
	1981	Schroder Sterling Fixed Interest Fund	n.a.
International	1980	The Currency Trust	£1.1m
		NEL International Managed Fund	£0.3m
	1981	RBC International Capital Fund	$2.7m
		Schroder Managed Currency Fund	n.a.
		Trans National Trust Ltd.	$3.9m
Insurance-linked	1979	Phoenix Sterling Exempt Gilt Fund	n.a.
		Phoenix Far East Fund	n.a.
		Phoenix International Currency Fund	n.a.
		Phoenix Fixed Interest Fund	n.a.
	1980	Providence Sterling Bond Fund	n.a.
		Providence Sterling Equity Fund	n.a.
		Providence International Bond Fund	n.a.
		Providence International Equity Fund	n.a.

Source: derived from Trevor, Matthews and Carey Ltd., *Channel Islands Fund and Unit Trust Review*, and *The Expatriate's Guide to Savings & Investment 1981–1982*, Financial Times Business Pub. Ltd.

cumstances. According to the Press Release 'Guernsey has been chosen as the site of the Royal Bank's first management subsidiary because of its favourable tax structure and the island's long history of political and social stability.' It would thus seem only natural for other established banks to follow this lead and to further diversify the island's business base.

(ii) In July 1980, Rothschilds set up Old Court International Reserves as a multi-currency cash investment fund in which any investor can choose to make investments in any of ten currencies, and to switch his holdings from one currency to another without incurring capital gains tax. This fund offers companies a new means of hedging against foreign currency exposure. As shares in the fund have a nominal value of 1 US cent and are priced in multiples of the various currencies equivalent to £10, currency investment is now available to the smallest investor. This fund raised over $95m. in its first year and merged with an existing fund to make a fund valued at £54m.

(iii) The formation of Trans National Trust Ltd. in May 1981 was a joint venture by Hambros Fund Managers (CI) Ltd. and the Allied Irish Investment Bank. This is notable *inter alia* for two aspects: it 'allows the Irish bank legitimately to side-step its country's exchange controls . . . [under which it] would have [been] required to invest 50% of its funds at home', and, the fund will be listed on the new UK Unlisted Securities Market, which has reduced the usual costs of setting up such a fund from around £100,000 to £40,000. The *Guernsey Evening Press and Star* further reported that 'it is considered that the fund will appeal especially to Irish expatriates looking for suitable offshore investment opportunities'.[2] This fund is registered in Guernsey but controlled in Switzerland.

(iv) The growth of management expertise on the island has resulted in the local management of offshore funds authorized in other offshore centres e.g. the Henderson American Offshore Fund, authorized in Hong Kong in 1980 is administered by Henderson Administration (Guernsey) Ltd..

(v) One of the aspects of the development of insurance has been an increase in insurance-linked funds: a development made easier in Guernsey as a result of Jersey's prohibitive ancient laws. The development of insurance-linked funds is easily understood given that there is an estimated world market of some 2½ million British expatriates, many of whom have an average of £400 per month to invest from their usually high salaries. Thus the Schroder Group launched five new offshore funds in November 1981 to be the investment outlets for two of its schemes—the International Bond (a single premium contract); and the Shroder International Plan (a 10-year-plus regular premium policy)—which constitute vehicles for accumulating life funds.

(c) Offshore Pension Funds

In the wake of exchange decontrol, the firm of actuaries Bacon and Woodrow came to Guernsey in the belief that Guernsey could become a particularly good centre for self-administered pension schemes. These schemes are exempt for Guernsey tax under S.40 (O) and (P) of the Income Tax (Guernsey) law, 1975, provided they are paid to a person not resident in Guernsey, and that the scheme is:

1) established in Guernsey (either by a Trust Deed or through a Trustee that may be a locally-based Bank or Trust Company);
2) under bona fide irrevocable trusts;
3) in connection with carrying on of business outside Guernsey;
4) solely to provide superannuation benefits for employees working outside Guernsey or for their widows/dependents;
5) recognized by employers and employees.

Under these provisions employers have greater freedom to provide benefits best suited to their company retirement policy and their employee needs, e.g. pensions would not be limited to two-thirds of salary, there can be 100 per cent commutation if required, and a lump sum can be given on return to the UK from overseas work and the fund can be readily supervised from the UK. While it is true that it is possible to set up a trust fund in the UK itself under S.218 of the UK 1970 Taxes Act, it is inoperative if one member for whom benefits are being provided is employed in the UK; moreover, income from UK equities, properties, unit trusts and annuities are subject to UK tax: only 'exempt gilts' and overseas investments escape UK tax. This business is likely to further develop in the near future.

Despite statements in previous years about the need for new legislation in the areas of insurance and finance, no new laws were introduced in the period under review. Some steps, however, were made in local tax laws and procedures to put right some local tax avoidance loopholes, these included:

i) 'Capital gains' made from underwriting. The existence on the island of a number of Lloyd's underwriters, whose investment activities in respect of their underwriting account gave rise, in the natural course of their business of protecting their capital reserves, to no tax liabilities in Guernsey with respect to 'capital gains' made will in future be treated by the States Income Tax Authority as 'profits' and therefore liable to Guernsey tax.
ii) 'The overdraft export system'. The 'overdraft export system' has been brought to an end whereby a resident, who is not solely or principally resident, so arranges his affairs that they do not make any remittances of income to Guernsey to avoid having any income chargeable to tax. In future such persons to qualify for local residence must be physically present for 91 days or more in the year of charge.
iii) The law which exempted non-resident dispositions from income tax on interest payable to them has been amended so that this concession no longer applies.

THE ISLE OF MAN

The new era began with a year of particular disappointment. Whereas the financial year 1979–80 witnessed an increase in Gross National Income of 15.2 per cent from £144.4m. to £166.4m., income from insurance, banking, finance and business services actually fell from £37.1m. in the previous year to £33.8m., a decline of 9.8 per cent: the GNP share of this sector fell from 25.7 per cent to 20.3 per cent. The Government Treasurer in his review of this period in June 1981 commented:

> Several possible reasons have been given for the setback that has occurred in the growth of the Island's finance industry. Although interest rates were high during the 1979/1980 financial year (Minimum Lending Rate peaked at 17% in late 1979), trading conditions were difficult with many of the local banks' customers in tourism, agriculture and fishing finding problems coping with loan repayments. At the same time the incoming Conservative

> administration and its budget of June 1979 marked a shift away from high income tax rates and towards high indirect taxes in the United Kingdom (VAT was increased to a standard rate of 15%). This change in the United Kingdom's fiscal stance coupled with the apparent ideological shift in favour of free enterprise and away from intervention by Government, reduced the relative attractiveness of the Isle of Man. In particular the relaxation of the UK's exchange control restrictions meant that an important advantage had been lost as the Isle of Man now had to compete with the rest of the world for the business that previously had preferred to remain within the Scheduled Territories.[3]

The fact that the above remarks could equally apply to the Channel Islands who did not suffer a similar reversal seems to underline the fragility of the Isle of Man's previous achievements. However this setback seems now to have been reversed in the subsequent two years. During the period 1979 to mid-1981, some eleven new banks were admitted, these being as follows:

1979	Meghraj Bank Ltd.
	Northern Bank (IOM) Ltd.
1980	First International Manx Bank Ltd.
	Gulf Banking and Trust Corporation Ltd.
	Mercantile Overseas Bank Ltd.
	Tyndall Bank (IOM) Ltd.
	Ulster Bank (IOM) Ltd.
1981	Bell International Ltd.
	Investment Bank of Ireland
	Lloyds Bank Finance (IOM)
	Roy West Trust Corporation (IOM)

The new intake increased the number of island banking institutions from thirty to forty-one. The pattern of new arrivals is much the same as before: there is still an absence of a large overseas non-UK bank which would give greater solidity to the global catchment possibilities for the finance sector. One interesting new arrival is the Roy West Trust Corporation (IOM), which, apart from the usual trust business, is intending to set up numbered bank accounts for its worldwide clientele who wish to take out life assurance policies. The life protection package 'does not require the disclosure of the name of the life assured, the beneficiaries, or the owner of the contract of insurance where the owner is other than the life assured to the Insurer or any other party.' Coverage consists of a one-year term insurance contract with minimum protection of $100,000 and a maximum limit of $500,000 on any one life and is intended for the beneficiaries of Trusts and related persons and the beneficial owners of companies managed by Roy West. The insurer will be the Fiduciary Life and General Insurance Company Ltd., a newly created wholly owned subsidiary of the Roy West Trust Group based in Douglas, IOM. The Roy West Group is a joint venture between the Royal Bank of Canada and the National Westminster Bank, the parent company being based in the Bahamas.

Despite the general initial setback, the island's bank deposits did increase

TABLE LV: Money on deposit in the Isle of Man as disclosed in the published accounts for 1980 by locally incorporated banking institutions

Name of banking institution	*Reporting date in 1980*	*Money on deposit (£m.)*
Isle of Man Bank Ltd.	31 Dec.	152.9
Commercial Bank of Wales Ltd.	31 Dec.	39.0
Williams & Glyn's Bank (IOM) Ltd.	30 Sept.	34.9
Savings & Investment Bank Ltd.	31 Dec.	28.2
International Finance & Trust Corp. Ltd.	30 Sept.	18.7
Celtic Bank Ltd.	31 Mar.	18.6
Singer & Friedlander	31 Dec.	12.9
Allied Irish Bank (IOM) Ltd.	31 Mar.	4.1
Total		309.3

TABLE LVI: Isle of Man company registrations in the years 1978–81

Year ending 31st March	*New registrations*	*Removals*	*Net increase*	*Total no. registered*
1978	1,789	183	1,606	6,201
1979	2,168	435	1,733	7,934
1980	2,385	549	1,838	9,772
1981	2,201	848	1,353	11,125

Source: Commercial Relations Office, Isle of Man.

significantly: the figures for mid-year 1978, 1979, 1980 and 1981 being respectively £315m., £409m., £650m. and £837m., an increase of 165.7 per cent on the 1978 base. As many of the financial institutions are private companies and not obliged to file public accounts, information about island deposit share is severely limited to the few that do. For what they are worth the following were obtained in respect of 1980, when the island deposits were £650m.

In the area of company registration, growth was substantial during this period, a net increase of 57.6 per cent being achieved as Table LVI indicates. Certain changes were made in respect of the domestic friction structure, the most important of which were as follows:

(*a*) In April 1980, Isle of Man officials replaced UK Customs and Excise Department officials as collectors of VAT so ending the situation where the affairs of island companies were naturally passed to the Department of Customs and Excise's computer at Southend. Under the terms of a new agreement the island now has the right to vary its VAT rate provided advance notice is given to the UK government.

(*b*) As from May 1980, the island's standard rate of income tax was finally reduced to 20p in the pound putting the Isle of Man on a par with its other British Isle competitors.

(*c*) The Income Tax Act 1980 gave the income tax assessor further powers to frustrate the avoidance of island taxes.

TABLE LVII: New offshore funds launched in the Isle of Man by type 1979–81

Type of fund	*Previous totals*	*1979*	*1980*	*1981*	*Cumulated total*
Gilts	2				2
Money market	—				
Bonds	1	1			2
Commodity	5	2	3	6	16
American	—				
Far East	3	1			4
European	—				
UK equities	4		1		5
International	11				11
Insurance-linked	—				
Investment trusts	—				
Totals	26	4	4	6	40

Source: mostly derived from company literature.

(*d*) The Exempt Insurance Companies Act 1981 was yet another attempt to attract captive insurance activities to the island. Under this new act, complete powers of discretion are given to the island Treasurer and the Assessor of Income Tax under S.1(1) to 'exempt the whole or part of the profits or income of an insurance company from liability to income tax under any enactment relating to income tax for the time being in force.' Previously only the underwriting profits were free. It is envisaged that a company would apply to be licensed as an insurance company under the 1974 Companies Act: authorization is automatic if the company is already authorized to carry on insurance business in the UK, but otherwise must be vetted by the Finance Board. It must have a paid-up share capital of not less than £50,000 and be able to demonstrate its re-insurance support. According to Mr. W. Dawson, the Island Treasurer:

> Considerable attention will be paid to the management of the company, because we have found from past experience that this is a critical factor, and that whatever ratios or other guidelines may be imposed, one is really in the hands of the management to ensure that the company is conducted in a proper manner. Generally, one would hope to ensure that the management includes someone with experience of the insurance industry, or that one of the local companies which have been set up to manage exempt insurance companies is being employed. As far as directors are concerned, it will normally be expected that at least half the directors of a company are resident in the Isle of Man.[4]

Tax exemption on profits arising solely on insurance risks undertaken outside the island is provided for. The annual fee for an insurance company licence will be set at £500 and a tax exemption certificate fee of £1,500 will also be levied.

During this period, a dynamic increase took place in new offshore fund flotations. Some fifteen new funds were launched, as Table LVII indicates, bringing the total number of Isle of Man registered publicized funds to forty-one. It is evi-

TABLE LVIII: Isle of Man offshore fund launchings by type, name and reported value 1979–81

Type of fund	*Year of issue*	*Name of fund*	*Reported value 1 December 1981*
UK equities	1980	The English Association Development Fund	£0.4m
Bonds	1979	Tyndall High Income Gilt Fund Ltd.	£2.6m
Far East	1979	Tyndall Pacific Fund International	$1.2m
Commodity	1979	The Coin Trust	£0.5m
		Normandy Metal Trust	£0.3m
	1980	The Chinese Fund	£0.1m
		Normandy Commodity Trust	£0.1m
		Surinvest Sapphire Trust	£1.2m
	1981	CAL Commodity and Currency Fund	£0.9m
		Cambridge Currency and Gold Trust	n.a.
		International Commodities Trust	£0.2m
		Petroman Oil Trust	£1.1m
		Vanguard Commodity Fund	£1.0m
		Wren Precious Metals Fund	£0.01m

Source: The Expatriate's Guide to Savings and Investment 1981–1982, Financial Times Business Publishing Ltd.

dent that the Isle of Man did not share in the gilt and UK equity and money market fund activity to the extent of the Channel Islands in this period. A definite specialization seems to have occurred in the direction of high risk commodity funds which accounted for nearly two-fifths of the total number of funds in 1981. The names of the new funds are given in Table LVIII. It is clear however that, numbers apart, the vast majority of these funds have rather low valuations compared to those in the Channel Islands.

A COMPARATIVE STATISTICAL SUMMARY OF BRITISH ISLE OFFSHORE DEVELOPMENT

Generally it would appear that, rather than undermining previous development achievements, the lifting of UK exchange controls has only led to a further consolidation of offshore centre financial activities. A comparative statistical review of these achievements is now provided in the areas of banking, company registration and offshore funds.

(a) Banking

Jersey has consistently been by far the largest banking centre. With the exceptions of the years 1975 to 1978, when its British Isle market share fell, by the end of the 1970s it had regained an earlier position where it accounted for about 75 per cent of the total. Apart from the mid-1970s, the Guernsey deposit share has declined somewhat, though both Guernsey and the Isle of Man recovered in 1980 from a relatively poor year in 1979. Nevertheless overall British Isle deposits

TABLE LIX: British Isle deposit growth and island centre market share 1973–81

Year	*Total deposits (£m.)*	*Percentage market share* Jersey %	Guernsey %	IOM %
1973	1,268	74.9	22.0	3.1
1974	1,520	69.7	27.0	3.3
1975	1,761	61.9	31.3	6.8
1976	2,811	69.4	22.4	8.2
1977	3,258	69.1	22.3	8.6
1978	4,657	75.2	18.1	6.8
1979	7,779	81.0	13.8	5.3
1980	10,150	75.9	17.7	6.4
1981	13,528	73.9	19.9	6.7

TABLE LX: Presence of the Top 100 and Top 300 world banks in each British Isle centre by position and country of bank origin

	Jersey			*Guernsey*			*Isle of Man*		
		No. in			*No. in*			*No. in*	
Country of bank origin	*Positions in Top 300*	*Top 100*	*Top 300*	*Positions in Top 300*	*Top 100*	*Top 300*	*Positions in Top 300*	*Top 100*	*Top 300*
United Kingdom	8:9:16:30: 53:159:205	5	7	8:9:16:30: 53:205	5	6	8:9:16:30: 53:129:174 205	5	8
United States	1:2:12:26: 58	5	5	21:26:46: 65:106	4	5			
France	4	1	1						
Holland	25	1	1						
Germany	147		1						
Luxembourg							251		1
Spain	121		1						
Ireland	175		1				175		1
Canada	28:56	2	2	28	1	1			
Kuwait							208		1
India	300		1						
Hong Kong	35	1	1						
Australasia				103		1			
		15	21		10	13		5	11

Source: positions extracted from *The Statist 71st Annual Review of World Banking 1981–1982,* Financial Times Business Pub. Ltd.

grew from £1,268m. in 1973 to £10,150m. in 1980, a staggering eightfold increase, as Table LIX reveals. The difference between the isle centres is again reflected in their shares of the Top 100 and Top 300 world banks as shown in Table LX. Given that in the year 1981 Jersey, Guernsey and the Isle of Man had respectively forty-nine, forty-two and forty-one banking insitutions, and, taking the ratio of the number of Top 100 banks to the total number of institutions as indicative of global offshore potential, the island rates are 30.6 per cent, 23.3 per cent and 12.2 per cent. In terms of direct representation from non-UK countries,

TABLE LXI: Annual British Isle deposit levels and average deposits per financial institution 1973–81

	Jersey			*Guernsey*			*Isle of Man*		
Year	*Deposits (£m.)*	*No. Inst.*	*Av. per Inst.*	*Deposits (£m.)*	*No. Inst.*	*Av. per Inst.*	*Deposits (£m.)*	*No. Inst.*	*Av. per Inst.*
1973	950	34	27.9	279	42	6.6	39	18	2.2
1974	1,060	35	30.3	410	44	9.3	50	19	2.6
1975	1,090	35	31.1	552	45	12.2	119	22	5.4
1976	1,150	39	29.5	631	43	14.7	230	24	9.8
1977	2,250	40	56.3	728	43	16.9	280	27	10.4
1978	3,500	42	83.3	842	42	20.0	315	30	10.5
1979	6,300	45	140.0	1,070	43	24.9	409	32	12.7
1980	7,700	46	167.4	1,800	43	41.9	650	37	17.6
1981	10,000	49	204.1	2,691	42	64.1	837	41	20.4

there are nine countries represented in Jersey (including a Swiss bank not in top 300), five in Guernsey (including representatives from Italy and Bermuda), and four in the Isle of Man (including Canadian representation). Guernsey benefits from a number of UK merchant banks which although not being in the Top 300 have extensive world networks: this is borne out in Table LXI which indicates the average deposit level per financial institution for the period 1973 to 1980. It is clear from Table LXI how much lower the deposit pull of Guernsey and especially the Isle of Man is as compared with Jersey. The figures also reveal how significant the establishment of foreign branch banks has been—spectacularly so in Jersey in 1979 and 1980, and to a lesser extent in Guernsey.

(b) Company Incorporations

As regards company incorporations, it is clear from Table LXII that once again Jersey is the largest centre, though its importance is not so relatively preponderant as in banking. On the other hand, the Isle of Man is the second largest centre, having increased its share relative to Jersey in recent years. In 1981, the individual centre shares of British Isle company incorporations were 47.5 per cent for Jersey, 31.7 per cent for the Isle of Man and 20.8 per cent for Guernsey.

TABLE LXII: British Isle company incorporations and individual island shares 1978–81*

	1978		*1979*		*1980*		*1981*	
Isle centre	*No. cos.*	*% Tot.*	*No. cos.*	*% Tot.*	*No. cos.*	*% Tot.*	*No. cos.*	*% Tot.*
Jersey	12,513	51.6	13,813	49.5	15,210	48.0	16,643	47.5
Guernsey	5,526	22.8	6,162	22.1	6,690	21.1	7,295	20.8
Isle of Man	6,201	25.6	7,934	28.4	9,772	30.9	11,125	31.7
	24,240		27,909		31,672		35,063	

*End-year figures.

(c) Offshore Funds

The number of offshore funds available and publicized in each of the island centres is indicated in Table LXIII for the years 1972, 1976 and 1981, together with the totals for offshore funds based in other world centres as derived from information in *The Expatriate's Guide to Savings and Investment 1981–1982.* Thus the British Isle centres accounted in 1981 for nearly 70 per cent of the total number of publicized offshore funds, whereas some ten years previously they had accounted

TABLE LXIII: Publicized offshore funds registered and based in the British Isle centres and other offshore centres 1972, 1976, and 1981

	1972			*1976*			*1981*		
Offshore centre	*No. funds*	*% B.I.*	*% World*	*No. funds*	*% B.I.*	*% World*	*No. funds*	*% B.I.*	*% World*
Jersey	24	50.0	26.0	52	55.3	33.5	109	51.4	35.6
Guernsey	13	32.5	16.9	19	20.2	12.3	63	29.7	20.6
Isle of Man	7	17.5	9.1	23	24.5	14.8	40	18.9	13.1
British Isle centres	40		51.9	94		60.6	212		69.3
Bermuda	9			15			24		
Caymans	2			3			5		
Hong Kong	8			20			35		
Luxembourg	11			11			16		
N. Antilles	4			6			6		
Switzerland	2			4			4		
Gibraltar				1			1		
Panama	1						1		
Singapore							1		
Turks & Caicos				1			1		
World total	77			155			306		

TABLE LXIV: Offshore funds available in the British Isle centres by type and centre 1981

Type of fund	*Jersey*	*Guernsey*	*Isle of Man*	*Total*
Gilts	22	6	2	30
Money market	9	6		15
Bonds	10	8	2	20
Commodity	5	2	16	23
US	14	7		21
Far East	9	3	4	16
European	2	1		3
UK equities	15	9	5	29
International	20	7	11	38
Investment trusts	3	5		8
Insurance-linked		9		9
Totals	109	63	40	212

for 52 per cent. In 1981, each British Isle centre offered more funds than any in the rest of the world. Despite some changes within the decade covered, the individual isle shares of British Isle issues had been roughly maintained. Within their total issues, different spreads of funds emerge, as are shown in Table LXIV.

It is evident that both Jersey and Guernsey have a good spread of funds over the various categories, and that the Isle of Man does not. Jersey has a definite lead as regards international and US funds and UK gilts, whereas Guernsey has a unique offering of insurance-linked funds, reflecting its unique position with regard to captive insurance and related insurance activities. The Isle of Man has a number of gaps, particularly in the areas of money market and US funds, but offers a considerable supply of commodity funds unmatched by any other centre.

ENVOI

What G.C. Powell said about Jersey in his 1980 Report holds good for all the islands in the future, i.e. that they 'should not become over complacent as to the inevitability of . . . growth taking place. The Island is in competition with other centres and has need therefore to have proper regard to the level of business costs and any other factors bearing on the ability to compete.'[5] Before developments in the rest of the world are considered in Part III, it is necessary to end this section with some comment on the selective strategy being adopted in respect to bank entry in the islands, and to refer briefly to some recent developments in UK attitudes towards offshore activity.

As regards the general philosophy of approach with respect to future development being based on consolidation by existing institutions, a cautionary note needs to be made: it should be remembered that offshore activity decisions are made by organizations which are, or are increasingly becoming, transnational in a global sense and therefore do not merely adhere to simple international/national responsibilities. Decisions in these areas are sometimes taken autonomously by independent subsidiaries or indeed branches, but it does not follow that both now and in the future, parental pressures may not, in certain circumstances, be made with respect to parental company advantage: this might not necessarily always coincide with competitive circumstances obtaining as between onshore and offshore centres. The island authorities will have to watch that the continuing evolution of their financial sectors is not frustrated by any consistent negative exercizing of such pressures with respect to their centres. There may be a future danger in assuming that the stability of the present institutions and island consolidation by such concerns will necessarily lead to the optimum pattern of island sector evolution in the long run. It does not necessarily follow that by confining new entry to representatives from as yet unrepresented onshore areas, they will avoid these long-term effects and so turn away institutions that may be more innovative ultimately. It is evident in the new circumstances that closer ties between the business community and the insular authorities need to be formalized. This has already led in Guernsey to the formation of an International Business Association and an advisory board for the finance industry which will give the industry more direct access to the States Advisory and Finance Committee (*Guernsey Evening Press and Star,* 5 April 1982 p.1).

As regards recent UK attitudes, comment is needed on:

a) an attempt to legislate against the British Isle havens via a Private Members bill;
b) the consultative document with regard to taxation of January 1981;
c) recent anticipations concerning the possible return of UK exchange control.

(*a*) On 20 October 1981, Mr. George Foulkes, the Labour MP for Ayrshire South, sought leave under the 10-minute rule to bring in a Private Member's bill to 'prohibit the transfer of funds from companies registered in the United Kingdom to subsidiaries of those companies or to companies of which they are subsidiaries, registered in the Channel Islands or the Isle of Man, "otherwise than in settlement of bargains at arm's length"'. The application was refused by 151 votes to 134 but did give some publicity to the alleged use of the islands for tax evasive purposes with respect to nominee directorships and 'sham' companies. In the debate it was alleged that the islands provided an easily accessible, English-speaking, comfortable bolt-hole for every kind of avoidance of UK taxes on the one hand and, on the other, that they relied on the UK for defence and travel abroad on British passports without, with the exception of the Isle of Man, paying any token contribution. Clearly, the strength with which these accusations were made was unfair, given the monitoring presence and influence of the Bank of England up to 1979 and the benefits to the British economy of investments deposited in the City of London. Mr Albert McQuarrie, Tory MP for Aberdeenshire East, opposed the introduction of the Bill and told MPs, 'I hope the House will see it as a publicity stunt which has no substance or merit and will leave the Channel Islands and the Isle of Man to get on with their own affairs.' The British Press tended to ignore this affair, with the exception of the *Daily Telegraph,* which had a leader on p.18 of its issue for 21 October 1981 in the following terms:

> Ever since the Norman Conquest, the Channel Islands have belonged to the Crown. They are not part of the United Kingdom and the Westminster Parliament has no right to tell them how to manage their tax affairs. The Isle of Man, too, is self-governing. But history and constitution apart, is there not something appealing to the British character about a slight anachronism, a touch of feudalism still in our midst? The islands, and all who live on them, add a richness to the British Isles which other States who have crushed out vestiges of local autonomy in the interests of strict uniformity lack. With 20 per cent taxes, good housekeeping and thriving economies, they deserve a pat on the back—not a kick.

Despite the anti-bias of Mr. Foulkes's accusations and the *Telegraph*'s somewhat unserious pro-bias, an issue nevertheless remains to which preliminary thoughts have been given by the UK Inland Revenue Board as indicated below.

(*b*) In January 1981 the UK Inland Revenue Board issued two Consultative Documents: *Tax Havens and the Corporate Sector* and *Company Residence.* The first document refers to the post exchange control situation since 1979 and argues that S.482 of the 1970 Taxes Act requires modification in the present context of free exchanges. However, wholesale repeal 'would seriously increase the risk of loss to the Exchequer by tax avoidance'. The document refers to the alleged growing use of tax havens for tax avoidance and the problems associated with the accumulation therein of profits and investment income and to legislation in the US, Germany, Japan, Canada and France, whereby onshore resident shareholders are made liable to tax on their proportionate share of the income of the offshore control foreign company. The Board of Inland Revenue selects as a possible scheme for the UK the application of the above approach but only to UK corporate shareholders with a direct or indirect interest of 10 per cent or more in the overseas company in cases where they are 'resident in a country with a "privileged tax system"' and 'it did not distribute by way of dividend to the shareholders a substantial proportion of its profits'. As a test of the 'legitimacy' of business activity, the Japanese Criteria is selected for possible application (see Part I Chapter III for a discussion of this). The subsequent draft legislation document that appeared in November 1981, entitled *International Tax Avoidance,* laid down further details for guidelines in this area (as discussed on pp.73–4). However legislation was not brought forward, as anticipated in the 1982 Finance Act following the unfavourable reception that was given to these proposals. This remains a matter for future determination.

Another part of the proposed new approach was 'a recasting of the terms on which a company is regarded as "resident" in the UK', for which the *Company Residence* document was issued. This indicated the need for a new realistic legal definition of 'residence' as there is no statutory UK definition, and the British Courts have equated 'residence' with the place of central management and control, weight being given to where formal meetings of directors are held: the latter is a nonsense in modern conditions of instant communication and rapid and easy transport. To end the artificiality brought about by modern circumstances, the Board proposes under S.4 of the document that 'without any change being made in the general law about company residence, companies should be taxed in the UK as residence on the basis of new statutory rules'. These rules would replace the present test of 'central management and control' with the concepts of 'central administration' and 'principal place of business'. 'Some modification of these rules might be required to deal with the special situation of companies operating in the financial and other services sectors, and they would not be appropriate to non-trading companies to which the existing law might continue to apply.' At the time of writing this issue had not been resolved.

(*c*) As was indicated in an earlier chapter, the *Royal Commission on the Constitution* 1969–73 endorsed the spirit of 'co-operative independence' which had been a general basis of constitutional relationships between the islands and the UK government over the years, declaring in relation to their use as tax havens that 'it is a matter for good sense and co-operation between the United Kingdom and Island Governments to ensure that any loss of tax to the UK Exchequer is kept to a minimum'. Evidently, decisions made in relation to (*b*) above will ensure that this remains the case, although the increasing importance of extra-UK business in the islands has been already noticed. Although the absence of exchange control does lessen the UK hold over the islands, they nevertheless remain dependent on many UK procedures and changes therein. Thus, *de facto,* listed banks under the UK Banking Act 1979 do have cheaper access to the London money markets; access to the new Stock Exchange Unlisted Company Register does cheapen British Isle offshore fund flotation costs; the UK requirement, as from 1 December 1981, for the statutory registration of insurance broker business under the 1977 Insurance Brokers' (Registration) Act, is seen to be needed to ensure an absence from Guernsey of firms that might not be registered if they attempted to set up in the UK and which used Guernsey's lack of controls as a loophole.

In the area of 'imperial contributions', the second area singled out for comment by the Royal Commission, responsible contributions continued to be made on a voluntary basis as they recommended (para. 1536, p.464). Thus following the Amoco Cadiz pollution disaster of 16 March 1978, the UK Department of Trade undertook operations in the interests of the South Coast of England and the Channel Islands that cost £1,074,804.44p. The UK considered it fair and reasonable that these costs be paid for on a 33⅓ per cent pro rata basis by the UK, Jersey and Guernsey. The sum of £358,268.15p. was duly paid by each of the Channel Island administrations. With respect to the allied area of the Common Purse Agreement between the Isle of Man and the UK, the large increases that occurred in VAT under the 1979 Finance Act brought out demands to scrap the tax, which was seen as being 'imposed' by the mainland, and to secure full control of domestic indirect taxes. As reported earlier in this chapter, the Isle of Man now separately administers this tax domestically and has secured a measure of freedom in the direction desired.

Finally, a degree of uncertainty obtains with respect to the continued absence of UK exchange controls, given that there may be a problem of capital flight during the run-up to the next UK general election, and there is anyway speculation concerning the possible reimposition of exchange controls in the event of the return of a Labour Government and possible UK withdrawal from the EEC. It is felt in some quarters that in the latter circumstances a unilateral end to 'co-operative independence' might arise, or that a new exchange control regime might not reinstate the privileged position the islands had in the period 1972 to 1979. These fears may have led to some present loss of revenue to the islands, particularly in relation to the transfer of trust registrations to centres outside the British areas of influence, such as Switzerland: it may still be the case in these circumstances that administration of such trusts continues to remain in the island centres. However, it should be borne in mind that it is now demonstrable that the islands are significantly globally orientated in their banking, trust and company management business. It is clear that the existence of foreign branch banks has made the Channels Islands particularly attractive deposit centres since the ending of exchange controls, and as these deposits are included by the Bank of England within the official UK banking statistics, they are of benefit to the UK economy. Table LXV reveals that the UK market share of British Isle offshore centre deposits declined slightly from 1.7 per cent in 1973 (the first year for which statistics are available for all the islands) to a low of 1.3 per cent in 1977, but have risen dramatically in importance since 1979 to about 4 per cent of the total. Over

TABLE LXV: The relative importance of British Isle centres' bank deposits to total UK deposits in the period 1973–81

Year	*Total UK deposits** *(£m.)*	*British Isle Centre deposits (£m.)*	*% Total UK deposits*
1973	74,603	1,268	1.7
1974	106,549	1,520	1.4
1975	116,034	1,761	1.5
1976	147,759	2,811	1.9
1977	168,331	3,258	1.9
1978	190,389	4,657	2.4
1979	213,721	7,779	3.6
1980	265,516	10,150	3.8
1981	351,286	13,528	3.9

*Derived from Table 3:1 of the *Bank of England Quarterly Bulletins* for the period. June figures.

the period 1973 to 1981, UK total deposits rose some 370 per cent, whereas British Isle centre deposits rose 966.9 per cent. Further UK benefits derive from the fact that the Islands' tourist industries to some extent divert UK holidaymakers away from foreign resorts: it has been estimated that Channel Island earnings from this source amount to £30m. alone. Lastly, UK tax avoidance by emigration is down to a mere trickle in the islands. In so far as it continues to happen, it is contained within areas in monetary union with the UK and so does not incur adverse consequences for the UK balance of payments as would be the case with emigration to Portugal, Spain or Florida.,

Furthermore, offshore activities in the island centres will, as elsewhere, be subject to a number of new onshore global pressures in the 1980s as indicated in Part III Chapter II.

REFERENCES

1. States Advisory and Finance Committee, *Economic Report for 1978, Billet d'État,* IX, 1979, para.41 p.239.
2. *Guernsey Evening Press and Star,* 8 June 1981, p.8.
3. Dawson, W., *Manx National Income 1979/1980—Commentary,* Isle of Man Treasury, 16 June 1981, p.3.
4. Dawson, W., 'A Detailed Consideration of the 1981 Exempt Insurance Act', conference paper presented to a Conference in the Isle of Man in November 1981, p.8.
5. Report on the Budget by the States' Economic Advisor, p.8, 16 October 1980.

PART III
The Global Pattern of Offshore Finance Centre Development Since 1970

'Tout chu [ce] qui vient de flot se retournera d'ebe'
Guernsey patois proverb *

Part I has already indicated the general rationale for transnational economic activities finding a home in an 'offshore' location and the factors that made this generally possible as a result of the telecommunication revolution, the evolution of the interbank and Eurocurrency markets, and the growth of worldwide financial branching networks. It was emphasized that the business possibilities thereby created in terms of international invisible exchange transformed many tax haven economies such that, as intermediate economies within the international trading system, they together established a new secondary trading system for transnational/international business. Part II has provided a series of British Isle case studies to demonstrate how a traditional 'guardian' onshore/offshore politico-economic friction matrix and 'currency bond' interact and how such structural transformation can be effected. This part will now outline the global pattern of such developments since the early 1970s. Chapter I will briefly indicate the individual development profiles of particular centres grouped on a regional basis. Chapter II will discuss recent changes in onshore attitudes to external invisible business and its location as between onshore and offshore sites.

*All that comes with the flood will return with the ebb. Riches too rapidly acquired, or ill-gotten, will disappear as quickly as they came. MacCulloch, Sir E., *Guernsey Folk Lore,* ed. by E.F. Carey, London, Elliot Stock, 1903, p.515.

CHAPTER I
The Development Decade of the 1970s: A Global Review of the Offshore Transformation of Tax Haven Centres

Earlier chapters in Part I have already explained how the 'push' factor of particular autonomous policy-imposed distortions created by US banking regulations were intensified in the early 1960s, and the 'pull' factor of a general need in all advanced economies for a wider geographical spread of activities to match that of individual industrial domestic parent companies that were expanding abroad, were of pivotal significance for much of the momentum behind early offshore development. US banks reacted to these circumstances primarily by expanding their own branch networks, whereas most European banks with the exception of many from the UK tended initially to prefer consortia. This latter preference arose due to the European banks' smaller portfolio of international companies and the fact that the consortium vehicle was ideally suited to the syndicated Euroloan market that emerged in the late 1960s and grew rapidly from US $4.7 billion in 1970 to US $82.8 billion by 1979: this was despite a hiatus in 1975 mostly conditioned by the ending in 1974 of the US Interest Equalization Tax, the termination of which was confidently expected to lead to the repatriation and transfer of a large part of the Eurobond business but not to the short-term end of the market, with the continued existence of Regulation Q which prohibited interest payments on deposits of less than thirty days, an expectation that proved in the event extremely optimistic.

Given the general onshore conditions previously outlined, Eurocurrency business and the arrangement of syndicated international loans became a diversification possibility not only for traditional tax haven enclaves such as Luxembourg, Switzerland, and Panama, but also for island states, many of which were newly independent and looking for development possibilities to exploit and/or were permitted to participate therein by a benevolent colonial master, or, subsequent to the 1973 oil crisis and the need to exploit the cycling and recycling of petrodollars, were ideally located to service the sudden rise to wealth of certain Middle East countries. As regards island states, development potential was often particularly viable in the case of former UK colonies which had had links with the City of London, which, despite the existence of UK exchange controls, had adopted a liberal 'open door' policy towards foreign bank entry to London both prior to 1970, and as part of a renewed domesic emphasis on banking competition after 1971, which encouraged non-resident trade, unlike the US and most other onshore centres: this had helped make the UK the dominant world centre for Eurocurrency activity, as well as a tax shelter for more than 4,000 non-UK resident companies by the early 1980s.

During the 1970s, a distinct reorientation took place in the pattern of syndicated Eurocurrency bank credits as Table LXVI demonstrates. While the impor-

TABLE LXVI: New syndicated Eurocurrency bank credits 1970–79 (in US$bn.)

	1970	*1971*	*1972*	*1973*	*1974*	*1975*	*1976*	*1977*	*1978*	*1979*
Industrial countries	4.2	2.6	4.1	13.8	20.7	7.3	11.3	17.4	29.1	27.5
Non-OPEC LDCs	0.3	0.9	1.5	4.5	6.3	8.2	11.0	13.5	26.9	35.4
OPEC countries	0.1	0.4	0.9	2.8	1.1	2.9	4.0	7.5	10.4	12.6
Communist countries	n.a.	0.1	0.3	0.8	1.2	2.6	2.5	3.4	3.8	7.3
Totals	4.7	4.0	6.8	21.9	29.3	21.0	28.8	41.8	70.2	82.8

Source: Morgan Guaranty Trust Company, *World Financial Markets.*

tance of industrial countries is to be noted in the years up to 1974, the significance of non-OPEC less-developed-country loans, and to lesser extent, OPEC-country loans became evident in the latter half of the period. These syndicated credits accounted for about half of total Eurocurrency bank lending, the remainder being unpublicized and contracted for in shorter maturities primarily to the private sector for trade financing or internationally related business.

It was shown in Table IV in Part I Chapter I that the official statistics given by the Bank for International Settlements indicate that offshore centres accounted for about 14 per cent of the use of Eurocurrency funds more or less throughout the 1970s. The above figure underestimates the global importance of offshore centres due to the narrow coverage of the reporting countries. More comprehensive estimates are published from time to time in the Morgan Guaranty Trust Company's monthly *World Financial Markets* from which the figures for 1970 and 1980 have been extracted in Table LXVII. It can be seen that participation in Eurocurrency business was confined to only seven offshore centres and ten onshore centres in 1970 but had spread more widely to twelve offshore centres and thirteen onshore centres by 1980. The market share of offshore haven centres grew from 13.0 per cent to over 34 per cent of the gross 1980 total at the expense of the onshore centres. Within the offshore group, the Bahamas and Caymans are the largest centre despite a decline, followed by Luxembourg, Singapore and Switzerland, with a new generation of centres in the Far Middle East in the ascendant. The other main feature demonstrated in the table is the relative decline in importance of onshore European centres from 71 per cent in 1970 to 59.7 per cent in 1980.

This shift away from W. Europe and N. America and new emphasis on Latin America and the Far East is confirmed by the statistics that emerge in Table LXVIII resulting from a regional breakdown being made of the identified borrower countries revealed in the Morgan Guaranty Trust Company's *World Financial Markets* Reports in relation to publicized Eurobonds and Bank Credits. Thus offshore centres in the latter areas have benefited as 'booking' centres for many of these loans, notwithstanding where they may have been 'arranged' within the global network of onshore external markets and offshore financial centres. The figures in Table LXVII are however given gross. Net figures, if available would net out repayments and refinancing of existing loans, stand-by credits not utilized etc., which result in double-counting globally.

Switzerland and Luxembourg are included with offshore centres in Table

TABLE LXVII: List of reported onshore and offshore Euromarket centres in 1970, 1975 and 1980 together with the reported size of their Eurocurrency activities and their percentage total market shares

	1970		*1975*		*1980**	
Market areas	*Centre size (US$bn.)*	*% Market share*	*Centre size (US$bn.)*	*% Market share*	*Centre size (US$bn.)*	*% Market share*
Onshore centres						
European centres:	82.6	71.0	304	62.7	789	59.7
UK	50.4	45.3	178	36.7	429	32.5
France	9.6	8.6	52	10.7	133	10.1
Germany	2.9	2.6	12	2.3	24	1.8
Italy	10.1	9.1	18	3.7	41	3.1
Belgium	4.9	4.4	19	3.9	64	4.8
Netherlands	4.2	3.8	19	3.9	54	4.1
Austria					16	1.2
Denmark					3	0.2
Ireland					3	0.2
Spain			3	0.6	11	0.8
Sweden	0.5	0.4	3	0.6	11	0.8
Rest of the world	14.2	12.7	34	7.0	82	6.2
Canada	8.7	7.8	14	2.9	31	2.3
Japan	5.5	4.9	20	4.1	51	3.9
Offshore centres						
Haven centres:	14.5	13.0	147	30.3	451	34.1
Luxembourg	2.5	2.2	30	6.2	107	8.1
Switzerland	6.1	5.5	18	3.7	37	2.8
Bahamas & Caymans	4.7	4.2	62	12.8	147	11.1
Bahrain			2	0.4	33	2.5
Hong Kong	0.4	0.4	9	1.9	30	2.3
Kuwait			2	0.4	6	0.5
N. Antilles					6	0.5
Panama	0.4	0.4	8	1.6	32	2.4
Philippines			1	0.2	2	0.2
Singapore	0.4	0.4	13	2.7	47	3.6
United Arab Emirates			2	0.4	4	0.3
Gross totals	101.3	100.0	485	100.0	1322	100.0

Source: Morgan Guaranty Trust, *World Financial Markets.*

*March figures.

LXVII, as indeed is Panama, because they do provide a comprehensive range of facilities for external trade activities to which their economies are substantially geared, unlike the UK, despite the importance of the City of London as a Euromarket centre; and France, despite the importance of Paris as the centre for Eurosterling. Moreover, Switzerland, Luxembourg and Panama belong to a first generation of countries that constituted a secondary trading system more continental in scope, which preceded the developments of the 1960s, having emerged in the inter-war period. Since the early 1960s they have become part of the new, more global, secondary trading system.

TABLE LXVIII: Regional dispersion of published Eurobond and bank credit borrowers 1970–80

Borrower countries	*% Share 1970–71*	*% Share 1972–74*	*% Share 1975–77*	*% Share 1978–80*
W. Europe	40.7	42.7	29.0	26.4
E. Europe	0.4	3.5	4.4	2.4
N. America	40.0	16.3	15.7	13.6
L. America	3.0	10.2	14.3	17.4
Far East	1.7	5.5	10.1	14.9
Middle East	1.3	2.5	2.6	0.5
Africa	1.7	4.1	3.5	1.5
Oceania	2.7	1.6	3.2	1.0
Multinational companies	0.2	2.6	1.7	0.1
Industrial institutions	7.4	5.2	9.4	5.3
Not specified	0.2	5.0	5.9	15.6
Value in US$bn.	11.2	82.4	176.1	347.7

Source: computed from Morgan Guaranty Trust Company, *World Financial Markets.*

TABLE LXIX: Number of foreign banks directly represented in London and New York 1970–80

	No. foreign banks in	
Year	*London*	*New York*
1970	161	75
1971	174	81
1972	213	85
1973	230	98
1974	262	114
1975	261	127
1976	263	144
1977	298	177
1978	311	208
1979	328	240
1980	351	249

Source: Parker, *The Banker,* February 1981.[1]

Table LXVII clearly establishes the pre-eminence of London by its one-third share of total deposits despite its decline since 1970. Given such statistics, it would seem that London might merit the title 'offshore centre'; however, given the definition as stated in Part I Chapter I, it would seem preferable to designate it as an onshore external centre given its relative position within the British economy. Certainly, relative to New York, it has consistently encouraged the presence of foreign banks as is evident from the statistics given in Table LXIX. Moreover, in addition to the 353 directly represented foreign banks in 1980, there were a further sixty-five institutions indirectly represented through a shareholding in one or more of twenty-nine joint venture banks or deposit-taking institutions. Table LXVII does not include all offshore financial centre locations or those tax havens that did not, but might yet, develop as centres of global importance. Moreover, not all offshore financial centre transformation was directly linked to the Eurocurrency business. As has already been indicated, there was a constant need for banks and other finance and industrial enterprises to extend their chain of world-wide representation and participation, to look out for tax-efficient bases for their increasingly global operations, to find means by which to penetrate industrial hinterlands and to overcome any invisible trade barriers if necessary in the process. Transnational financial business had to follow and pursue clients, potential depositors and markets, continuous access to which was essential if they were to maintain their competitiveness within a world trading system. The scope for financial vehicle innovation was wide, yet there was still, at the country level, a tendency to maintain strict exchange controls combined with vigorous tax laws by which to constrain international currency flows. However, possibilities for frictioneering to exploit the anomalies and asymmetries in the international friction structure were there and added to in the 1970s by the spread of political independence to formerly colonial areas, and, by the paternalist encouragement given by some colonial centre countries, such as the UK, to the newly independent periphery states. Options were opened up for tax haven offshore financial centre development in an unprecedented way. Traditional havens or newly independent but aspiring havens had the choice of attempted development based on:

a) zero tax with or without double taxation treaties with other countries;
b) low taxes with or without double taxation treaties with other countries;
c) a combination of (*a*) or (*b*) with special tax and/or other privileges with regard to specific business of an international character (banking, insurance, shipping, offshore funds) or domestic industry undertaken by international business within local free trade zones.

The pursuit of any of the above required the importation of foreign expertise, the supply of which was limited. Moreover, for the offshore hinterland of each continental region, possibilities of development were not open to all states. Mere provision of a low or zero friction economic environment does not ensure development without political stability and continued confidence in future political stability being present: this applied to newly independent areas such as were within the Caribbean region as much as to sophisticated centres that became internally threatened, as was the case in the Lebanon. Furthermore, despite an appropriate design of offshore domestic friction structures, failure to appreciate the needs of multinational business to impress on onshore tax regimes and others the 'legitimacy' of their activities by the provision of local supervision of their activities led in many cases to very short run gains followed by a low reputation that circumscribed development or postponed substantial financial sector growth until a due period of time had elapsed and local supervisory powers had been instituted.

As the global dispersion of actual and potential centres exhibited a regional clustering pattern, often originating from geographical time-zone and continental proximity advantages, the evolution and development of each prime centre will be reviewed in relation to its region as a whole and its constellation of lesser centres. Some thirteen centres will now be discussed in relation to four main regions within the limits of available published data. The regions and their respective centres are as follows:

1. *The Caribbean Basin:* Bermuda, the Bahamas, the Caymans, Netherlands Antilles, Panama;
2. *Europe:* Switzerland and Luxembourg;
3. *The Middle East:* Bahrain, the United Arab Emirates;
4. *The Far East and Oceania:* Hong Kong, Singapore, the New Hebrides (Vanuatu), the Norfolk Islands.

1. THE CARIBBEAN BASIN

This area has been and is notable for a considerable number of actual tax haven locations and therefore potential sites for offshore finance centres. The area is geographically interposed between two rich continents, with Canada and the United States to the north and west, and Central and South America with their areas of political instability and oil *nouveaux riches* to the south. Furthermore Panama which borders on this area is crucially located at a geographical global interface between the west and the east. All aspiring havens are largely within the same time zone of operation as the all important world capital market of New York, to which they all to a greater or lesser extent have proximity, as well as to other important onshore US regional capital markets.

Primary features of the area as a whole during the 1970s include the exclusion in 1972 of all the British associated states from the rescheduled Sterling Area, a general economic dependency on the North American onshore hinterland such that many previous currency bonds with sterling became linked to the US dollar, incipient political unrest, a failure to appreciate the importance of reputation and the need for local regulations to promote long-term offshore banking developments which, at the end of the decade, was crucial when much business from Switzerland and the Middle East sought a haven from the political fears created by the Iran and Afghanistan crises.

Within this area some five main centres have emerged as being of international significance as offshore finance centres—Bermuda, the Bahamas, the Caymans, the Netherlands Antilles and Panama. These will be separately considered below. There are, however, many other haven centres that have had financial centre aspirations which were not realized in the 1970s. Two potential centres have not had such pretensions and have pursued nationalistic policies with regard to localization of banking: Jamaica (since 1966), and Trinidad and Tobago (since 1970). Moreover, both these latter centres have been subject to intermittent political instability.

Of the tax haven centres that failed to develop into offshore finance centres, many merely owe their attractiveness to US and UK tax treaties whereby inter-onshore provisions have been extended to colonial areas, thereby permitting their use as a base for holding companies, as has been the case in Antigua, Dominica, Grenada, Montserrat, St. Kitts, St. Lucia, and St. Vincent. Some extensions of provisions were discretionary, as was the case between the UK and the British Virgin Islands, where one such agreement was terminated without renewal in 1972; in other cases special relationships were permitted, as in the case between the US and the US Virgin Islands, where a foreign corporation is allowed to satisfy its US tax obligations by paying tax on its world-wide income to the authorities of those islands. The significance of Montserrat depends on its double taxation agreements not only with the UK and the US, but also with Denmark, New Zealand and Sweden; that of the British Virgin Islands depends on similar arrangements with Denmark, Japan, Norway, Sweden and Switzerland. In some cases tax haven development was specifically recommended by the out-going colonial master country, as was the case with the Turks and Caicos Islands and the UK-sponsored Jakeway Report of 1970, though lack of resources and communications severely hampered their immediate viability as such.

Several centres made initial attempts that were foolhardy in that they encouraged 'shell' type operations which gave them a bad reputation both with reputable bankers and with important onshore tax authorities which subsequent legislative attempts to rectify did not reverse. Thus Anguilla developed a reputation under its permissive laws in the early 1970s for 'off-the-peg' banks and shady company-broking activities. Attempts were made to change this by means of the Companies Act (Amendment) Ordinance of 1976, and measures in 1977 that prohibited undesirable business registration: some 125 companies were deregistered, and a licence fee of US$500 was imposed on offshore companies having the word 'bank' in their incorporated title. St.Vincent introduced new legislation in 1977 to provide for tax exemption of offshore companies but in 1979 the US Comptroller of Currency saw fit to name some twenty-five 'shell' banks as operating from that island of which US nationals were told to be wary.

In the case of many potential centres, their relative remoteness and lack of economic development notwithstanding, ability to act autonomously is often severely constrained and frustrated by the artificial constitutional associations that were imposed when 'self-determination' was granted. Many of these 'colonial marriages of convenience' were arranged by the former Colonial Office in Whitehall, London, in the hope that groups of islands could function effectively as political and administrative units. Many of these arrangements failed to take into account age-old animosities and rivalries, e.g. Anguilla was linked to St. Kitts and Nevis, with whom it had had hostile relationships since the eighteenth century: after a long battle it seceded from this relationship and managed, with reluctant Whitehall consent, to regain its status as a Crown Colony as from 1 January 1981. Similar requests have been made in respect of the Anguilla/Barbuda link, the Nevis/St. Kitts link, and the Grenadine/St. Vincent link. Moreover, other islands such as Montserrat, the British Virgin Islands (twenty islands), the Turks and Caicos Islands (thirty islands), have sought ways to perpetuate their dependency status in the shadow of the nationalistic Bahamas. Thus, despite the fact that all the above-mentioned islands offer tax haven advantages for offshore activities in varying degrees, they have not become offshore finance centres.

Two main candidates for achieving future offshore centre status would appear to be Barbados and the Turks and Caicos Islands. Barbados is perhaps the largest of the lesser potential centres. It is a low tax area which has given special concessions to business since 1965 under the International Business Companies Act prior to achieving independence in November 1966. Its currency was once linked to sterling but is now linked to the US dollar. It has a tax treaty network which includes the UK, the US, Denmark, Norway, Sweden, Switzerland and Canada. It was a late entrant into offshore banking, being initially handicapped by its bad name acquired through an early unregulated development which resulted in two of its islands being used allegedly as a conduit for the illegal gains of organized crime in North America. However, given a well-developed infrastructure, political stability and first-class communications, a new attempt was made in 1979 with the introduction of an Offshore Banking Act. Although this Act does impose a 2½ per cent tax on profits, unlike the Bahamas and the Caymans, by the end of 1980 some six international banks had taken up representation on the island, including three Canadian, two American and one British. The Turks and Caicos Islands may develop in the near future following injections of British aid for their tourist industry and the institution of new Banking Ordinances in July 1979 regulating the licensing of offshore banks and imposing fines for unauthorized disclosure of financial information.

As regards potential continental enclave states bordering on the area, two possibilities exist for the future: Costa Rica and Mexico. In the case of the former, pensioners are allowed to live there tax-free, the country is politically stable, although, with two exceptions, all its banks are nationalized: development thus seems unlikely in the immediate future. Mexico however did make some tentative moves in the direction of external financial sector development following the rapid development of its capital market in the latter 1970s, one feature of which was the creation of its unique investment instrument—the petrobond: a

TABLE LXX: Main characteristics of Caribbean Basin major offshore centres for non-resident companies or trusts

Tax haven provisions	*Bermuda*	*Bahamas*	*Caymans*	*N. Antilles*	*Panama*
No tax	X	X	X		
No tax on foreign source income					X
Low tax				X	
Best for					
(a) Trusts	X	X	X		
(b) Holding cos.				X	
(c) Shipping cos.					X
No exchange control					X
No tax treaties	X	X	X		X
US tax treaty				X	
No-tax guarantee	X	X	X		
Bank secrecy		X	X		X
Numbered bank accounts		X			X
No financial disclosure					X
Bearer shares		X	X	X	X

Source: extracted from table on p. 155 in M. Malone, *How To Do Business Tax Free,* Delaware, Enterprise Pub. Inc., 1976.

freely negotiable participation certificate giving the bearer rights to a specific quantity of Mexican oil at a fixed coupon rate of interest and having a redemption value indexed to the price of oil. A new law that came into force in early January 1982 permits the setting-up of offshore banking units dealing with exclusively external activities. Initially this has been met with a cool reception because of Mexico's high operation costs and inferior communications relative to other centres in the area, and the existence of local withholding taxes combined with a lack of tax treaties to mitigate their effect on local foreign investment.

A discussion is now given of the major centres of the area, the main characteristics of which are summarized in Table LXX.

Bermuda

The territory of Bermuda contains some one hundred islands but centres on a group of seven connected by bridges. It is within easy air access to New York (1½ hours) and the UK (6½ hours). It is the oldest self-governing colony, having a tradition that goes back to 1620, having achieved full self-government in 1968. For many years it has been dependent on tourism, especially from the US, and financial services. Bermuda was the pioneer of the exempt company: this dates back to the 1950 Exempted Companies Act which places no restrictions on the nationality of shareholders or directors of companies incorporated locally but trading and doing business externally. There is a minimum share capital of BD$12,000, all of which must be subscribed. It offers to these companies a no-tax guarantee up to the year 2006: the number of such companies grew from 2,019 in 1970 to 3,328 in 1976 and to 5,088 by 1980. An Overseas Investment Tax is levied at 5 per cent on the purchase of foreign exchange with local currency for purposes of investment.

During the 1970s, while it has been an undoubted offshore financial centre of world standing, the development of Bermuda has been atypical due to its exclusive attitude to bank entry. Unlike other offshore centres it is not a centre for branches or subsidiaries of foreign banks. All banking, both local and international, has been confined to just four banks: two well established, the Bank of Bermuda (dating from 1889) and the Bank of N.T. Butterfield and Son (dating from 1858); and two created in 1969, the Bermuda National Bank (40 per cent owned by the Bank of Nova Scotia) and the Bermuda Provident Bank (31 per cent owned by Barclays Bank International). Banks may only be incorporated by Act of Parliament and at least 60 per cent of shares must be Bermuda owned.

During the 1970s two developments are to be noted. Firstly , a stock exchange dealing in local securities was opened in Feburary 1971 which aided its development as a centre for offshore funds, the number of which rose from nine in 1972 to twenty-four in 1981, making it the fifth largest centre for such funds, as was shown in Table LXIII in Part II Chapter VI. Secondly, it became the largest centre in the world for captive insurance companies. Captive insurance had begun in a small way in Bermuda in the 1960s, but received a boost in 1969 with the passing of the Bahamian Insurance Act which caused some two hundred Bahamian captives to seek sanctuary in Bermuda, a least half of which were estimated to have been US and Canadian corporations. By mid-1980 this number had increased to over 1,000 out of an estimated world total of 1,500. This development occurred despite Bermuda's omission in 1972 from the Rescheduled Sterling Area and the flight and subsequent development of captives in Guernsey and, in addition, the loss of the previously dominant British trust business; and the loss of political confidence caused by the murder of the Police Commissioner in 1972, the assassination of the Governor in 1973 and riots in December 1977. The development of captive insurance is likely to be checked by favourable tax changes in the US states of Colorado and Tennessee and new anti-avoidance rules in the US, under which US owned captives established outside the USA will be classified as Controlled Foreign Corporations (CFCs) and will achieve no tax savings unless:

a) a foreign corporation owns at least 50 per cent of the captive and US risks are not more than 75 per cent of the total;
b) a foreign corporation owns at least 75 per cent of the captive;
c) at least 50 per cent is owned by other shareholders who may be US, but none of which holds less than 10 per cent *and* US risks are limited to 75 per cent;
d) 75 per cent or more is owned by other shareholders who may all be US, each of whom owns less than 10 per cent of the captive.

An automated international futures exchange is to open in 1982, in which 600 seats will be offered at $12,500 each to be cleared by London's International Commodity Clearing House and backed by major international banks.

The Bahamas

The Bahamas consists of a chain of 700 islands of which thirty are inhabited. Half of its 240,000 population live on New Providence where its capital, Nassau, is located. For a tax haven that was described in 1972 as 'probably past its zenith'[2] it has done spectacularly well and during the 1970s became the largest Eurocurrency centre outside London. The beginnings of its pre-eminence go back to 1970, when twenty-two US commercial banks opened branches in Nassau to avoid the high establishment expenses of a London operation, and to set up a low-cost launching-pad for Euro-dollar operations in the same time zone as New York but avoiding US restrictions on direct capital exports. Seventeen of the above mentioned banks had no previous international experience. By the end of 1972 a total number of 339 banking licences had been issued. Independence was achieved in 1973 after which the Bahamian Monetary Authority was replaced by a Central Bank in 1974. Throughout the 1970s active supervision of the registered banks has led to considerable numbers of licences being revoked as is indicated in Table LXXI. By 1980 there were about 300 banks, of which 108 were operating in the Eurocurrency market, including eighty-five branches of US banks, whose assets increased from $38.3bn. in 1975 to $89.7bn. by the end of February 1980. While much of this operation, perhaps 75 per cent, was arranged through onshore bank head offices and transacted through a Bahamian nameplate operation, this has begun to change under pressure from onshore control banks and foreign tax authorities, thus during 1980 two US banks, Citibank and Morgan Guaranty, issued Certificates of Deposit through their Nassau branches, each issue being

TABLE LXXI: Bahamian Bank and Trust Company licensing and revocations 1973–79 (revocations shown in brackets)

	Public				Restricted					Non-active				
End year	*Bank & trust*	*Bank*	*Trust*	*Total*	*Bank & trust*	*Bank*	*Trust*	*Nominee trust*	*Total*	*Bank & trust*	*Bank*	*Trust*	*Total*	*Total number of licences*
1973	45(3)	134(14)	12(1)	191(18)	10(3)	23(7)	49(6)	20	102(16)	7	14(1)	8	29(1)	322(35)
1974	40(7)	124(11)	10(2)	174(20)	9(2)	21(3)	36(6)	30	96(11)	5(2)	14(2)	8(2)	27(6)	297(37)
1975	39(4)	122(10)	9(1)	168(15)	6(1)	20	30(7)	30	86(8)	7	12(3)	2(6)	21(9)	275(32)
1976	40	118(1)	10(1)	168(2)	5	20	28(1)	28(1)	81(2)	4(1)	8	1	13(1)	262(5)
1977	43(1)	126(9)	9(1)	178(11)	5	18(1)	27(2)	31(2)	81(5)	4(3)	9(3)	1(1)	14(7)	273(23)
1978	47(3)	133(1)	10(1)	190(5)	5	17(1)	27(4)	33	82(5)	3	9	1	13	285(10)
1979	54	137	10	201	5	16(1)	30	36	87(1)	4	7(1)	1	12	300(2)

Source: Central Bank of the Bahamas Quarterly Review, December 1979, Tables 1.18 and 1.19.

worth \$100m. It was stated that this was both cheaper, being free from the Federal Reserve Board's reserve requirements (a CD costing 9 per cent on Wall Street can be issued through Nassau at 8¾ to 8⅞ per cent) and given a concomittant issue in New York of negotiable instruments could be traded directly on the US markets. At the end of the period the disturbances in Iran and Afghanistan, and even political fears regarding Switzerland, have placed a higher global premium on security of deposit from which Nassau has benefited such that more than thirty Swiss bank branches and subsidiaries have become located in Nassau.

Nassau is very diversified as a centre, having had a long tradition as a centre for trusts and companies since the early 1950s, when it followed Bermuda's exempt company example. By 1975 some 14,000 companies had been incorporated. There is a tax-free zone in the Freeport area on the island of Grand Bahama, where companies are guaranteed freedom from taxes until 1990, and from import or stamp duties until the year 2054. Shipping registration under 'flags of convenience' provisions has been available since the end of 1976. The Bahamas is a no-tax area without tax treaties but with numbered bank account facilities and recently intensified bank secrecy laws. Towards the end of the 1970s it was evident that its Eurolending business was beginning to be threatened by certain US States which were opening their doors to international banking—Florida, Delaware 'the Luxembourg of the USA', Main and South Dakota. Some such loss seems inevitable for these and other reasons to be explained in the next chapter. William Allen, the Governor of the Bahamian Central Bank, is now considering the future establishment of an offshore stock exchange, a commodity exchange, and a foreign exchange centre. Apart from concentrating new promotional efforts outside the USA by looking for business, especially trust accounts, in Latin America and in Europe, captive insurance is regarded as a new development possibility, despite the previous unfortunate experience that resulted from the 1969 Insurance Act referred to in the discussion of Bermuda above. Thus, in September 1979, Bahamas Underwriters Services Inc. with a sister company in the Caymans became the first management company to specialize exlusively in captive insurance.

The Caymans

Being 500 miles due south of Miami and equidistant from North, South and Central America, the Caymans are at a strategic geographical commercial interface. They are a no-tax, no tax-treaty area, where no-tax guarantees are given. Until 1959, they were administered by Jamaica and became a Crown Colony in 1962. Modern company and trust legislation was introduced in 1966 with the Banks and Trust Companies Regulation Law, and in 1967 with the Cayman Trust Law, after which trusts flourished and foreign banking was encouraged. By 1972, there were reported to be over 2,500 companies and more than 600 exempt trusts served by fifty licensed banks. By 1980 these had grown to 320 international banks, the majority of which were restricted to offshore activities, 6,000 exempt trusts and more than 12,000 companies.

Much of the initial impetus for development came from a number of companies that have either abandoned the Bahamas or, together with Bahamian companies, set up 'shell' companies in the Caymans as a bolthole in case the political climate of the Bahamas deteriorated. One of the distinct advantages of the Caymans has been that, despite a population that is 20 per cent European, 25 per cent African, and the remainder multiracial, there has been political, social and racial harmony. As regards commercial activity, no disclosure of information is required, exempt companies do not have to file an annual return of shareholders, 'no par value' shares can be issued, and with Exchange Control approval bearer shares can be issued to non-residents. Exempted trusts are permissible, provided the beneficiaries are resident and domiciled outside the Caymans, and can have a perpetuity of a hundred years with up to fifty years tax exemption guaranteed. The 1967 Trust Law states that no law subsequently enacted can impose any tax or duty on income or realised gains on any property forming such a trust. One innovatory method of attempted onshore tax avoidance is that all the rights of beneficiaries may be vested in the local Registrar of Trusts so that, theoretically, none has any legal or equitable rights to any income or property that might otherwise be taxed onshore. Communications are good with Miami, Texas, Kingston Jamaica and San Jose (Costa Rica). Tourism has grown from virtually nothing in 1966 to 178,800 in 1980, three-quarters of which come from the USA. The Confidential Relationship (Preservation) Law of 1976 provides for prosecution in the event of disclosure of information. Exchange Control was abolished on 17 March 1980. In 1979 an insurance law was passed for the licensing and control of assurance and insurance. A ship registration business has also been attracted to the island.

The Netherlands Antilles

Formerly the Dutch West Indies captured in the 1630s, the Netherlands Antilles consist of the Leeward Islands of Curacao, Aruba and Bonaire, situated some forty to seventy miles off the coast of Venezuela and much further north and east of Puerto Rico, the Windward Islands of St. Maarten, St. Eustatius and Saba. For offshore purposes it is the Leeward Islands that are of interest, especially Curacao and Aruba, both of which have free zone areas for external business where specially low rates of tax on profits are applicable. Otherwise, the group is a low tax area and an integral part of the Kingdom of the Netherlands, confirmed as such by a 1954 Dutch Statute, yet fully autonomous in internal affairs. The existence of double taxation provisions with the USA, the UK, Holland and Denmark, reduce or remove withholding tax liability on interest or dividends remitted to Curacao: thus the one with the US reduces the level of withholding tax from 30 per cent to 15 per cent. These tax treaties permit remission of interest by parent companies to their Antilles subsidiaries without withholding taxes, an advantage the islands have over Luxembourg in respect of the use of subsidiary companies for parent company financing. Moreover, since 1967, an increasing number of Eurocurrency loans have been taken up by NA based subsidiaries of major US and other foreign corporations, the proceeds of which have been used for intercompany financing by way of loans.

Special tax facilities have been available under the Profits Tax Ordinance

1940, which have made the islands a centre for investment and holding companies in the area of finance and real estate. These tax advantages are available to limited liability companies who may issue bearer shares. Since 1963 special tax facilities have been available to stimulate the establishment of ocean shipping and aviation companies. Since 1970 the banking sector has been regulated under National Ordinance No. 138, as revised by No. 23 1976, since when some thirty or more offshore banks have been licensed as well as eighty-two credit institutions. Tighter supervision of offshore banks is being planned as well as the encouragement of international insurance companies.

Panama

Its crossroads location between Central and South America, and the international transport focus given to it by its canal linking the Atlantic to the Pacific, has for many years provided it with the opportunities for offshore frictioneering. Panama became independent from Colombia in 1903 and the canal was opened by the US in August 1914. While in theory it has its own currency, the balboa, the US dollar circulates freely: indeed, US banking in Panama goes back to the arrival of Citibank in 1904. Since 1927 its company law has encouraged company formation which by 1981 had reached some 50,000 on the register. Since 1948 there has been a Free Trade Zone at Colon at the Atlantic entrance to the canal, where more than 800 companies by 1976 and 1,000 by 1979 have become established following the 1957 Investment Incentives Act. Panama is a no-tax area for offshore business deriving foreign-source income but does have taxes on Panamanian-source income. Law No. 9 1964 specifically includes no-tax provisions for invoicing products handled abroad, directing transactions abroad, distributing dividends or participation activities abroad, receiving interest, commission and similar fees from financial operations conducted abroad. Following a series of financial scandals in the 1960s, a Cabinet Decree (No. 238 of July 1970) set up a National Banking Commission in lieu of the absence of a central bank to supervise and license banking activities and to re-establish Panama's reputation as a financial centre. The latter resulted in a clean-up operation wherein the 247 registered banks were cut down to about twenty. In 1974 an amendment law, Law No. 93, resulted in a three-category licence system: 'general' (for local and foreign banking), 'international' (exclusively offshore), and 'representative' (mere representative presence). In that year thirty banks were registered as class 1; thirteen as class 2; and three as class 3. By 1981 these numbers had increased to forty-five, twenty-five and nine respectively.

Much of the offshore development of Panama resulted from its being used as the Latin American branch of the Eurodollar market for channelling and recycling such funds: it has not developed into a Latin American dollar centre. Legislative provisions now permit local depositing of funds with foreign bank subsidiaries that have general licences. Bank secrecy is enforced and numbered accounts are available. Deposits rose from $420m. in 1970 to $34 billion in 1980. The business emphasis is now shifting increasingly towards the use of Panama as a centre of Latin American regional and subregional activity. Thus many US and European banks use it to service their South American regional Euromarket portfolios and Latin American banks use it to funnel Eurofunds into their national systems.

Panama has thus become a very diversified centre and moreover, since the Reinsurance (Companies) Law No. 72, 1976, has sought to encourage reinsurance business activity, since when thirty-four underwriting companies have become registered and a Latin American Reinsurance Syndicate, PLAR, has been formed: reinsurance has grown from USA $20m. in 1976 to US $100m. in 1981. Some politico-economic uncertainty arose before the US handing back of the Canal Zone in October 1979. The stability of the State now rests to some extent on its ability to run the canal to the satisfaction of its international users.

2. EUROPE

Political upheavals since the nineteenth century have resulted in periodic migrations of refugees seeking to transfer their often considerable financial assets to places which promised political and fiscal security and neutrality. Several European enclave states were able to offer such refuge, of which some were relatively large, such as Switzerland and Luxembourg, and others relatively small such as Liechtenstein, Monaco, Gibraltar and more recently Andorra and Campione. In addition the relatively liberal atttitude of the United Kingdom towards external entrepôt business and the existence of its satellite British Isle havens provided a slightly more remote location for continental European funds and those of a growing number of expatriates globally based. In reality, the activities of many of the above-mentioned locations were co-operatively organized between the individual haven and a contiguous state e.g. Andorra is a co-principality ruled by the Bishop of Urgel and the President of France; Campione is an Italian enclave surrounded by Switzerland; Monaco is in monetary union with France but not fiscally sovereign with regard to French tax payers; Liechtenstein has had a close customs relationship with Switzerland since 1924, and has additional close monetary and exchange control relationships with that country; Gibraltar, the Channel Islands and the Isle of Man all have close ties with the United Kingdom as has already been outlined.

Our survey of developments in the 1970s will concentrate on Luxembourg and Switzerland and largely ignore the above-mentioned continental enclave centres as they did not develop diversified external financial sectors that became globally based. For example, Andorra has no registered foreign banks and only six domestic ones; Gibraltar tended to discourage the establishment of offshore banks in this period (an attitude that has very recently changed) although it is a centre for international shipping as a result of the 1965 Merchant Shipping (Taxation and Concessions) Ordinance, and for exempt companies under the Company (Taxation and Concessions) Ordinance 1967, and insurance companies are offered a 25-year income tax holiday—only five banks were registered here during the 1970s.

A few comments, however, need to be made regarding Liechtenstein although, again, it has not really developed as an offshore finance centre, only three banks being established there. Liechtenstein is a sovereign state situated between

Austria and Switzerland, which has been in customs union with Switzerland since 1923. Its currency is the Swiss franc and it is subject to Swiss turnover tax, import and stamp duties, and exchange control regulations. It has been a centre for holding companies and domiciliary companies, of which there are two forms, the Aktiengesellschaft and the Anstalt. Since a law of 1928 it has been a centre for trusts and is the only European country to recognize the Anglo-Saxon trust concept. Following a series of financial scandals—the 1977 Crédit Suisse scandal involving the Liechtenstein company Texon Finanzanstalt known as 'the Chiasso Affair', and the scandal involving the Weisskredit Bank in Lugano—it adopted strict controls in 1980 with regard to the presentation and auditing of accounts and changed the rules concerning membership of company boards requiring the presence of at least one local member who must be either a qualified accountant or a lawyer.

Unlike centres in many of the other global regions, the European centres tend to be only partially low tax ones, rarely no-tax ones, and do not combine their offshore activities with free trade zone activities.

Luxembourg

Luxembourg has been in economic union with Belgium since 1922 and its external monetary relations are handled by the Belgian National Bank. The internal absence of a central bank has helped to attract to it foreign commercial banks because there is consequently no internal imposition of minimum reserve requirements on bank liabilities. Moreover, since 1929, there has been a law giving holding companies tax exemption, with the exception of a registration tax of 1 per cent of subscribed capital and an annual *taxe d'abonnement* equivalent to 0.16 per cent of the actual value of shares issued, making it for such companies the 'Gibraltar of the North'.

During the 1970s, Luxembourg became the fourth largest Eurocurrency centre after London, the Bahamas and Caymans, and Paris. Its central West European position enabled it to service the particular needs of particular countries during this period. The main features of its development have been in this respect threefold.

a) Its importance in relation to West Germany as the centre for the Euro-Deutschmark market, and as a business base for Scandinavian banks doing business in West Germany, their major export market. The beginnings of this connection go back to 1967 with the arrival of the Dresdener Bank which set up Compagnie Luxembourgeoise de Banque, which was followed by twenty-eight others. Proximity to Frankfurt, low office costs and the absence of the Bundesbank's minimum reserve requirements, created considerable attractions. Thus, about 45 per cent of Luxembourg's Euromark business is settled in Deutschmarks.

b) Its importance in relation to Belgium as a backdoor for Belgian investment money. Belgium has been a major source of funds for borrowers on the Eurobond market, much of which has been channelled via Luxembourg: indeed, the 'Belgian postman' has been the proverbial name given to the

TABLE LXXII: Luxembourg quoted securities 1970–80

End year totals	*Shares*	*Domestic bonds*	*International bonds*	*Total quoted securities*
1970	165	47	432	644
1971	170	45	509	724
1972	172	44	590	806
1973	165	47	630	842
1974	159	44	667	870
1975	152	47	779	978
1976	152	50	961	1,163
1977	162	57	1,108	1,327
1978	165	58	1,176	1,399
1979	169	63	1,260	1,492
1980	178	67	1,312	1,557

traditional Eurobond investor. Consequently, the Belgian bank Kredietbank Luxembourgeoise is often a major participant in the Luxembourg market.

c) As a conduit for Swiss banks Luxembourg has become a useful location for Swiss subsidiaries as a way round their own domestic capital controls, which are not applied in Switzerland on a consolidated balance sheet basis.

Thus, during the 1970s, the primary importance of Luxembourg has been as a centre for Eurocurrency activity. It has provided the Eurobond market with its main geographical home and has become more concerned with international issues than most other centres in the world. As a result of its acquired expertise in the new Euromarkets, its importance changed during the 1970s from being primarily a money marketplace to being a centre for medium-term investment. Central to this development has been the importance of its stock exchange. This exchange was founded under a special law of 1927 by which its transactions were granted exemption from turnover tax and stamp duty. It is a bankers' bourse, 80 per cent of its shares being owned by twelve banks locally established. During the 1970s this exchange became the international listing centre for Eurobonds due to its low listing fees, unbureaucratic and speedy procedures for admission, and its lack of withholding taxes and low brokerage rates. The importance of international bonds in Luxembourg is indicated in Table LXXII. Thus, whereas in 1970 international bonds accounted for 67 per cent of quoted securities, by 1980 this share had risen to 84.3 per cent: this development was no doubt aided by the attitude of some onshore states at this time, such as the UK, which banned the domestic launching of international bonds. The growth of international banks is indicated in Table LXXIII. Thus the number of registered banks rose from thirty-seven to 111. The relative and increasing importance of the German banks is indicated, closely followed by that of the Scandinavian and Swiss banks. The presence of these international banks has made Luxembourg an important arranging centre for loans and has given it a high capacity to syndicate quite substantial loans e.g. in 1978, three syndicates were arranged exclusively by and with Luxembourg banks for an aggregate single loan of DM 1 billion.

TABLE LXXIII: Banks in Luxembourg by nationality 1970–80

Country of origin	*1970*	*1971*	*1972*	*1973*	*1974*	*1975*	*1976*	*1977*	*1978*	*1979*	*1980*
Belgium/Luxembourg	14	14	14	14	13	12	12	12	12	12	12
France	4	4	4	4	5	5	5	6	6	6	8
Germany	3	6	12	16	16	16	15	20	24	28	30
Italy					1	1	2	3	4	5	6
Japan				1	2	2	2	3	4	4	4
Scandinavia				2	3	3	8	10	13	14	14
Switzerland	5	5	5	5	5	6	7	8	8	9	7
United States	7	8	10	16	15	15	12	13	12	12	11
Other countries	1	2	2	4	6	6	6	6	6	9	9
Joint ventures etc.	3	4	4	8	10	10	9	9	8	9	10
End year totals	37	43	51	70	76	76	78	90	97	108	111

Source: Commissariat au Controle des Banques.

Luxembourg's other attractions include the fact that its location permits a close proximity to foreign business for the subsidiaries set up by multinational companies to service corporate customers and gives facility to the refinancing of credit lines to such customers more cheaply. Given Luxembourg's tax neutral structure, it is therefore ideal for co-ordinating international company operations. International tax agreements have been concluded with Austria, Belgium, Brazil, France, Germany, the Netherlands, Ireland, the UK and the USA (although holding companies are excluded from the benefits of this tax treaty network). In comparison with other European countries, Luxembourg allows subsidiaries greater freedom in relending their revenues, especially to the US. It has less stringent capital requirements and allows debt-equity ratios as large as 10 to 1.

Towards the end of the 1970s, it was being used as a centre in which to list small oil and gas-related business as a means of providing access to the unofficial London market, where over-the-counter trading is forbidden if such companies are unlisted elsewhere and have not been in existence for at least three years. The growth of banking has fostered the development of other institutions and markets, e.g. by the end of the 1970s it had seventy-seven investment funds. A deterioration in the profitability of wholesale operations led to six innovations:

a) in 1979 value added tax on gold transactions was abolished just after West Germany and Switzerland applied it, which has encouraged the development of a gold market, which now has a daily fixing worth $35,000;

b) a stamp duty of 10.1 per cent has now been removed to encourage the development of a local market in dollar Certificates of Deposit;

c) under a new agreement which extends the sixty-year-old economic union with Belgium until 1991, there will be greater monetary autonomy under the aegis of a new Luxembourg Monetary Institute, although the parity between the Belgian and Luxembourg francs will be maintained;

d) the establishment of fiduciary accounts following new bank secrecy laws will encourage investment banking and portfolio management without the exchange control measures found in Switzerland;

e) changes in holding company law will allow such companies to invest in money market instruments and precious metals;
f) encouragement is being given to the use of Luxembourg as a base for foreign pension funds: this has already attracted a number of such funds from the US.

The above-mentioned frictioneering changes indicate an evident willingness on the part of the Luxembourg authorities to diversify financial sector activities and to benefit from the adverse economic circumstances and changes of policy attitude being experienced in Switzerland, which will now be considered.

Switzerland

Switzerland is a small landlocked confederation of twenty cantons and six half cantons, each with a considerable degree of individual sovereignty, such that the net tax position of any particular location for economic activity is affected by federal, cantonal and communal taxes. Within the federation, however, Zurich is the major financial centre, with Geneva and Basle being lesser centres.

For many decades Switzerland has acted as a haven of refuge for international capital. Neutrality during two World Wars, a generally sound and convertible currency with an absence of foreign exchange controls, the multi-lingual character of its people and its central European location, its stable political system, the importance attached to bank secrecy, and its reputation for reliability and trustworthiness, have all conspired to make it the significant 'money-box' centre for international funds. A special feature of Swiss development has been the existence of numbered (note, *not* anonymous) bank accounts and secrecy laws that date back to 1934, which were introduced to protect Jewish accounts from investigation by Nazi agents. Under Article 47 of the Swiss Banking Law, disclosure of information is not only open to civil action but is a punishable offence. Moreover, tax evasion is not regarded as a criminal offence as it is in the US and many other countries, so that divulging of information to foreign tax authorities is regarded as a contravention of Swiss law, even where a client elects to waive this right, as the *Financial Times,* 19 November 1981, reported in the case of *St. Joe Minerals* v. *the US Securities and Exchange Commission.* Above all it is this security feature of Switzerland and confidence in it that has proved attractive to international funds for the country has by no means been a zero tax, zero friction, financial centre. As a result, an abundance of excess savings over the needs of domestic credit demand ensures a considerable supply of funds for intermediation and external investment within the international banking and financial system. This is promoted by five main provisions.

a) An extensive network of double taxation agreements in relation to withholding taxes, as is indicated by Table LXXIV. Some twenty-two countries are involved as compared with only eight in the case of the Luxembourg network. The 35 per cent Swiss withholding tax chargeable on interest earned from bank deposits and bonds is reduced according to the terms of each specific agreement. However, these benefits under a 1962 law are limited to persons and companies having bona fide Swiss residence.

TABLE LXXIV: Comparative tax treaty networks and withholding tax provisions in Switzerland and Luxembourg

Withholding taxes / Recipient	Switzerland		Luxembourg		
	Interest on bonds & deposits (%)	*Dividends (%)*	*Domestic bonds & interest (%)*	*Dividends* (portfolio) (%)*	*Dividends (large holdings) (%)*
Resident corporations and individuals	35	35	5	15	
Non-resident corporations and individuals in –					
(a) Non-treaty countries	35	35	5	15	15
(b) Treaty countries					
Austria	5	5	5	15	15
Belgium	10	15	5	15	10
Canada	15	15			
Denmark	0	0			
Finland	0	5			
France	10	5	5	15	5
Germany	0	15	0	15	10
Ireland	0	10	0	15	5
Italy	12.5	15			
Japan	10	15			
Malaysia	10	15			
Netherlands	5	15	0	15	2.5
Norway	5	5			
Pakistan	15	35			
Portugal	10	15			
Singapore	10	15			
S. Africa	35	7.5			
Spain	10	15			
Sweden	5	5			
Trinidad & Tobago	10	20			
United Kingdom	0	15	0	15	5
United States	5	15	0	7.5	5

Source: Tables 12.3 and 16.6 of Kemp, *A Guide to World Money and Capital Markets.*
*Holding-company dividends are exempt.

b) The existence of zero tax companies, of which there are two kinds: holding companies, in which the main purpose must be the holding of shares in other companies, which pay no income tax whether federal or cantonal provided their entire income is so derived; and domiciliary companies, which must be registered in Switzerland for external trade purposes and can, at the discretion of the authorities, be given the same tax privileges as the above. All companies must have a majority of resident Swiss citizen shareholders and be registered with the Commercial Registrar.

c) Fiduciary accounts. Given an at-source tax of 35 per cent on the interest from domestic investments, Swiss banks began to offer trust balances on a commission basis for discretionary investment abroad in the 1960s as Euromarket transactions qualified as external investments. These deposits became relatively popular during the 1970s, especially for trustee accounts,

TABLE LXXV: The Swiss foreign bond market 1970–80

Year	*Foreign bonds launched in Switzerland US$m.*	*World foreign bond market US$m.*	*Swiss market as a % of total*
1970	312.5	2445.8	12.8
1971	867.1	3490.8	24.8
1972	1014.5	4384.6	23.1
1973	1535.3	5349.8	28.7
1974	972.4	7722.8	12.5
1975	3529.0	12300.8	28.7
1976	5443.5	18943.3	28.7
1977	4959.3	16610.2	29.8
1978	7608.9	21542.1	35.3
1979	9479.5	19979.6	47.4
1980	7454.7	17458.9	42.7

Source: OECD

securities and investment in precious metals. By the end of 1980 these equalled approximately 25 per cent of the banking system's combined assets. Under this facility, a client deposits money in a Swiss bank at his own risk which the bank places on his behalf on the Euromarkets, frequently through subsidiary banks in Luxembourg. These funds are not included in the Swiss bank's balance sheet for the technical reason that they do not represent risks incurred. These funds grew from Sw.Fr.5bn. at the end of 1977 to Sw.Fr.172.6bn. by October 1981 when some 333 banks and finance companies out of 557 were managing fiduciary accounts, foreign banks holding 40 per cent of the total. One reason for the rapid increase was large sums of petro-money from OPEC seeking an investment outlet. Given domestic problems associated with a government budget deficit, these deposits have been threatened with a 5 per cent withholding tax.

d) Foreign bonds. Whereas other centres such as London have not permitted the domestic issue of foreign bonds by foreign borrowers, Switzerland has, and their importance has grown during the 1970s as Table LXXV indicates, such that the Swiss share of the foreign bond market has grown from 12.8 per cent in 1970 to 42.7 per cent in 1980. These issues are not entirely unregulated as they require the approval of the Swiss National Bank when they are for amounts over Sw.Fr.10m. with a maturity duration of more than one year. Switzerland has become an important placement centre in this respect for Japanese companies.

e) Following the Washington Agreement of 1968, which established a two-tier market for gold, an official market and an open sector market, a free gold market was set up in Zurich which flourished.

In general the 1970s have been an uneasy decade for Switzerland. Circumstances have caused an intensification of domestic economic frictions that constrained and channelled external development in the early part of the decade; various international scandals in the mid-1970s in relation to Swiss accounts brought some international disrepute to the country; and, since the mid-1970s, attempts have been made to assert federal powers of supervision over the banking system. Moreover, given a number of budgetary difficulties and a demand from local socialists for controls, the government has sought to seek out new areas of taxation that have included international finance activities, the activation of which, or the threat of which, have created for the first time incipient fiscal instability.

At the beginning of the 1970s, due to imported inflationary pressures and difficulties associated with large inflows of foreign funds, controls were placed on finance activities that included the abolition of interest payments on foreign time deposits of less than three months maturity, a 50 per cent increase in stamp duty on international security trading, and a limit being placed on forward sales of Swiss francs to foreigners. Since 1975 a concerted attempt has been made by the Federal Banking Commission to try to introduce banking regulations with regard to reporting statistics and auditing of accounts. Since 1977 a new code of conduct has been operated, determining the kinds of money a bank may accept and how bank secrecy should be handled with respect to 'illegal' capital deposits: failure to adhere to this code incurs a Sw.Fr.10m. fine. As a result of US pressure there is now an agreement to assist in the identification of illicit deposits resulting from organized crime—although Austria has recently passed legislation enabling anyone to open a bank account under a false name!

Since the late 1970s, there has been a certain amount of fiscal instability resulting from new taxes and new tax proposals being continually under discussion. Whereas the ban on interest payments on many foreign sight and short-term time deposits and the forward sale restrictions were lifted in early 1980, a 5.6 per cent gold sales tax was introduced. However, the introduction of the latter had the inevitable result that sales from the Big Two (South Africa and the Soviet Union) shifted to London and other centres, a trend which was intensified when Swiss customs officials allowed details of monthly gold imports and exports to become available to the Press. As a result this tax was subsequently withdrawn at the end of December 1981. New bank capital ratios were introduced as from December 1980, which obliged banks for the first time to meet minimal capital ratio requirements on *consolidated* balance sheets with higher levels introduced for foreign loans and advances. Moreover, new banks must have a capital base of at least Sw.Fr.2m. To encourage some repatriation of Swiss franc offshore lending activities a series of measures were announced in September 1980: foreign central banks were allowed to participate in Swiss franc private placement financings; persons domiciled and resident abroad could take sub-participation in Swiss franc credits to foreigners and buy into private placements; thenceforth non-franc credits arranged in Switzerland can have a multicurrency option under which borrowers can for certain periods during the life of the credit draw funds in Swiss francs; a limited secondary market for private placement will be allowed to develop within Switzerland. In the early 1980s fiscal instability has been created by the threat of new changes, e.g. in 1980 a proposal was put forward to introduce a 5 per cent withholding tax on fiduciary accounts which was followed in 1981 with an alternative proposal of imposing a stamp duty of between 0.10 and 0.15 per cent per annum which was endlessly debated; in early 1981, Willi Ritchard, the socialist Finance Minister, announced proposals to tax bank deposits,

TABLE LXXVI: The number of registered banks in Switzerland and the growth of total and foreign bank balances 1970–79

Year	*No. registered banks*	*Total bank balances (Sw.Fr.m.)*	*Foreign banks asset balance (Sw.Fr.m.)*	*Foreign banks liabilities balance (Sw.Fr.m.)*
1970	578	209950,5	70836,2	60737,4
1971	587	246268,5	90609,4	77525,2
1972	592	265496,7	96703,7	80590,5
1973	584	276605,1	95820,8	80962,9
1974	570	286676,1	92818,9	78694,4
1975	563	322963,2	112535,7	88022,0
1976	550	347710,5	122068,1	96620,0
1977	550	369625,6	125885,9	95937,8
1978	551	398540,1	134720,4	104323,1
1979	554	438170,9	159208,9	117310,4

Source: Les Banques Suisses en 1979, Table 16, p. 37, Swiss National Bank.

including foreign bank deposits; socialist party proposals have also included the ending of criminal treatment of breaches of secrecy, the right of fiscal and justice departments to demand information from banks in relation to tax evasion and deposits from Third World personalities or governments held in personal accounts, compulsory deposit insurance, and disclosure of information requirements concerning non-bank affiliate companies. A 1981 Federal Law permits exchange of information with other countries in the event of criminal cases so long as 'grave prejudice' to the Swiss economy is not thereby incurred. It is clear that the old order of stability no longer obtains.

The importance of foreign banking is indicated by Table LXXVI which indicates how, as the number of banks have declined over the 1970s given the concentration of domestic banking business, so the importance of foreign bank assets to total assets rose from 33.7 per cent in 1970 to 36.3 per cent in 1979. Of the total 554 banks registered in 1979, twenty-nine were canton banks; five were large banks, there were 178 other banks (eighty-one of which were foreign owned); eighty were finance companies (forty-two of which were foreign owned, of which forty-one were external); there were fifteen branches of foreign banks, and twenty-five private banks.

3. THE MIDDLE EAST

While this area has been one of actual and incipient war and political unrest throughout the 1970s, development of finance centres has nevertheless been important due to the accelerated development prospects brought about by the *nouveaux riches* oil-exporting countries after the oil price rise and their need to recycle surplus petro-dollars after 1973. Moreover, the general economic development activities in the area subsequent to this event brought in their train considerable numbers of foreign expatriate managers and skilled workers who require institutions through which to locate their excess earnings in low tax high security parts of the world. The lack of developed indigenous banks in the area with global expertise made the satisfaction of these requirements of necessity dependent on that of Western banks and the free Eurocurrency markets as intermediators, particularly in the Gulf region. Furthermore, this area had a latent financial development potential given its global time zone location in which its business hours overlap the closing of Tokyo, the Asian dollar markets of the Far East, the financial markets of Europe, and finally, the opening of New York at the end of its day: in addition it provides Saturday and Sunday opening, unlike most of these regions.

While a number of centres could have developed given the possibilities of offshore/external financial trade presented to the region, in the event Bahrain emerged as the focal development centre. Given its previous development, clearly Beirut in the Lebanon, although geographically distant from the Gulf, would, in normal circumstances, have been expected to be a beneficiary centre despite a past that had not been unblemished (a moratorium on new bank licences being in force since the collapse of the Intro Bank in 1966). However its civil war of 1975–76 and the continuous instability of its aftermath, both economic and political, did not allow it to develop its planned free bank zone, although its indigenous financial development continued being fed by the remittance of \$100m. to \$150m. per month from Lebanese workers in the Gulf. The resulting unrest created a vacuum in the western part of the Middle East, as a result of which many offshore companies moved to Athens to set up tax-exempt companies known as 'Law 89 offices' under that law passed in 1967 or shipping companies in Piraeus under Law 378 of 1968. Several Lebanese banks showed interest at this time in opening offices in Cyprus, but no banking licences were issued: in November 1981, however, the Cyprus authorities did agree to set up an offshore banking zone to service Middle Eastern clients.

Given that Saudi Arabia did not seek to become a leading financial centre and indeed pursued a policy of 'Saudi-ization' of its banks, and that Kuwait only allowed locally owned banks to operate within its borders, the obvious candidates for offshore development became Bahrain and the United Arab Emirates, although some incentives were offered in Egypt (under Law No.43 1974), Jordan (under a Decree of 1975), and Tunisia (under Law No.63 1976) which however did not attract significant numbers of clients. Kuwait has developed a very diversified financial sector that includes the most developed Eurobond market in the area and has launched a number of World Bank bond issues denominated in Kuwaiti dinars: a special feature of the former is a bondholder option to redeem at specified dates before maturity. In many ways however, the main features of Kuwait reveal it to be more of an onshore external centre and not an offshore centre, and so arguably should not have been included as such in Table LXVII.

Naturally large sums of money tended to go direct from Arab countries to the London, Zurich and New York markets by-passing Eurobond/currency participation in local regional centres. Thus, by 1981 there were twenty-five Arab banks in London compared to only twenty in Bahrain, including privately-owned commercial banks, part or wholly state-owned institutions, consortia and joint venture banks. The latter category included the bringing together of OPEC capital with European and/or American banking expertise, as well as joint wholly Arab banks such as Gulf International (owned by the governments of Bahrain, Iraq, Kuwait, Oman, Qatar, Saudi Arabia and the United Arab Emirates), and the Bank of Credit and Commerce International (owned by the governments of the United Arab Emirates, Bahrain and Saudi Arabia). Within the space of a comparatively short time indigenous Arab banking had developed from a few small banks to a significant number with world-wide reputations of integrity. Thus, whereas in 1980 only fifteen Arab institutions were included in *The Banker's* Top 500, by 1981 the number had increased to thirty-six. The second largest bank is the Saudi Arabian bank, the National Commercial Bank of Jeddah, which since 1979 has conducted much of its international operations by proxy through a wholly-owned subsidiary in Bahrain known as Saudi National Commercial Bank (SNCB), providing medium-term Saudi riyal finance either directly to corporate clients or indirectly through their banks.

Bahrain

Bahrain is an island state at the centre of the Gulf area and lies within 300 miles of states such as Abu Dhabi, Dubai, Kuwait, Qatar and Saudi Arabia. Before the rapid rise in oil prices in 1973, its economy though oil based had been developed since the mid-1960s with a view to becoming a service centre for its surrounding economies. A free trade zone had been established at Mina Sulman, its main port, and air and telecommunications had been established to that end. It became fully independent in 1971, after having had a special treaty relationship with the UK. Thereafter Bahrain remained politically stable and free from particular political allegiances. It has no central bank but the Bahrain Monetary Agency (BMA) was set up in 1973. As part of a government move to diversify the economy away from its heavy dependence on oil production and refining, offshore banking was encouraged as from October 1975, since when a remarkable growth has occurred such that Bahrain has become a centre similar to Luxembourg or Switzerland in its regional area.

Under the licensing system adopted, offshore banking units (OBUs) could be set up, paying no taxes and exempt from all reserve requirements for an annual fee of $25,000. Under the conditions of the licence an OBU must be a full branch of its parent bank or must satisfy the BMA of the commitment of the parent bank to its office; the office must be fully staffed and actively engaged in the business which is written in the books of the branch. In the case of existing fully licensed banks who apply for an OBU licence for their non-resident business, arrangements must be made for separate accounting records as approved by the BMA. OBUs are not allowed to deal with residents of Bahrain, with the exception of the Government, its Agencies, the fully licensed banks and any development projects approved by the BMA. As is indicated in Table LXXVII, the growth of OBUs and of their balances was quite spectacular. Growth was so rapid that the BMA imposed a moratorium on new licensing during the period July/December 1979. Its convenient time zone location filled a gap and completed a world money market link, following on from Singapore in the morning and affecting the London market's opening bids and carrying the structure of

TABLE LXXVII: Growth of OBUs, liability balances and geographical classification 1975–81 in Bahrain

		Liability balances					
End year	*No. OBUs*	*Total (US$bn.)*	*Arab countries (US$m.)*	*North America (US$m.)*	*Western Europe (US$m.)*	*Offshore⁺ centres (US$m.)*	*Other (US$m.)*
1975	2	1.7					
1976	26	6.2	2,578	214	2,277	923	222
1977	33	15.7	8,255	419	4,995	1,539	493
1978	42	23.4	11,666	1,891	7,018	1,850	1,016
1979	51	27.8	16,143	828	7,873	1,936	984
1980	58	37.5	24,236	358	9,311	2,339	1,222
1981*	65	39.8	26,143	287	8,994	2,880	1,466

Source: Bahrain Monetary Agency, *Quarterly Statistical Bulletin,* March 1981, and *Annual Report,* 1980, p. 23.

*March figures ⁺Bahamas, Hong Kong, Singapore, Lebanon

world interest rates through the West's weekend. Bahrain thus became an important centre in the global interbank network: interbank funds account for approximately 70 per cent of OBU liabilities. It has become an important arranging centre both for Arab governments and major US banks for multi-currency loans particularly to North African and the Far Eastern countries, and, as such, it is an offshoot of the Eurodollar market and a centre through which to tap the Arab deposit market, given its onshore doorstep hinterland of half a dozen of the wealthiest countries in the world. Its rigorous licensing provisions have been set to ensure its long run development as an active funding centre and not to become a 'post-box' operation as is often the case with Caribbean centres. A Bahraini dinar Eurobond market was launched in 1977, the main features of which are that they are option bonds payable in US dollars and interest and/or principal payable in that currency, free of withholding tax and in bearer form. Differentials between the Eurodollar and Bahraini dinar (BD) interest rates are smoothed over by a swap arrangement between the two currencies at an effective cost of 12 per cent to avert excessive 'dollarization' of deposits in particular circumstances, even though the BD is linked to the Special Drawing Right value at 1 BD = 2.10 SDRs. The existence of the OBUs have played a very positive part in reducing the wide margins which previously applied to large transactions in Gulf currencies; enabling the issue of capital in these currencies to take place; and, in providing a forward market for both the Kuwaiti dinar and the Saudi riyal for periods up to one year. The latter has been particularly important in giving greater certainty to foreign contractors involved in Saudi Arabian development programmes whose future earnings might otherwise be subject to unacceptable currency exchange exposure. Table LXXVIII reveals the importance of the different currencies utilized in OBU transactions on the liability side. The dominance of the US dollar is clear, accounting for some 63 per cent of OBU liabilities in 1980, as compared with the 25 per cent share of regional currencies.

In the wake of the Shah of Iran's overthrow there were considerable outflows of

TABLE LXXVIII: Currency classification of offshore banking units' liabilities (US$m) in Bahrain 1976–80

Year end	*OBU liabilities*	*US$*	*Regional* currencies*	*DM*	*Swiss francs*	*Others*
1976	6,214	4,471	1,168	175	258	142
1977	15,701	11,269	3,567	252	330	283
1978	23,441	15,459	6,720	383	295	584
1979	27,764	17,538	8,113	609	546	958
1980	37,466	23,631	9,366	786	1,101	2,582

Source: Bahrain Monetary Agency, *Quarterly Statistical Bulletin,* March 1981.
*Saudi riyals, Kuwaiti dinars, UAE dirhams, Qatar riyals, Bahrain dinars.

regional money to higher-yielding foreign currency assets. Previously this market had been used both by Saudi Arabia and Kuwait. Towards the end of the 1970s something like half the Saudi money supply was deposited in Bahrain. However, both countries took measures which have reduced their activity in this market: the Central Bank of Kuwait imposed exchange control restrictions and liquidity requirements in February 1979 to stem the outward drain of short-term funds, thereby limiting OBU access to the Kuwaiti dinar, deposits of more than one month held outside Kuwait being henceforth not regarded as liquid and therefore part of a 25 per cent mandatory liquidity ratio. The Saudi Arabian Monetary Agency perversely and unexpectedly revalued its riyal at this time when devaluation seemed likely. Furthermore, the United Arab Emirates' central bank also brought in restrictions at this time. Naturally, therefore, business in regional currencies other than riyals has tended to atrophy but a substantial increase in non-dollar Eurocurrencies has developed and institutional ties have been forged with Germany and Switzerland. Moreover, the recent arrivals of Japanese and Asian banks hoping for corporate business with their compatriot firms have helped to make up for Bahrain's decline as a regional centre. In addition, links have been forged with other centres, e.g. two Bahraini banks have joined the Arab Latin American Bank—Arlabank—based in Peru (which is 60 per cent Arab owned and 40 per cent Latin American owned); the Saudi-owned Arab Solidarity Bank was established in the Cayman Islands in 1978 under the management of the State Bank of India.

At the end of March 1981 the Bahraini finance sector comprised nineteen commercial onshore banks, two specialized banks, sixty-five OBUs, nine investment banks, forty-one representative offices and six brokers—147 institutions in all—the national parentage of which is shown in Table LXXIX.

A further aspect of offshore development has been the registration of Exempt Companies under the provisions of Resolution No.25 of 1977 of the Ministry of Commerce and Agriculture, which releases such companies from requirements under the Commercial Company Law No. 28 1975 with respect to local majority share ownership provided they trade in the Gulf but not locally, maintain a physical presence in Bahrain, rent office and residential accommodation, employ workers and hold an annual general meeting, have a minimum subscribed capital of BD 20,000 and pay an annual registration fee of BD 2,500: these provisions are available for a period not exceeding twenty-five years. In 1978, 1979 and 1980, registrations were made of seventeen, twenty-four, and sixteen com-

TABLE LXXIX: National parentage and type of banking representation in Bahrain, March 1981

Countries	*OBUs*	*Commercial banks*	*Specialised banks*	*Rep. banks*	*Investment banks*	*Brokers*	*National totals*
Bahrain	12	4	2	2	6		26
S. Arabia		1					1
UAE	1	1					2
Oman	1						1
Jordan	1	1					2
Iraq		1					1
Iran	1	2					3
Egypt	1						1
India	2						2
Pakistan	2	2					4
Malaysia	1						1
Hong Kong	3						3
Korea	1						1
Japan	1			15			16
Philippines	1			1			2
Australia				2			2
United Kingdom	10	3		2		6	21
France	6	1		4			11
Luxembourg	1				1		2
Belgium	1						1
Holland	1	1		1			3
West Germany				3			3
Spain	1			1			2
Switzerland	3			3			6
Italy				1			1
Greece				1			1
Yugoslavia				1			1
Canada	2			2			4
United States	8	2		5	2		17
Bermuda	1						1
Cayman Islands	1						1
Peru	1						1
Brazil	2			1			3
Totals for types of financial representation	66	19	2	45	9	6	147

Source: derived from pp. 1–4 of *Alnaqd* (Quarterly Publication of Bahrain Monetary Agency), Vol. No. 2, Issue No. 5, March 1981.

panies respectively. In 1980, public subscriptions were permitted for such companies. So great was the interest in these companies from local and Kuwaiti investors that oversubscription occurred. Thus it was announced in early 1982 that a public share issue by the Bahrain International Bank (BIB) was more than 400 times oversubscribed, with potential investors being prepared to put up US $11.8bn. for the 28 million $1 shares on offer. As a result of this and other public launchings, the BMA announced a twelve-month moratorium on the formation of new offshore banking units and investment companies in February 1982. Perhaps this is also to allay frequent allegations that are made that the centre is now 'over-banked'.

TABLE LXXX: Local and foreign bank representation in the United Arab Emirates 1975 and 1980

	No. banks end 1975			*No. banks end 1980*		
	Local	*Foreign*	*Total*	*Local*	*Foreign*	*Total*
Abu Dhabi	6	21	27	12	24	36
Dubai	7	23	30	17	25	42
Sharjah	4	16	20	8	20	28
Ajman	2	4	6	3	10	13
Umm al Quain	2	4	6	3	9	12
Ras al Khaimah	4	6	10	7	16	30
Fujeirah	1	3	4	2	9	11
Totals	26	77	103	52	113	165

Source: United Arab Emirates, *Currency Board Annual Reports.*

The United Arab Emirates

The United Arab Emirates (UAE) were established in 1971 being a federation of the seven emirates which formerly comprised the Trucial States. Six of the emirates—Abu Dhabi, Ajman, Sharjah, Umm al Quwain and Ras al Khaimah—are located along the southern coast of the Arabian Gulf, the seventh, Fujeirah, is located on the coast of the Gulf of Oman. Naturally, given this federation, each emirate has its own finance centre although as Table LXXX indicates, Abu Dhabi, Dubai and Sharjah are by far the most significant. A boom period between 1973 and 1977 unfortunately ended in a banking crisis in which two banks were forced to close and massive capital outflows took place. This was just one year after the first Restricted Licence banks (some twelve in number) had been created, which had been a counter measure to the establishment of OBUs in Bahrain. This event and the institution of foreign exchange controls prevented any significant offshore development from taking place. In 1979 the IMF suggested the setting up of a Central Bank to replace the Currency Board System which was a remnant from colonial times. Foreign exchange restrictions curb offshore lending as they require any bank lending UAE dirhams up to three months to non-resident banks to deposit 15 per cent of the amount involved interest-free with the monetary authority, thereby effectively raising the price of dirhams. Not surprisingly, of the original twelve Restricted Licences only three or four banks at any one time since 1976 have been operative. It is possible that during the 1980s a more coherent attempt at offshore development may be made, in which case it will probably be necessary to concentrate the external financial sector rather than maintain the present diffusion of activity.

4. THE FAR EAST AND OCEANIA

While East Asia has been dominated in the past by Hong Kong, during the 1970s, Singapore rose as an offshore banking centre in South East Asia and became in size the main Far East centre despite the more sophisticated financial diversification of the former. Several small island states in Oceania emerged as satellite areas for Hong Kong, in particular Vanuatu (called the New Hebrides until July 1980) and the Norfolk Islands. Modest and competitive developments occurred in the Philippines after mid-1977 when offshore banking units were allowed but that country has constrained external financial sector activities by not allowing foreign banks, with the exception of four, to set up domestic branches.

The Asia-Pacific area has in general benefited from the existence of a large number of free trade zones, as discussed in Part I Chapter I, which required finance and centres for investment. It has also been an area where increasingly many onshore governments have sought Eurofinance to ease their international debt problems. An important feature behind offshore centre development has been the production vacuum and positive externality provided by the fact that, for most of the 1970s, Japan played a passive role with respect to the potential evolution of Tokyo as an onshore external finance centre: liberalized exchange control regulations were not issued until 1 December 1980. Prior to Feburary 1979 non-residents were prohibited from purchasing Japanese securities with maturities of less than five years and one month. No locally-based Eurodollar or Euroyen market was allowed to develop until December 1980. The Japanese monetary authorities deliberately discouraged such activities because it was felt that the domestic bond market, on which the central government was reliant as a source of funds, would become diffused. Thus, Euroyen bonds were not permitted until 1977 and only eleven issues were allowed up to 1980, each of which required the prior approval of the Ministry of Finance and were not issued in Japan.

Hong Kong

Hong Kong is a British Crown Colony which has full responsibility for its internal affairs and exercises considerable autonomy in external matters with minimum control from London. For many years its proximity to mainland China has given it an economic importance as an entrepôt trade centre far beyond its small size, such that it has become the main point of contact between the West and that continent in respect of financial and trade affairs. Furthermore, 90 per cent of its land area—the New Territories—is on lease from China and adjoins on the mainland that country's province of Guangdong, a lease that is due to expire on 9 June 1997.

In addition to its Chinese associations and its location within the growth area of the Pacific basin, Hong Kong possesses other advantages that have furthered the importance of financial activities: it has had great political stability, despite the various wars that have occurred in the Far East area and the recent influx of Vietnamese; its governmental system is non party-political and it is administered by a governor appointed by the British monarch, who acts with the advice of executive and legislative councils over which he presides; the basic economic philosophy pursued has been one of *laissez-faire,* although this does not extend to making the economy a tax haven as such or one without regulations, though the foreign exchange market itself is unrestricted; lastly, some nine free trade zones have been established to encourage foreign investments which contributed to its industrial success as a Newly Industrialized Country.

The financial importance and offshore significance of Hong Kong is of very recent origin. In 1946 some thirty banks were present, almost all exclusively devoted to the entrepôt trade. With the collapse of trade with China following the UN embargo at the time of the Korean War in the early 1950s, the island's economic strategy began to concentrate on the development of domestic manufacturing industries, particularly export-oriented light industries and their finance. Certain decisions were made in the mid-1960s which gave financial stability to the colony. In July 1964, a Deposit Rate Agreement was made, in the absence of a central bank, by which all licensed banks agreed to a measure of self-regulation with respect to the stabilization of interest rates on time deposits to be operated under the aegis of the Exchange Banks' Association (EBA). Following a number of bank failures that culminated in that of the Canton Trust in 1965, a moratorium on new full bank licences was imposed, which, with the exception of the allowed entry of Barclays Bank in 1972, was maintained until March 1978. For this reason, as well as a general trend towards business concentration, the numbers of local banks fell from eighty-eight in 1964 to seventy-three in 1970. During the latter part of the 1960s no retaliation was made with respect to the institution in Singapore of the Asian Dollar Market (to be discussed) and that country's adoption of a lower withholding tax on foreign investments which inaugurated Singapore's offshore development. From 1969 onwards a number of innovations took place which nevertheless made Hong Kong a prime world finance centre. The main developments are summarized chronologically below:

1969, the Far East Stock Exchange was opened (the first stock exchange, the Hong Kong Exchange, was opened in 1871);
1971, the Kam Ngan Exchange was opened;
1972, the Kowloon Exchange was opened;
Hong Kong was excluded from the Scheduled Territories of the Sterling Area;
1973, the Hong Kong currency became linked to the US dollar as from February;
First issues made of Hong Kong dollar Certificates of Deposit;
1974, a gold market was formed;
the currency link with the US dollar was severed in November and allowed to float separately;
1975, a Commodity Exchange was set up;
1977, offshore Hong Kong dollar bonds (Eurobonds) first issued;
revival of dollar Certificates of Deposit;
1979, Commercial Paper Market opened with issues on behalf of the Mass Transit Railway Corporation.

Given the moratorium on bank entry referred to, the setting up of finance companies, or deposit-taking companies (DTCs) as they are locally designated, became the only route by which a presence in Hong Kong could be *de novo* effected. Since 1976, DTCs have been regulated by a Deposit-Taking Companies Ordinance, under which they are precluded from obtaining deposits under HK

$50,000 and from operating current account facilities, but are not subject to the prudential supervision imposed on full banks. As a result, many bank consortia-owned finance companies have been established, funded by shareholder deposits documented outside the colony. Local banks may use 'memorandum' accounts where foreign currency offshore transactions can be entered and remain free of all tax provided the funds are externally located.

As regards taxation, Hong Kong is very far from being a no-tax haven, although taxes are lower than most onshore areas. Company profits have been subject to a standard rate of 17 per cent (reduced to 16.5 per cent 1981/82) which, in 1977, was extended to include profits from offshore financial operations which do not require the 'substantial intervention of a branch elsewhere'. Domestic social programmes have promoted new tax proposals that have created fiscal instability and uncertainty. There were plans to introduce a dividend withholding tax and, after the 1978 Official Code on Unit Trusts and Mutual Funds, a 0.3 per cent stamp duty on sales and redemptions of unit trusts, but these were eventually shelved. Offshore currency market development was constrained during the 1970s due to the continued existence of the 15 per cent withholding tax and lack of double taxation agreements which tended to discourage foreign investors, who found Singapore a lower tax centre for their activities. Moreover, periodic weaknesses in the external value of the Hong Kong dollar have restricted the actual development of potential financial instruments. Thus, Hong Kong has tended to concentrate on being a centre for syndicated loans, especially in relation to the borrower countries in this region of the world: in 1981 it was the fourth largest centre for loan syndication after London, New York and Paris, with sixty-one such loans (compared with only nine in Singapore) valued at US$3,523m.

During this period a modest development of offshore funds took place, the number of publicized funds increasing from one in 1968 to thirty five by 1981: about a third of these are investments spread throughout the Far East region, with additionally ten exclusively in Japan and three in Australasia.

Major developments have occurred in the banking sector since the mid-1970s. In an effort both to promote and yet to control the banking sector, the ban on new bank licences was lifted in March 1978 after being in operation for thirteen years: at this time seventy-four banks were licensed of which only thirty-one were foreign owned. Foreign banks were now able to register but were restricted to the establishment of just one branch. In the eighteen-month period of new registration to August 1979, no less than forty banks were admitted. By 1980 there were 115 banks of which seventy-two were foreign and Hong Kong had become 'The London of the East'. However, the banking sector continued to be dominated by the Hongkong and Shanghai Bank with a 50-60 per cent share of total deposits (including the Hang Seuk Bank, its subsidiary) and the Bank of China and its twelve sister banks being responsible for a further 30 per cent. What became disturbing to the authorities was the growth to 342 of the DTCs and the difficulties, actual and potential, resulting from the creation of credit process in which they were involved: DTC assets grew from HK$52 billion in 1978 to HK$121 billion by the end of 1980, their deposits from the non-bank public in Hong Kong increasing nearly fourfold to approximately HK$40 billion, whereas licensed bank balances only doubled to HK$256 billion and their non-bank deposits increased by only 40 per cent to HK$87 billion. It was evident that the DTCs had been used as a means of avoiding the EBA interest rate fixing arrangement. Consequently, the Financial Secretary carried out a number of reforms to curtail the DTCs. First of all the EBA was made a statutory body which all banks were required to join: it was now renamed the Hong Kong Association of Banks and henceforth the interest rates set applied to all short-term deposits. Secondly, DTCs were thenceforth restricted in their activities to deposits of three months maturity or more, whereas previously they had been unrestricted and it was estimated that 90 per cent of their deposits had been short-term. Thirdly, a new category of DTC, the merchant bank, was introduced which would be free to take deposits of any maturity provided the initial deposit is HK$500,000 or more, the level of paid-up capital being increased from HK$2.5m. to HK$75m. for such institutions. Furthermore, the Financial Secretary proposed six new criteria against which future applications for DTC licences would be considered:

1) the applicant would have to be subject to adequate supervision by recognized banking authorities of its country of incorporation;
2) it would have to have traded as a DTC for at least three years;
3) the owners would have to be reputable, and the beneficial owner of any holding of 10 per cent or more would have to be identifiable and reputable;
4) the management of a company would have to be in 'fit and proper hands';
5) the company would have to be in good standing in the Hong Kong money markets;
6) it must have 'substantial assets (net of contra items) on its books in Hong Kong with a record of steady growth and prudent trading for at least three years'.

At the end of May 1980 the moratorium on new bank licences in force since 1979 was lifted. Five criteria were now introduced for foreign banks seeking a Hong Kong banking licence and for local institutions wishing to obtain bank status:

a) the bank must be incorporated in a country whose monetary authorities exercise 'effective prudential supervision' and do not object to the bank having a Hong Kong licence;
b) the bank must have total assets (less contra items) of more than HK$10bn.;
c) an acceptable form of entry reciprocity must be available to Hong Kong banks in the applicant bank's country of origin;
d) it must be a limited company, incorporated in Hong Kong, and not the subsidiary of a licensed bank, with a paid up share capital of at least HK$100;
e) it must have been in the business of taking deposits and granting credit to the public in Hong Kong for at least ten years and have been registered under the DTC Ordinance since 1976 or for at least ten years, whichever is the shorter.

The minimum assets criterion is subject to annual review and will be based on the annual league tables published in *The Banker*. These criteria are designed to prevent a rush of new registrations. Other changes include the unification of the four local stock exchanges in the near future and new regulation of insurance to encourage the establishment of an international reinsurance industry.

In recent years the competitive edge of Singapore has been felt and appreciated and new measures have been introduced mindful of this fact. Attempts have been made to develop new financial instruments, e.g. in 1980 the European Asian Bank, Fuji Bank, the Bank of Tokyo and Chase Manhattan launched US-dollar denonimated Certificates of Deposit once it became clear that Hong Kong Government tax officials would exempt these issues from the 15 per cent local withholding tax. Finally, in an effort to maintain and enhance Hong Kong's position in the area, withholding taxes on all foreign currency deposits were abolished at the end of February 1982 and the withholding tax on Hong Kong dollar deposits was reduced from 15 to 10 per cent. Mr Paul Myners of Rothschild was reported in the *Financial Times* of 25 February 1982 (p.1) as having declared that:

> The tax has acted as a disincentive to deposit gathering in Hong Kong because there was no clear legal opinion on the tax. As a result, Singapore developed as a funding centre at the expense of Kong Kong. Now there will no longer be any problem about Hong Kong's strong emergence as a funding centre.

However, given that there are another fifteen years until the 1997 lease termination deadline, there are likely to be intermittent bouts of uncertainty concerning the future of the colony. The intention is to resolve the issue well before the above date. At present the situation would seem to be as described in the *Sunday Telegraph* of 10 January 1982 (p.2):

> Chinese officials see Hong Kong's future as an important city-state administered by the British Government as a free trade area and commercial centre, but with sovereignty vested in the People's Republic.
>
> The overall Chinese plan is to organize, well in advance of 1997 . . . a formal transfer to Peking of sovereignty of Hong Kong island and the narrow coastal strip of mainland China in Kowloon.
>
> The Chinese Government will then, officials claim, request Britain to continue to administer the former colony for between 30 and 45 years.

In the future, the onshore taxation adopted by China may well be crucial to the continued profitability of many finance sector activities. A draft of its new law would seem to indicate that it will be higher than other developing countries in the region, such as Indonesia, Malaysia and the Philippines, with the exception of joint venture projects and new special economic zone areas.

Singapore

As its business hours overlap San Francisco and Tokyo at the start of the day, and subsequently Hong Kong, the Middle East and Europe, Singapore has an ideal location within the world time zone finance chain. It is a small island city-state lying off the tip of the Malay Peninsular and is an important staging-post between north and south and east and west. Singapore became independent on 3 June 1959, but was initially federated with Malaysia. At independence two banking systems were inherited: British and foreign banks, and local banks which since the 1930s had formed local money and capital markets that had made Singapore to some extent independent from London. Once the break with Malaysia had been confirmed in 1965, a series of steps were taken to explore the frictioneering possibilities of its South East Asia location. The main activities promoted and events of significance are summarized below in chronological order:

1968, the Asian Dollar Market was set up;
1969, an open registry was established for shipping offering tax exemption and tonnage tax rebates in return for the hiring of 25 per cent of crews locally;
a gold market was established;
1970, the formation of the Monetary Authority of Singapore (MAS);
the introduction of secret numbered bank accounts;
merchant banking permitted;
Banking Act;
1971, the Asian Dollar Bond Market was opened;
1972, Discount Houses were first permitted;
1973, stamp duty was abolished on international earnings;
Asian Dollar Bonds were made tax-exempt;
Singapore's stock exchange was made independent from that of Malaysia;
free trading in the gold market was permitted for residents and non-residents;
1975, the first Negotiable Certificates of Deposit (NCDs) were issued;
1976, the commission on fees on offshore letters of credit was reduced from 40% to 10%;
Asian Dollar Bonds and Asian Currency Unit deposits held by non-residents were made exempt from estate duty;
1977, the first Floating Ratc Certificates of Deposit (FRCDs) were issued;
trading in call options commenced;
1978, the freeing of exchange controls;
the first U.S. dollar Certificates of Deposit were issued;
1979, a gold futures market was set up—the Gold Exchange of Singapore;
1980, stamp duty on investment was abolished;
an Asian Dollar commercial paper market was introduced;
1981, the first Singapore Dollar Floating Rate Certificates of Deposit were issued.

The starting point for offshore development came in November 1968, when the government adopted a suggestion made by the local branch of the Bank of America and set up the Asian Dollar Market. Banks were henceforth allowed to set up specific internal departments called Asian Currency Units (ACUs) to handle offshore non-Singapore dollar currency business free from exchange controls and banking regulations and benefiting from a reduction of income tax from 40 per cent to 10 per cent on offshore income, whether remitted or not: this effectively undercut the Hong Kong 15 per cent tax on foreign currency deposit interest. ACUs were permitted to offer credit facilities to Singapore residents, but could not accept fixed deposits of less than S$250,000 or any savings deposits and

TABLE LXXXI: Withholding taxes applicable in Singapore

	Interest %	*Dividends* %
Residents of non-treaty countries	40	40
Residents of treaty countries		
Australia	10	0
New Zealand	15	0
Japan	15 or 0*	0
Malaysia	40	0
Philippines	15	0
Thailand	25 or 10*	0
Belgium	15	0
Denmark	15 or 10*	0
France	10 or 0*	0
Germany	10	0
Italy	12.5	0
Netherlands	10	0
Norway	40	0
Sweden	15 or 10*	0
Switzerland	10	0
United Kingdom	15	0
Israel	15	0
Canada	15	0

Source: Table 25.3 of Kemp, *A Guide to World Money and Capital Markets.*
*lower rates applicable to approved industrial loan interest.

so were at some disadvantage as compared with fully licensed banks, although they were not subject to reserve requirements.

Unlike Hong Kong, the main emphasis of development in Singapore was the establishment of a funding as opposed to a syndication centre. Moreover, in contrast to Hong Kong, where there were no double taxation agreements, Singapore developed a tax treaty network with Japan, the EEC countries, Switzerland and other centres. In the Asian Dollar market no withholding taxes apply to either interest or dividends. Otherwise, the withholding taxes indicated in Table LXXXI are applicable. The 1970 Banking Act prescribed a threefold system of licensing—full, restricted and offshore: the growth of the financial institutions is indicated in Table LXXXII between 1970 and March 1981. During the 1970s the number of offshore banks increased from none in 1970 to 50 by March 1981, merchant banks increased from two to thirty-nine in the same period, representative offices from none to forty-five. In terms of ACUs, their value rose spectacularly from US$30.5m. in 1968 to about US$71bn. by the end of 1981. Over 70 per cent of both sources and assets were in the interbank market. It is estimated that about 90 per cent of these were in US dollars. The Asia-Pacific region has benefited from the existence of this market as more than 80 per cent of Singapore's offshore funds are utilized in the region itself.[4] Seventy per cent of loans are to governments in the area, particularly Indonesia, South Korea, Malaysia, the Philippines, Taiwan, Thailand and Singapore itself. Moreover, many Asian businesses have also benefited that are small and family-owned and so would not have qualified for Eurocurrency loans from Europe directly. In the making of these loans LIBOR (London interbank offer rate) or SIBOR

Table LXXXII: Financial institutions in Singapore 1970, 1975 and 1981

		1970		*1975*		*1981**
Banks						
Local full licence		11		13		13
Foreign banks		26		57		87
(a) full	26		24		24	
(b) restricted	0		12		13	
(c) offshore	0		21		50	
Merchants banks		2		21		39
Representative Offices						
banks		8		38		45
merchant banks		0		1		4
Asian Currency Units		14		66		120
banks	14		52		85	
merchant banks	0		13		34	
others	0		1		1	
Discount Houses		0		4		4
International Money Brokers		0		5		7

Source: Monetary Authority of Singapore Annual Reports.

*March figure.

(Singapore interbank offer rate) is taken as the base, with floating spreads ranging from 1 to 3 per cent (higher than London) over base rate and participation fees ranging from 1/8 per cent to 3/8 per cent plus front-end fees of between ½ to 1 per cent. Syndication business gradually began to grow, particularly with South Korea and Taiwan.

In terms of numbers of banks, Singapore became the fourth largest world centre after London, New York and Hong Kong, although many 'overbanking' allegations have been made. Thus the *Asian Wall Street Journal* of 20 November 1981 estimated that more than '30 are unprofitable but maintain an office because the banks' officials feel that Singapore is a centre in which international banks must have a presence . . . Margins can be wafer-thin . . . with 20% of Singapore's banks handling some 80% of all available business.' It is alleged by such sources that much of this activity is 'artificial' and in reality arranged in Hong Kong and that the Asian Dollar Market will eventually level out at the $100 billion level. Despite such assertions there has, in recent years, been a steady flow of new business in particular from Japan whose bankers are denied a domestic offshore market and who, since 1978, have made Singapore their second largest destination for overseas investment. These banks have largely contributed to Singapore becoming the largest centre for Asian Dollar Certificates of Deposit after London and New York: in 1980 there were twenty-six Japanese licensed banks responsible for more than three-quarters of the estimated value of S$200.7m. of these instruments. The Japanese growth since 1978 is largely attributable to new Japanese banking regulations, which required Japanese banks to match the maturities of their assets and liabilities within specified limits. The need to match long-term lending to long-term borrowing led directly to the issuance of three-year floating rate Certificates of Deposit on the Singapore market by these banks.

In addition to the stimulus given by Japanese banks, there was a growth of

Arab interest with the advent in 1979 of the National Commercial Bank of Saudi Arabia and in 1981 with that of the National Bank of Kuwait, both of which have interests in syndication activity. Furthermore, an important local bank, the United Overseas Bank Ltd., has recently been trying to form a link with a West Coast US bank. The government too, has been determined to extend the reputation of Singapore and the quality and scope of the financial services it can offer, in fact to turn it into a 'financial supermarket for Southeast Asia'. Some of its new policies include the following:

a) In 1981 new rules were issued to encourage Singapore's development as an insurance centre (in 1980 the value of insurance activities stood at S$471m.).
b) An open-door policy has been adopted to attract professional expertise including lawyers specializing in loan syndication, foreign brokers and fund managers. In the latter case 50 per cent of management fees will now be allowed as a tax deductable expense. It is recommended that more pension funds be set up and turned over to private investment managers.
c) The Economic Development Board has tried since 1980 to promote research and development by offering special tax incentives, including double deduction for R.&D. expenses. An attempt is being made generally to promote Singapore as a capital goods base (oil field equipment and agricultural machinery) for trade with China to complement Hong Kong's consumer goods base.

It has become clear that aspects of the previous friction structure have impeded development as a result of the ossification caused by the bank licensing system. It has been claimed that restrictions on the raising of funds locally acts as a deterrent to syndication participation. Suggestions for change include the following:

1. Taxation and other incentives to help the growth of Singapore as a fund management centre. Corporation tax rates in Hong Kong are levelled at 16.5 per cent, much lower than Singapore's 40 per cent. In addition, money remitted from abroad escapes tax in Hong Kong. Banks in Singapore have suggested that offshore income for authorized unit trusts or investment companies should bear the same 10 per cent concessionary rate of tax as the ACUs.
2. Changes should be made in the classification of bonds, notes and floating rate certificates held by banks to offer greater flexibility in asset management.
3. Limitations on lending for property development should be lifted.
4. Taxes on interest earned through bank deposits should be abolished. Banks' liquidity ratios should be lowered from 26 to 16 per cent. The threshold at which a company must make a general bid for another company should be raised to 30 per cent ownership rather than 20 per cent.
5. Banks should be permitted to enter the stockbroking business.
6. Finance houses should be allowed to deal in gold and foreign exchange.

Oceania

Whilst this area would appear to be rather remote for mainstream offshore banking, some development nevertheless occurred during the 1970s. The initial attempts were made in Norfolk Island, the Cocos (Keeling) Islands, Christmas Island and Papua New Guinea, which were largely nipped in the bud by the tightening of Australian tax and exchange control rules in 1973. Prior to that date, as these islands had been within the Australian exchange control net, it had been possible for Australian companies to borrow external funds via an island-located company, such that interest paid was considered as a deduction for internal Australian tax purposes which thereby avoided Australian withholding tax. Subsequent to 1973 only one haven emerged to be of any international significance which may yet achieve offshore centre status: the New Hebrides. These consist of some eighty islands and were an Anglo-French condominion until becoming the Republic of Vanuatu in July 1980. The origin of development here lies in the decision by the British administration to regularize the activities of some fringe financial ventures which began to exploit the no-tax, no tax-treaty, no exchange control environment that existed at the end of the 1960s. The resulting legislation, the 1970 Banking Regulation Act, and the 1971 Company Regulation Act, and Trust Companies Regulation Act, and the 1973 Insurance Regulation, while giving extensive powers of discretion to the government in terms of incorporation permissions and granting of exempt company status, provided an outwardly respectable image which enabled Vila, the capital on the island of Efat, to develop as a satellite centre for Hong Kong as a loan booking centre for the latter's residents desiring to avoid Hong Kong's 15 per cent interest tax: by 1980 it had become a base for 500 exempt companies with links mainly with Hong Kong or Australia. To service this activity an invasion of international accountancy firms and trust companies took place. From a base of one domestic bank in 1969 some fifty had become established by 1981, although only six of these have a physical presence, the rest being 'brass-plate' operations. In 1979 a new communications satellite station brought direct telex and telephone links which have enabled it to better exploit its time zone advantages: one hour ahead of Sydney, two hours ahead of Tokyo and nineteen ahead of San Francisco, which might prove a more convenient loan booking centre for Asian banks rather than the Caribbean. Despite some political unrest resulting from secessionist tendencies within its constituent islands, the recent advent of independence should result in a more autonomous development promotion strategy. In 1981 attempts were made to develop as a new registration centre for flags of convenience vessels by setting a scale of fees below that of Liberia.

SYNOPSIS

Our review of the 1970s has revealed how the emergence of the Eurocurrency markets, shifts in the location of international wealth, and the spread of political independence to formerly colonial areas combined to result in a network of onshore external centres and gave rise to the potential/actual, general/selective offshore financial transformation of existing tax havens and newly independent aspiring tax havens: a development option that was sometimes combined with export free manufacturing zones and/or 'flags of convenience' shipping registers. The autonomous policy-imposed distortions initially created by the US monetary policies of the 1960s, tempered by periodic instrumental policy-imposed distortions in several onshore centres as well as some offshore centres, created a need for transnational business and banking to disintermediate therefrom. Tax havens were able to satisfy this need to compete for this business on the basis of competition by frictioneering and an economy orientation towards positive noninterventionist policies that emphasized low tax, low friction production conditions and a permissive but not promiscuous attitude towards the requirements of multinational banking and certain types of financial markets and the provision of financial instruments and vehicles not otherwise available onshore, or only available under strict controls.

Regionally, development was necessarily 'unconditionally place-bound' given the practical considerations to be located near specific onshore wealth/capital market hinterlands and time zone conveniences of business linkage thereto for investment placing and switching activities. Four primary regions of activity emerged:

1) the Caribbean area and Central America for servicing North and South America;
2) European enclave states and independent islands for servicing European business interests;
3) the Gulf area for servicing the Middle Eastern oil surplus countries;
4) Hong Kong and Singapore with the sub-region of Oceania for servicing the Asian-Pacific area.

Within each region the viability of many activities relied on the tacit or complicit, passive attitude of one or more important onshore economies in particular centres, e.g. Luxembourg and its reliance on permissive Belgian and German attitudes; the Caribbean area and US authority attitudes; Bahrain and the positive activities of Saudi Arabia; the Far East and the negative attitude of Japan towards an indigenous onshore external market. Within these regions, political and fiscal stability, consistent political will and reputable financial regulations have been seen to be the touchstones for sustained development commitment by the international banking community and the international community of tax authorities: these elements have largely determined which of the many aspiring newly independent candidates have been favoured and which have not. With the exception of European continental enclave states, most territories have 'dollarized' their currency bonds especially after, in the case of formerly British colonies, the rescheduling of the Sterling Area in June 1972. The US dollar has therefore extended its role as the pre-eminent master currency in the world trading system. Only a few havens were linked to negotiated currency states, e.g. Luxembourg with Belgium; Switzerland has been the only centre with a neutral currency to which only Liechtenstein has been directly linked.

Each of the above mentioned regions have had at least one primary offshore centre which has acted as the regional centre for surplus funds: the four such 'money-box' centres being Panama, Switzerland, Bahrain and Hong Kong. Around each of these regional primary offshore centres were clustered a group of secondary offshore centres which acted essentially as 'turntable centres' both regionally and inter-regionally, supporting and promoting transnational investment and business activities. The main secondary offshore centres were for the Caribbean area and Central America—Bermuda, the Bahamas, the Caymans, and the Netherlands Antilles; for the European region—Luxembourg, Liechtenstein, Jersey and Guernsey; for the Gulf area the United Arab Emirates; in the Far East—Singapore, Vanuatu (formerly the New Hebrides). A few centres may be regarded as transitional secondary centres or potentially so, these being Barbados, the Turks and Caicos Islands, the Isle of Man, the Lebanon. Finally, there are a number of peripheral tax haven centres that do not as yet have a significant global importance but are nevertheless contributors to the world network of offshore activity to a greater or lesser degree: these are Andorra, Anguilla, Gibraltar, Monaco, Nauru, Puerto Rico, St. Vincent, Montserrat, the Philippines and the British and American Virgin Islands. In addition there are a number of potential centres which may well develop in the 1980s, these being Mexico, Cyprus, Campione, Costa Rica, Tunisia, Egypt, Malta and Jordan.

The above-mentioned offshore network of four primary centres, eleven secondary centres, four transitional secondary centres and eleven peripheral tax havens are interconnected with each other and interposed between onshore external centres and onshore domestic capital centres and individually constitute intermediate economies within the world trading system to a greater or lesser extent, and collectively provide an alternative secondary trading system that is global in scope for the location of international invisible activities and earnings.

REFERENCES

1. Parker, C., 'The 'Big Apple' Maintains Its Pace', *The Banker,* February 1981, p.113. See Colville, J.R., 'London—Europe's Financial Centre', *The Banker,* July 1966, p.467, which indicates that in mid-1966, there were more than 100 foreign banks established in London compared with 65 in New York, 48 in Paris, 25 in Frankfurt and 17 in Zurich; and that British banks had nearly 4,500 branches overseas compared with only 160 with respect to US banks.

2. Doggart, T., 'Tax Havens—The Landscape Changes', *The Banker,* April 1972, p.543.

3. Kemp, L.J., *A Guide to World Money and Capital Markets,* London, McGraw-Hill Book Company (UK) Ltd., 1981.

4. Bhattacharya, A.K., 'How Far Does Asia Benefit from the Asian Dollar Market?' *The Banker,* November 1976, p.1225.

The reader is referred to the following general sources of information with regard to offshore centres:

Chown, J.F., *Offshore Financial Centres,* 4th edn., revised by M. Cook, a Banker Research Unit Survey, London, Financial Times Business Publishing Ltd., 1981.

Doggart, C., *Tax Havens and Their Uses,* EIU Special Report No.105, London, Economist Intelligence Unit Ltd., September 1981.

The Banker Surveys of Offshore Investment Centres published in August 1970, April 1972, May 1974 and April 1977.

Individual centre information is available in Central Bank and National Monetary Authority Annual Reports and in periodic articles and special supplements published in *The Banker, Financial Times,* and *Investors Chronicle and Financial World.*

CHAPTER II
The Restructuring of the International Friction Matrix in the 1980s

While the structure of the international friction matrix in the 1980s is likely to continue to create a demand for the existence of offshore haven financial centres and their associated financial services, the relative global importance of such centres and perhaps, for some centres, the local absolute importance of such activities will be crucially affected by a restructuring process that may result in this decade being the development decade for onshore external centres. The following two areas of change will shape the extent of this development bias and the possible repatriation loss to offshore centres as onshore positive non-interventionist policies elicit more low or zero friction external invisible trade: (1) onshore changes of attitude in respect of the taxation of offshore invisible trade activities; (2) The onshore financial de-regulation process and the spread of onshore external centres. These two aspects will now be separately discussed.

(1) ONSHORE CHANGES OF ATTITUDE IN RESPECT OF THE TAXATION OF OFFSHORE INVISIBLE TRADE

Taxation of multinational corporations, whether in the business or finance sectors, has come under increasing international and national scrutiny as onshore governments have found a need to preserve and/or increase their national tax bases and to generally plug external tax leakage. In 1979, the twenty-four nation OECD Committee on Fiscal Affairs published a report on this subject—'Transfer Pricing and Multinational Enterprises'—which offered some guidelines of approach to governments. In general the 'arm's length' pricing method for treating transactions within multinational groups was endorsed. However the difficulty of applying such criteria in many practical cases leads to long and detailed negotiations between individual companies and tax administrations which the Committee considered could be alleviated by the application of one of three alternative criteria:

i) The 'comparable and controlled price'. This method is only appropriate for raw materials and basic commodities in which there is a relatively free market and for some compound products such as chemicals.
ii) The 'resale price'. This method works backwards from the reseller's price via 'an appropriate mark-up percentage'. This is not ideal where there is much value added at the reseller stage.
iii) The 'cost-plus' criterion merely adds a margin of profit to the cost of production. However, different markets bear different costs, and loss-leader techniques may be utilized so that costs in these circumstances are notoriously subjective.

In practice a 'residual' method tends to be adopted whereby negotiations take place without publicity. Within America, however, there is a move to adopt a 'unitary basis' for taxation, under which a company's entire earnings from its principal or 'unitary business' wherever derived would be taken and a part apportioned for local taxation. Some thirty-six states believe that they have this right, of which twelve claim the right to tax foreign companies by a process of 'worldwide combination'. If these latter methods were generally adopted current patterns of multinational trade would clearly be radically undermined as indeed would the routing of incomes thereby earned through offshore haven centres. Moreover, radical proposals have been put forward in Washington by the IRS. As summarized by *The Economist* of 20 June 1981 (p.105), these include desires to:

> Emphasise that the burden of proving the substance of a tax-haven transaction is put squarely on the taxpayer; make a specific disallowance of tax deductions attributable to activities in tax havens unless the taxpayer comes up with clear and convincing evidence that the underlying transactions took place, and that the amount of the deduction is reasonable.
>
> Discourage taxpayers from taking high risks on the chance that they will not be caught cheating by imposing a fixed (but no-fault) penalty on large deficiencies resulting from tax-haven transactions.
>
> End the existing income tax treaties with the Netherlands Antilles, the Channel Islands and the British Virgin Islands plus other havens.
>
> Prevent further abuse by being selective in negotiating tax treaties with countries with which America does not have a significant trade or investment relationship; not go into full-scale treaties with known tax havens; sign limited treaties with havens, and include exchange of information provisions to override local bank secrecy laws and similar practices.
>
> Ensure that the information needed to run the tax system properly—and to prosecute offenders—is available by getting the bank secrecy override provisions into every tax treaty (a provision likely to give the Swiss a heart attack).
>
> Review the workings of treaties regularly to make sure they are not being abused.
>
> Put pressure on abusive havens to sign exchange of information agreements by, say, increasing the withholding of taxes on payments made by American businesses into those havens.

Co-ordinated onshore policy seems imminent in respect of international tax authority discussions, information exchanges, and the simultaneous audits of the same company at the same time by two or more national tax authorities. The offshore future of particular transnational financial vehicles may also be constrained by new tax judgments in the Courts, e.g. in 1977 captive insurance companies were threatened by a decision of the US Internal Revenue Service which denied their bona fide activity and regarded them as a self-insurance device which made the tax-deductability of premiums and loss reserves doubtful. Since the *IRS* v. *Carnation Company* case, firms have sought out other insurance and reinsurance external to their in-house activities which have increased the cost of the operation. As Moore has recently observed:

> The consensus view is that companies should not only use captives if the parent wants to go into the insurance business, is a foreign corporation not subject to sub-part F of the IRS code and can therefore shelter the captive's underwriting and investment income offshore for tax purposes, is cash heavy, and has a foreign source of income from countries in which it is paying higher taxes than it can get credit on in its domiciled country.[1]

Despite the above, it is clear that inland revenue authorities do not have things all their own way, as was indicated by the temporary withdrawal of the UK Board of Inland Revenue's intended legislative proposals (previously discussed) from the 1982 Finance Bill as a result of strong opposition from multinational firms who intimated the complete removal of their international finance functions to offshore bases in the event of the implied threat to groups' internal financing arrangements and the possible clawbacks of past relieved tax resulting from the 'yellow peril' document (referring to the cover colour of the Board's draft proposals).

Governments will continue to attack and seek to foreclose the use of vehicles that exploit national friction structures in an officially considered undesirable manner. The plugging of loopholes surrounding inter-onshore economy exchange might, as a result of an intensified pressure, drive more business offshore or divert its international registration/location. The above mentioned Finance Bill attacked two such loopholes:

'Double-dip' leasing. International frictioneering activity had been centred round provisions whereby assets which may not have originated in the UK could be leased abroad (especially in the US) in such a way as to qualify for a 25 per cent tax allowance in the UK and a further allowance abroad. If funnelled through a UK bank, the effective interest charge could be reduced by 2 per cent or more. The Bill reduced this tax allowance from 25 per cent to 10 per cent.

Tax credit relief available to banks under the 'tax-spared' system. The use of tax credits against withholding tax paid abroad permits banks to make loans at lower margins than would otherwise be possible but such credits sometimes exceed the tax attributable to profits from overseas lending. In addition under certain double taxation agreements, e.g. with Malaysia, India and Brazil, the UK tax credit is available even when the foreign government waives its rights to levy withholding taxes. This enables banks in some cases to lend at less than the cost of such funds. It was estimated that £80m. were being lost to the UK Exchequer as a result of this. The Bill therefore proposed to gear the tax credit only to that part of the interest on the foreign loan which actually represents the bank's margin between its lending rate and its cost of funds.

Recent and future decisions in court cases may lead to 'daisy chain' redistribution of the location of offshore activities to avoid proximity to particular onshore tax regimes. This may particularly result from the very radical judgments made in the English Courts in 1981. In the UK the distinction between evasion and avoidance has become increasingly blurred. After many years in which the Inland Revenue has urged the Courts to ignore the form that a series of transactions takes and to look only at the overall effect of these transactions, the Courts in 1981 finally conceded to this view. Techniques of tax avoidance increasingly involved interconnected transactions between artificial persons such as limited liability companies without minds of their own but under the direction of a single mastermind. For the first time in *W.T. Ramsay Ltd.* v. *IRC* (1981) 2 WLR 449, the precedent was established that liability to tax should be determined by considering the reality of the end result of a scheme and to ignore any pre-ordained series of transactions, whether or not they included the achievement of a legitimate commercial end. This was confirmed in judgments given the same year in the cases of *Eilbeck* v. *Rawling* and *IRC* v. *Burmah Oil.* In future, therefore, no matter how safe a scheme may appear technically, there is a strong risk that the law will henceforth extend to counteract it. It is believed that this judgment will crucially affect more than 1,000 companies and wealthy individuals who were clients of tax avoidance organizations, some of which involved offshore bases.[2]

(2) THE ONSHORE DE-REGULATION PROCESS, THE INTERNATIONALIZATION OF DOMESTIC FINANCIAL MARKETS AND THE SPREAD OF ONSHORE EXTERNAL CENTRES

Of central importance in this area are the implications of the overdue proposed reforms of the US banking system and the liberalization of this and other countries' banking systems that will to some extent in the near future defrictionize international onshore invisible exchange, as interpenetration of more onshore capital and money markets takes place.

Part I Chapter I has already indicated the domestic restrictions hampering intra-state and inter-state banking in the US. Some liberalization of the US domestic financial centres took place in the 1970s such that by 1980 there was a disposition of foreign banks as shown in Table LXXXIII. It is clear that New York, San Francisco (California), Chicago (Illinois), and Miami (Florida) had become the main centres of representation. The type of presence effected depended

TABLE LXXXIII: Foreign banks located in the US by state and type in 1980

State	*Branches*	*Subsidiaries*	*Agencies*	*Other**	*Total*
New York	75	20	58	6	159
California		16	81		97
Illinois	31	2		1	34
Florida			12		12
Georgia			9		9
Washington	8				8
Pennsylvania	5				5
Massachusetts	4				4
Oregon	4				4
Hawaii			2		2
Texas				1	1
Total	127	38	162	8	335

Source: Federal Reserve Board.[3]

*including investment companies.

on the attitudes adopted in each state, e.g. New York passed legislation in 1961 to enable branches of foreign banks to be formed, whereas California did not permit this, the emphasis there being on agencies and representative offices. Changes effected by some states in the 1970s laid the foundation for offshore banking in the 1980s and the growth of regional external onshore markets not restricted to Edge Act small enclave development.

At the beginning of the 1970s, New York and the regional US centres owed their standing in world finance more to the fact that they were commerce centres for the largest of the world economies rather than as centres of foreign exchange and international finance. Despite its importance, New York was very largely US orientated in its activities until the early 1970s, after which a deepening involvement in foreign exchange business occurred. This trend stemmed initially from the massive increase in oil imports in the early 1970s and the need to protect US foreign interests' currency exposure by hedging, forward trading, swaps and currency future operations that occurred when the adjustable peg system of exchange rates was replaced *de facto* by floating exchange rates. Between April 1977 and March 1980, the daily trading volume on the New York foreign exchange market increased from $5bn. to $23bn. Interbank dealing and the activities of international foreign exchange brokers came to the fore, such that the New York Federal Reserve Bank declared in 1981: 'New York . . . has been transformed from a regional market to a major link between Europe and the Far East that now rivals London as the leading centre for global foreign exchange dealings.'[4] As a result of this, foreign banks became keener to set up in New York and give added depth and liquidity to its dealings. Foreign bank representation at the branch level was, however, only permitted on a reciprocal basis: only Canadian banks had the option of setting up subsidiary companies. Even in this state, however, local usury laws persisted, which caused some US banks to relocate certain activities elsewhere and to seek expansion in states that were prepared to accommodate their wishes, e.g. Citicorp transferred its credit card business to South Dakota; Morgan Guaranty and Chase Manhattan persuaded the State of Delaware to pass a generous tax and banking act which would benefit subsidiary operations in that state.

California's general prosperity proved an attractive location for retail deposit business and the fact that it also provides a foreign exchange and money market facility after New York closes. Moreover, its Pacific location was of interest to Japanese, British and continental European banks. By mid-1981, the *Financial Times* reported that there were seventeen full-service state chartered bank foreign subsidiaries, eighty-five agencies and one branch office holding 17 per cent of the total state bank assets, plus 250 local banks and twenty-one Edge Act Bank representatives from other US states.[5]

The State of Illinois, the centre for the Midwest, with Chicago as the US centre for financial futures trading, was the first centre of any size to pass an International Banking Act. This 1973 Act extended equal treatment to foreign banks as that accorded Illinois banks but limited their branching activities and confined their location to the 'Loop' district of Chicago. By 1981 foreign bank representation comprised thirty branches and twenty representative offices: local banks included two top banks, six regional banks and 1,000 neighbourhood banks.

TABLE LXXXIV: Foreign bank and Edge Act bank representation in Miami September 1980

Foreign bank representation	Edge Act bank representation	Year formed
Banca de Bilbao	Citizens and Southern International Bank	1969
Banco do Brasil	Bank of America International of Florida	1971
Banco Central	Citibank Interamerica	1971
Banco do Estado de Sao Paulo	Irving Interamerican Bank	1971
Banco de la Nacion Argentina	Wells Fargo Interamerican Bank	1971
Banco de la Provincia de Buenos Aires	Bank of Boston International of Miami	1972
	Chase Manhattan International Banking	1972
Banco de Vizcaya	Banca's Trust International	1974
Banco de Santandar	Northern Trust Interamerican Bank	1974
Banco Exterior de Espana	Morgan Guaranty International Bank	1977
Banco Internacional de Costa Rica	Marine Midland Interamerican Bank	1978
	Chemical Bank International of Miami	1979
Banco Real	Manufacturers Hanover Bank International	1979
Banko Hapoalim	New England Merchants Bank International	1979
Bank Leumi le-Israel	Continental Bank International (Miami)	1979
Bank of Nova Scotia	Republic New York International Banking	1979
Bank of Tokyo	American Security Bank International	1980
Israel Discount Bank	*Banco de Bogota	1980
Lloyds Bank International	*Banco de Santander International	1980
Royal Bank of Canada	J. Henry Schroder International Bank	1980
Standard Chartered Bank	First Union International Bank	to open
	Riggs Bank International	to open
	Security Pacific International Bank	to open
	United California Bank	to open

Source: Greater Miami Chamber of Commerce.

*Foreign owned.

Finally, in 1977, the State of Florida adopted an International Banking Act which, for the first time, permitted foreign branches to open representative offices and agencies and under a 'competitive equality law' these are ensured to enjoy any improvements resulting from legislation passed at the federal level: local taxes were reduced almost to zero on international banking transactions as from 1980. The defrictionizing of the local friction structure led to Miami's development as a mini Hong Kong for Latin American business. This is aided by the fact that almost 60 per cent of its local population are Latin American and the city tends to be a first port of call for incoming Latin American visitors. Both Edge Act banks and foreign banks became attracted to this centre for this reason, the latter also being drawn there too as a base from which to service corporate business in the prosperous south east areas of the United States. Representation from these two sources is indicated in Table LXXXIV.

As at September 1980, there were nineteen foreign banks registered in Miami: six from Latin America, five from Spain, three from Israel, two from Canada and the UK and one from Japan. In addition there were twenty-four Edge Act banks exclusively dealing with foreign trade. To further promote Miami as an international finance centre, a European Trade Office was opened in Stuttgart in November 1980 as well as a Trade Promotion Office in Latin America. In 1980 a local Banking Commission abolished a tax on intangibles and a documentary stamp tax, so that no state or city taxes were henceforth applied to international financial business.

At the federal level, a series of changes ushered in an entirely new era of banking: (1) the International Banking Act 1978; (2) the 1979 amendment to the 1919 Edge Act; (3) the Depository Institutions Deregulation and Monetary Control Act 1980; (4) the 1981 International Banking Facilities Provisions.

1) This Act was introduced to foster 'competitive equality' between domestic and foreign banking on a 'national treatment' basis. Foreign branches could now be opened either under Federal or state laws, but provisions were made for the regulation and supervision of such banks, in particular with regard to common reserve requirements, and reporting regulations in respect of foreign bank holding companies. Interstate branching was now possible on an Edge Act basis. For the first time FDIC insurance was mandatory on foreign bank domestic deposits of less than $100,000.[6]
2) The Edge Act legislation was amended in 1979 to abolish the previous requirement that each Edge operation had to be separately capitalized and thereby enabled 'master' Edge concentration of such offices under one office to take place. The requirement that clients must be non-resident within the meaning of the US immigration and tax laws was retained.
3) The Depository Institutions Deregulation and Monetary Control Act 1980 tackled many of the reform questions previously noted and placed some new regulations on foreign banks with respect to monetary control and the ability of the Federal Reserve Board to impose reserve requirements thereon. The main provisions include the gradual lifting of maximum rates of interest under Regulation Q and the final abolition of that regulation in 1986.
4) In 1969 at the time of the imposition of the Voluntary Foreign Credit Restraint Program, one governor of the Federal Reserve Board put forward the idea of a 'foreign window' facility in which foreign deposits might be booked and exempted from reserve requirements and Regulation Q, and from which foreign loans could be advanced, as an alternative to the emigration of such business to the overseas branches of US banks, or the loss of such business to foreign banks operating in London and the other emerging Eurocurrency centres. This idea was rejected in 1974 after some deliberation as being outweighed by the negative implications assumed for the conduct of domestic monetary policy. The idea resurfaced in 1977, however, when Walter Wriston, Chairman of Citibank, put forward the idea of creating onshore tax exempt facilities (variously referred to as domestic international banking units, DIBs, or international banking facilities, IBFs) to help to overcome failing US financial international competitiveness. The state legislature of New York freed international loan activities from state and city taxes and regulations in 1978, but this required approval from the Federal Reserve Board for implementation which was sought in 1979. After considerable delay and the passing of the Monetary Control Act that gave the Fed. the legal authority to reduce reserve requirements to zero, final agreement in principle was announced in November 1980. A specific plan was approved on 8 June 1981 for im-

> plementation as from 3 December 1981. Henceforth US banks would be able to compete openly and directly in the Eurocurrency markets from onshore US offices without using or having to set up foreign subsidiaries outside the reach of their bank regulators, so avoiding complicated paper work. Dealings in these markets would be on the basis of the entire capital strength of the banks involved and not just the smaller capital of offshore subsidiaries, thereby making these transactions slightly cheaper. Moreover, these dealings would theoretically enjoy a superior 'country risk' associated with US operations. Thus, it was thought that this might make possible Eurocurrency participation by the smaller US banks which could not previously afford the costs of external branch formation, so that the effective size of these markets would be enlarged.
>
> According to the finalized scheme the Fed would grant the following concessions: (*a*) no reserve requirement: usually a 3 per cent reserve requirement had been enforced under Regulation D; (*b*) no interest rate ceilings as imposed under Regulation Q; (*c*) a minimum withdrawal/deposit limit was set at \$100,000 (the initial, proposed limit was \$500,000); (*d*) banks would be exempted from a 48-hour notice-of-withdrawal rule and foreign banks and official institutions may place 'overnight' funds in IBFs; (*e*) banks need only notify the Fed. two weeks in advance that they want to start an IBF and agree to abide to the rules. They must also ensure that their customers understand the rules.

In addition to the above, funds are subject to insurance against bank failure and subject to the Federal Deposit Insurance Corporation to prevent 'seepage' or 'leakage' between the domestic and offshore banking systems; and to prevent any undermining of domestic monetary policy, IBF business must be entered in separate books which are inspected by the Fed.: no separate housing is required for such activity. Exemption of IBFs from local tax is left with State Governments. Initially, the States of New York, Connecticut, California, Florida, Georgia and Maryland passed legislation to make such exemptions: legislation in several other states including Hawaii, Illinois and Massachusetts is pending at the time of writing. New York was the first to start business on 3 December 1981.

The scheme as initially introduced has certain freedoms and restrictions that will condition its use. It is unique in that deposits may be taken in the local currency (US dollars) as well as in foreign currencies, whereas such schemes in other parts of the world have usually specifically excluded the use of domestic currencies. There are, however, a number of 'buts'. To ensure that financial activities are restricted to non-residents, IBFs are prohibited from issuing negotiable Certificates of Deposits, bankers' acceptances or other negotiable instruments and can only offer time deposits; they are expected to support only operations outside the US and to extend credit only to such operations (it is not desired that US companies place funds in IBFs by routing them through their foreign subsidiaries); deposit facilities offered to foreign non-bank residents are subject to minimum maturity requirements or a required two business days' notice prior to withdrawal, and to minimum deposits and withdrawals of \$100,000 to preserve the wholesale nature of the business. The above restrictions clearly put IBFs at a competitive disadvantage as compared with foreign offshore locations, even

TABLE LXXXV: Assets in foreign branches of US banks 1973–80 (in $bn.)

Year	*UK*	*Bahamas / Caymans*	*Other*	*Total*
1973	61.7	23.8	36.4	121.9
1974	69.8	31.7	50.4	151.9
1975	74.9	45.2	56.4	176.5
1976	81.5	66.8	71.1	219.4
1977	90.9	79.1	88.9	258.9
1978	106.6	91.7	108.5	306.8
1979	130.9	109.0	124.3	364.2
1980*	137.1	119.4	124.5	381.0

Source: Federal Reserve Bulletin

*October figures.

though it is proposed in the near future to exempt them from insurance cover costs in line with the position of foreign branches of US banks.

It is believed that by promoting international banking on US soil, part of the multi-billion dollar Eurodollar market will be repatriated and give the US authorities a greater say in its control. Estimates are published by the Fed. of the assets held in the foreign branches of US banks as shown in Table LXXXV. The importance of London and the Bahamas/Caymans is evident. The question remains as to how much is likely to be repatriated and to what extent the new IBF facility will add to the size of the market. Two factors must be taken into consideration in answering these questions. Firstly, while there may be benefits from enjoying US sovereign risks, some mistrust may exist and banks may not wish to keep all their offshore eggs in one onshore basket. Moreover, non-US banks may be thought to provide greater confidentiality for depositors, added to which the example of the Iranian assets freeze is evidence that bank deposits may be interfered with for political ends. Secondly, there are good business reasons, as has already been shown, for a geographical dispersion of activities due to *inter alia* nearness to depositors and borrowers and time zone locational advantages. Ashby has given estimates of the possible shifts in the global location of the Eurocurrency markets in the 1980s as shown in Table LXXXVI.[7] Some loss of London's pre-eminence seems inevitable, although the London money markets are open for a large part of the time when New York is closed and have at present distinct advantages with respect to syndicated loans, insurance etc., though this is being eroded by international competition and London's present higher operating costs as compared with New York. Ashby estimates that by the end of the decade London's share of the gross world wide market will decline from 32 per cent to 20 per cent. As regards the Bahamas and Cayman Islands, it is expected that their share may fall from 11 per cent to just over 2 per cent with about $100bn. in assets held by US bank branches eventually being repatriated. While this loss is inevitable, it is thought that no overall reduction in the volume of total business done in these centres will occur. To begin with, it is unlikely that all Eurobusiness will leave their shores. On the one hand, IBFs themselves are restricted to foreign business only, deposits from and loans to US customers that are at present offshore will tend to stay offshore; moreover, some banks may well be wary of onshore disclosure and record-keeping, and nationals from certain

TABLE LXXXVI: Possible shifts in the global location of the Eurocurrency markets as indicated by the estimated percentage shares of the gross worldwide market in 1980, 1985 and 1990

	Percentage shares		
	1980	*1985*	*1990*
London	32	25	20
Bahamas and Caymans	11	5	2
New York	0	12	18
Others	57	58	60
	100	100	100

Source: Grinlays Bank.

countries may be wary of the onshore US centres and London in the wake of the asset freezes that took place during the Iranian 'hostages' and Falklands crises. On the other hand, the Caribbean centres, in particular the Bahamas, have recently become a prime centre for offshore Geneva-based banks following increased investor uncertainty in Switzerland due to fiscal instability in that country and uncertainties resulting from the recent political difficulties in Iran, Afghanistan and Poland: some twenty-five of these banks have recently set up in this area. Morover, Arab investors have been increasingly using Bahamian companies as vehicles for overseas investment. Private client business may increasingly be attracted to the area given their reinforced secrecy laws. Furthermore, perhaps of greater significance than IBFs will be the development of money markets in Miami. Given that Edge Act banks can open branches without having to boost their capital base, new developments may take place at the nearby port of Tampa with its free trade zone and proximity to Panama. A knock-on effect may result in the Caribbean from the need in the above region for trust business associated with these developments.

Given the above and similar estimates, the staff of the Federal Reserve Board have concluded that eventual IBF balances may be in the range $80bn. to $120bn., with half coming from domestic banking offices and half from foreign offices: this may be an underestimate as other commentators have put forward a top level of $200bn. In terms of New York, US banks were given thirty days in which they could transfer their assets into IBFs without having to comply with Fed. regulations governing the movement of funds between banks and their offshore subsidiaries. In the first six weeks, Salomon Brothers (as reported in the *Financial Times,* 8 February 1982, p.16) estimated that more than $60bn. worth of assets had been attracted thereto: $33bn. belonging to US banks, and $28bn. from foreign banks, 260 banks being involved. Most of the US bank total was transferred from branches in London, Luxembourg and Nassau. This represented about 5 per cent of the Euromarket world-wide. Mr. James Bordon of Chase Manhattan commented that 'The World offshore market is bound to gravitate towards New York'. It remains to be seen whether some of the 'buts' mentioned above are abolished and how many other US states actualize the

New York example. US success in this area might well pressurize Japan or Germany to follow suit and existing Eurocurrency centres may further liberalize local currency transactions with non-residents from reserve requirements. If this trend materializes, the 1980s will become a decade of growth for onshore external markets. In each case, though, 'country-risk' considerations may be as important as cost considerations.

Globally, it would seem that the immediate future will be a continuation of the recent past, and that onshore the internationalization process will continue to forge ever closer links between domestic and international capital markets, further reinforcing the interlinked global business networks already formed and emphasizing the increasing dominance of the international markets over national domestic markets. It is probable that overseas expansion will continue to be an integral part of the overall strategy of banking corporations, and that in order for particular national banks to obtain participation in this, further liberalization of onshore domestic financial systems will occur. Each at present restricted onshore economy, if it is to participate in this process, will be forced to re-examine its domestic financial friction structure in the light of worldwide developments and its needs, revisions which will tend to further the greater, if not conditional, interpenetration of onshore banking systems. *Per se* this will tend to create internal pressure to expand and create more onshore external markets. Where such changes occur there will be a tendency for domestic banks to seek to extend their global office network and to increase their assets held overseas to offer international services which can meet the new foreign competition at home. Two countries where this is already taking place are Canada and Spain: Australia is in the early stage of such a re-assessment process.

Canada

The new Canadian Bank Act that came into effect on 1 December 1980 may prove typical in respect of the liberalization of onshore financial systems. Under this act, foreign banks may incorporate subsidiary banks in Canada only if as favourable treatment is offered to Canadian banks in the jurisdiction of the parent bank country. Licensing is on an annual basis for the first five years of operation, after which three-year licences may be issued. No limit is laid down as to the number of branches permitted in Canada, although prior approval is required. Overall entry is conditioned within a set limit that the foreign banking sector must not exceed 8 per cent of all banks' domestic assets and that a minimum authorized capital of $5m. is observed of which half must be fully paid; initial and all subsequent increases in authorized capital must be approved with an upper limit of twenty times the original authorized capital. These reciprocal provisions have enabled full banking licences to be issued to Canadian banks in Japan, Hong Kong and Switzerland where previously Canadian banks could not obtain full status. From mid-1981 until March 1982, forty-seven foreign bank approvals had been made in Canada. In return Hong Kong had allowed Canadian chartered banks to establish full operations, Japan had allowed the five largest Canadian banks to open branches in Tokyo, and the Royal Bank of

Canada had been allowed to acquire the Banque Occidentale pour l'Industries et le Commerce (Suisse) (to be called the Royal Bank of Canada (Suisse)) to fill a gap in that bank's global network.[8]

Spain

Spain has liberalized its banking system with a series of reforms since 1977, permitting the introduction of foreign banks and the creation of new domestic financial instruments. A decree of 1978 permitted the new entry of foreign banks which by 1982 had risen from four to thirty. These new entrants have been the instigators of new instruments such as acceptances and floating rate loans. By the autumn of 1981, foreign banks had built up a loan portfolio two-thirds the size of the fifty indigenous banks. Foreign banks may not open more than three branches and deposits in pesetas from customers cannot exceed 40 per cent of their assets, guarantees cannot exceed three times their net worth and no investment in equities is permitted. There is a 4 per cent turnover tax on borrowings in the peseta interbank market.[9] To increase their international competitiveness, Spanish banks extended their networks to New York, San Francisco, Miami and Latin America: the Banco de Santander developed more than a hundred offices throughout the latter region. In order to finance the internationalization of their capital bases, some Spanish banks placed parts of their capital on the international stock markets, e.g. The Banco Hispano-Americano, Spain's third largest commercial bank, placed nearly 3 per cent of its capital on the London stock exchange to raise $18.5m. for this purpose in early 1982.[10]

All highly developed onshore economies, whether with liberalized financial systems or not, will tend to become subject to these and other types of financial penetration as the following examples indicate from recent changes in the UK, Japan, and the US.

> *The UK.* Changes in the methods of central government finance favouring a greater reliance on commercial bill finance made the Bank of England in mid-1981 substantially increase the list of banks whose bills are 'eligible' for discounting, such that the number of these banks nearly doubled to ninety-six. Most of the new admissions were foreign banks: seventeen were from the US, seven each from Japan and France, three from Germany, two each from Switzerland and Holland, and one each from Belgium and Ireland.
>
> *Japan.* Japan is increasingly being faced with the *de facto* internationalization of the yen and the growth of its importance within the world financial system, e.g. the increased use of the yen as a reserve currency by the central banks of the Middle East and South East Asia and international investors.[11] The liberalization of the Japanese banking system, especially if an onshore external market were to develop based on yen and/or dollars, would clearly make Tokyo the major financial centre of Asia. Although this is not at present intended, some changes in this direction are already apparent, e.g. the Tokyo Stock Exchange is considering lifting the ban on foreign membership to allow foreign-owned securities houses to become members of the

exchange;[12] Citibank, the largest US bank, has begun to expand in Japan, having opened six branches there by the end of 1981, more than any of the other sixty-four foreign banks then present, having made a heavy capital commitment to a new computer and communication systems and having made provisions for non-Japanese money market operations in which it hopes to expand as Japanese companies develop their role in international finance. Citibank has also created two consumer credit ventures, two leasing companies, a consultancy company and a company servicing yen travellers' cheques for itself and three large Japanese citybanks.[13] Furthermore, the Japanese authorities are expected to raise the $5bn.–$6bn. ceiling limits imposed on foreign bank currency, swaps between foreign currencies and yen.

The US. The US is perceived as being a major target market, especially as a result of its banking system reforms, which will make small regional banks prime takeover targets both for domestic banks and as a means of foreign banks gaining US entry. The *Financial Times* of 21 December 1981 (p.24) reported that UK institutions had taken private placements ranging from 3 per cent to 13 per cent in such banks already.

The further development of hybrid financial institutions and multinational joint ventures is likely to emphasize the development of new types of institution with multi-purpose 'in-house' capabilities, combining banking services with investment facilities, insurance etc., or acting on a specialist basis within chosen market areas, e.g. the Sanwa Bank of Japan established a 50:50 joint venture finance company with the US Citicorp in Switzerland in 1981 to be named Sanwa Finanz (Schweiz) AG, as a means of opening up new business for the Japanese bank in underwriting bond issues by Japanese companies mostly in Swiss francs.

It would therefore seem as a result of the above-mentioned developments that the prophesy made by Giddy and Allen in 1979[14] that 'international banking will merge with domestic banking to form a single, global wholesale banking market' is about to manifest itself, as more domestic wholesale banking markets become opened-up to new financial and non-financial institutions, both internal and foreign, and local oligopolies lose their previously privileged protected positions. Concomitant with this Giddy and Allen expect an 'unbundling' of financial services which have previously been jointly provided, e.g. direct ties between deposit-taking and loan-extending facilities, and in addition a proliferation of special-purpose package contracts and financial instruments. Furthermore they anticipate that:

> The apparent trend toward large banks absorbing smaller ones, which has some economic logic as geographical barriers to entry are broken down, will encounter a countervailing tendency for relatively small, specialized international financial institutions to emerge and sometimes succeed.
>
> This unconventional belief arises because there are few economies of scale in wholesale banking, and because sharply lower costs for information access and processing, shared funds transfer facilities, combined with fewer regulatory barriers to entry and the unbundling of services, will enable

> more smaller institutions to try their hand at providing a specialized banking service . . .
>
> The new small international banks will not necessarily participate in the highly competitive Eurocurrency market . . . Small banks will be entrepreneurs—they will use their specialized contacts and knowledge and new technology to create for themselves a niche of banking. They will be innovators, risk takers and packagers of services.[15]

Globally, there will be changes in the balance of banking power between individual nations. It is likely, for instance, that American banks will continue to decline in importance relative to Arab banks. The latter have grown significantly in absolute terms in recent years, e.g. the Gulf International Bank owned by seven Arab governments doubled its assets in 1980 and was managing loans over $12,000m. or four times its 1978 figures; the Arab Banking Corporation set up in January 1980 grew to $2,000m. by the end of its first year's trading; the Saudi International Bank, founded in August 1975, is now the largest of the London consortium banks and in 1981 was involved in the management of twenty-two floating rate note and Certificate of Deposit issues and forty-two loans for sovereign and corporate borrowers with a total value of $12bn. By mid-1981 Arab banks were participating in almost 45 per cent by volume of all Eurocurrency credits as compared to about 10 per cent in the previous year. The location strategies adopted by these banks in the future will have a significant effect on particular centre results. These activities might be tempered by evolving concepts of Islamic banking that may alter the operational criteria of Arab banking and the cycling of petro-funds.

The growth of onshore external markets may well result in future attempts to exert controls on the Euromarkets which have been threatened since the international crisis surrounding the Bankhaus Herstatt and the Franklin National Bank failures of the mid-1970s as well as subsequent cases of improvement subsidiary financial activity. Onshore surveillance is likely to be more comprehensive and parental control thereby more effective if this method is resorted to rather than controls exercised on a banking centre basis. This change combined with a general adoption of the guidelines laid down by the Basle 'Concordat' and the EEC directive (discussed in Chapter I Part I) will thereby introduce a greater degree of global uniformity in reserve and capital requirements and lessen the scope for international bank frictioneering activities. A *sine qua non* for the effective discharge of such onshore supervision would appear to be concomitant acceptance of the consolidation of accounts, such that the assets and liabilities of all parts of a group of banking companies are aggregated, with intra-group items being offset against each other: this would prevent the use of subsidiary companies located in areas with no or very low solvency requirements for gearing up the overall lending capacity and creating thereby an equity capital pyramid, and thus '"blind spots" on the world map of banking supervision'[16] would be very largely eliminated. Such a change was accepted in principle by the EEC Group of Bank Supervisory Authorities—the Groupe de Contact—and ratified by the central bank governors of the Group of Ten and Switzerland in May 1979. This was followed by discussions on this and other matters by the first world conference of supervisory authorities held in London in July 1979.

This is not the place in which to attempt an assessment of the future prospects of the Eurocurrency markets. However, it is to be noted that financial innovation continues to be found therein, although individual governments may attempt to circumscribe the impact of particular developments. Thus, the early 1980s saw the emergence of such new financial vehicles as zero coupon Eurobonds and Eurodollar interest rate futures. Zero coupon bonds bear no interest, are priced at a deep discount, but offer prospects of capital gains and so are attractive to investors where such profits may be exempt from taxation. Several issues were made in early 1982 but when advantage was taken by investors in Japan to use them as a capital gain exempt tax vehicle and tax shelter, after the month of February 1982 (when some $780m. had been invested alone) the Japanese authorities halted sales. Nevertheless, these coupons do have an appeal in respect of investment from offshore centres. Eurodollar interest rate futures is yet another US innovation, the first of which was launched on Chicago's International Monetary Market in December 1981 and called a Eurodollar Certificate of Deposit Contract: it provides for delivery on a quarterly basis of $1m. in three-month Eurodeposits at a prime bank which allows the investor to hedge against interest rate or exchange rate positions.

Although initial reactions have been muted, it is highly likely that financial futures will become a feature of the 1980s as a hedge against future price movements of particular assets or for speculative purposes: fluctuating exchange rates and interest rates make this seem inevitable. Thus, the Chicago Board of Trade exchange has witnessed already a growth of financial futures from 2 per cent by volume of its total activities in 1977 to 33 per cent by the end of 1981. Mergers are already taking place between commodity trading companies, stock exchange companies and banking interests, so that in future the line between securities and commodity trading is likely to become increasingly blurred. In addition to currencies, interest rates, bonds, mortgages and treasury bills already introduced, and the new Eurodollar contract, trading in domestic bank certificates of deposit was introduced in 1981, and stock indices futures markets are planned in Kansas, the two New York exchanges, and the Chicago Mercantile Exchange. The latter exchange is to have an Indices and Options Market, as options futures are being increasingly permitted by the US Commodities Futures Trading Commission (CFTC). An added attraction is that in 1981 the domestic US tax liability on short-term gains was reduced to a flat rate of 32.5 per cent compared to a previous rate of between 50 and 70 per cent. The London International Financial Futures Exchange (LIFFE) is scheduled to open in September 1982. LIFFE contracts will be in three-month US dollar and sterling time deposits based on a notional twenty-year 12 per cent gilt-edged stock and four currencies against the dollar. The attractiveness of this particular market will, however, depend on the attitudes taken by the Inland Revenue Board with respect to the taxing of these activities.[17]

If there is to be 24-hour trading in financial futures throughout the world, time zone gaps need to be filled—some of them by certain offshore centres. Working parties in Hong Kong and Singapore are now considering extending each centre's commodities trading ordinances to include the new financial contract investment vehicles, including currency futures in £ sterling, US dollars,

Deutschmarks, yen and Swiss francs, and interest rate futures in Eurodollars and sterling. A feasibility study has been conducted for Singapore by the Continental Illinois National Bank and Trust Company, individuals from which have intimate experience of Chicago's International Monetary Market exchange. Bermuda is setting up in 1982 the first computerized futures exchange, INTEX, providing a 24-hour dealing service in futures contracts with traders linked thereto via computer terminals in their offices: fourteen types of contracts are planned.

Other areas of financial futures development have already emerged including gold futures. This developed in Chicago in 1975 when the US ban on owning gold bullion was lifted. Markets were subsequently opened in New York, Singapore (November 1978), Hong Kong (March 1980), Sydney and Japan (March 1982). Finally, following the lifting of the UK ban on UK ownership of gold bullion in October 1979, Europe's first exchange for forward trading in gold was opened in London on 19 April 1982, thereby completing a global ring of such exchanges. The introduction of gold options trading was begun in 1976 by Crédit Suisse and is also beginning the diversification of this market.[18]

Another transnational growth industry with bank and non-bank international corporate network connections is international leasing, either of the cross-border type or via foreign subsidiary companies. This activity has current appeal due to the fact that industrial and commercial companies, especially those involved with aircraft, ships, computers, and major industrial plant, obtain the use of such assets with a low capital outlay. Leases may be 'leveraged' to combine equity with debt interest in proportions of 1 to 5 or lower, the debt interest being financed by money market funds such as yen bond funds in Australia. Specialist leasing firms, as well as subsidiaries of UK merchant banks and US investment banks, have recently become involved in the growth of this phenomenon. In particular, this development has appealed to multinational firms in high risk countries where the separation of asset use from asset ownership may have distinct advantages. Leasing has been given a new boost in the US due to the coming into force as from 13 August 1981 of the Economic Recovery Tax Act which has laid down more liberal rules with regard to official recognition of 'true leases', and has made more generous 'safe harbour' provisions, heightened the value of tax benefits by accelerating the depreciation periods on all equipment and the granting of investment tax credits (ITCs), lowered the equity risk from 20 per cent of the asset cost to 10 per cent, and allowed 'wash leases', whereby tax benefits of companies with tax losses and recent equipment purchases may be transferred within ninety days to companies with tax shelter.[19] Clearly, provided offshore centres can offer more competitive terms to allow local or external local incorporation of such trading companies, a distinct boost to their company registrations and earnings therefrom could be effected.

In the area of insurance and reinsurance a number of Lloyds of London style markets have now been set up around the world. The New York Insurance Exchange was set up in March 1981 and others are planned for Chicago and Florida as well as significant joint-venture Arab schemes in the Middle East. These are promoted by, and will themselves promote, transnational institutional linkages for defensive and competitive reasons.

Other forms of financial business traditionally conservative in their investment portfolios are likely to become increasingly worldwide in outlook. Thus, US corporate pension funds now invest 2 per cent of their $600bn. of assets abroad. Ehrlich[20] expects the foreign investment proportion to grow at a rate of ½ per cent per annum to about 7 per cent by 1990. Given an estimated 10 per cent growth rate of total assets to $1,400bn., this would suggest $100bn. being then invested abroad. This development has occurred since the passing in 1974 of the Employee Retirement Income Security Act (ERISA) which directed fund managers to diversify their portfolios and thereby opened up the overseas investment spectrum. These trends may have significance for offshore centre deposits and trust finance.

ERISA requires that indicia (evidence) of ownership of foreign assets held for employee benefit plans must be maintained in locations subject to the jurisdiction of US courts, except as otherwise authorized by regulation of the Secretary of Labor. Rules made in 1977 and amended as from 30 March 1981 permit indicia to be held abroad if the related assets are under the management and control of a US bank, insurance company, or investment adviser/manager registered with the Securities and Exchange Commission or in the custody of a foreign bank or other specified type of foreign entity, as long as the custodian is supervised or regulated by a government agency or regulatory authority in the host country. Some US banks already provide global master custodianship services, using their own foreign branches in countries in which they are represented as subcustodians and other foreign banks where this is not the case. These services include safekeeping the indicia, the collection of dividends and interest, currency translation, and centralized reporting of all investments and income, no matter who may be managing different parts of the plan funds.

As many onshore countries have withholding taxes (although these may be partially mitigated by double-taxation agreements) and have government barriers to the withdrawal at will by foreign investors of earnings or liquidation proceeds (of the 140 member countries of the International Monetary Fund covered in its 1980 Annual Report on Exchange Arrangements and Exchange Restrictions, only twenty-three had no restrictions of any kind on capital payments), the use of offshore centres may well be increasingly resorted to for investment in offshore funds or for the location of investment companies, especially when they are combined with free trade zones that encourage foreign low tax or no tax investments. Banks are using international commingled funds for this purpose.[21] Moreover, some US states such as Alaska and Vermont have passed enabling legislation to permit foreign investment of public employee pension funds, though as yet they are in the minority. The future for offshore pension funds and offshore investment of onshore pension funds would seem to be encouraging.

The internationalization process will be furthered by the actions of important national and supranational institutions. Thus, in early 1982, the Export–Import Bank of the US (Eximbank) decided to offer potential borrowers in less developed countries the option of financing their purchase of US capital goods in Japanese yen, due to the lower level of interest rates in Japan.[22] The World Bank is increasingly seeking to encourage 'co-financing' development projects in the Third

World: in 1981 it circulated some 500 leading financial institutions on the subject. In June 1981 it was managing $4bn. in co-finance projects that included $1.7bn. from private banks.

The increased competitive pressures implied by the above developments will still give in many instances cost advantages to offshore centres and security advantages for non-Eurocurrency business, although it is evident that if the concentration of development lies in the expansion and repatriation of offshore Eurocurrency activities via onshore external markets, the relative importance of offshore centres in this area will decline. The question is, will its decline only be relative? Clearly, there is a danger that the smaller centres may become less viable as financial centres if scale factors and more assertive onshore fiscal protection policies pre-empt their operational advantages, although continued political stability and low taxes have a pulling power of their own for external trust business and overseas trading company registration. In some centres there is still scope for further relaxation of local friction structures, e.g. in March 1982 the twenty-four offshore bankings units in Manila were allowed to handle for the first time the foreign currency remittances of 200,000 Filipino expatriates working abroad. They were given this business because they were better equipped to handle it given their widespread networks, especially in the Middle East, where about three-quarters of these workers are employed: they can now open and maintain peso accounts to pay the workers' beneficiaries from these remittances.

The 1980s might prove to be crucial for centres that come in conflict with the onshore countries with which they are in monetary union, e.g. when Belgium unilaterally devalued the Belgium/Luxembourg joint franc by 8.5 per cent in March 1982, it led to a demand by Luxembourg for exchange rate guarantees in the event of future devaluations and for a separate valuation of Luxembourg's gold and foreign reserves held by the Banque Nationale de Belgique and there was some discussion about an independent Luxembourg currency as a result. It has also been publicized that the Isle of Man is studying the implications of breaking its links with sterling and withdrawing from the sterling area if the UK reintroduces exchange controls.[23] Furthermore, in the medium to long term, it is not clear what the implications for the British Isle centres would be if full monetary union were to be achieved in Europe. In the event of special arrangements not being made in such a context the islands would be individually faced with the prospect of full integration with the UK or unilateral independence or bilateral union or integration with each other.

The above considerations and trends seem to suggest that individual centre restrictive entry might have to be more flexible with respect to innovation, new institutional entry and the creation of new enabling and commercial laws. Otherwise, the institutional ambitions and global linkages of locally incorporated institutions will be crucial if they are to have a share in the new developments. To take two recent examples in relation to Guernsey: Henry Ansbacher, a small merchant banker, as part of a move to develop itself into a major trade-oriented financial services group, announced in February 1982 new ties with Touche Remant, one of the City of London's largest fund managers, managing £900m. of investment trusts and controlling £1.3bn. funds, including pension funds with a

20 per cent stake in R.P. Martin, the City moneybrokers; and a take-over of Seascope, a leading ship and insurance broker. The resultant broadened base of this bank may well have an important contribution to make to the expansion of corporate business in banking, offshore funds and insurance. Also in February 1982, it was announced that three actuarial consultancy firms—Bacon and Woodrow (established in Guernsey), Duncan C. Fraser and R. Watson and Sons—have combined to launch a European operation called EURACS (European Actuarial Consultancy Services) and have agreed with the Banque Bruxelles Lambert, the second largest bank in Belgium, to acquire its pension consultancy division to offer a comprehensive consultancy advice service for multinational companies. This may well be of significance for the development of offshore pension funds on the island of Guernsey.

It is likely that many island centres will further develop consultancy and management services. Thus, the *Guernsey Evening Press and Star* announced on 27 July 1981 that:

> A new overseas marketing base for its Channel Islands managed funds is being opened in the crown colony of Gibraltar by Hambros Bank Ltd. of the UK.
>
> Hambros Bank (Gibraltar) has been set up with £750,000 capital and which will primarily offer a full range of merchant banking services.
>
> Hambros (Gibraltar), like Hambros in Jersey and Guernsey—total assets of £120m.—is a wholly owned subsidiary of the UK parent. It is the first UK merchant bank to be granted an offshore licence in Gibraltar.
>
> In addition to marketing offshore funds the bank sees 'the Rock' as an attractive place for captive insurance companies and intends to offer tax advice to clients in this field.
>
> Mr. D.J. Thomason, a director of Hambros Bank in London, has said that apart from general banking facilities to non-residents, the main areas of business would be investment advice and banking services for tax-exempt companies in Gibraltar and various services to expatriates living in Spain and close to Gibraltar.
>
> It is also hoped to secure new business in Morocco.

The same issue of the above-mentioned Guernsey paper also announced:

> Britannia International Investment Management Ltd. has announced the opening of a representative sales office in the Cayman Islands.
>
> The office has been licensed, by the Cayman Islands Protection Board, to provide investment advice and consultancy services. It is located in the premises of the Washington International Bank and Trust Ltd. in George Town.
>
> Britannia International Investment Management, based in Jersey, is a member of the Britannia group of investment companies, whose managed funds exceed £500m.
>
> Of this total £70m. is managed in Jersey.
>
> The new offshore office will provide information and investment advice on Britannia's full range of services.

Finally, perhaps the quote from Rothschild given below, though made in a general context, encapsulates the incipient dilemma for offshore centres and their development strategies for the remainder of the 1980s:

> competitiveness does not consist exclusively in the ability to serve given demand patterns at low prices, but to a large and growing extent in the creation of demand for 'new' products through product innovation, . . . marketing strategies etc. Supply does not—as the market equilibrium model suggests—simply adjust to an exogenous international demand structure; on the contrary, the structure of international trade flows is constantly modified by the supply side through the activities of 'pioneering' export innovators who discover openings for new products and product differentiation. Other exporters and exporting countries may then, as 'imitators', follow this lead and score successes by adjusting to the structured opportunities so revealed.[24]

It is likely that offshore centres will continue to rely on imported US and UK financial innovative expertise to pioneer, diversify and maintain their financial offerings to transnational enterprise and to retain their individual global importance and the significance of the international secondary invisible trading system.

REFERENCES

1. Moore, J., 'Captive Companies. Survey: Reinsurance', *Financial Times,* 7 September 1981, p.VII. See also Bawcutt, P.A., *Captive Insurance Companies: Establishment, Operation and Management,* Cambridge, Woodhead-Faulkner, 1982.
2. See Taylor, T.P.D., 'Tax Planning and Tax Avoidance after Ramsay', a series of five articles in the following issues of *Taxation:* 10 October, 17 October, 24 October, 31 October and 7 November, 1981.
3. Berger, F.E., 'The Emerging Transformation of the US Banking System', *The Banker,* September 1981, p.35.
4. Revey, P., 'Evolution and Growth of the United States Foreign Exchange Market', *Federal Reserve Bank of New York Quarterly Review,* Vol.6, No.3, Autumn 1981, p.32.
5. *Financial Times,* 24 June 1981.
6. See Bellanger, S., 'Optimism Gives Way to Realism in the 1980s'; and, Walmsley, J., 'Moving towards Competitive Equality', *The Banker,* February 1980. Also Wright, C.F., 'Changes in the Structure of American Banking and Finance—A New Era of Competition', *Barclays Review,* February 1982.
7. Ashby, D.F.V., 'Will the Eurodollar Market Go Back Home?' *The Banker,* February 1981, p.98. See also Morgan Guaranty Trust Company, 'International Banking Facilities', *World Financial Markets,* November 1981, pp.6–11; Financial Times Survey, 'Financial Services in New York', *Financial Times,* 3 December 1981, pp.15–19; and, Ireland, J., 'International Banking Facilities', *The Banker,* July 1981, pp.51–6.
8. Anon, 'Canadian Banks Look Abroad for Growth', *The Banker,* March 1982, p.5; see also LaBrosse, J.R., 'Canada's New Banking Law', *The Banker,* March 1981, pp. 37–41.
9. Financial Times Survey, 'Spanish Banking', *Financial Times,* 23 March 1982, pp.I, II and VII.
10. *Financial Times,* 24 March 1982, p.24.

11. Egashira, K., 'The Internationalisation of the Yen', *The Banker,* March 1982, pp.37–41. See also Gregory, G. 'Foreign Banking in Japan – in Search of a Broader Role', *The Banker,* June 1979; and, Pringle, R., 'The Glint of Steel behind Tokyo's International Role', *The Banker,* August 1981, pp.77–81.

12. *Financial Times,* 5 February 1982, p.32.

13. *Financial Times,* 10 December 1981.

14. Giddy, I. and Allen, D., 'International Competition in Bank Regulation', *Banca Nazionale del Lavoro Quarterly Review,* No.130, September 1979, p.315.

15. Giddy and Allen, op.cit., pp. 320–1.

16. Colje, H., 'Bank Supervision on a Consolidated Basis', *The Banker,* June 1980, pp. 29–34.

17. Holland, M., 'Tax Implications for Banks', *The Banker,* April 1982, pp.123–9. See this issue for other articles on the London Financial Futures Exchange.

18. Financial Times Survey, 'Gold Futures', *Financial Times,* 20 April 1982, pp.25–30.

19. Clark, T.M., 'The Dawn of International Leasing', *The Banker,* April 1982, pp.57–67. See this issue for other articles on this subject by N. Johnson and R. Hawkins.

20. Ehrlich, E., 'International Diversification by United States Pension Funds', *Federal Reserve Bank of New York Quarterly Review,* Vol.6 No.3, Autumn 1981, p.2.

21. Ehrlich, op.cit., p.6.

22. *Financial Times,* 2 February 1982, p.4.

23. *Financial Times,* 23 February 1982, p.1. See also Dawson, W., 'Implications of an Independent Manx Currency', Isle of Man Treasury, 1977.

24. Rothschild, K.W., 'Export Structure, Export Flexibility and Competitiveness', *Weltwirtschafliches Archiv,* Band III, Heft 2, 1975, p.225.

Bibliography

Adams, C.W., 'Secret Account or Foreign Trust?' *The Banker,* April 1972.

Anstead, D.T. and Latham, R.G., *The Channel Islands,* revised by E.T. Nicholle, third edition, W.H. Allen, London, 1893.

Ashby, D.F.V., 'Challenge from the New Euro-centres', *The Banker,* January 1978.

______'Will the Eurodollar Market Go Back Home?' *The Banker,* February 1981.

Baker, J.C., *International Bank Regulation,* Praeger, New York, 1978.

Baldwin, R.E., *Non-tariff Trade Distortions of International Trade,* Allen and Unwin, London, 1971.

Bank of America, *Captive Insurance Companies,* pamphlet, n.d.

Bank of England, 'UK Exchange Control: A Short History', *Bank of England Quarterly Bulletin,* Vol. 7, No. 3, September 1967.

______'The Investment Currency Market', *Bank of England Quarterly Bulletin,* Vol. 16, No. 3, September 1976.

Bank Research Unit, *Who is Where in World Banking 1981–82,* Financial Times Business Publishing Ltd., London, 1981.

______*Who Owns What in World Banking 1981–82,* Financial Times Business Publishing Ltd., London, 1981.

The Banker, 'Canadian Banks Look Abroad for Growth', March 1982.

______'Jersey in Two Minds', July 1973.

______'Jersey Still Dithering', February 1974.

______'Survey: London $ CDs', June 1976.

______'Survey: Offshore Investment Centres', August 1970, April 1972, May 1974 and April 1977.

______'Survey: Technology in Banking', March 1980.

Bawcutt, P.A., *Captive Insurance Companies: Establishment, Operation and Management,* Woodhead-Faulkner, Cambridge, 1982.

Bellanger, S., 'Optimism Gives Way to Realism in the 1980s', *The Banker,* February 1980.

Berger, F.E., 'The Emerging Transformation of the US Banking System', *The Banker,* September 1981.

Bergsten, C.F. *et al., American Multinationals and American Interests,* Brookings Institution, Washington, D.C., 1978.

Bertrand, R., 'The Liberalisation of Capital Movements—An Insight', *Three Banks Review,* No. 132, December 1981.

Bhagwati, J.N., 'The Generalised Theory of Distortions and Welfare', ch.4 of *Trade, Balance of Payments and Growth,* ed. J.N. Bhagwati *et al.,* North Holland, Amsterdam 1971.

______'Alternative Theories of Illegal Trade: Economic Consequences and Statistical Detection', *Weltwirtshafliches Archiv,* Band 117, Heft 3, 1981.

Bhattacharya, A.K., 'How Far Does Asia Benefit from the Asian Dollar Market?' *The Banker,* 1976.

Blackstone, L. and Franks, D., *The UK as a Tax Haven: A Guide to New Tax Planning Opportunities,* Economist Intelligence Unit Special Report No. 95, March 1981.

Blander, M., 'Why Banks Choose to Work Together', *The Banker,* March 1981.

Board of Trade Journal, 'Direct and Trade Investment in the Non-sterling Area', Vol. 194, No. 3710, 26 April 1968.

Bonnar, D.K., 'Fitting into the Banking Jigsaw', Finance Supplement, July 1978, *Jersey Evening Post.*

Brown, W.P., 'Who uses Offshore Centres? International Banks', *The Banker,* April 1977.

Cairncross, Sir A., *Control of Long-term International Capital Movements,* The Brookings Institution, Washington D.C., 1973.

Caouette, J.P., 'Hong Kong and Singapore—A Survey: Time Zones and the Arranging Centre', *Euromoney,* July 1978.

Caporaso, J.A., 'Industrialization in the Periphery: The Evolving Global Division of Labor', *International Studies Quarterly,* Vol. 25, No. 3, September 1981.

Caves, R.E., 'International Corporations: The Industrial Economics of Foreign Investment', *Economica,* Vol. 38, 1971.

Chown, J.F., 'Who Uses Offshore Centres 1. Multinational Companies', *The Banker,* April 1977.

______*Offshore Financial Centres,* fourth edition revised by M. Cook, a Banker Research Unit Survey, Financial Times Business Publishing Ltd., London, 1981.

Clark, R. and Cherrington, M., 'Telecommunications and Financial Markets', *The Banker,* March 1980.

Clark, T.M. 'The Dawn of International Leasing', *The Banker,* April 1982, pp. 57–67.

Colje, H., 'Bank Supervision on a Consolidated Basis', *The Banker,* June 1980.

Colville, J.R., 'London—Europe's Financial Centre', *The Banker,* July 1966.

Coombes, J., *Capital Transfer Tax,* Professional Books, London, 1977.

Corner, D.C. and Stafford, D.C., *Open-end Investment Funds in the EEC and Switzerland,* Macmillan, London, 1977.

Davis, S.I., *The Euro-Bank: Its Origins, Management and Outlook,* Macmillan, London, 1976.

Dawson, W., *Implications of an Independent Manx Currency,* Isle of Man Treasury, 1977.

Dean, J.W. and Giddy, I.H., 'Strangers and Neighbors: Cross-Border Banking in North America', *Banca Nazionale del Lavoro Quarterly Review,* June 1981.

Dematte, C., 'International Financial Intermediation: Implications for Bankers and Regulators', *Banca Nazionale del Lavoro Quarterly Review,* March 1981.

Doggart, C., *Tax Havens and Their Uses,* Economist Intelligence Unit Special Report No. 105, London, 1981.

Doggart, T., 'Tax Havens—The Landscape Changes', *The Banker,* April 1972.

Dunning, J.H., 'Explaining Changing Patterns of International Production: In Defence of the Eclectic Theory', *Oxford Bulletin of Economics and Statistics,* Vol. 41, 1979.

______and Pearce, R.D., *The World's Largest Companies 1962–78,* Financial Times, London, 1980.

Egashira, K., 'The Internationalisation of the Yen', *The Banker,* March 1982.

Ehrlich, E., 'International Diversification by United States Pension Funds', *Federal Reserve Bank of New York Quarterly Review,* Vol. 6, No. 3, Autumn 1981.

Evans, P., *Dependent Development: The Alliance of Multinational State and Local Capital in Brazil,* Princeton University Press, Princeton, 1979.

______'Beyond Center and Periphery: A Comment on the Contribution of the World System Approach to the Study of Development', *Sociological Inquiry,* Vol. 49, No. 4, 1979.

Fair, D., 'The Independence of Central Banks', *The Banker,* October 1979.

Finger, J.M., 'Tariff Provisions for Offshore Assembly and the Exports of Developing Countries', *Economic Journal,* Vol. 85, 1975.

______'Offshore Assembly Provisions in the West German and Netherlands Tariffs: Trade and Domestic Effects', *Weltwirtschaftliches Archiv,* Band 113, Heft 2, 1977.

Firn, J., 'External Control and Regional Development', *Environment and Planning,* Vol. A, No. 7, 1975.

Frankel, A.B., 'International Banking: Part I, Business Conditions', *Economic Review of Federal Reserve Bank of Chicago,* September 1975.

Gammie, M., *Tax Strategy for Companies,* second edition, Oyez, London, 1981.

Giddy, I. and Allen, D., 'International Competition in Bank Regulation', *Banca Nazionale del Lavoro Quarterly Review,* September 1979.

Goodman, L.S., 'The Pricing of Syndicated Eurocurrency Credits', *Federal Reserve Board of New York Quarterly Review,* Vol. 5, No. 2, Summer 1980.

Gregory, G., 'Foreign Banking in Japan—In Search of a Broader Role', *The Banker,* June 1970.

Griffiths, B.N., *Invisible Barriers to Invisible Trade,* Macmillan, London, 1975.

Hanson, D.G., *Service Banking,* Institute of Bankers, London, 1979.

Hayes, A., 'The 1970 Amendments to the Bank Holding Company Act: Opportunities to Diversify', *Federal Reserve Bank of New York Monthly Review,* February 1971.

Hermann, A.H., 'The EEC's Kidglove Approach to Tax Havens', *The Banker,* April 1972.

Heyting, W.J., *The Constitutional Relationship between Jersey and the UK,* Jersey Constitutional Association, Jersey, 1977.

Hofmann, H., 'Euromarkets in the Eighties. Survey: Euromarkets', *Investors Chronicle,* 12 September 1980.

Holland, M., 'Tax Implications for Banks', *The Banker,* April 1982.

Interbank Research Organisation, *The Regulation of Banks in the Member States of the EEC,* Sijthoff and Noordhoff, Leyden, 1978.

Ireland, J., 'International Banking Facilities', *The Banker,* July 1981.

Isle of Man Bank Ltd., *The Isle of Man: A Small Independent Land at the Centre of the British Isles,* Isle of Man Bank Ltd., Douglas, Isle of Man, 1980.

Jacob, J. Esq., *Annals of the Bailiwick of Guernsey,* Vol. I, Marshall and Simpkins, London, 1830.

Johns, R.A., 'The Locational Implications of Resource Scarcity for Fisheries Development', Discussion Papers in Economics No. 6, Department of Economics, University of Keele, March 1974.

Jones, J.F.A. (ed.), *Tax Havens and Measures Against Tax Evasion and Avoidance in the EEC,* Associated Business Programmes, London, 1974.

Kelly, J., *Bankers and Borders: The Case of American Banks in Britain,* Ballinger, Cambridge, Mass., 1977.

Kemp, L.J., *A Guide to World Money and Capital Markets,* McGraw-Hill Book Company (UK) Ltd., London, 1981.

Kermode, D.G., *Devolution at Work: A Case Study of the Isle of Man,* Saxon House, London, 1979.

Kerr, C.F. and Donald, P., 'Some Aspects of the Geography of Finance in Canada', *Readings in Canadian Geography,* edited by R.M. Irving, Holt, Rinehart and Winston, Toronto, 1965.

Kidder, K., 'Bank Expansion in New York State: The 1971 Statewide Branching Law', *Federal Reserve Bank of New York Monthly Review,* November 1971.

Kindleberger, C.P., *The Formation of Financial Centers: A Study in Comparative Economic History,* Princeton Studies in International Finance No. 36, Princeton University, 1974.
Kinvig, R.H., *The Isle of Man: A Social, Cultural and Political History,* Liverpool University Press, Liverpool, 1975.
Knechtle, A.A., *Basic Problems in International Fiscal Law,* Translated from the German, edited and revised by W.E. Weisflog, HFL, London, 1979.
Krul, N., 'Financial Markets and Economic Nationalism', ch. 6 of *The New Economic Nationalism* edited by O. Hieronymi, Macmillan Press, London, 1980.
Kunreuther, J.B., 'Banking Structure in New York State: Progress and Prospects', *Federal Reserve Bank of New York Monthly Review,* April 1976.

LaBrosse, J.R., 'Canada's New Banking Law', *The Banker,* March 1981.
Lees, F.A., *Foreign Banking and Investment in the US,* Macmillan, London, 1976.
Le Hérissier, R.G., *The Development of the Government of Jersey 1771–1972,* States of Jersey, Jersey, 1972.
Le Rossignol, S.J., *Notes on Banking and Political Events in Jersey,* Jersey, 1915.
Lindbeck, A., 'The Changing Role of the Nation State', *Kyklos,* Vol. 28, Fasc. 1, 1975.
Lipson, C., 'The International Organisation of Third World Debt', *International Organisation,* Vol. 35, No. 4, Autumn 1981.
Loveridge, Sir J., *The Constitution and Law of Guernsey,* La Société Guernesiaise, Guernsey 1975.

MacCulloch, Sir E., *Guernsey Folk Lore,* ed. by E.F. Carey, London, Elliot Stock, 1903.
McCarthy, I.M., 'Offshore Banking Centres: Benefits and Costs', *Finance and Development,* December 1979.
Mackay, J.A., *The Pobjoy Encyclopoedia of Isle of Man Coins and Tokens,* second edition, Pobjoy Press, Surrey, 1978.
Madeuf, B. and Michalet, C., 'A New Approach to International Economics', *International Social Science Journal,* Vol. xxx, No. 2. 1978.
Mann, D., 'The Role of British Banks After the End of Exchange Control', *The Banker,* January 1980.
Marshall-Fraser, W., 'The Coinages of the Channel Islands' *La Société Guernesiaise Report and Transactions 1948,* Guernsey, 1948.
______'A History of Banking in the Channel Islands and a Record of Bank Note Issues', *La Societe Guernesiaise Report and Transactions 1949,* Guernsey, 1949.
Mendelsohn, M.S., 'Eurobond Survey', *The Banker,* November 1976.
Merriman, P., 'Pensions for International Executives', *Multinational Business,* Issue No. 2, 1981.
Mills, J., *Building Society Law,* Steven and Son, London, 1976.
Montagnon, P., 'Syndicated Credits: Extending the Era of 'Megadollar' Deals. Survey: The Euromarkets', *Investors Chronicle,* 18 September 1981.
Moore, J., 'Captive Companies. Survey: Reinsurance', *Financial Times,* 7 September 1981.
Morgan Guaranty Trust Company, 'International Banking Facilities', *World Financial Markets,* November 1981.

Ossola, R., 'The Vulnerability of the International Financial System: International Lending and Liquidity Risk', *Banca Nazionale del Lavoro Quarterly Review,* September 1980.

Palamountain, E., 'Thoughts on Offshore Funds', *The Banker,* August 1970.
Paltzer, E.F., 'Internationalization of Banking by Foreign Bases and Addresses', ch. XI

of *The Development of Financial Institutions in Europe, 1956–1976,* edited by J.E. Wadsworth, *et al.,* Sijthoff, Leyden, 1977.

Parker, A., *Exchange Control,* third edition, Jordan and Sons, London, 1978.

Parker, C., 'The "Big Apple" Maintains its Pace', *The Banker,* February 1981.

Philip, K., 'On Location of Production, Factor Movements, etc., as Affected by the Social and Fiscal Policies of Individual Countries and Economic Communities' and comment thereon by Hufbauer, G.C., 'Taxation and Public Expenditures in an Open Economy', ch. 8 of *The International Allocation of Economic Activity,* edited by B. Ohlin, *et al.,* Macmillan, London, 1977.

Ping, H.R., 'Bargaining on the Free Trade Zones', *New Internationalist,* No. 85, March 1980.

Pocock, H.R.S. (ed.), *The Memoirs of Lord Coutanche,* Phillimore Press, Sussex, 1975.

Powell, G.C., *Economic Survey of Jersey,* States of Jersey, Jersey, 1971.

______'The Position of the Channel Islands with their Special Status for the EEC', ch. 9 of *Tax Havens and Measures against Tax Evasion and Avoidance in the EEC,* edited by J.F. Avery Jones, Associated Business Programmes, London, 1974.

______'Does Jersey Have a Future as an Offshore Financial Centre?' *The Banker,* May 1974.

Pringle, R., 'Why American Banks Go Overseas', *The Banker,* November 1966.

______'The Glint of Steel Behind Tokyo's International Role', *The Banker,* August 1981.

Quarmby, E., *Banknotes and Banking in the Isle of Man 1788–1970,* Spink and Son Ltd., London, 1971.

Revey, P., 'Evolution and Growth of the United States Foreign Exchange Market', *Federal Reserve Bank of New York Quarterly Review,* Vol. 6, No. 3, Autumn 1981.

Rothschild, K.W., 'Export Structure, Export Flexibility and Competitiveness', *Weltwirtschafliches Archiv,* Bank III, Heft 2, 1975.

Sargeaunt, B.E., *An Outline of the Financial System of the Isle of Man Government,* Douglas, Isle of Man, 1925.

Saunders, R.M., *Tax Planning for Business in Europe,* Butterworths, London, 1977.

______*Principles of Tax Planning,* Finax Publications, London, 1978.

Sennet, W.E., 'What is a Captive?' and 'Advantages and Disadvantages of Captives and Preconditions for Successful Operation', *Papers in Risk Management, No. 5: Captive Insurance Companies,* Keith Shipton Developments Ltd., London, 1976.

Sethi, S. and Cuhney, A.F., 'The Domestic International Sales Corporation (DISC): Problems and Prospects', in *Management of the Multinationals,* edited by S.P. Sethi and R.H. Holton, Free Press, New York, 1974.

Sharp, P., *UK Fiscal Implications of International Trade,* Institute of Chartered Accountants, London, 1976.

Simon's Taxes Vol. F—Double Taxation Relief and Agreements, third edition, London, 1976.

Smith, A., 'The Informal Economy', *Lloyds Bank Review,* July 1981.

Solly, H.W., *Anatomy of a Tax Haven. Vol. 1: The Isle of Man,* second edition, 1980; *Vol. 2: Manx Income Tax,* 1979, Shearwater Press, Isle of Man.

Statist 71st Annual Review of World Banking, Financial Times Business Publishing Ltd., London, 1981.

Strange, S., *Sterling and British Policy: A Political Study of an International Currency in Decline,* Oxford University Press, Oxford, 1971.

Sumption, A., *Taxation of Overseas Income and Gains,* third edition, Butterworths, London, 1979.

Syckoff, E.L., *US Taxation of Foreign Trusts: US Taxation of International Operations Service,* Prentice-Hall, Englewood Cliffs, N.J., 1979.

Taylor, T.P.D., 'Tax Planning and Tax Avoidance after Ramsay', a series of five articles in the following issues of *Taxation:* 10 October, 17 October, 24 October, 31 October and 7 November, 1981.

Thring, P. and Taylor-Jones, M., 'Harmonising Bank Annual Accounts in the European Community', *The Banker,* June 1981.

Vaubel, R., 'Free Currency Competition', *Weltwirtschafliches Archiv,* Band 113, Heft 3, 1977.

Veale, F.W., 'Open Door to Expansion of Finance Industry', *Guernsey Evening Press and Star,* 14 October 1975.

Wadsworth, J.E., *et al.,* 'Part D—The Official Regulation of Financial Institutions', *The Development of Financial Institutions in Europe,* Sijthoff, Leyden, 1977.

Wallerstein, I., 'Dependence in an Interdependent World: The Limited Possibilities of Transformation within the Capitalist World Economy', paper presented at Conference on Dependence and Development in Africa, Ottawa, Canada 1973.

______'Semi-peripheral Countries and the Contemporary World Crisis', *Theory and Society,* Vol. 3, 1976.

______'A World-System Perspective on the Social Sciences', *British Journal of Sociology,* Vol. 27, 1976.

______'Semiperipheral Countries and the Contemporary World Crisis', ch. 5 of *The Capitalist World Economy,* Cambridge University Press, Cambridge, 1979.

Walmsley, J., 'Moving Towards Competitive Equality', *The Banker,* February 1980.

Watts, H., *The Branch Plant Economy: A Study of External Control,* Longmans, London, 1980.

Wood, D. and Byrne, J., *International Business Finance,* Macmillan, London, 1981.

Woolley, P.K., 'Britain's Investment Currency Premium', *Lloyds Bank Review,* July 1974.

Wright, C.F., 'Changes in the Structure of American Banking and Finance—A New Era of Competition', *Barclays Review,* February 1982.

Yassukovich, S.M. 'Multinational Companies and Offshore Centres', *The Banker,* May 1974.

PERIODICALS

Individual centre information is available in Central Bank and National Monetary Authority Annual Reports. The following contain regular information of general interest:

Bank of International Settlements, Basle, *Annual Reports.*

IMF *Annual Reports on Exchange Restrictions.*

Morgan Guaranty Trust Company's *World Financial Markets.*

Further information is available in periodic articles and special supplements published regularly in *The Banker, The Financial Times,* and the *Investors Chronicle and Financial World.* The following Financial Times Surveys were specifically referred to in this book:

'Financial Services in New York', 3 December 1981;

'Spanish Banking', 22 March 1982;

'Gold Futures', 20 April 1982.

GENERAL REPORTS

OECD Committee on Financial Markets, *Standard Rules for the Operation of Institutions for Collective Investment in Securities,* OECD, Paris, 1972.

______ *Experience with Controls on International Operations in Shares and Bonds,* OECD Secretariat, Paris, 1981.

______ *Regulations Affecting International Banking Operations,* Directorate for Financial and Fiscal Affairs, OECD, Paris, 1981.

COUNTRY REPORTS

The United Kingdom

UK Board of Inland Revenue. *Company Residence: A Consultative Document,* January 1981.

______ *Tax Havens and the Corporate Sector: A Consultative Document,* January 1981.

______ *International Tax Avoidance,* November 1981.

UK Monopolies and Mergers Commissions, *Reports on the Proposed Mergers — The Hongkong and Shanghai Banking Corporation, Standard Chartered Bank Ltd., and The Royal Bank of Scotland Group Ltd.,* January 1982.

Royal Commission on the Constitution, 1969-1973. *Relationships Between the United Kingdom and the Channel Islands and the Isle of Man,* Part XI of Vol.1 of the Report together with the relevant extract from Vol.2, the Home Office, HMSO, London, 1973.

UK Institute of Directors. *Submission on the Inland Revenue Consultative Document on Tax Havens* of January 1981.

The United States

Department of the US Treasury: *Report to Congress on Foreign Government Treatment of US Commercial Banking Organizations,* 1979.

The British Isle Centres

Financial Times, *The Expatriate's Guide to Savings and Investment 1981–82,* Financial Times Business Publishing Limited, London, 1981.

Trevor, Matthews and Carey Ltd.. *The Channel Islands Investment and Unit Trust Review.*

Jersey

Jersey Statistical Digest 1980- . States of Jersey. Jersey.

States Economic Advisor's *Reports on the Budget 1970–1982.*

Hellyer, E.P., *Rapport au Comité Nommé Le 19 Août 1927 Pour Faire L'étude de La Revision de La Législation Financière de L'Isle.* 4 November 1927.

Report and Recommendations of the Special Committee of the States of Jersey Appointed to Consult with Her Majesty's Government in the UK on All Matters Relating to the Government's Application to Join the European Economic Community, States of Jersey, Jersey 1967.

Coopers and Lybrand, *Report on Financial Institutions registered under the Depositors and Investors (Prevention of Fraud) (Jersey) Law 1967,* unpublished, Jersey, 29 October 1973.

Policy Advisory Committee, *Report and Proposition Regarding the Scale and Pattern of Development in the Island over the Next Five Years,* States of Jersey, Jersey, 8 January 1974.

______ *Report and Proposition Regarding Economic Strategies and Immigration Control Policies,* States of Jersey, Jersey, 9 May 1978.

Commercial Relations Department, *Commercial Law Reform Report No. 1: Report on Insolvency with Draft Insolvency Law,* Jersey, August 1973.

______*Report No. 2: Report on Company Law Reform with Draft Company Law,* Jersey, October 1975.

______*Report No. 3: Report on Trusts with Draft Trusts and Trustees (Jersey) Law,* Jersey, 24 October 1975.

______*Report No. 4: Report on Mortgages of Moveable Property with Draft Chattel Bonds (Jersey) Law 197,* Jersey, 24 October 1975.

Falle, R., *Some Notes on the Jersey Currency,* Local History Collection File, Jersey Public Library, undated and unpublished.

Guernsey

1972 Economic Development Plan, Billet d'État, XI 1972.

Economic Policy Document, Billet d'État, XIV 1974.

States of Guernsey Advisory and Finance Committee, *Economic Reports for 1975–82,* various *Billets d'Etat* 1976–82.

Isle of Man

Isle of Man Digest of Economic and Social Statistics 1980-

Report of the Joint Working Party on the Constitutional Relationship between the Isle of Man and the United Kingdom ('The Stonham Report'), 1969.

Royal Commission on the Constitution 1969–73, *Isle of Man—Joint Evidence of the Home Office and Tynwald,* HMSO.

P.A. International Management Consultants, *Economic Survey of the Isle of Man,* London, 1975.

______*Review of the Isle of Man/UK Common Purse Agreement,* London, August 1976.

Dawson, W., *Usury: A Memorandum,* Isle of Man Treasury, 29 December 1976, unpublished.

______*Manx National Income 1979/1980: A Commentary,* Isle of Man Treasury, 16 June 1981, unpublished.

______*A Detailed Consideration of the 1981 Exempt Insurance Act,* conference paper presented to a conference in the Isle of Man in November 1981, unpublished.

Index